Compliance by Design in AI Systems

Compliance by Design in AI Systems

Shifting Compliance in AI System Development and Deployment Left

Bjørn Aslak Juliussen

Faculty of Law, UiT The Arctic University of Norway

Edward Elgar PUBLISHING

Cheltenham, UK • Northampton, MA, USA

Published by

Edward Elgar Publishing Limited
The Lypiatts
15 Lansdown Road
Cheltenham
Glos GL50 2JA
UK

Edward Elgar Publishing, Inc.
William Pratt House
9 Dewey Court
Northampton
Massachusetts 01060
USA

Authorised representative in the EU for GPSR queries only: Easy Access System Europe – Mustamäe tee 50, 10621 Tallinn, Estonia, gpsr.requests@easproject.com

A catalogue record for this book is available from the British Library

Library of Congress Control Number: 2026931768

This book is available electronically in the **Elgar**online
Law subject collection
https://doi.org/10.4337/9781035390731

MIX
Paper | Supporting responsible forestry
FSC® C014540

ISBN 978 1 0353 9072 4 (cased)
ISBN 978 1 0353 9073 1 (eBook)
ISBN 978 1 0353 9074 8 (ePub)

Printed and bound in the UK by Short Run Press Ltd, Exeter EX2 7LW

Contents

List of figures

List of tables

Preface

"Without prejudice to" is a term frequently used in EU technology regulations. Regulation 2024/1689 (The Artificial Intelligence (AI) Act) is "without prejudice to" the General Data Protection Regulation (GDPR), and recent cybersecurity regulations such as the Network and Information Security (NIS) 2 Directive and the Cyber Resilience Act (CRA) are without prejudice to both the GDPR and the AI Act. However, in situations where these regulations and directives enter into effect simultaneously, compliance with these rule sets would entail prioritising different design choices in technological solutions. These choices would, to a varying degree, enhance or diminish the end goals of the different applicable rule sets. This book explores the research question of whether it is possible to develop a *compliance by design* approach to processing personal data in AI systems compliant with the requirements of the GDPR, the AI Act, and specific relevant cybersecurity regulations.

The book examines the research question through several sub-research questions. The approach examines whether compliance with the identified legal requirements could be achieved through alterations to the methodologies applied when developing and maintaining developed AI systems. Thus, the first sub-research question examines the main methods and methodologies utilised for developing AI systems and managing their lifecycle post-deployment. After such an examination, relevant legal requirements are analysed during the different phases of the lifecycle of an AI system: data collection and model training, deployment, and when trained AI models are fine-tuned on AI-as-a-Service (AIaaS) platforms.

The book identifies that one methodology frequently applied to developing and maintaining AI systems, Machine Learning Operations (MLOps), has the potential to implement and embed several relevant legal requirements, including, but not limited to, the principle of accuracy in the GDPR, the requirement for accuracy under the AI Act, the right to receive meaningful information about the logic involved in automated decision-making, and the purpose limitation principle. MLOps is a concept without a clear, authoritative definition. However, the methodology includes automatic, semiautomatic, and manual processes for regularly training AI models across the development and deployment phases.

Moreover, the book also addresses the question of how to achieve compliance with different rule sets that enter into effect at the same time. Based on the findings of the legal and technical examinations, *proportionality by design*, based on the principle of proportionality, is developed as a framework providing an overview, an interpretative source, and a basis for best practices for AI development and use.

Acknowledgements

This book analyses whether it is possible to align two different disciplines – law and computer science – in order to ensure compliance with data protection regulation, the AI Act, and cybersecurity regulations when developing and deploying AI systems.

Since the first proposal of the AI Act was made public in April 2021, AI regulation has become a highly discussed and political issue. This book goes beyond the discussions of whether AI regulation hinders innovation and technological development. The book takes the stance that the AI Act and the other regulations analysed are in force and asks the question of how AI system developers under the scope of the regulations could comply with the regulations. In order to analyse this question, the book argues that a *compliance by design* approach should be pursued. The overall idea with compliance by design is to implement compliance assessments in the development process and to assess legal and regulatory questions earlier in the process – to shift the compliance assessments *left* in the development process.

The book analyses EU regulations. However, the development methodologies analysed are not EU-specific. Thus, the relevance of this book is not solely European, but might also be relevant for other jurisdictions.

The law is up to date as of 1 August 2025.

I would like to thank the team at Edward Elgar Publishing for making this book possible, for their efficiency and attention to detail in producing this book.

I would also like to thank Asbjørn Strandbakken, Dag Johansen, Jon Petter Rui, and Sabine Gless for helpful comments and suggestions. Any errors or inconsistencies are mine alone.

Finally, I would like to thank Ingrid for your constant motivation, distraction, and support.

List of abbreviations

AG	Advocate General
AI	Artificial Intelligence
AIaaS	AI as a Service
API	Application Programming Interface
CI/CD/CT	Continuous Integration/Continuous Delivery/Continuous Training
CJEU	Court of Justice of the European Union
CNIL	Commission Nationale de l'informatique et des Libertés
CoE	Council of Europe
CRA	Cyber Resilience Act
CSIRT	Computer Security Incident Response Team
DDoS	Distributed Denial-of-Service (Attack)
DPA	Data Protection Authority
DPIA	Data Protection Impact Assessment
EC	European Commission
ECHR	European Convention on Human Rights
ECtHR	European Court of Human Rights
EDPB	European Data Protection Board
EEA	European Economic Area
ENISA	European Network and Information Security Agency
EU	European Union
FHE	Fully Homomorphic Encryption
FLOPs	Floating Point Operations
GDPR	General Data Protection Regulation
ICT	Information and Communications Technology
IEC	International Electrotechnical Commission
IoT	Internet of Things

ISMS	Information Security Management System
ISO	International Organization for Standardization
KPI	Key Performance Indicator
LED	Law Enforcement Directive
LIME	Local Interpretable Model-agnostic Explanations
LLM	Large Language Model
ML	Machine Learning
MLOps	Machine Learning Operations
NIS	Network and Information Security
OECD	Organisation for Economic Co-operation and Development
PET	Privacy Enhancing Technology
TFEU	Treaty of the Functioning of the European Union
WP29	Working Party Number 29
XAI	Explainable Artificial Intelligence

1. Introduction

1.1 COMPLIANCE BY DESIGN IN AN AI CONTEXT

The overall focus of this book is whether and to what extent specific technology-related regulations from the European Union (EU), namely data protection,[1] cybersecurity,[2] and Artificial Intelligence (AI) regulation[3] could be efficiently complied with during the development and deployment of AI systems.

In recent years – particularly since the public release of commercial large language models (LLMs) at the end of 2022 – AI systems have transitioned from an entrenched research sphere to an integral part of our everyday lives.[4] Recent decisions from European data protection authorities (DPAs)[5] suggest

[1] Regulation (EU) 2016/679 of the European Parliament and of the Council of 27 April 2016 on the protection of natural persons with regard to the processing of personal data and on the free movement of such data, and repealing Directive 95/46/EC (General Data Protection Regulation) [2016] OJ L 199/1.

[2] Directive (EU) 2022/2555 of the European Parliament and of the Council of 14 December 2022 on measures for a high common level of cybersecurity across the Union, amending Regulation (EU) No 910/2014 and Directive (EU) 2018/1972, and repealing Directive (EU) 2016/1148 (NIS 2 Directive) [2022] OJ L 333/80; Regulation (EU) 2024/2847 of the European Parliament and of the Council of 23 October 2024 on horizontal cybersecurity requirements for products with digital elements and amending Regulations (EU) No 168/2013 and (EU) 2019/1020 and Directive (EU) 2020/1828 (Cyber Resilience Act) OJ/L 2024/2847.

[3] Regulation (EU) 2024/1689 of the European Parliament and of the Council of 13 June 2024 laying down harmonised rules on artificial intelligence and amending Regulations (EC) No 300/2008, (EU) No 167/2013, (EU) No 168/2013, (EU) 2018/858, (EU) 2018/1139 and (EU) 2019/2144 and Directives 2014/90/EU, (EU) 2016/797 and (EU) 2020/1828 (Artificial Intelligence Act) [2024] OJ L 2024/1689.

[4] Yupeng Chang et al. "A survey on evaluation of large language models". In: *ACM Transactions on Intelligent Systems and Technology* (2023). doi: https://doi.org/10.48550/arXiv.2307.03109.

[5] Garante per la protezione dei data personale. *ChatGPT: Italian DPA notifies breaches of privacy law to OpenAI.* url: https://gpdp.it/home/docweb/-/docweb-display/docweb/9978020#english. Last accessed: 01.08.2025. Data Protection

that commercial LLMs such as ChatGPT[6] potentially breach several of the requirements in the General Data Protection Regulation (GDPR).[7] The security of the processing of personal data under the GDPR and the overall cybersecurity of a system – including AI-based systems – are closely interlinked. For instance, a breach of the security of an AI system would also, in many incidents, involve a breach of the security of the processing of personal data, according to Article 32 of the GDPR. However, specific cybersecurity regulations aim not only to secure the data processed but also to ensure the operational resilience of the (AI) system. Consequently, adherence to not only data protection regulations but also general and sector-specific cybersecurity regulations is essential for both the security of AI systems and the security of the personal data processed within AI systems.

Moreover, in 2024, the EU adopted the AI Act, which delineates specific regulations for AI systems.[8] The overall purpose of the AI Act, according to Article 1 of the Act, is "to improve the functioning of the internal market and promote the uptake of human-centric and trustworthy AI, while ensuring a high level of protection of health, safety, and fundamental rights ensured in the Charter" of Fundamental Rights of the EU.

This book explores the research question of whether it is possible to concurrently develop a *compliance by design* approach to processing personal data in AI systems compliant with the requirements of the GDPR, the AI Act, and specific relevant cybersecurity regulations – when developing and governing deployed AI systems.

The remainder of the introduction is structured as follows. In section 1.2, the background and context, including related works, of the book are presented. In section 1.3, the research question, including relevant sub-research questions, is elaborated. Section 1.4 defines the scope of the book, including its limitations. In section 1.5, the nature and scope of the interdisciplinary research

---

Commission. *Data Protection Commission launches inquiry into Google AI model.* url: https://www.dataprotection.ie/en/news-media/press-releases/data-protection-commission-launches-inquiry-google-ai-model. Last accessed: 01.08.2025.

[6] OpenAI. *ChatGPT.* url: https://chat.openai.com/. Last accessed: 01.08.2025.

[7] Regulation (EU) 2016/679 of the European Parliament and of the Council of 27 April 2016 on the protection of natural persons with regard to the processing of personal data and on the free movement of such data, and repealing Directive 95/46/EC (General Data Protection Regulation) [2016] OJ L 199/1.

[8] Regulation (EU) 2024/1689 of the European Parliament and of the Council of 13 June 2024 laying down harmonised rules on artificial intelligence and amending Regulations (EC) No 300/2008, (EU) No 167/2013, (EU) No 168/2013, (EU) 2018/858, (EU) 2018/1139, and (EU) 2019/2144 and Directives 2014/90/EU, (EU) 2016/797, and (EU) 2020/1828 (Artificial Intelligence Act) [2024] OJ L 2024/1689.

methodology of the book are presented. Finally, section 1.6 contains the outline of the whole book.

1.2 BACKGROUND, CONTEXT, AND RELATED WORK

The current section will contextualise the research undertaken in the book within the broader domain of related work. Overall, the book situates itself within two principal domains of related research:

1. Research on "by design" requirements, i.e., approaches such as privacy by design, data protection by design, and security by design. Such approaches underscore the proactive implementation of privacy, data protection, and cybersecurity requirements into the design and development phases of various technological systems.[9]

---

[9] Lee A Bygrave. "Security by design: Aspirations and realities in a regulatory context". In: *Oslo Law Review* 8 (3 2021), pp. 126–177. doi: https://doi.org/10.18261/olr.8.3.2; Information Registratiekamer and Privacy Commissioner Ontario. *Privacy-enhancing technologies: The path to anonymity.* Tech. rep. Achtergrondstudies en Verkenningen 5B, vols. I and II, Rijswijk, 1995; ENISA. *Privacy Enhancing Technologies.* 2022. url: https://www.enisa.europa.eu/news/enisa-news/promoting-data-protection-by-design-exploring-techniques. Last accessed: 01.08.2025. Mireille Hildebrandt. "Legal protection by design: Objections and refutations". In: *Legisprudence* 5.2 (2011), pp. 223–248. doi: https://doi.org/10.5235/175214611797885693; Karen Yeung. "Hypernudge: Big Data as a mode of regulation by design". In: *The Social Power of Algorithms.* New York: Routledge, 2019, pp. 118–136. doi: https://doi.org/10.1080/1369118X.2016.1186713; Deirdre K Mulligan and Kenneth A Bamberger. "Saving governance-by-design". In: *California Law Review* 106.3 (2018), pp. 697–784. doi: https://doi.org/10. 15779/Z38QN5ZB5H; Lachlan Urquhart and Tom Rodden. "A legal turn in human computer interaction? Towards 'Regulation by Design' for the Internet of Things". In: *Towards 'Regulation by Design' for the Internet of Things (March 11, 2016)* (2016). doi: https://dx.doi.org/10.2139/ssrn.2746467; Monika Zalnieriute, Lyria Bennett Moses, and George Williams. "Rule of law by design?" In: *Tulane Law Review* (2021); Dirk Helbing et al. "Ethics of smart cities: Towards value-sensitive design and co-evolving city life". In: *Sustainability* 13.20 (2021), p. 11162. doi: 10.3390/su132011162; Karen Yeung, Andrew Howes, and Ganna Pogrebna. "AI governance by human rights–centered design, deliberation, and oversight: An end to ethics washing". In: *The Oxford Handbook of Ethics of AI.* Ed. by Markus D Dubber, Frank Pasquale, and Sunit Das. Oxford: Oxford University Press, 2020, pp. 77–106. isbn: 9780190067397. doi: 10.1093/oxfordhb/9780190067397.013.5. eprint: https://academic.oup.com/book/0/chapter/290657408/chapter-ag-pdf/44521952/book_34287_section_290657408.ag.pdf. url: https://doi.org/10.1093/oxfordhb/9780190067397.013.5; Denisa Reshef Kera.

2. Research on methodologies concerning the development and governance of the complete lifecycle of AI systems, with a specific focus on existing research on Machine Learning Operations (MLOps). This research

---

"experimental algorithmic citizenship in the sandboxes: An alternative to ethical frameworks and governance-by-design interventions". In: *Proceedings of the III Ibero-American Conference on Smart Cities (ICSC-2020)* (2020); Mireille Hildebrandt. "The public (s) on life: A call for legal protection by design". In: *The Onlife Manifesto: Being Human in a Hyperconnected Era*. Cham: Springer, 2015, pp. 181–193. doi: https://doi.org/10.1007/978-3-319-04093-6_19; Ugo Pagallo. "Cracking down on autonomy: Three challenges to design in IT law". In: *Ethics and Information Technology* 14 (2012), pp. 319–328. doi: https://doi.org/10.1007/s10676-012-9295-9; Ugo Pagallo. "On the principle of privacy by design and its limits: Technology, ethics and the rule of law". In: *European Data Protection: In Good Health?* Ed. by Serge Gutwirth et al. Dordrecht: Springer, 2012, pp. 331–346. isbn: 978-94-007-2903-2. doi: 10.1007/978-94-007-2903-2_16. url: https://doi.org/10.1007/978-94-007-2903-2_16; Paolo Balboni et al. "Designing connected and automated vehicles around legal and ethical concerns: Data protection as a corporate social responsibility". In: *SETN Workshops*. 2020, pp. 139–151. doi: https://doi.org/10.5281/ zenodo.7291693; Iwona Karkliniewska. "Building transparency and robustness of AI/ADM management in public sector". In: *AIxPA@ AI* IA*. 2022, pp. 1–7; Sandra Wachter, Brent Mittelstadt, and Chris Russell. "Why fairness cannot be automated: Bridging the gap between EU non-discrimination law and AI". In: *Computer Law & Security Review* 41 (2021), p. 105567. ISSN: 0267-3649. doi: https://doi.org/10.1016/j.clsr.2021.105567. url: https://www.sciencedirect.com/science/article/pii/S0267364921000406; Marco Almada. "Human intervention in automated decision-making: Toward the construction of contestable systems". In: *Proceedings of the Seventeenth International Conference on Artificial Intelligence and Law*. 2019, pp. 2–11. doi: https://doi.org/10.1145/ 3322640.3326699; Marco Almada. "Regulation by design and the governance of technological futures". In: *European Journal of Risk Regulation* (2023), pp. 1–13. doi: https://doi.org/10.1017/err.2023.37; Joshua A Kroll. "The fallacy of inscrutability". In: *Philosophical Transactions of the Royal Society A: Mathematical, Physical and Engineering Sciences* 376.2133 (2018), p. 20180084. doi: https://doi.org/10.1098/rsta.2018.0084; Anthony Aguirre et al. "AI loyalty by design: A framework for governance of AI". In: *Oxford Handbook on AI Governance*. Ed. by Justin B Bullock et al. Oxford: Oxford University Press, 2021, pp. 320–344. doi: https://doi.org/10.1093/oxfordhb/9780197579329.013.70; Pieter van Gelder et al. "Safe-by-design in engineering: An overview and comparative analysis of engineering disciplines". In: *International Journal of Environmental Research and Public Health* 18.12 (2021), p. 6329. doi: 10.3390/ijerph18126329; Pieter Van Cleynenbreugel. "By-design regulation in the algorithmic society: Promising way forward or (EU) constitutional nightmare in-the-making?" In: *Inaugural Conference of the IACL Research Group on Algorithmic State Market & Society–Constitutional Dimensions*. 2019. doi: https://doi.org/10.1017/9781108914857.011.

domain focuses on frameworks, methodologies, and practices aimed at automating the deployment, management, and maintenance of ML models in operational environments.[10]

Diver defines "compliance by design" as "meeting the requirements of a specific field of substantive doctrinal law within the design of the code, insofar as that field targets its norm at digital artefacts".[11] Compliance by design thus refers to the commonalities of approaches such as privacy by design,[12] data protection by design in Article 25 (1) of the GDPR,[13] and security by design.[14]

The purpose of the book is not to take the current compliance by design approach and simply insert it into the AI field. Rather, the approach of the book is to devise a potentially more appropriate framework that builds on current compliance by design approaches, privacy by design, data protection by design, and security by design, and to include the specific requirements in the AI Act. These requirements are then implemented in current methodologies for developing and managing the lifecycle of AI systems. The aim and purpose of such an approach is to come one step closer from a retroactive, ex-post focus of compliance in AI systems to a proactive, ex-ante approach where several of these requirements are implemented before, during, and after an AI system is trained, deployed, and maintained.

The "by design" approach of the book should, thus, be understood as broader than the design of code or the "design" phase of a development methodology. In the book, the term "design" is applied as a term encompassing a broad

---

10 Xinrui Zhang and Jason Jaskolka. "Conceptualizing the Secure Machine Learning Operations (SecMLOps) Paradigm". In: *2022 IEEE 22nd International Conference on Software Quality, Reliability and Security (QRS)*. 2022, pp. 127–138. doi: 10.1109/QRS57517.2022.00023; Cedric Renggli et al. "A data quality-driven view of MLOps". In: *arXiv preprint arXiv:2102.07750* (2021). doi: https://doi.org/10.48550/arXiv.2102.07750.

11 Laurence Diver. *Digisprudence: Code as Law Rebooted*. Edinburgh: Edinburgh University Press, 2022, p. 26. isbn: 9781474485340. doi: doi:10.1515/9781474485340.

12 Information Registratiekamer and Privacy Commissioner Ontario. *Privacy-Enhancing Technologies: The Path to Anonymity*. Tech. rep. Achtergrondstudies en Verkenningen 5B, vols. I and II, Rijswijk, 1995.

13 Regulation (EU) 2016/679 of the European Parliament and of the Council of 27 April 2016 on the protection of natural persons with regard to the processing of personal data and on the free movement of such data, and repealing Directive 95/46/EC (General Data Protection Regulation) [2016] OJ L 199/1.

14 Lee A Bygrave. "Security by design: Aspirations and realities in a regulatory context". In: *Oslo Law Review* 8 (3 2021), pp. 126–177. doi: https://doi.org/10.18261/olr.8.3.2.

understanding, including development and deployment, and the methodologies applied to develop and maintain deployed AI systems.

A theoretical rationale outlining both compliance by design and, more generally, "regulation by design" is the transition from a passive approach where regulation is presented as rules by the state that is enacted and enforced by the state to an active approach where regulation is presented as having a purpose beyond simple enforcement, i.e., that regulation should modify behaviour.[15]

In related work concerning *by design* requirements in regulation, Murray and Scott have presented a framework of control within the active approach of regulation by design.[16] Murray and Scott present four categories of control within "by design" requirements in regulation: (I) hierarchical (law), (II) community-based (community norms), (III) competition-based (markets), and (IV) design-based (computer code). Moreover, they present three methods of control: standard-setting, information-gathering, and behaviour-modification.[17] Murray and Scotts' work outlines that design can be incorporated within the law, meaning that technological solutions must be designed in a specific manner in order to be compliant. However, Murray and Scott also highlight that the technology itself can be designed in a behaviour-modification manner that affects users like the effect of formal law. The focus of this book is on the hierarchical level and on the standard-setting level. The focus of the book is, hence, how the specific legal requirements could be implemented within a specific technological solution: AI systems.

A focus on how data protection and privacy by design could be implemented in technology through amendments to the methodologies used to develop the technology is not a new concept. Hoepman has related work within software engineering and has introduced specific privacy by design strategies and patterns.[18] Design patterns are defined as "fundamental structural organisation or schema for software systems. They [the design patterns] provide a set of predefined subsystems, specify their responsibilities, and include rules and

---

15 Kostina Prifti et al. "Regulation by design: Features, practices, limitations, and governance implications". In: *Minds and Machines* 34.2 (2024), p. 13. doi: https://doi.org/10.1007/s11023-024-09675-z.

16 Andrew Murray and Colin Scott. "Controlling the new media: Hybrid responses to new forms of power". In: *The Modern Law Review* 65.4 (2002), pp. 491–516.

17 Ibid.

18 Japp-Henk Hoepman. "Privacy design strategies". In: *ICT Systems Security and Privacy Protection. SEC 2014. IFIP Advances in Information and Communication Technology*. Ed. by Nora Cuppens-Boulahia et al. 2014. doi: https://doi.org/10.1007/978-3-642-55415-5_38.

guidelines for organising the relationships between them".[19] Hoepman defines design strategies as a: "fundamental approach to achieve a certain design goal. It favours certain structural organisations or schemes over others. It has certain properties that allow it to be distinguished from other (fundamental) approaches that achieve the same goal".[20] Overall, Hoepman's approach is characterised by attempting to translate the specific privacy and data protection by design principles into strategies that could be implemented when conceptualising the design and architecture of a software system. Unlike Hopeman's approach, the approach in the book specifically focuses on AI systems, and not traditional software systems. Although the current privacy and data protection by design approaches are used as a first step, the suggested approach in the book is tailored to AI systems, and specific requirements in the AI Act are also included, in addition to data protection and cybersecurity regulation requirements.

In recent years, a wide range of legal research has been conducted on compliance by design. Examples include broader concepts of "by design", for instance, "democracy, rule of law and human rights by design" as suggested by Nemitz.[21] In the paper, Nemitz suggests that the developers of AI systems should perform an impact assessment on how the specific system under development would affect democracy, the rule of law, and human rights. Similarly, Hildebrant has suggested "legal protection by design",[22] a framework "as a way to ensure that the technological normativity that regulates our lives: first is compatible with enacted law, or even initiated by the democratic legislator, second, can be resisted, and third, may be contested in a court of law".[23] Such "by design" approaches go beyond the mere detailed legislation, and implement fundamental and comprehensive approaches to implementing principles, values, and fundamental rights into the design of technology. However, a specific aspect of such "meta-compliance by design" that is not, as far as publicly

---

19 *TOGAF Standard, Version 9.2. 22 Architecture Patterns.* https://pubs.opengroup.org/architecture/togaf9-doc/arch/chap22.html. Last accessed: 26.08.2024.

20 Japp-Henk Hoepman. "Privacy design strategies". In: *ICT Systems Security and Privacy Protection. SEC 2014. IFIP Advances in Information and Communication Technology.* Ed. by Nora Cuppens-Boulahia et al. 2014. doi: https://doi.org/10.1007/978-3-642-55415-5_38.

21 Paul Nemitz. "Constitutional democracy and technology in the age of artificial intelligence". In: *Philosophical Transactions of the Royal Society A: Mathematical, Physical and Engineering Sciences* 376.2133 (2018), p. 20180089. doi: https://doi.org/10.1098/rsta.2018.0089.

22 Mireille Hildebrandt. "Legal protection by design: Objections and refutations". In: *Legisprudence* 5.2 (2011), pp. 223–248. doi: https://doi.org/10.5235/175214611797885693.

23 Ibid.

available literature suggests, addressed in the current related work is the alignment between the positive existing regulation – including the requirements in the AI Act – and the methodologies applied when developing and managing the lifecycle of AI systems. Such aspects are important to address and will be addressed in this book, for the following reasons:

1. In order to move from a retroactive, ex-post assessment of whether technology – and more specifically AI systems – comply with specific regulations, it is important to build on existing and well-used methodologies for developing AI systems and managing the lifecycles of deployed AI systems.
2. Since technology undoubtedly has normative decision-power, sometimes similar to formal legislation, it is important to implement existing positive legislation into AI systems in order to reduce a potential regulatory and democratic debt such AI systems could entail in the future.
3. It is crucial to apply existing methodologies when developing AI systems to be compliant with positive legislation to ensure that formal legislation can be effectively implemented in practice, and not just in books.

In the current literature, there are distinct differences between the literature on compliance by design from a legal and governance perspective and the literature from a computer science and technology perspective. This difference in literature is especially visible in terms of the granularity of the end goal potentially achieved by the development process. While legal and governance literature often focuses on open-ended high-level end goals such as democracy, rule of law, and human rights, computer science research often focuses on a specific end goal, such as explainability or a specific principle in data protection law, such as data minimisation.[24] The degree of implementability also differs between the two distinct fields of literature, where computer science often presents a more practical and technical solution to a specific end goal. The framework presented in the book will attempt to bridge these two current fields of related work. In order to achieve a specific end goal, e.g., purpose limitation under the GDPR, it is necessary to interpret the low-level detailed design goal – purpose limitation – in line with primary law such as the Charter of Fundamental Rights.[25] Furthermore, it is necessary to fit the results from

---

[24] Kostina Prifti et al. "Regulation by design: Features, practices, limitations, and governance implications". In: *Minds and Machines* 34.2 (2024), p. 13. doi: https://doi.org/10.1007/s11023-024-09675-z.

[25] European Union. Charter of Fundamental Rights of the European Union, 26 October 2012, 2012/C 326/02.

such a legal analysis within a framework applied when developing AI systems. The book will attempt to present such an approach.

There is currently active research on how to implement various technical standards and cybersecurity standards in methodologies for developing and deploying AI, such as within the MLOps framework.[26] However, the current line of research mostly focuses on standards from standardisation bodies such as the International Standardisation Organisation (ISO) and not EU regulations on data protection, cybersecurity, and AI. Thus, the book builds on existing research while also presenting a novel approach, since the requirements implemented in the book relate to regulations rather than technical standards.

The novelty of the book is mainly related to the implementation of existing "by design" frameworks within a new technology, AI and the subfield of machine learning (ML). Moreover, the book presents a novel approach where "by design" requirements are implemented in the MLOps framework. Lastly, the book applies an interdisciplinary approach towards interpreting and implementing the requirements for AI systems under the AI Act. It also highlights to what extent these requirements could be integrated effectively into the ongoing workflows for developing and maintaining deployed AI systems.

1.3 RESEARCH QUESTION

The primary research question (RQ) of this book is:

> How can data protection regulation, specific cybersecurity regulations, and requirements in the AI Act be implemented and complied with during the development and deployment of AI systems?

In order to comprehensively analyse the primary research question, it is necessary to formulate several specific sub-research questions:

---

[26] Cedric Renggli et al. "A data quality-driven view of MLOps". In: *arXiv preprint arXiv:2102.07750* (2021). doi: https://doi.org/10.48550/arXiv.2102.07750; Matteo Testi et al. "MLOps: A taxonomy and a methodology". In: *IEEE Access* 10 (2022), pp. 63606–63618. doi: 10.1109/ACCESS.2022.3181730; Willem-Jan van den Heuvel and Damian A. Tamburri. "Model-driven ML-Ops for intelligent enterprise applications: Vision, approaches and challenges". In: *Business Modeling and Software Design*. Ed. by Boris Shishkov. Cham: Springer International Publishing, 2020, pp. 169–181. doi: https://doi.org/10.1007/978-3-030-52306-0_11; Xinrui Zhang and Jason Jaskolka. "Conceptualizing the secure machine learning operations (SecMLOps) paradigm". In: *2022 IEEE 22nd International Conference on Software Quality, Reliability and Security (QRS)*. 2022, pp. 127–138. doi: 10.1109/QRS57517.2022.00023.

1. What are the main methods and methodologies utilised for developing AI systems and managing their lifecycle post-deployment?
2. Which specific requirements in the regulations above are especially relevant for an AI system's data collection and model training phase, and how could these requirements be met?
3. Which requirements in the regulations above are especially relevant for the inference stage of a deployed AI system, and how can these requirements be met?
4. How do existing data protection and cybersecurity regulations, as well as the AI Act, apply to AI as a Service (AIaaS), and how can compliance be ensured in this context?
5. Is it possible to implement the relevant requirements for AI systems in the GDPR, specific cybersecurity regulations, and the AI Act within the methodologies identified in sub-RQ 1?
6. Is it possible to ensure concurrent compliance with data protection and cybersecurity regulations, as well as the requirements in the AI Act, through a fundamental rights compliance approach based on the Charter of Fundamental Rights of the European Union?

1.4 SCOPE AND LIMITATIONS

This book analyses several EU regulations and directives, primary EU law concerning the fundamental right to privacy and data protection in the Charter[27] Articles 7 and 8, and the rights under the European Convention on Human Rights (ECHR)[28] Article 8, in conjunction with existing methodologies for developing AI systems. The analysis results in a suggestion of a framework to implement specific regulatory requirements in the development and deployment process of AI systems.

The analysis of both the laws and regulations and the methodologies for developing AI systems, as well as the resulting framework, assumes a set of predefined restrictions that both delimit and form the scope of the book.

First, the book is situated within the jurisdictional context of EU law, including the rights of Article 8 in the ECHR. However, the rights of the ECHR are only applied to interpret EU law, in accordance with the principle outlined in Article 52 (3) of the Charter. The book will not analyse the Council of Europe

---

[27] European Union. Charter of Fundamental Rights of the European Union, 26 October 2012, 2012/C 326/02.

[28] Convention for the Protection of Human Rights and Fundamental Freedoms (European Convention on Human Rights) (ECHR).

Framework Convention on Artificial Intelligence.[29] The reason behind this delimitation is that the book is placed within the context of EU law. Although the European Commission has signed the Framework Convention on behalf of the EU, the convention is aligned with the AI Act and does not contain more detailed and specified rules than the AI Act, interpreted in line with the Charter.[30]

The selection of EU law as the regulatory scope for analysis in the book is primarily due to the leading role the EU has as a regulator of technology. Existing examples of EU regulation, notably the GDPR, often serve as a source of inspiration for jurisdictions outside Europe when implementing regulations in similar fields, known as the Brussels effect.[31] Moreover, the relationship between the Charter of Fundamental Rights and the ECHR has gained increasing attention recently due to the process of the EU accession to the ECHR.[32] The EU is – as of Q3 2025 – not a party to the ECHR. However, in March 2023, the 46 member states of the Council of Europe (CoE) and the EU reached a technical agreement on the EU's accession to the Convention.[33] Issues regarding the EU's common foreign and security policy remain to be

---

29 Council of Europe Treaty Series – No. 225. *Council of Europe Framework Convention on Artificial Intelligence and Human Rights, Democracy and the Rule of Law.* url: https://rm.coe.int/1680afae3c. Last accessed: 01.08.2025.

30 European Commission. *Commission signed the Council of Europe Framework Convention on Artificial Intelligence and human rights, democracy and the rule of law.* url: https://digital-strategy.ec.europa.eu/en/news/commission-signed-council-europe-framework-convention-artificial-intelligence-and-human-rights. Last accessed 16.09.2024.

31 Anu Bradford. "The Brussels effect". In: *Northwestern University Law Review* 107 (2012), p. 1. url: https://ssrn.com/abstract=2770634; See, for instance, the Brazilian law *Lei Geral de Proteção de Dados Pessoais* of 2018. https://lgpd-brazil.info/. Last accessed: 01.08.2025.

32 Delegation of the European Union to the Council of Europe. *Major progress on the path to EU accession to the ECHR: Negotiations concluded at technical level in Strasbourg.* url: https://www.eeas.europa.eu/delegations/council-europe/major-progress-path-eu-accession-echr-negotiations-concluded-technical-level-strasbourg_en?s=51. Last accessed: 01.08.2025.

33 Delegation of the European Union to the Council of Europe. *Major progress on the path to EU accession to the ECHR: Negotiations concluded at technical level in Strasbourg.* url: https://www.eeas.europa.eu/delegations/council-europe/major-progress-path-eu-accession-echr-negotiations-concluded-technical-level-strasbourg_en?s=51. Last accessed: 01.08.2025. Stian Øby Johansen et al. "The revised draft agreement on the accession of the EU to the ECHR: Third time's a charm?" In: *European Papers–A Journal on Law and Integration* 9.2 (2024), pp. 641–646. doi: https://doi.org/10.15166/2499-8249/774.

negotiated in the 46 + 1 group consisting of the 46 members of the CoE and the EU.[34] If the EU becomes a full member of the Convention in the future, as this technical agreement marks an important step towards that goal, EU regulations and directives might be put under the scrutiny of the European Court of Human Rights (ECtHR). Thus, it is important both to focus on the rights of the Charter and to analyse the Charter in line with the ECHR in the book.

Second, in order to place the methodologies applied to develop AI systems and manage deployed AI systems in context, it is necessary to have some initial focus on the methodologies applied to develop traditional software systems. Although it is a very different process to develop an AI system and a traditional software system, the development process and lifecycle management of AI systems share some inspiration from traditional software engineering. There exist various methodologies for the process of developing software systems. Recently, agile methods, such as Scrum,[35] have gained popularity due to their ability to enhance creativity during software system development. Prior to the widespread adoption of agile methods, plan-driven methodologies were more commonly used. Plan-driven software system development methodologies refer to a structured approach to developing a software system. The key characteristics of all plan-driven software system development processes include repeatability and predictability, a well-defined and structured process, comprehensive documentation, upfront system architecture, detailed planning, process monitoring, control, risk management, verification, and validation.[36] Chapter 2 of this book will focus on development methodologies for AI systems. However, in order to do so, descriptions of some aspects of traditional software development are necessary to exemplify how some aspects of software engineering could be applied to – potentially – more efficiently comply with various regulatory requirements in AI system development and deployment.

---

[34] Council of Europe. *EU accession to the ECHR ("46+1" Group)*. url: https://www.coe.int/en/web/human-rights-intergovernmental-cooperation/accession-of-the-european-union-to-the-european-convention-on-human-rights. Last accessed: 01.08.2025.

[35] Lind Rising and Norman S. Janoff. "The Scrum software development process for small teams". In: *IEEE Software* 17.4 (2000), pp. 26–32. doi: https://doi.org/10.1109/52.854065.

[36] Marcelo Marinho Marcelo, John Noll Ita Richardson, and Sarah Beecham. "Plan-driven approaches are alive and kicking in agile global software development". In: *2019 ACM/IEEE International Symposium on Empirical Software Engineering and Measurement (ESEM)*. IEEE. 2019, pp. 1–11. doi: https://doi.org/10.48550/arXiv.1906.08895.

The right to privacy and the right to data protection are not absolute rights, and these rights may, therefore, lawfully be interfered with if certain specific conditions are fulfilled. Many of the specific regulations analysed in the book have exemptions from their scope for national security purposes, and also specific exemptions for the right to life, protected under Article 2 of the Charter. Examples of such exemptions include the exemption for national security and military objectives from the scope of the AI Act, according to Article 2 (3) of the AI Act. The book will delimit its scope against both specific AI systems used for military and national security purposes. The reasoning behind this delimitation is mainly to put the key focus of the book on the requirement under the scope AI Act and the other analysed examples of secondary law. The scope of the analysed regulations, therefore, functions as a natural delimitation of the scope of the book.

In addition to the fundamental rights outlined in the Charter, this book will focus on the domains of data protection regulation, cybersecurity regulation, and AI regulation. The selection of these specific areas of law is based on several reasons. Privacy and data protection have a long and rich legislative history in the EU, dating back to the Data Protection Directive from 1995.[37] The concept of privacy by design, which involves incorporating privacy strategies in the design of technology, was first introduced in the mid-1990s.[38] As privacy and data protection are considered fundamental rights under Articles 7 and 8 in the Charter, and given the available case law from the Court of Justice of the European Union (CJEU), as well as the long history of privacy by design, privacy and data protection have been chosen as the subject of analysis in the book.

Cybersecurity requirements are essential demands for nearly any software system or AI system. However, the legislative initiatives from the EU, specifically regarding cybersecurity, are relatively new, dating back to the NIS Directive from 2016.[39] The introduction of EU cybersecurity initiatives is a response to the vulnerability of cyberspace and its increasing importance in

---

[37] Directive 95/46/EC of the European Parliament and of the Council of 24 October 1995 on the protection of individuals with regard to the processing of personal data and of the free movement of such data [1995] OJ L 281/31.

[38] Ann Cavukian. *Privacy by Design: The 7 Foundational Principles.* Tech. rep. Information and privacy commissioner of Ontario, Canada, 2009.

[39] Regulation (EU) 2019/881 of the European Parliament and of the Council of 17 April 2019 on ENISA (the European Union Agency for Cybersecurity) and on information and communications technology cybersecurity certification and repealing Regulation (EU) No 526/2013 (Cybersecurity Act) [2016] OJ L 151/15 and Directive (EU) 2022/2555 of the European Parliament and of the Council of 14 December 2022 on measures for a high common level of cybersecurity across

society. Due to the importance of embedded cybersecurity in software and AI systems, and since cybersecurity regulation is a prioritised policy area in the EU, cybersecurity regulation has been chosen as a subject of analysis in the book.

Moreover, AI regulation is such a recent policy area that although the AI Act entered into force on 1 August 2024, it does not apply before 2 August 2026, with some of the requirements applying from 2025 and 2027, according to Article 113 of the AI Act. The AI Act categorises AI systems based on their intended purposes, ranging from prohibited systems to high-risk, minimal-risk AI systems, as well as requirements for general-purpose AI models and general-purpose AI models with systemic risk. As high-risk AI systems are subject to the most substantial requirements, they are the key focus of this book. When an AI system processes personal data, the provider of the system must – potentially– comply with data protection regulation, cybersecurity regulation, and the AI Act simultaneously. This is a challenging task, and it is, therefore, an interesting research question to focus on how such legal consideration could be properly taken into account throughout the entire AI system development process and lifecycle of AI systems.

1.5 METHODOLOGY

This book is the result of interdisciplinary research at the intersection of computer science and law. These disciplines possess distinct characteristics and are traditionally separated into diverse categories of science and research. Given the different nature of these disciplines, it is necessary to develop and formulate a specific research methodology that aligns with the objectives of this book.

Computer science is traditionally categorised within the realm of natural science. Science could be described as a process where various phenomena are systematically examined. The primary objective of such systematic studies is to test hypotheses through reproducible experiments. Computer science, as a part of the natural sciences, typically employs the hypothetico-deductive method,[40] wherein the exploration of a phenomenon leads to the formulation of a hypothesis that provides an explanatory framework. This hypothesis is subsequently subjected to empirical testing through a series of experiments or formal verification through mathematics. If the experimental outcomes or

---

the Union, amending Regulation (EU) No 910/2014 and Directive (EU) 2018/1972, and repealing Directive (EU) 2016/1148 (NIS 2 Directive) [2022] OJ L 333/80.

40 Anton E. Lawson. "Hypothetico-deductive method". In: *Encyclopedia of Science Education*. Ed. by R Gunston. Dordrecht: Springer, 2015. doi: https://doi.org/10.1007/978-94-007-2150-0_260.

formal verifications align with the hypothesis, the hypothesis is supported. However, if the results diverge from the hypothesis, the hypothesis is falsified or weakened, necessitating the formulation of an alternative hypothesis.

With specific regard to the research methodology applied in computer science, the Association for Computing Machinery (ACM) established a task force in 1989 to formulate and present a specific research methodology framework tailored to computer science.[41] The methodological framework established by the task force comprises three main paradigms, namely theory, abstraction, and design. The theory paradigm of the computer science research methodology has its basis in mathematics and consists of establishing a description — a hypothesis — testing the hypothesis in experiments, and analysing the experimental results. The theory paradigm involves using formal methods, models, and empirical evaluation to advance the understanding of computational systems. The hypothesis testing could also be conducted in more formal manners, e.g., through mathematical testing. The abstraction paradigm, also known as modelling, builds on the outcomes of the theory phase, generating new hypotheses, constructing models, making predictions, designing experiments, collecting data, and analysing the results obtained from the experiment. The final part of the framework, the design paradigm, draws inspiration from engineering principles and encompasses a systematic approach to constructing a system to solve a specific problem. The design paradigm includes stating the system's requirements, stating the specifications of the system, designing and implementing the system, and carrying out thorough testing.

In contrast, law is a discipline focusing on textual interpretations rather than experimental evaluation. The methodology is primarily concerned with interpreting various legal sources to establish a norm, applying this norm to the facts of the case, and assessing the hierarchy of norms, in case different norms could apply to the same facts.[42] Legal research methodology is often concerned with hypotheses, assumptions, and the meta-narratives that underpin the legal methodology.[43]

When comparing legal research methodology to computer science research methodology, the two methodologies exhibit some similarities, but also several distinctive differences. In an experimental computer science methodology, the objective is to construct an artefact or a system in a specific use-case domain

---

41 Peter J Denning et al. "Computing as a discipline". In: *Communications of the ACM* 32.1 (1989), pp. 9–23.

42 Hans Petter Graver. "Vanlig juridisk metode? Om rettsdogmatikken som juridisk sjanger". In: *Tidsskrift for rettsvitenskap* 2 (2008). doi: https://doi.org/10.18261/ISSN1504-3096-2008-02-01.

43 Christina Ramberg. *Erfarenheter som kan vara til nytta för doktorandar i juridik*. Stockholm: Jure Forlag, 2003.

to demonstrate its feasibility using scientific methods.[44] A similarity between legal research methodology and computer science research methodology is that they both test the validity of different approaches to problems. While the legal research methodology tests such validity by interpreting legal sources, the computer science research methodology tests it through various experimental evaluations.

The research presented in this book combines legal research methodology with a computer science methodology and employs a methodological approach that is interdisciplinary in nature. Legal research on privacy, data protection, cybersecurity regulation, and AI regulation often adopts a retrospective approach where an operational system is analysed. In contrast, computer science research often aims to design effective solutions to real-life problems. In such a process, compliance issues risk not being given the necessary attention.

From a legal research perspective, the book situates itself within the principle of *lex lata* and legal dogmatics, describing the law in force.[45] In specific parts of the book where the analysis of the law in force results in suggestions for improvements or alterations of the current regulations, the principle of *lex ferenda* will be applied.[46] It is explicitly indicated in the book if the analysis results in specific suggestions for the improvement of laws and regulations in force.

Within the legal research methodology applied in the book, the aim is to identify, specify, and clarify the primary current and near-future legal considerations related to developing and deploying AI systems within data protection, cybersecurity, AI regulation, and the overarching constitutional boundaries for processing personal data and using AI within the Charter interpreted in line with the ECHR. Given the advent nature of the field and the consequent scarcity of traditional legal sources such as case law, the identification, specification, and clarification of the issues cannot lead to definitive conclusions in every case. Nevertheless, to ensure methodological rigour in relation to the legal analysis, the legal analysis will be grounded in related judgements from the ECtHR and the CJEU regarding various forms of data processing.

---

44 Timothy Colburn. "Methodology of computer science". In: *The Blackwell Guide to the Philosophy of Computing and Information*. Ed. by Luciano Floridi. Hoboken: Blackwell Publishing, 2003, pp. 318–326. doi: https://doi.org/10.1002/9780470757017.ch24.

45 Jan M Smits. "What is legal doctrine? On the aims and methods of legal-dogmatic research" In: *Rethinking Legal Scholarship: A Transatlantic Dialogue*. Ed. by Rob van Gestel, Hans-W Micklitz, and Edward L Rubin. Cambridge: Cambridge University Press, 2017, pp. 207–228.

46 Hugh Thirlway. "Reflections on *lex ferenda*". In: *Netherlands Yearbook of International Law* 32 (2001), pp. 3–26. doi: 10.1017/S0167676800001148.

Despite the inherent challenges related to the lack of traditional legal sources, the legal analysis will be based on existing judgements from the CJEU and the ECtHR regarding the constitutional boundaries of fundamental and human rights. These analyses will attempt to prognosticate how these judicial bodies that decide and delineate the overall constitutional and fundamental rights boundaries in Europe, in the future, may assess privacy and data protection boundaries regarding the development and deployment of AI systems.

In a computer science context, the book is grounded in the subfield of system research, research related to software systems development methodologies, and AI research. Abstraction is applied to describe the currently used development methodologies for AI systems. Based on the combination of this abstraction and the analysis of the legal sources, the book suggests specific approaches to implement the necessary legal constraints in the development methodologies for AI systems and the methodologies applied to update deployed AI systems.

1.6 OUTLINE

Overall, the structure of the book focuses on three different components: The data component, the model component, and the AI-as-a-Service (AIaaS) component.

The data components address specific data protection, cybersecurity, and AI Act issues when collecting training data and applying the training data to train an AI model.

The model component focuses on the same three legal topics when applying a trained AI model to draw inferences in a deployed setting.

The last component focuses on legal constraints when an AI model is applied in a commonly used business model known as AIaaS, where an AI model is rented from a platform provider, running it on a cloud computing platform. Key legal issues in such a setting include controllership status under the GPPR and AI governance issues with AI infrastructure and data sharing.

All three chapters, to some extent, also focus on whether and how identified legal aspects could be implemented in a methodology applied for AI development and lifecycle management known as MLOps.

The chapters of the book are structured as follows:

- Chapter 2 focuses on the first sub-research question of how AI-based systems and ML systems are developed and maintained during their lifecycles. The chapter functions as a necessary step in order to analyse how data protection, cybersecurity regulation, and AI regulation compliance could be implemented in the development and lifecycle management of AI systems. The last section of Chapter 2 presents the data component, model component, and the AIaaS component as an overall structure of the remainder of the book. All of these stages include data protection, cybersecurity regulation, and AI Act requirements issues.

- Chapters 3, 4, and 5 will analyse data protection, cybersecurity regulation compliance issues, and AI Act requirements in the data component, model component, and overall AI system component of AI system development and deployment. These three chapters focus on sub-research questions 2–4. In all of these chapters, the relevant requirements under data protection regulation, cybersecurity regulation, and the AI Act will be analysed. Chapters 2 and 3 also contain a subsection on how the various legal requirements potentially could be implemented through alterations to the MLOps framework, sub-research question 5.
- In Chapter 6, the focus is on sub-research question 6 and how the principle of proportionality and the fundamental right to data protection relate to the overlap in scope of the GDPR and the AI Act. Chapter 6 establishes an explanatory taxonomy that attempts to function as an interpretative tool and a basis for best practice when AI systems enter the scope of the GDPR, the AI Act, and the rights of the Charter simultaneously.
- In Chapter 7, the enforcement of the GDPR, the AI Act, and the proportionality by design concept from Chapter 6 are analysed. The concepts of self-enforcement, enforcement through enforcement authorities, and enforcement in courts are examined.
- Lastly, Chapter 8 summarises the overall findings and concludes. Chapter 8 also focuses on how the findings of the book could be investigated further in future research.

2. The development and lifecycle of AI-based systems

2.1 INTRODUCTION

The forthcoming chapter functions as a prerequisite for the analyses in the subsequent chapters. Initially, the chapter will explain how – typically – an AI system is developed from data and algorithms that are applied to train an AI model. The current chapter and the book will especially focus on a subfield of AI, ML. Subsequently, a comparison is made between developing traditional software and developing AI systems. The rationale behind this comparison is to describe how some elements of more traditional software development and software lifecycle management have inspired methodologies applied for developing AI systems and managing the lifecycle of deployed AI systems. Then, the next section of the chapter provides a detailed explanation of the MLOps framework. The last section summarises the overall findings of the chapter and concludes.

2.2 DEFINING AI: FROM TAXONOMIES TO LEGAL DEFINITIONS

While the recent surge in public interest in AI might create the impression that AI is a very new and emerging research field, AI has a rich historical lineage dating back to the 1950s.[1] From the birth of the field of AI in approximately the late 1950s and early 1960s, and continuing to the mid-1990s, the dominant trajectory of AI centred around expert systems.[2] In expert systems, the fundamental premise is that every aspect of learning and intelligence should be meticulously defined, enabling a learning component (a machine) to simu-

[1] John McCarthy et al. "A proposal for the Dartmouth summer research project on artificial intelligence, August 31, 1955". In: *AI Magazine* 27.4 (2006), pp. 12–12.

[2] CS Krishnamoorthy and S Rajeev. *Artificial Intelligence and Expert Systems for Engineers*. Boca Raton: CRC Press, 2018, p. 18.

late these aspects.[3] Currently, such a predefined solution to AI is not widely pursued.

At present, the focus has shifted towards the practical application of ML. ML refers to various methodologies where algorithms, comprising a standardised set of mathematical and statistical rules, are deployed to identify similarities within extensive datasets.[4] These identified patterns are applied to learn from unseen data and thereby perform tasks such as predictions, recommendations, and content generation, without explicit pre-programmed instructions. An ML solution to a problem typically comprises three main components:

1. The dataset that is applied as a basis for learning.
2. The problem – e.g., classification, regression, or clustering – and the specifically selected ML algorithm to solve the problem.
3. Performance metrics, e.g., accuracy, to assess whether the trained ML model performs sufficiently on unseen data.[5]

One commonality across the AI field is the focus on scientific taxonomies of the different types of AI systems and the different methods such systems employ.[6] In the AI Act adopted by the European Union (EU) in 2024, AI systems are now legally defined. This definition – in one of the first specific AI

---

[3] Dan Patterson. *Introduction to Artificial Intelligence and Expert Systems.* Englewood Cliffs: Prentice Hall, 1990, p. 10.

[4] Michael I Jordan and Tom M Mitchell. "Machine learning: Trends, perspectives, and prospects". In: *Science* 349.6245 (2015), pp. 255–260. doi: https://doi.org/10.1126/science.aaa8415.

[5] Tom M Mitchell. *Machine Learning.* New York: McGraw-Hill, 1997, p. 2; Christoph Molnar. *Interpretable Machine Learning.* Lulu.com, 2020.

[6] Tadas Baltrušaitis, Chaitanya Ahuja, and Louis-Philippe Morency. "Multimodal machine learning: A survey and taxonomy". In: *IEEE Transactions on Pattern Analysis and Machine Intelligence* 41.2 (2018), pp. 423–443. doi: https://doi.org/10.48550/arXiv.1705.09406; Pooja Rani et al. "Taxonomy of machine learning algorithms and its applications". In: *Journal of Computational and Theoretical Nanoscience* 17.6 (2020), pp. 2508–2513. doi: https://doi.org/10.1166/jctn.2020.8922; Ines Chami et al. "Machine learning on graphs: A model and comprehensive taxonomy". In: *The Journal of Machine Learning Research* 23.1 (2022), pp. 3840–3903. doi: https://doi.org/10.48550/arXiv.2005.03675; Frank Emmert-Streib and Matthias Dehmer. "Taxonomy of machine learning paradigms: A data-centric perspective". In: *Wiley Interdisciplinary Reviews: Data Mining and Knowledge Discovery* 12.5 (2022), e1470. doi: https://doi.org/10.1002/widm.1470.

regulations globally – is similar to the one from the Organisation for Economic Co-operation and Development (OECD).[7]

With a legal definition of AI, we can move beyond the various scientific taxonomies of AI and AI systems to a precise definition that places an autonomous system either within or outside of the scope of the AI Act and thereby within or outside the scope of the requirements in the AI Act. The definition of an AI system in Article 3 (1) of the AI Act reads as follows:

> [A] machine-based system designed to operate with varying levels of autonomy and that may exhibit adaptiveness after deployment and that, for explicit or implicit objectives, infers, from the input it receives, how to generate outputs such as predictions, content, recommendations, or decisions that can influence physical or virtual environments.

Several provisions of the definition of AI systems according to Article 3 (1) of the AI Act necessitate some elaboration. The definition in Article 3 (1) is further explained and expounded in recital 12 to the AI Act. The next paragraphs aim to interpret the specific subparts of the definition in line with recital 12.

First, an AI system must be "designed to operate with varying levels of autonomy". Recital 12 underscores the importance of separating AI systems from more traditional software systems or programming approaches. Consequently, the definition outlined in Article 3 (1) should exclude systems reliant exclusively on rules defined solely by natural persons for automatic execution of operations. The reference to varying levels of autonomy is to be understood as a condition for AI systems to have "some degree of independence of actions from human involvement and of capabilities to operate without human intervention", according to recital 12, to fall within the scope of the definition in Article 3 (1) of the AI Act. Thus, the requirement necessitating AI systems to be "designed to operate with varying levels of autonomy" serves as a separating factor between traditional software systems and AI systems, aligning with the purpose of the definition from the EU lawmaker, expressed in recital 12 to the AI Act.

Second, according to the definition of AI systems under Article 3 (1) of the AI Act, AI systems "may exhibit adaptiveness after employment". This adaptiveness refers to the self-learning capabilities inherent in some AI systems, i.e., the capability to evolve while deployed in an operational setting, as specified in recital 12 to the AI Act.

---

[7] Organisation for Economic Co-operation and Development (OECD). *OECD, AI Principles Overview.* Paris: OECD. url: https://oecd.ai/en/ai-principles. Last accessed: 01.08.2025.

The inclusion of "explicit or implicit objectives" in the definition in Article 3 (1) of the AI Act refers to the fact that the output of the AI system might be both explicitly defined by the AI system provider or more implicitly determined, according to recital 12. Furthermore, recital 12 to the AI Act presupposes that the objectives of AI systems may deviate from the intended purpose of the system, especially if the AI system is deployed in a context different from the one intended by the AI provider.

One of the most important parts of the definition of AI systems in Article 3 (1) of the AI Act is the requirement that AI systems must "infer" outputs from the inputs they receive. The "infer" requirement is further explained in recital 12 to the Act. According to the EU legislator, the inference aspect of the definition pertains to the process of obtaining the outputs of the systems, such as predictions, content, recommendations, or decisions, from the input data. Additionally, as outlined in recital 12, "inference" also encompasses the process of deriving models and/or algorithms from data during model training. Inference includes ML and logic- and knowledge-based approaches that infer from encoded knowledge or symbolic representation of the task to be solved, according to recital 12.

In order to get a more comprehensive understanding of such "inference" in ML, it is necessary to provide a brief overview of the most frequently used types of ML.

2.3 MACHINE LEARNING

2.3.1 Comparing a Technical and a Legal Definition of AI

ML adopts a distinct approach to problem-solving compared to traditional programming of a software system. Rather than relying solely on predefined rules and human-programmed algorithms, ML apply data and specific ML algorithms to address known or unknown problems. An approach to defining ML, expressed technically, is Mitchell's definition:

> A computer program is said to learn from experience E with respect to some class of tasks T and performance measure P if its performance at tasks in T, as measured by P, improves with experience E.[8]

This formal definition emphasises that ML is characterised by the evolving nature and improving tasks with experience. In Mitchell's definition, the reference to a "computer program" is analogous to the reference to ML algorithms and ML models in the examples below.

---

8 Tom M Mitchell. *Machine Learning*. New York: McGraw-Hill, 1997, p. 2.

Table 2.1 Comparison between a technical definition of ML and the AI Act Article 3 (1)

Mitchell's definition	AI Act Article 3 (1)
Learn from experience E	"[I]nfer from the input it receives" and "[E]xhibit adaptiveness"
The task of class T	"[O]utputs such as predictions, content, recommendations, or decisions"
Performance measure P	"[C]an influence physical or virtual environments"
Improves with experience E	"[O]perate with varying levels of autonomy"

Mitchell's definition was first published in 1997.[9] A potential insightful task is to compare the specific subparts of such a technical definition with the definition adopted by the European legislator in the AI Act of 2024. Such a comparison aims to evaluate the extent to which the foundational elements of a technical definition of ML appear in the legal definition of AI systems in the AI Act. Table 2.1 below compares the formal definition by Mitchell to AI Act Article 3 (1).

A finding in Table 2.1 is the alignment between all elements in the technical definition in the legal definition outlined in Article 3 (1) of the AI Act. While not every component possesses an exact equivalent, e.g., the performance measure P is not precisely the same as the possibility of influencing physical or virtual environments. However, the underlying concepts have exhibited similarities across the two definitions. It is, therefore, a viable path to explore additional parts of the formal definition by Mitchell in order to provide insight into the AI Act's definition of AI systems.

The solution to a problem – or the class of tasks T – is often discovered through discerning known or unknown patterns in the data. ML systems are mostly categorised into one of three categories: supervised, unsupervised, or reinforcement learning systems.[10] Each of these different categories represents a different approach to learning from data to solve problems.

2.3.2 Supervised, Unsupervised, and Reinforcement Learning

A supervised ML system can be analogously compared to the method used to teach a child how to read. In the pedagogical process of teaching someone how

9 Ibid.

10 Michael I Jordan and Tom M Mitchell. "Machine learning: Trends, perspectives, and prospects". In: *Science* 349.6245 (2015), pp. 255–260. doi: https://doi.org/10.1126/science.aaa8415.

to read, an individual who masters the task of reading explains to the person under training the correlation between specific sounds and their corresponding letters or groups of letters. Similarly, in supervised ML, the training data are pre-annotated by an annotator. The annotated training data provides the ML algorithms with a guideline on how specific inputs should be classified or clustered.[11] The aim of the trained ML model is to classify, cluster, or do a similar task with the data, where the new data is mapped to a similar category or cluster as the annotated data. The trained ML model achieves this by mapping input data to desirable outputs.

Suppose that a supervised ML approach is applied for a classification task. In the training process, the ML algorithm is exposed to data points and produces a score for each category it is going to classify. The objective of the learning process is for the category to have the highest score for the correct category. A computable function is used to measure the error between the output of scores and the desired score of the correct classification, known as an error or loss function. During the ML process, the internal adjustable parameters of the ML algorithm are adjusted to reduce the error or loss function to an acceptable level. The adjustable parameters are also referred to as weights. To adjust the loss function properly, each adjustable parameter – weight – of the algorithm is computed to indicate how adjusting the weight would increase or decrease the loss function. The overall aim of the learning is to optimise the loss function.

To illustrate how supervised ML might be applied to solve a problem or a task, suppose that a financial institution wants to develop a technical solution to predict which debtors have a high risk of defaulting on their credit. In such a situation, a supervised ML approach could be applied. The first step to develop a supervised ML model would be to collect data on customers defaulting, customers not defaulting, and data about these two groups of customers, e.g., income, address, and previous credit defaults. This data is then split into three sets: training data, validation data, and test data. The training data is used as input in a supervised ML algorithm to develop a credit default supervised ML model that maps the input data to desirable outputs, whether or not the data meets a debtor default threshold. The input data, e.g., income and credit history, is mapped to the target output, whether the customer defaulted or not. The validation data is used during the model development process to tune the parameters of the model on unseen data. The validation data can be applied to ensure that the model does not overfit on the training data and also performs well on unseen data. The model can then be applied to new, unseen data, the test data, to assess how well the model generalises to new, unseen data. After

11 Christoph Molnar. *Interpretable Machine Learning*. Lulu.com, 2020.

this training process, the model can be applied to predict a customer's credit risk.

In contrast to supervised ML systems, which require the use of pre-annotated datasets, unsupervised ML systems operate without such pre-annotated data, as suggested by the term "unsupervised". Instead, these systems employ ML algorithms that identify similarities within extensive datasets autonomously. One method of unsupervised learning is clustering, where data exhibiting similar characteristics are sampled into clusters, while data that deviates from such clusters is deemed an anomaly.[12] Such a clustering process could be applied for purposes such as sorting data, optimising different alternatives, or recommending a specific marketing campaign to a specific customer or group of customers. Another method of unsupervised learning is dimensionality reduction, where high-dimensional data, i.e., data with a lot of features, is reduced to a lower number of features while retaining as much of the important information as possible from the original data.[13] The lower-dimensional data is then applied to train a model.

In reinforcement learning systems, the output generated by the ML algorithm is subject to classification by an annotator, discerning it as either correct or incorrect. Additionally, the ML system receives feedback in the form of a "reward" for correct outputs or a "penalty" for incorrect ones.[14] A reinforcement learning setting often exhibits more flexibility compared to settings where supervised or unsupervised learning is applied. Unlike the initial premise suggesting immediate feedback following each decision, reinforcement learning often operates within a dynamic setting where rewards or penalties are dispensed after a chain of decisions is performed by the agent (referred to as the "machine"). The agent's primary objective is to maximise the cumulative reward over time. An example of a task where a reinforcement learning solution could be applied is where a reinforcement agent plays Tetris or other games, or where a mechanical robot performs a task on a factory floor.

The next subsections will address two other subsets of ML commonly used, deep learning methods and large language models (LLMs).

---

[12] Muhammad Usama et al. "Unsupervised machine learning for networking: Techniques, applications and research challenges". In: *IEEE Access* 7 (2019), pp. 65579–65615. doi: 10.1109/ACCESS.2019.2916648.

[13] Jose Manuel Pena et al. "Dimensionality reduction in unsupervised learning of conditional Gaussian networks". In: *IEEE Transactions on Pattern Analysis and Machine Intelligence* 23.6 (2001), pp. 590–603.

[14] Iqbal H Sarker. "Machine learning: Algorithms, real-world applications and research directions". In: *SN Computer Science* 2.3 (2021), p. 160. doi: https://doi.org/10.1007/s42979-021-00592-x.

2.3.3 Deep Learning

Deep learning is a subset of ML. Similar to the approaches described above, the overall aim of deep learning is to learn representations from data.[15] Deep learning, however, allows the models to learn such representations through multiple processing layers known as neural networks, a network of interconnected layers. The "deep" in deep learning refers to the number of layers in the neural networks. These layers have a backpropagation algorithm that is applied to change the parameters of the current layer based on the computations from the previous layer.[16]

The ML methods elaborated in the previous subsections are limited when processing natural raw data. Previously, a task such as image recognition or speech recognition through ML required a feature extractor that extracted a feature from the raw data, the image or sound recording, to be a suitable representation that the learning subsystem could apply to detect or recognise a pattern.[17]

In deep learning, such feature extraction is not necessary because the learning infrastructure, the layers of the network, themselves automatically discover the representations in the raw data, e.g., the image or audio recording, needed for detection or classification. For image recognition, a typical deep learning process would commence with the first layer learning features from the edges of the image; the second layer focusing on motives in the image, zeroing in on specific arrangements; and the third layer targeting learning representations of specific combinations of motives of the image, etc. These layers are not annotated by a human or preprogrammed; they are learned by a general-purpose learning procedure in the layers of the neural network.

In supervised learning, many of the methods used apply linear classifiers to categorise the input data. Such linear classifiers are sensitive to small changes in the input data. In complex recognition tasks – such as image and speech recognition – small changes to the input data might not entail an actual change in the output data category, and other little variations might represent a different output category. For instance, if an image of a white wolf and a polar bear both have a similar background, a linear image recognition model might classify the two as similar. Opposite, if one image of a polar bear is in an icy background and another is in an urban zoo setting, the linear image classifier might classify them as different animals. Deep learning offers the possibility to account

15 Yann LeCun, Yoshua Bengio, and Geoffrey Hinton. "Deep learning". In: *Nature* 521.7553 (2015), pp. 436–444. doi: https://doi.org/10.1038/nature14539.

16 Ibid.

17 Ibid.

for such irrelevant changes in the setting (the same background) while being sensitive to relevant changes in the input data (two different animals).

The next subsection will address another subset of ML, less dependent on pre-trained human-annotated input-output mapping, LLMs.

2.3.4 Large Language Models (LLMs)

LLMs are a subset of deep learning consisting of AI algorithms trained on vast text datasets and specifically developed to perform language-related tasks.[18] ChatGPT is an example of an LLM developed based on a transformer-based architecture.[19] The "large" in large language models refers to the size of the neural network applied in the deep learning architecture of LLMs.[20]

In LLMs, the input data is text. In order for the ML models to compute outputs from the inputs, the text has to be transformed into numeric inputs. This processing operation is known as word embedding. When embedding a value in a word, words frequently used together in the text, for instance, the words banana and apple, are embedded with more similar values than the two words banana and car.[21]

The text generation in LLMs is, in essence, a classification problem. The LLM predicts the next word with the highest probability to fit in the context based on the data the LLM has been pre-trained on. The classes the LLM model could choose from are the number of tokens, fundamental elements of letters that words in a given language consist of.

Generative language models, such as ChatGPT, predict such words from massive training data and a pre-trained method known as self-supervised learning. When ChatGPT was trained, massive amounts of text from the Internet were scraped. The self-supervised learning process then removed the last word in a sentence, and the ML model predicted the outcome of the word. In such a context, the actual next word is present, and the output might be self-supervised to the ground truth, the actual word of the sentence that was scraped from the Internet. This process is repeated on massive amounts of text data.

---

[18] Andreas Stöffelbauer. *How Large Language Models Work from Zero to ChatGPT.* url: https://medium.com/data-science-at-microsoft/how-large-language-models-work-91c362f5b78f. Last accessed: 01.08.2025.

[19] OpenAI. *ChatGPT.* url: https://chat.openai.com/. Last accessed: 01.08.2025.

[20] Marco Del Pra. *Large Language Models.* url: https://medium.com/@marcodelpra/large-language-models-1a6eec644b30. Last accessed: 01.08.2025.

[21] Michael Phi. *Illustrated Guide to Transformers: Step by Step Explanation.* url: https://towardsdatascience.com/illustrated-guide-to-transformers-step-by-step-explanation-f74876522bc0. Last accessed: 01.08.2025.

In GPT models, the G stands for "Generative", referring to the next word prediction in the language models, and the P stands for "Pre-trained", referring to the training process explained in the former paragraph. The T stands for "Transformer", a model architecture that will be explained in the following paragraphs.

A transformer architecture consists of an encoder and decoder.[22] Both of these parts are composed of a neural network consisting of layers. The encoder and decoder architecture attempts to solve the dependencies of context in next-word prediction. When predicting the next word in a sentence, the probability of a specific next word is not only dependent on the words of that specific sentence but also potentially on the words sixteen words earlier in the sentence or a context from the former paragraph of the text. The encoder-decoder architecture allows LLMs to assign value to more important parts of a sequence of words to assess the probability of the next word in a specific context.

The encoder is tasked with storing the sequences of input data (the text) in a continuous representation that reflects what the encoder has "learned" from the input text. In this process, the encoder learns which words often appear together, in which order these words appear together, and if some words in a specific order are questions and whether some are answers. The encoder stores the information of which words appear together more often in a numerical matrix. The encoder then computes the probability between 0 and 1 of how a specific word attends to the other words of the sentence.[23]

The task of the decoder is to generate the next words in the sequence of words. The decoder builds on the scores from the encoder, where the probability of the next word based on previous words of a sentence is calculated and chooses the word with the highest probability each time, one word at a time. The probability is calculated based on both the previous outputs and the outputs from the encoder as inputs.[24]

To summarise, language creation through LLMs is possible because of vast amounts of text data that are pre-trained in a model to calculate the probability of the next word. When LLMs are put into an AI system, it is also necessary to include various filters to prevent the generation of content that is dangerous, hateful, or overly biased.

The unique characteristics of ML, including its reliance on data and iterative learning, necessitate modifications to traditional software system development

---

[22] Ashish Vaswani et al. *Attention Is All You Need.* 2023. arXiv: 1706.03762.

[23] Michael Phi. *Illustrated Guide to Transformers: Step by Step Explanation.* url: https://towardsdatascience.com/illustrated-guide-to-transformers-step-by-step-explanation-f74876522bc0. Last accessed: 01.08.2025.

[24] Marco Del Pra. *Large Language Models.* url: https://medium.com/@marco-delpra/large-language-models-1a6eec644b30. Last accessed: 01.08.2025.

methodologies where computer functionality is programmed and developed by natural persons. Such adaptations to development methodologies will be addressed in the next subsection.

2.4 THE DIFFERENCE IN DEVELOPING TRADITIONAL SOFTWARE AND AI SYSTEMS

The development of an AI system shares certain parallels with, yet also diverges significantly from, the development of traditional software systems. Traditional software systems necessitate explicit programming for their functionalities, whereas AI systems infer functionality through the training data and the models developed by the data through algorithms.[25] This results in varying levels of autonomy within AI systems, a characteristic acknowledged in the definition of AI systems in the AI Act discussed above. Another distinction between traditional software and AI-based software systems lies in the impact of data: in traditional software systems, data only affects the output, while in AI systems, data can influence the model upon which the system is based, thereby affecting the overall system, even after the AI system is deployed.

Another difference between traditional software systems and AI systems is the nondeterministic nature of AI systems. While a software system is intended to have the same input-output mapping in similar instances, the nondeterministic nature of an AI system might result in similar input receiving different output, or the same output.

In terms of explainability, explaining the output of traditional software systems is generally a more straightforward task compared to AI-based systems. Given the potential impact of data on the model and, consequently, on the entire AI systems, continuous monitoring of the AI systems and the trained ML model becomes imperative upon deployment. In contrast, traditional software systems do not demand the same level of ongoing monitoring in order to explain the output of the system. The explainability of the outputs of AI systems is further addressed in Chapter 4, section 4.5, of the book.

[25] Prince Jain. "Interaction between software engineering and artificial intelligence – a review". In: *International Journal on Computer Science and Engineering* 3.12 (2011), p. 3774.

2.5 MLOps: FROM DEVELOPMENT TO LIFECYCLE MANAGEMENT

2.5.1 Preprocessing of the Data

In an AI system, the functionality is inferred from the training data and the ML algorithms, rather than being explicitly programmed by a human developer. The forthcoming subsection will concentrate on a specific methodology for developing ML-based systems, known as Machine Learning Operations (MLOps). To fully comprehend the MLOps methodology, it is first necessary to examine the typical workflow involved in developing a solution to a problem or set of tasks in a ML project.[26]

As previously mentioned, an ML process commences with a known or unknown problem or a set of tasks and employs data and an ML algorithm to address the problem. The ML algorithm is used to train an ML model that is applied to infer outputs from unseen data. Consequently, the initial phase of an ML process typically involves the collection and processing of data. The raw data collected during this phase often contains outliers, i.e., data points that significantly differ from other data points, and may lack sufficient quality for direct application in the ML process.[27]

To enhance the utility of the data, preprocessing steps are often undertaken to remove outliers and erroneous data points from the dataset. Depending on the specific requirements of the problem at hand, further processing may be necessary to extract only the necessary data to train the ML algorithm. The refined data then serves as the foundation for the learning and problem-solving capabilities of the ML system.[28]

Upon the completion of the data collection and cleaning of the dataset, it may be necessary to analyse the data to understand the specific attributes and characteristics of the data. In instances where the ML process commences with a pre-trained ML model, and the learning process merely involves fitting the finished trained model to an adjusted data environment, it may not

---

[26] Sridhar Alla and Suman Kalyan Adari. "Beginning MLOps with MLFlow". In: *Begin. MLOps with MLFlow* (2021). doi: https://doi.org/10.1007/978-1-4842-6549-9.

[27] Kai Zhang and Minxia Luo. "Outlier-robust extreme learning machine for regression problems". In: *Neurocomputing* 151 (2015), pp. 1519–1527. doi: https://doi.org/10.1016/j.neucom.2014.09.022.

[28] Felix Neutatz et al. "From cleaning before ML to cleaning for ML". In: *IEEE Data Engineering Bulletin* 44.1 (2021), pp. 24–41.

be necessary to use all the data for model refinement.[29] However, in other scenarios, a thorough analysis of the data might be required to identify biases or discern any identifiable patterns within the data. This data analysis phase ensures that the ML model is capable of making accurate predictions or inferences, thereby enhancing the overall effectiveness of the ML process.[30]

2.5.2 Model Training

Following the preprocessing of the data in the dataset, it is often necessary to preprocess the data further before training the ML algorithm. The training of an ML model typically necessitates the separation of the data into training, testing, and validation datasets.[31] In order to better understand the purposes of these datasets, consider an example where ML is employed for image classification, categorising images of animals as either pets or wild animals.

Initially, the image data is segregated into training, testing, and validation datasets. In the case of a supervised ML approach, a human annotator first categorises a portion of the images as either pets or wild animals in the training dataset. After this manual annotation, the ML algorithms classify the unlabeled data using the annotated training data.

The ML algorithm utilises the annotated data to classify the images, categorising them into two groups – pets and wild animals – based on their similarities with the classified examples. A loss function – i.e., a function that measures the error between a classification and the human-annotated classification – is used together with the validation dataset to assess the accuracy of the classification performed by the ML algorithm.[32] The parameters of the algorithm can be adjusted to achieve a result from the loss function that meets the desired level of accuracy.

29 Sanket Vaibhav Mehta et al. "An empirical investigation of the role of pre-training in lifelong learning". In: *Journal of Machine Learning Research* 24.214 (2023), pp. 1–50. url: http://jmlr.org/papers/v24/22-0496.html.

30 Jianglin Huang, Yan-Fu Li, and Min Xie. "An empirical analysis of data pre-processing for machine learning-based software cost estimation". In: *Information and Software Technology* 67 (2015), pp. 108–127. doi: https://doi.org/10.1016/j.infsof.2015.07.004.

31 Sotiris B Kotsiantis, Dimitris Kanellopoulos, and Panagiotis E Pintelas. "Data preprocessing for supervised learning". In: *International Journal of Computer Science* 1.2 (2006), pp. 111–117.

32 Qi Wang et al. "A comprehensive survey of loss functions in machine learning". In: *Annals of Data Science* 9 (2022), pp. 187–212. doi: https://doi.org/10.1007/s40745-020-00253-5.

Finally, the testing dataset, which consists of data that the ML model has not previously encountered, is used to evaluate the performance of the trained ML model. This last step ensures that the model's ability to classify new, unseen data is accurately assessed.

Achieving generalisation in ML is a complex task. Generalisation refers to the ability of an ML model to perform equally well on unseen data as it does on the training data.[33] Overfitting, a common issue in ML, occurs when the model fits too precisely to the training data, thereby limiting its ability to make accurate predictions on unseen data.[34] To mitigate the risk of overfitting, it may be necessary to separate a larger part of the training data as validation data and test data. This allows for early detection of a lack of generalisation and overfitting during the ML process. Overfitting might also be addressed by augmenting the training datasets with more specialised data points. This enhances the model's ability to generalise from the training data to unseen data, thereby improving the predictive performance of the ML model.

2.5.3 Model Deployment

After the ML training is finished, the model is deployed in the setting where the model is intended to operate. Typically, data scientists are responsible for the model training, while software engineers and operational teams are responsible for implementing the trained model into the application it is going to function.

In both the training phase of the ML model and the subsequent implementation of the trained model into the application, the adoption of MLOps could be a beneficial methodology. In order to get a thorough understanding of the MLOps methodology, it is necessary to have an overview of DevOps – a foundation of the MLOps framework.

2.5.4 DevOps – A Basis for MLOps

DevOps is a methodology that seeks to integrate software system **dev**elopment with **op**eration**s**. Operations refer to the internal teams responsible for monitoring and fixing internal bugs in deployed software systems. DevOps was established in response to practices where the internal teams responsible

[33] Birk Torpmann-Hagen et al. "Segmentation consistency training: Out-of-distribution generalization for medical image segmentation". In: *2022 IEEE International Symposium on Multimedia (ISM)*. New York: IEEE, 2022, pp. 42–49.

[34] Tom Dietterich. "Overfitting and undercomputing in machine learning". In: *ACM Computing Surveys (CSUR)* 27.3 (1995), pp. 326–327.

for developing a software system and those responsible for operating deployed systems were siloed within organisations. DevOps attempts to merge these two teams and also introduces automatic monitoring of development and deployment practices.[35]

The DevOps approach is based on the agile approach to software system development. The DevOps approach consists of four principles:

1. Automation of the software system development lifecycle. The automation is achieved through automated testing and automation of manual tasks in the software system development and deployment/operations.
2. Effective collaboration across both development and operations teams.
3. Continuous improvement through performance metrics.
4. Focusing on end-user needs both in the development and in the operations phases.[36]

The overall rationale behind DevOps – collaboration between development teams and operations teams – is illustrated in Figure 2.1. The figure illustrates that if and when an internal bug is identified by the team monitoring the deployed software system (the bottom part of the circle), the software system would reenter some parts of the development phase in order to rectify the bug. The figure is a simplification. In cases where a bug is identified in the testing phase, the normal procedure often involves reentering the implementation phase and resolving the bug.

2.5.5 MLOps – An Extension of DevOps to ML

MLOps is an extension of DevOps, tailored specifically for ML workflows. There is no unified definition of MLOps – despite an increasing interest in industry and academic circles. The overall aim of the MLOps methodology is to improve the efficiency of an ML model by automating processes. While DevOps caters to all software systems, MLOps is designed to address the challenges and requirements of ML systems. Similar to DevOps, a key focus of MLOps is the automation of manual processes involved in both the model training and the integration of these trained ML models into operational AI

[35] Christof Ebert et al. "DevOps". In: *IEEE Software* 33.3 (2016), pp. 94–100. doi: 10.1109/MS.2016.68.

[36] Mali Senapathi, Jim Buchan, and Hady Osman. "DevOps capabilities, practices, and challenges: Insights from a case study". In: *Proceedings of the 22nd International Conference on Evaluation and Assessment in Software Engineering 2018*. New York: Association of Computing Machinery, 2018, pp. 57–67. doi: https://doi.org/10.48550/arXiv.1907.10201.

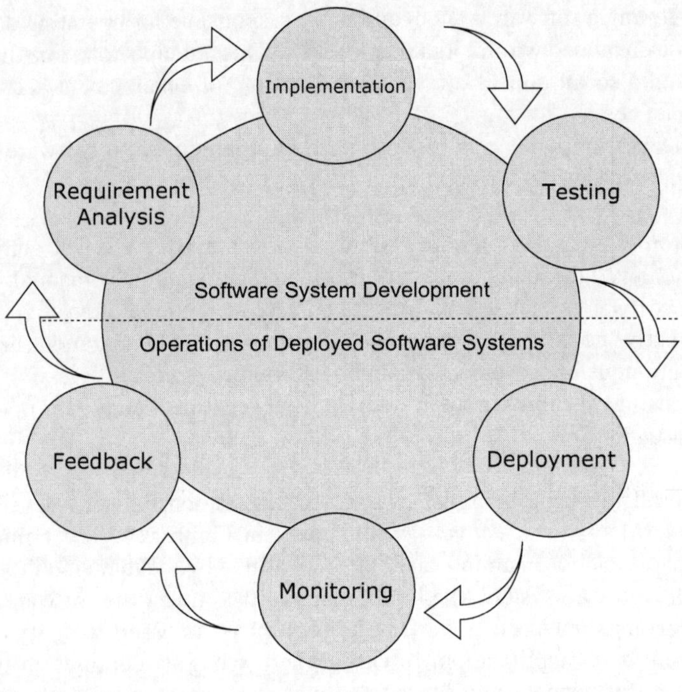

Figure 2.1 Illustration of DevOps

systems. The integration of the trained ML model into a functional AI system can take various forms. It could be either a completely manual implementation, a continuous model delivery process, or a continuous integration/continuous delivery/continuous training of pipelines.[37] Regardless of the approach, the overarching goal of MLOps is to facilitate an efficient transition from ML model training to the deployment of the model in an operational AI system.

The applicability and utility of MLOps could be illustrated with an example. A company that rents out e-scooters in a city region wants to utilise an ML model to have algorithm-based pricing of their services. The pricing is based on an ML model that uses weather data, rented scooters, and the current time as input data. The ML model is implemented in the software system of the rental company and the company's mobile application. Suppose that the company uses a pre-trained model that is not updated with current real-time

37 Sibanjan Debeeprasad Das and Pradip Kumar Bala. "What drives MLOps adoption? An analysis using the TOE framework". In: *Journal of Decision Systems* 33.3 (2024), pp. 376–412. doi: https://doi.org/10.1080/12460125.2023.2214306.

data from the application. In such instances, the ML model could risk being outdated in its intended use, due to cyclical variations of demand because seasons change. MLOps is a methodology for both automating the update of the ML model and including pipelines from the model training to the application in order to have a real-time updated ML model implemented in the AI system it is intended to operate within.

The effect of the deployed ML model becoming outdated due to changes in the data in the setting where the model is deployed is known as concept drift or concept shift, and it is a common challenge within statistics and ML.[38] As a result of the concept drift, the performance of the model decreases, as it was trained on data that no longer accurately reflects the conditions encountered by the deployed model.

Another example of concept drift is if a recommender system on social media fails to introduce new content. In such a scenario, the recommended content will eventually become stale and uninteresting for social media users.

There are various forms of concept drift. The concept drift described in the first example above is a recurring cyclical concept drift due to the change of seasons. Other recurring concept drifts could be more difficult to predict, e.g., due to inflation in market prices or similar. Another type of concept drift is a sudden concept drift, for instance, because sensors collecting real-time data used in a deployed ML model malfunction. In addition, another type of concept drift is a gradual concept drift, e.g., a social media user is gradually starting to be more interested in different content from recommender systems.

To mitigate concept drift, there are two main approaches: a passive approach and an active approach. In the active approach, the aim is to detect the concept drift in the data and to mitigate it by retraining the model or refining the data. In a passive approach, the model is continuously retrained independently of whether a concept drift is detected or not.[39]

In a fully manual implementation in MLOps, no parts of the process of integrating the ML model into an AI system are automated. The ML model training, the implementation of the finished trained ML model into a working AI system, and the testing of whether all functionality is kept during the

---

[38] Jan Zenisek, Florian Holzinger, and Michael Affenzeller. "Machine learning-based concept drift detection for predictive maintenance". In: *Computers & Industrial Engineering* 137 (2019), p. 106031. doi: https://doi.org/10.1016/j.cie.2019.106031.

[39] Meng Han et al. "A survey of active and passive concept drift handling methods". In: *Computational Intelligence* 38.4 (2022), pp. 1492–1535. doi: https://doi.org/10.1111/coin.12520.

operations of the AI system are fully manual processes. These processes are all manually executed, requiring significant human intervention and oversight.[40]

In continuous model delivery, the ML side of the process is automated. Pipelines, i.e., infrastructural elements that modify the data flowing through them as it progresses along the pipeline, are often used. In a continuous model delivery, one or more of these pipelines extend from the ML training phase to the implementation of the ML model in the deployed AI system. Such a setup makes it possible to update the ML model and retrain the model even after it is deployed, thereby ensuring that the model remains current and effective.[41]

Continuous integration / continuous delivery / continuous training (CI/CD/CT) of pipelines is an MLOps practice where the pipelines are automatically tested during the model training phase and subsequently deployed into the operational AI system. These pipelines form an integral part of the ML architecture, facilitating the rapid development of new pipelines. This approach ensures that the internal ML model in the operational AI system is consistently updated and optimised, resulting in a potential enhancement in the overall performance of the ML system and preventing concept drift.[42]

Continuous integration/continuous delivery are terms known from DevOps. Continuous Training (CT) is an MLOps-specific term where the data processed in a deployed ML model is used to automatically retrain the model to keep the trained ML model updated to the environment in which it is going to function.[43] In CT, the production data of a deployed ML model is collected and used for retraining, and not just to draw inferences on a finished trained ML model.

Another key feature of MLOps that intends to lower the negative effect of inherent shortcomings in developed solutions – a concept known as technical

---

[40] Sridhar Alla and Suman Kalyan Adari. “Beginning MLOps with MLFlow”. In: *Begin. MLOps with MLFlow* (2021). doi: https://doi.org/10.1007/978-1-4842-6549-9.

[41] Damian A Tamburri. “Sustainable MLOPs: Trends and challenges”. In: *2020 22nd International Symposium on Symbolic and Numeric Algorithms for Scientific Computing (SYNASC)*. 2020, pp. 17–23. doi: 10.1109/SYNASC51798.2020.00015.

[42] Sridhar Alla and Suman Kalyan Adari. “Beginning MLOps with MLFlow”. In: *Begin. MLOps with MLFlow* (2021). doi: https://doi.org/10.1007/978-1-4842-6549-9.

[43] Satvik Garg et al. “On continuous integration/continuous delivery for automated deployment of machine learning models using MLOps”. In: *2021 IEEE Fourth International Conference on Artificial Intelligence and Knowledge Engineering (AIKE)*. New York: IEEE, 2021, pp. 25–28. doi: https://doi.org/10.1109/AIKE52691.2021.00010.

debt[44] – is to continuously monitor the ML model; to have standardised templates for the overall ML project from the initial data collection to deployment and post-deployment monitoring, versioning models, code, logs, and weights trained on different data sets; and to use specific standardised infrastructure for the ML project.[45] As specific AI regulation comes into effect, some of these requirements will be regulatory requirements. The focus of the book is on whether such regulatory requirements could be implemented in the MLOps framework.

In summary, MLOps is a methodology that facilitates the integration of pipelines between the ML model development and the implementation of the ML model in an AI system or application. The automation of these pipelines enables continuous updates to the ML model within the AI system where it has been deployed. This ensures that the ML model remains a current and effective internal part of the system it is intended to operate within.

2.6 SUMMARY AND NEXT STEPS

In each of the phases described above – collecting the data into the dataset, preprocessing the data, training the ML algorithm, deploying the trained ML model, and lifecycle management of the deployed AI system – numerous choices and decisions are involved. Some of these decisions are made by natural persons who design and choose the specific solutions within the AI system, and some decisions are inferred from the AI system itself.

AI systems deployed in real-life use cases potentially enter the scope of various regulations. The book will focus on specific parts of data protection regulation, cybersecurity regulation, and the AI Act during the phases of data collection, model training, and model deployment. The current subsection will address and explain the specific structure of the overall book – focusing on the data component, the model component, and the AI-as-a-Service (AIaaS) component as a guiding structure for the book, as illustrated in Figure 2.2.

The forthcoming three chapters will analyse specific legal and regulatory aspects regarding personal data protection, cybersecurity, and requirements in the AI Act. The chosen structure, whereby legal requirements from various

---

[44] Edith Tom, Aybüke Aurum, and Richard Vidgen. "An exploration of technical debt". In: *Journal of Systems and Software* 86.6 (2013), pp. 1498–1516. doi: https://doi.org/10.1016/j.jss.2012.12.052.

[45] Willem-Jan van den Heuvel and Damian A. Tamburri. "Model-driven ML-Ops for intelligent enterprise applications: Vision, approaches and challenges". In: *Business Modeling and Software Design*. Ed. by Boris Shishkov. Cham: Springer International Publishing, 2020, pp. 169–181. doi: https://doi.org/10.1007/978-3-030-52306-0_11.

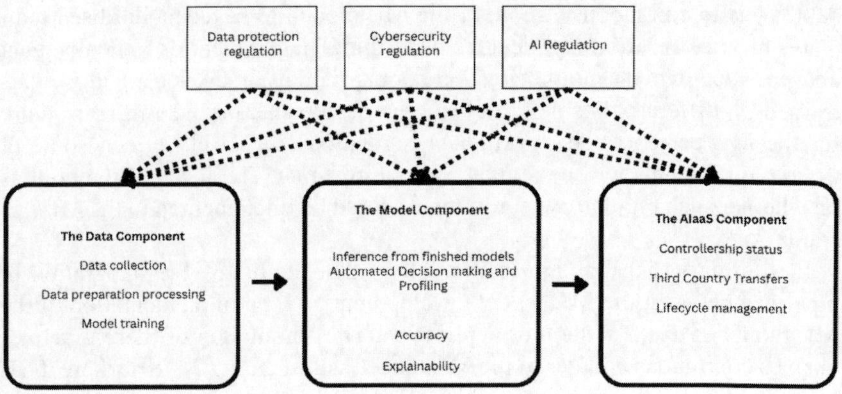

Figure 2.2 *Illustration of the components of the book*

regulations and directives are organised under three distinctive components, namely, a data component, a model component, and an AIaaS component, facilitates cross-fertilisation between the different regulations.

For instance, accuracy is a fundamental principle under both the GDPR and the AI Act. The accuracy of an AI system is predominantly dependent on the quality of the training data. In instances where an AI system enters the scope of both the GDPR and the AI Act, it is potentially a viable approach to assess such aspects together. The accuracy of the AI system is closely linked to the quality of the training and data processed in deployed models, and accuracy across different regulations will, therefore, be addressed in the data component of the book.

Comparable instances also arise in the model inference stage of an AI system. For instance, transparency requirements outlined in Article 86 of the AI Act share several similarities with the right to information concerning the logic involved in automated individual decision-making under the GDPR. Consequently, it is a feasible approach to address such legal and technical aspects together in a chapter addressing the model inference stages of an AI system.

Moreover, there are relevant cybersecurity requirements in the AI Act, in the GDPR Article 32, and in specific cybersecurity regulations and directives. Cybersecurity requirements are relevant in all three phases of developing and deploying an AI system, especially when the AI model is implemented in an overall system together with different Application Programming Interfaces (APIs) and with the use of AIaaS. Cybersecurity issues are one example of regulatory requirements that will be addressed in the chapter regarding legal requirements when a trained ML model is utilised on AIaaS platforms. In Chapter 5, legal issues regarding the lifecycle management of deployed AI systems will also be addressed.

All three chapters will present relevant data protection, cybersecurity, and AI Act requirements. The legal analyses are distinctive for every regulation. However, there is a natural alignment between the regulations that makes it a viable approach to assess them together in the three overall chapters that correspond with the three overall phases when developing and deploying an AI system: data collection, inference, and deployment of a trained model in an overall system.

3. The data component: towards compliant processing of (personal) data in AI system development

3.1 INTRODUCTION

The previous chapter has elaborated on the workflow of a typical ML project where data and ML algorithms are applied to develop an ML model capable of detecting patterns in unseen data, thus facilitating the model to draw inferences.[1] The present chapter shifts the focus towards compliant data processing throughout the model training phase, including compliant collection and processing of training data. ML models require data to be developed. Thus, it is relevant to assess how the data could be lawfully collected and processed during the model training process. Specifically, the structure of the current chapter is divided into three parts focusing on data protection regulation interpreted in line with primary EU law, cybersecurity regulation, and requirements in the AI Act.

In the current chapter, the terms "AI system development", "AI model development", "ML model development", and "model training" will be applied. All these terms carry distinct and specific nuances. However, in the following sections, they will be applied interchangeably as a matter of variety.

The specific regulations analysed in the current chapter – although they have different purposes and end goals – overlap in their scope in some specific circumstances. For instance, a provider developing a high-risk AI system processing personal data would need to comply with the requirements for high-risk AI systems in the AI Act, cybersecurity requirements for products with digital elements that are also high-risk AI systems in the CRA, and the requirements in the GDPR concurrently. It is thus a viable approach to assess the different data-related requirements in these regulations in the same chapter. The current chapter will focus on the compliant collection and processing

1 Iqbal H Sarker. "Machine learning: Algorithms, real-world applications and research directions". In: *SN Computer Science* 2.3 (2021), p. 160. doi: https://doi.org/10.1007/s42979-021-00592-x.

of the training, testing, and validation data applied to develop ML models. Compliant processing of data processed in a deployed model to draw inference is the focus of the next chapter in the book, Chapter 4.

This chapter is organised as follows:

Section 3.2 analyses data protection regulation and AI system development, and the focus is on the lawful collection and processing of training data constituting personal data under the scope of the GDPR and EU primary law. In order to analyse the compliant collection and processing of training data, it is necessary to analyse the GDPR in line with the requirements for interfering with the right to data protection in the Charter. The analysis in section 3.2 is structured in accordance with the requirements for interference in a fundamental right in the Charter, legality, and the principle of proportionality.

Section 3.3 analyses specific data-relevant requirements in the AI Act, especially data governance requirements. The requirements are analysed from a compliance by design perspective, where the focus is on how to comply with the data governance requirements in the AI Act during AI system development. The data governance requirements in the AI Act refer to requirements in the regulation to ensure sufficient quality of the data throughout the AI systems' lifecycles.

Section 3.4 provides specific details on data-relevant requirements in cybersecurity regulations in relation to AI system development. High-risk AI systems that are part of a "product with digital elements" need to comply with the cybersecurity requirements of CRA. In general, cybersecurity attacks on AI systems could either attack the model in order to extract training data or other types of data or perturb the data used to lower the precision of the AI model. Since data is an important component of the cybersecurity of AI systems, section 3.4 will focus on data-relevant requirements in the CRA. The focus is especially on mitigating measures for one attack type referred to as "data poisoning attacks" and on how to mitigate the risk of data poisoning attacks during AI system development.

After the specific data relevant legal requirements for AI system development have been identified and analysed, the focus of the chapter shifts to whether it is possible to implement some of the identified legal requirements in the MLOps framework, in section 3.5.

Lastly, section 3.6 summarises the overall findings of the chapter.

3.2 AI SYSTEM DEVELOPMENT AND DATA PROTECTION LAW: THE FUNDAMENTAL RIGHT STRUCTURE AS A GUIDELINE

3.2.1 Introduction

An AI system and an AI project consist – as previously stated – of datasets and an algorithm that is trained to develop a model. The trained AI model is then applied to unseen data – data the model has not been trained on. In the EU acquis, personal data protection is a fundamental right in Article 8 of the Charter.[2] This fundamental right is operationalised through a comprehensive regulation, the GDPR.[3] The current subsection will focus on the compliant and lawful processing of personal data during the training of an AI model in accordance with both the fundamental right to data protection (primary law) and the operationalisation of this fundamental right in the GDPR (secondary law).

To analyse the compliant processing of training data that constitutes personal data, it is necessary to analyse the requirements of the GDPR in line with the fundamental rights in the Charter and corresponding case law from the CJEU. In a consistent corpus of case law from the CJEU, the rights and obligations of the GDPR are interpreted in line with the Charter Articles 7 and 8.[4] An AI system developed in breach of the fundamental rights of the Charter will never be compliant under the EU acquis, even though the system complies with secondary law. Hence, it is necessary to analyse the GDPR in line with the Charter to develop a compliance by design approach to personal data processing during AI system development.

---

2 European Union, Charter of Fundamental Rights of the European Union, 26 October 2012, 2012/C 326/02.

3 Regulation (EU) 2016/679 of the European Parliament and of the Council of 27 April 2016 on the protection of natural persons with regard to the processing of personal data and on the free movement of such data, and repealing Directive 95/46/EC (General Data Protection Regulation) [2016] OJ L 199/1.

4 Joined Cases C-92/09 and C-93/09 Volker and Markus Schecke GbR, Hartmut Eifert v Land Hessen, joined party Bundesanstalt für Landwirtschaft und Ernährung ECLI:EU:C:2010:662 paragraph 47; Joined Cases C-203/15 and C-698/15 Tele2 Sverige AB v. Post- och telestyrelsen and others, Judgement of 21 December 2016 (Grand Chamber) (ECLI:EU:C:2016:970) para 115; Case C-2017/16 Ministerio Fiscal, Judgement of 2 October 2018 (Grand Chamber) (ECLI:EU:2018:788) para 52; Joined Cases C-511/18, C-512/18 and C-520/18 La Quadrature du Net and Others v Premier minister and Others, Judgement of 6 October 2020 (Grand Chamber) (ECLI:EU:C:2020:791) para 112.

According to Article 52 (3) of the Charter, "in so far [...] the Charter contains rights which correspond to rights guaranteed by the Convention for the Protection of Human Rights and Fundamental Freedoms, the meaning and scope of those rights shall be the same as those laid down by the said Convention. This provision shall not prevent Union law providing more extensive protection". The ECHR is a minimum requirement for the fundamental rights under the Charter. In order to identify the scope of the fundamental right to data protection in an AI context under EU primary law, it is, therefore, necessary to also analyse some specific examples of case law from the ECtHR regarding Article 8 of the ECHR. The chapter, therefore, analyses the right to private life in Article 8 of the ECHR, the right to private life in Article 7 of the Charter, and the right to data protection in Article 8 of the Charter in an AI system development context, with the main focus on the right to data protection in Article 8 of the Charter.

The legal analysis of the data protection requirements for lawful collection and processing of personal data during AI system development is structured in line with the requirements for interfering in the right to data protection, the structure of lawful interference in a fundamental right: legality and the principle of proportionality.[5] In order to lawfully interfere with the right to data protection, the interference must not breach the essence of the right; be provided for on the basis of a lawful legal basis; pursue a legitimate aim; and be necessary, suitable, and proportionate *stricto sensu*, according to Article 8 (2) and 52 of the Charter and the case law cited in the preceding paragraphs.[6] An interference in a fundamental right must pass all the subtests above to not

---

5 Jeremy McBride. "Proportionality and the European Convention on Human Rights". In: *The Principle of Proportionality in the Laws of Europe*. Ed. by Evelyn Ellis. Oxford: Hart Publishing, 1999, p. 23; Aharon Barak. *Proportionality: Constitutional Rights and Their Limitations*. Cambridge, UK: Cambridge University Press, 2021; Matthias Klatt and Moritz Meister. *The Constitutional Structure of Proportionality*. Oxford: Oxford University Press, 2012; Mordechai Kremnitzer, Talya Steiner, and Andrej Lang. *Proportionality in Action: Comparative and Empirical Perspectives on the Judicial Practice*. Vol. 22. Cambridge, UK: Cambridge University Press, 2020, p. 1.

6 Aharon Barak. *Proportionality: Constitutional Rights and Their Limitations*. Cambridge, UK: Cambridge University Press, 2012, p. 342; Mordechai Kremnitzer, Talya Steiner, and Andrej Lang. *Proportionality in Action: Comparative and Empirical Perspectives on the Judicial Practice*. Vol. 22. Cambridge, UK: Cambridge University Press, 2020, p. 1; Matthias Klatt and Moritz Meister. *The Constitutional Structure of Proportionality*. Oxford: Oxford University Press, 2012; Jeremy McBride. "Proportionality and the European Convention on Human Rights". In: *The Principle of Proportionality in the Laws of Europe*. Ed. by Evelyn Ellis. Oxford: Hart Publishing, 1999, p. 23.

constitute a violation of the right. If a measure is both in accordance with the law, pursues a legitimate aim, and is suitable and necessary, the last part of the proportionality assessment is to test whether the interference is proportionate *stricto sensu.*

By organising the legal analysis in line with these specific criteria, it is possible to analyse the collection and processing of personal data in AI system development in a manner that complies with both primary and secondary law, a compliance by design approach. Moreover, the subtest of the principle of proportionality could be described as a common core of the fundamental rights to privacy and data protection in the Charter and ECHR Article 8. As a result of structuring the legal analysis according to these subtests, it is possible to develop an approach in line with the rights of the Charter and Article 8 of the ECHR.

The next subsections are organised as follows:

Subsection 3.2.2 analyses how the processing of personal data to develop an AI model interferes with the fundamental right to data protection.

An interference breaching the "essence" of the right to data protection could never be compliant. Subsection 3.2.3, therefore, analyses the requirements for the essence of the right to data protection in relation to the processing of personal data for AI system development.

The next subsections – subsections 3.2.4–3.2.8 – focus on the compliant processing of training data constituting personal data in the GDPR and the Charter. Such an analysis is conducted on the basis of the requirements for interfering with the right, namely, lawfulness, legitimate aim, suitability, necessity, and proportionality *stricto sensu.* Various relevant requirements in the GDPR for the processing of personal data for AI system development are interpreted together with the different requirements in interfering with Charter rights, to develop an analytical structure that complies with secondary and primary law concurrently.

Lastly, subsection 3.2.9 summarises the overall findings of the subsections.

3.2.2 Interference with the Right to Data Protection and AI System Development

The right to privacy and the right to data protection are fundamental rights according to Articles 7 and 8 of the Charter of Fundamental Rights of the European Union.[7] Within the EU, the GDPR contains specific rules that

---

[7] European Union, Charter of Fundamental Rights of the European Union, 26 October 2012, 2012/C 326/02.

operationalise the rights under the Charter. According to recital 1 of the GDPR, the regulation refers only to Article 8 of the Charter.

The right to private life and the right to data protection in Articles 7 and 8 of the Charter carry distinct nuances and are not essentially interrelated.[8] There are differences across these rights, in relation to both the scope and limitation of the rights and their material content. The CJEU has also recognised that Articles 7 and 8 are distinct rights carrying different aims and scopes, yet with a close connection.[9] The main objective of the current chapter is the compliant processing of personal data to develop and train an AI model. In the CJEU, Articles 7 and 8 of the Charter are often assessed together as part of the same assessment of interference and the lawfulness of the interference.[10] Therefore, the remainder of the chapter will focus on judgements where both Articles 7 and 8 are assessed, with the key focus on Article 8 of the Charter. The book will, therefore, not examine the distinctions between Articles 7 and 8 of the Charter further.

The right to a private life is a human right according to Article 8 of the ECHR.[11] The ECHR is analysed under an EU law lens in the current chapter because the ECHR is a minimum requirement of the Charter rights, according to Article 52 (3) of the Charter. Within the scope of the ECHR, the collection, storing, and processing of personal data would constitute an interference with

---

8 Orla Lynskey. "Deconstructing data protection: The 'added-value' of a right to data protection in the EU legal order". In: *International & Comparative Law Quarterly* 63.3 (2014), pp. 569–597. doi: https://doi.org/10.1017/S0020589314000244; Juliane Kokott and Christoph Sobotta. "The distinction between privacy and data protection in the jurisprudence of the CJEU and the ECtHR". In: *International Data Privacy Law* 3.4 (Sept. 2013), pp. 222–228. ISSN: 2044-3994. doi: 10.1093/idpl/ipt017. eprint: https://academic.oup.com/idpl/article-pdf/3/4/222/2160080/ipt017.pdf. url: https://doi.org/10.1093/idpl/ipt017.

9 Judgement of the Court (Grand Chamber) of 21 December 2016 in Joined Cases C-203/15 and C-698/15, Tele2 Sverige AB (C-203/15) v Post- och telestyrelsen, and Secretary of State for the Home Department (C-698/15) v Tom Watson, Peter Brice, Geoffrey Lewis, ECLI:EU:C:2016:970.

10 Judgement of the Court 20 May 2003 in joined cases C-465/00, C-138/01, and C-139/01 Österreichischer Rundfunk and others ECLI:EU:C:2003:294 paragraphs 72–80 and Judgement of the Court 9 November 2010 joined Cases C-92/09 and C-93/09 Volker and Markus Schecke ECLI:EU:C:2010:662 paragraph 47 et seq.; Herke Kranenborg. "Protection of personal data". In: *The EU Charter of Fundamental Rights: A Commentary*. Ed. by Steve Peers et al. Oxford: Hart Publishing, 2014, pp. 223–266 on p. 230. doi: http://dx.doi.org/10.5040/9781849468350.ch-009.

11 Convention for the Protection of Human Rights and Fundamental Freedoms (European Convention on Human Rights) (ECHR).

Article 8 of the ECHR.[12] Further processing of collected personal data would constitute another interference.[13] The ECHR has a traditional vertical human rights protection structure, where the ECtHR assesses whether a state has disproportionately interfered with an individual's rights. However, personal data is frequently processed by private actors, and not just states, to develop AI systems. In order to assess the private parties' obligations, the focus will be on the fundamental rights of the Charter, where the ECHR functions as a minimum requirement.

The current subsections will analyse secondary law in line with primary law in the Charter to suggest a manner of processing personal data in AI system development that complies with both secondary and primary law. Before the GDPR could be analysed in line with the Charter, the horizontal nature of the right to data protection regulation in the Charter needs to be analysed. According to the wording of Article 51 (1) of the Charter, the provisions of the Charter are relevant for the EU institutions and the member states only when they are implementing Union law. Moreover, according to Article 51 (2), the Charter does not extend the field of application of Union law beyond the powers of the Union. A literal interpretation of the Charter Article 8 in line with Article 51 would entail that the associated obligations of the right relate only to the EU institutions and member states, and not, e.g., a private controller processing personal data to develop an AI system. Traditionally, the subject of obligations in human rights conventions – such as the ECHR – has been governments. Human rights have functioned as guarantees against disproportionate state interference. However, the fundamental right of data protection of the Charter also includes private parties as a subject of obligation through a horizontal effect established by the CJEU. In order to fully develop a compliance by design approach that includes the GDPR and the Charter, it is important to establish the aspects of this horizontal effect, including in which instances the horizontal effect comes into effect. The next subsection will analyse case law from the CJEU to establish the function and limitation of the horizontal effect of Article 8 of the Charter.

3.2.3 The Horizontal Effect of the Charter Rights

Generally, and not with specific regard to the right to data protection in Article 8 of the Charter, the horizontal effect of the Charter rights and related obligations is a disputed issue with conflicting views both in the legal literature and

---

[12] Y.G. v Russia, Judgement of 30 August 2022 Application No. 8647/12 paragraph 40).

[13] Y.G. v Russia, Judgement of 30 August 2022 Application No. 8647/12 paragraph 44).

internally in the CJEU among the advocates general.[14] On the one hand, those refusing the direct horizontal effect of the Charter – the binding effect the Charter has on private parties – argue that the wording of Article 51 (1) of the Charter binds only the EU institutions and EU member states, that the system of the Charter where limitations only could be provided for by law calls for the Charter to be binding only for institutions with legislative power, i.e., the EU institutions and the member states.[15] Finally, the ones opposed to the direct binding effect by the Charter argue that the fundamental right protection is efficient enough through the member states' duty to protect the fundamental rights in legislation.[16] The view of the ones opposing the direct effect con-

---

14 Opinion of Advocate General Trstenjak on 8 September 2011 in Case C-282/10, ECLI: EU:C:2011:559 paragraphs 80–87, and Opinion of Advocate General Trstenjak delivered on 29 March 2007 in Case C-80/06 ECLI:EU:C:2007:200 paragraph 69; Juan Ignacio Ugartemendia. "The horizontal effect of the EU Charter of Fundamental Rights in the case law of the Court of Justice". In: *Fundamental Rights Challenges: Horizontal Effectiveness, Rule of Law and Margin of National Appreciation.* Ed. by Cristina Izquierdo-Sans, Carmen Martínez-Capdevila, and Magdalena Nogueira-Guastavino. Cham: Springer International Publishing, 2021, pp. 11–21. isbn: 978-3-030-72798-7. doi: 10.1007/978-3-030-72798-7_2. url: https://doi.org/10.1007/978-3-030-72798-7_2; Opinion of Advocate General Villalón on 18 July 2013 in Case C-176/12 AMS or Association de Médiation Sociale ECLI:EU:C:2013:491 paragraphs 28 et seq.; Tobias Mast and Christian Ollig. "The lazy legislature: Incorporating and horizontalising the Charter of Fundamental Rights through secondary Union law". In: *European Constitutional Law Review* 19.3 (2023), pp. 462–486. doi: 10.1017/S1574019623000238.

15 Opinion of Advocate General Trstenjak on 8 September 2011 in Case C-282/10, ECLI: EU:C:2011:559 paragraphs 80-87, and Opinion of Advocate General Trstenjak delivered on 29 March 2007 in Case C-80/06 ECLI:EU:C:2007:200 paragraph 69.; Juan Ignacio Ugartemendia. "The horizontal effect of the EU Charter of Fundamental Rights in the case law of the Court of Justice". In: *Fundamental Rights Challenges: Horizontal Effectiveness, Rule of Law and Margin of National Appreciation.* Ed. by Cristina Izquierdo-Sans, Carmen Martínez-Capdevila, and Magdalena Nogueira-Guastavino. Cham: Springer International Publishing, 2021, pp. 11–21. isbn: 978-3-030-72798-7. doi: 10.1007/978-3-030-72798-7_2. url: https://doi.org/10.1007/978-3-030-72798-7_2.

16 Opinion of Advocate General Trstenjak on 8 September 2011 in Case C-282/10, ECLI: EU:C:2011:559 paragraphs 80-87, and Opinion of Advocate General Trstenjak delivered on 29 March 2007 in Case C-80/06 ECLI:EU:C:2007:200 paragraph 69.; Juan Ignacio Ugartemendia. "The Horizontal Effect of the EU Charter of Fundamental Rights in the Case Law of the Court of Justice". In: *Fundamental Rights Challenges: Horizontal Effectiveness, Rule of Law and Margin of National Appreciation.* Ed. by Cristina Izquierdo-Sans, Carmen Martínez-Capdevila, and Magdalena Nogueira-Guastavino. Cham: Springer International Publishing,

cludes that the Charter rights could be indirectly binding for private parties only through rules in secondary law implementing an obligation to protect the Charter rights.

On the other hand, those arguing that the Charter could have a direct horizontal effect base their arguments on the fact that such a direct horizontal effect is a fundamental principle of EU law from before the entry into force of the Charter and the Lisbon Treaty. It would be counterintuitive if a fundamental rights instrument and Article 51 (1), which is intended to enhance fundamental rights protection, is applied to diminish the protection by excluding a horizontal effect. Moreover, through a literal interpretation of Article 51 (1), it is argued that the wording does not address the horizontal effect, but the binding nature of the Charter.[17]

In the data protection field and within Article 8 of the Charter, the CJEU has established a direct binding horizontal effect of the Charter.[18] The effect is established by the CJEU by activating the Charter right via secondary data protection regulation. Since the secondary law activates the EU institution's competence, the secondary data protection law functions as a trigger for the horizontal effect of the Charter right.[19] Such an activation is in line with Article 51 (1) of the Charter. The court's case law regarding data protection law where the horizontal effect of the Charter right has been activated by the

---

2021, pp. 11–21. isbn: 978-3-030-72798-7. doi: 10.1007/978-3-030-72798-7_2. url: https://doi.org/10.1007/978-3-030-72798-7_2.

[17] Opinion of Advocate General Villalón on 18 July 2013 in Case C-176/12 AMS or Association de Médiation Sociale ECLI:EU:C:2013:491 paragraphs 28 et seq.; Juan Ignacio Ugartemendia. "The Horizontal Effect of the EU Charter of Fundamental Rights in the Case Law of the Court of Justice". In: *Fundamental Rights Challenges: Horizontal Effectiveness, Rule of Law and Margin of National Appreciation*. Ed. by Cristina Izquierdo-Sans, Carmen Martínez-Capdevila, and Magdalena Nogueira-Guastavino. Cham: Springer International Publishing, 2021, pp. 11–21. isbn: 978-3-030-72798-7. doi: 10.1007/978-3-030-72798-7_2. url: https://doi.org/10.1007/978-3-030-72798-7_2.

[18] Judgement of 13 May 2014 in Case C-131/12 Google Spain, ECLI:EU:C:2014:317, paragraph 68; Tobias Mast and Christian Ollig. "The lazy legislature: Incorporating and horizontalising the Charter of Fundamental Rights through secondary Union law". In: *European Constitutional Law Review* 19.3 (2023), pp. 462–486. doi: 10.1017/S1574019623000238.

[19] Tobias Mast and Christian Ollig. "The lazy legislature: Incorporating and horizontalising the Charter of Fundamental Rights through secondary Union law". In: *European Constitutional Law Review* 19.3 (2023), pp. 462–486. doi: 10.1017/S1574019623000238.

CJEU has been described as secondary law functioning "as a gateway for the constitutionalisation of private law by the judiciary".[20]

Since data protection law is both a part of secondary law and a right according to primary law, the activation of the horizontal effect of the Charter rights by the CJEU is both logical and appropriate. First, it would be illogical if secondary law contained more and more extensive rights than primary law. Second, since the EU law is activated by the secondary law, the horizontal effect of the Charter rights is in accordance with Article 51 (1) of the Charter. However, the CJEU has – as of 2025 – not established the right of Article 8 as a right with general horizontal effect outside examples where secondary law is activated. Other regulations than the data protection regulations – e.g., the CRA and the AI Act – have frequent references to fundamental rights. The horizontal effect of the AI Act is examined further in Chapter 6 of the book.

Within the Charter and corresponding case law from the CJEU, the CJEU has held – in a consistent body of case law – that any processing of personal data by a third party may constitute an interference with Articles 7 and 8 of the Charter.[21] Therefore, processing personal data by anyone other than the data subject would constitute an interference with the right to data protection. When personal data is processed as part of the training data to develop an AI model, the controller would need to respect the requirements for interference, namely, respect for the essence of the right, lawfulness, legitimate aim, necessity, suitability, and proportionality *stricto sensu*.[22]

---

[20] Aqilah Sandhu. *Grundrechtsunitarisierung durch Sekundärrecht: zur Reichweite des mitgliedstaatlichen Grundrechtsschutzes im Anwendungsbereich von Öffnungsklauseln am Beispiel des europäischen Datenschutzsekundärrechts.* Tübingen: Mohr Siebeck, 2021, p. 188. doi: https://doi.org/10.1628/978-3-16-160897-1; Tobias Mast and Christian Ollig. "The lazy legislature: Incorporating and horizontalising the Charter of Fundamental Rights through secondary Union law". In: *European Constitutional Law Review* 19.3 (2023), pp. 462–486. doi: 10.1017/S1574019623000238.

[21] Judgement of the Court Fourth Chamber 17 October 2013, Schwarz, C-291/12, EU:C:2013:670, paragraph 25.

[22] Matthias Klatt and Moritz Meister. *The Constitutional Structure of Proportionality.* Oxford: Oxford University Press, 2012; Aharon Barak. *Proportionality: Constitutional Rights and Their Limitations.* Cambridge, UK: Cambridge University Press, 2021; Jeremy McBride. "Proportionality and the European Convention on Human Rights". In: *The Principle of Proportionality in the Laws of Europe.* Ed. by Evelyn Ellis. Oxford: Hart Publishing, 1999, p. 23; Mordechai Kremnitzer, Talya Steiner, and Andrej Lang. *Proportionality in Action: Comparative and Empirical Perspectives on the Judicial Practice.* Vol. 22. Cambridge, UK: Cambridge University Press, 2020, p. 1.

3.2.4 The Scope of Personal Data Protection

Since the horizontal direct effect of Article 8 of the Charter is activated by secondary law functioning as a trigger, it is important to establish the activating scope of secondary data protection regulation. According to the CJEU, the *processing* of *personal data* is regarded as an interference with Articles 7 and 8 of the Charter.[23] It is, thus, crucial to analyse and define the scope of these two concepts in EU law.

Personal data is defined in Article 4 (1) of the GDPR as "any information relating to an identified or identifiable natural person [the] ('data subject')". The term "identifiable" is further explained in the same article as the possibility for both the direct and the indirect identification of a natural person, particularly by reference to an identifier such as a name, an identification number, location data, an online identifier or to one or more factors specific to the physical, physiological, genetic, mental, economic, cultural, or social identity of a natural person. To determine whether a natural person is identifiable, an account should be taken of all the means reasonably likely to be used, such as singling out, either by the controller or by another person, to identify a natural person directly or indirectly. To ascertain whether means are reasonably likely to be used to identify a natural person, account should be taken of all objective factors, such as the cost of and the amount of time required for identification, taking into consideration the available technology at the time of the processing and the technological developments, according to recital 26 of the GDPR.

In a judgement from 9 November 2023, the CJEU gives some guidance on the interpretation of personal data under Article 4 (1) of the GDPR. The case concerned the question of whether a Vehicle Identification Number (VIN) constituted personal data.[24] A VIN is an alphanumeric code assigned to a vehicle by the manufacturer. The CJEU held that the question of whether this alphanumeric number constitutes personal data is dependent on whether there are any reasonable means that enable the identification of a natural person from that number. The question of whether a piece of information constitutes personal data would, therefore, depend on whether this piece of information combined with other information enables the identification, and whether such identification is a means reasonably likely to be used.

An important clarification from the CJEU in the VIN judgement is that the outcome of the identifiability assessment could differ between actors, for instance, between the manufacturer in the example above and another entity

---

[23] Judgement of the Court Fourth Chamber 17 October 2013, Schwarz, C-291/12, EU:C:2013:670, paragraph 25.

[24] Judgement of the Court (Third Chamber) of 9 November 2023 in case C-319/22 Gesamtverband Autoteile-Handel eV v Scania CV AB ECLI:EU:C:2023:837.

that does not have access to the information that enables identification from the alphanumeric code. There is an ongoing scholarly debate on whether the identifiability criterion should be assessed from a relative or an absolute approach.[25]

According to the relative approach, the identifiability criterion and the potential nature of data as personal data depend on the means reasonably likely to be used by the one holding the data or another person to re-identify a natural person.[26] The absolute approach considers the identifiability in an abstract manner while evaluating the robustness of the method applied to de-identify the data.[27] The development in the CJEU – in both the VIN judgement, the judgement of the Court in the ongoing Grand Chamber case T-557/20,[28] and the IAB Europe case[29] – supports the relative approach where the identifiability of the data has to be assessed in terms of the holder of the data, i.e., the reasonably means applied by the person attempting to identify a natural person. The relevant assessment in the relative approach does not test the general integrity of the de-identifiability method applied. The relative approach of the concept of personal data in the GDPR supports a purpose-oriented inter-

---

25 Frederik J Zuiderveen Borgesius. "Singling out people without knowing their names – Behavioural targeting, pseudonymous data, and the new Data Protection Regulation". In: *Computer Law & Security Review* 32.2 (2016), pp. 256–271. ISSN: 0267-3649. doi: https://doi.org/10.1016/j.clsr.2015.12.013. url: https://www.sciencedirect.com/science/article/pii/S0267364915001788; Michèle Finck and Frank Pallas. "They who must not be identified – Distinguishing personal from non-personal data under the GDPR". In: *International Data Privacy Law* 10.1 (Mar. 2020), pp. 11–36. ISSN: 2044-3994. doi: 10.1093/idpl/ipz026. eprint: https://academic.oup.com/idpl/article-pdf/10/1/11/33151834/ipz026.pdf. url: https://doi.org/10.1093/idpl/ipz026.

26 Michèle Finck and Frank Pallas. "They who must not be identified – Distinguishing personal from non-personal data under the GDPR". In: *International Data Privacy Law* 10.1 (Mar. 2020), pp. 11–36. ISSN: 2044-3994. doi: 10.1093/idpl/ipz026. eprint: https://academic.oup.com/idpl/article-pdf/10/1/11/33151834/ipz026.pdf. url: https://doi.org/10.1093/idpl/ipz026.

27 Frederik J Zuiderveen Borgesius. "Singling out people without knowing their names – Behavioural targeting, pseudonymous data, and the new Data Protection Regulation". In: *Computer Law & Security Review* 32.2 (2016), pp. 256–271. ISSN: 0267-3649. doi: https://doi.org/10.1016/j.clsr.2015.12.013. url: https://www.sciencedirect.com/science/article/pii/S0267364915001788.

28 Judgement of the General Court (Eight Chamber, extended composition) of 26. April 2023 in Case T-557/20 Single Resolution Board (SRB) v European Data Protection Supervisor (EDPS).

29 Judgement of the Court (Fourth Chamber) 7 March 2024 in the Case C-604/22 IAB Europe v Gegevensbeschermingsautoriteit ECLI:EU:C:2024:214.

pretation of the GDPR. If the purpose of the GDPR enters into effect for the question referred to a preliminary ruling, the CJEU is likely to interpret the information as personal data. The outcome of the identifiability assessment could, therefore, depend on who attempts to re-identify natural persons and needs to be assessed on a case-by-case basis.

The GDPR does not apply to anonymous data or data that has been properly anonymised, according to recital 26 of the GDPR. According to recital 26, the GDPR does not apply to "anonymous information, namely information which does not relate to an identified or identifiable natural person or to personal data rendered anonymous in such a manner that the data subject is not or no longer identifiable". The concept of anonymous information, thus, covers data that has never been personal data (anonymous data) and personal data processed in a manner where identifiability is no longer possible with reasonable means (anonymised data). However, the GDPR apply to pseudonymous data which is data that is processed "in such a manner that the personal data can no longer be attributed to a specific data subject without the use of additional information, provided that such additional information is kept separately and is subject to technical and organisational measures to ensure that the personal data are not attributed to an identified or identifiable natural person", according to Article 4 (5) of the GDPR. There are several examples of scholarly works on the scope of GDPR relating to the concept of anonymous information.[30] The recent development in the CJEU combined with the technological advancements, however, makes the concepts of personal data and anonymous information concepts that need to be assessed on a case-to-case basis and in the specific context the data is processed. The book will, therefore, assess the concept of

---

[30] Michèle Finck and Frank Pallas. "They who must not be identified – Distinguishing personal from non-personal data under the GDPR". In: *International Data Privacy Law* 10.1 (Mar. 2020), pp. 11–36. ISSN: 2044-3994. doi: 10.1093/idpl/ipz026. eprint: https://academic.oup.com/idpl/article-pdf/10/1/11/33151834/ipz026.pdf. url: https://doi.org/10.1093/idpl/ipz026; Emily M Weitzenboeck et al. "The GDPR and unstructured data: Is anonymization possible?" In: *International Data Privacy Law* 12.3 (Mar. 2022), pp. 184–206. ISSN: 2044-3994. doi: 10.1093/idpl/ipac008. eprint: https://academic.oup.com/idpl/article-pdf/12/3/184/45690911/ipac008.pdf. url: https://doi.org/10.1093/idpl/ipac008; Robert Aufschläger et al. "Anonymization procedures for tabular data: An explanatory technical and legal synthesis". In: *Information* 14.9 (2023), p. 487. doi: https://doi.org/10.3390/info14090487; Tao Huang and Shuyuan Zheng. "Using differential privacy to define personal, anonymous and pseudonymous data". In: *IEEE Access* (2023). doi: https://doi.org/10.1109/ACCESS.2023.3321578; James Casaletto et al. "Federated analysis for privacy-preserving data sharing: A technical and legal primer". In: *Annual Review of Genomics and Human Genetics* 24 (2023), pp. 347–368. doi: https://doi.org/10.1146/annurev-genom-110122-084756.

anonymous information and the scope of the GDPR only in specific contexts, specifically in relation to third-country transfers in Chapter 5. To summarise, personal data is information that enables the identification of natural persons. The identification needs to be assessed in terms of reasonable means applied to identify a natural person in a relative manner.

Personal data needs to be *processed* in order for the scope of the GDPR to enter into effect, as stated in Article 1 of the GDPR. According to the GDPR Article 4 (2), "processing" is defined as "any operation or sets of operations which is performed on personal data or on sets of personal data, whether or not by automated means". Therefore, activities such as collecting, storing, using, sharing, adapting, or altering data fall under the scope of the GDPR, provided that the data processed meets the definition of personal data. In relation to the development and deployment of an AI system, both the use of personal data to train an algorithm to develop an AI model and the application of personal data on a finished trained and deployed AI model would be regarded as processing, according to Article 1 and the definition of processing in Article 4 (2) of the GDPR.

The broad definition of both "personal data" and "processing" has given rise to claims that, in light of increases in technology towards easier identification of natural persons, datafication, and improvements in data analytics, the GDPR has evolved into the "law of everything".[31] Moreover, the same scholars argue that the definition of the identifiable criterion has resulted in almost every piece of information being regarded as personal data.[32] Notwithstanding these broad definitions and technological developments towards easier identification, there exist examples of data that do not meet the definition of personal data and thus do not enter the scope of the GDPR. For instance, data about weather and temperature, not allowing for identification of natural persons or data concerning companies or public authorities – in general – are outside the definition of personal data in Article 4 (1) of the GDPR.[33]

To recapitulate, the processing of personal data is regarded as an interference with both Articles 7 and 8 of the Charter. The two terms "processing" and "personal data" are interpreted in a dynamic manner by the CJEU. Personal data is information that enables the identification of a natural person, while processing is defined as any operation performed on personal data. The next

---

31 Nadezhda Purtova. "The law of everything: Broad concept of personal data and future of EU data protection law". In: *Law, Innovation and Technology* 10.1 (2010): 40–81. doi: 10.1080/17579961.2018.1452176.

32 Ibid.

33 Regulation (EU) 2018/1807 of the European Parliament and of the Council of 14 November 2018 on a framework for the free flow of non-personal data in the European Union [2018] OJ L 303/59.

subsections will presuppose that there has been an interference in the rights of the Charter through the processing of personal data, and analyse the requirements for lawful interference when processing personal data to develop an AI model, commencing with the requirement that the interference needs to respect the essence of the right.

3.2.5 The Essence of the Right to Data Protection and AI System Development

Processing of personal data to develop an AI system in line with secondary law, but in breach of the essence of a right in the Charter, would never be a compliant approach due to the lex superior nature of the fundamental right to data protection. The analysis of whether some specific measures in relation to personal data processing as a part of AI system development need to be implemented in line with the "essence" requirement is not just an academic exercise. The case law of the CJEU has several examples of personal data processing operations being stopped from one day to another as a result of a judgement from the CJEU. Such examples include the transfer of personal data to third countries in the two Schrems judgements[34] and alterations to processing practices in relation to the retention of communication data.[35] Although these judgements did involve processing operations being stopped from one day to another due to breaches of the essence of the right, the examples from the case

---

34 Judgement of the Court (Grand Chamber) of 6 October 2015 in case C-362/14 Maximillian Schrems v Data Protection Commissioner, joined party: Digital Rights Ireland Ltd ECLI:EU:C:2015:650; Judgement of the Court (Grand Chamber) 16 July 2020 in Case C-311/18 Data Protection Commissioner v Facebook Ireland Ltd, Maximillian Schrems ECLI:EU:C:2020:559.

35 Judgement of the Court (Grand Chamber) of 8 April 2014 in Joined Cases C-293/12 and C-594/12, Digital Rights Ireland Ltd (C-293/12) v Minister for Communications, Marine and Natural Resources, Minister for Justice, Equality and Law Reform, Commissioner of the Garda Síochána, Ireland, The Attorney General ECLI:EU:C:2014:238 paragraph 40; Judgement of the Court (Grand Chamber) of 21 December 2016 in Joined Cases C-203/15 and C-698/15, Tele2 Sverige AB (C-203/15) v Post- och telestyrelsen, and Secretary of State for the Home Department (C-698/15) v Tom Watson, Peter Brice, Geoffrey Lewis, ECLI:EU:C:2016:970; Judgement of the Court (Grand Chamber) of 6 October 2020 In Joined Cases C-511/18, C-512/18, and C-520/18, La Quadrature du Net (C-511/18 and C-512/18), French Data Network (C-511/18 and C-512/18), Fédération des fournisseurs d'accès à Internet associatifs (C-511/18 and C-512/18), Igwan .net (C-511/18) v Premier ministre (C-511/18 and C-512/18), Garde des Sceaux, ministre de la Justice (C-511/18 and C-512/18), Ministre de l'Intérieur (C-511/18), Ministre des Armées (C-511/18),ECLI:EU:C:2020:791.

law illustrate the need for developing processing operations, particularly when an opaque and potentially invasive form of processing such as AI is applied, in line with the fundamental right to data protection.

Contrary to the Council of Europe (CoE) and the ECHR, the right to data protection is distinct in Article 8 of the Charter, separated from the right to a private life in Article 7 of the Charter. Article 7 has the following wording: "Everyone has the right to respect for his or her private and family life, home and communications". While Article 8 of the Charter reads as follows:

1. Everyone has the right to the protection of personal data concerning him or her.
2. Such data must be processed fairly for specified purposes and on the basis of the consent of the person concerned or some other legitimate basis laid down by law. Everyone has the right of access to data which has been collected concerning him or her, and the right to have it rectified.
3. Compliance with these rules shall be subject to control by an independent authority.

In addition to the requirements for interference with the right to data protection under Article 8 (2) of the Charter, the conditions in Article 52 of the Charter must be fulfilled for the interference in Article 8 of the Charter to be lawful. According to Article 52 (1) of the Charter, any interference or limitations to the rights within the Charter must be provided for by law and respect the "essence" of the rights and freedom. Limitations may be made only if they do not restrict the essence of the right, are necessary, and genuinely meet the objectives of general interests recognised within the Union or the need to protect the rights and freedoms of others.

The possibility to interfere with Charter rights closely resembles the conditions for interfering with Article 8 (1) ECHR, according to Article 8 (2) ECHR, namely, lawfulness, legitimate aim, necessity, suitability, and proportionality *stricto sensu*.[36] However, an interference in a fundamental right or freedom in the Charter also has to "respect the essence of those rights and freedoms", under Article 52 (1) to be lawful. The "essence" requirement has led to specific

36 Tor-Inge Harbo. "The function of proportionality analysis in European law". In: *The Function of Proportionality Analysis in European Law*. Leiden: Brill Nijhoff, 2015, p. 201; Antonio Troncoso Reigada. "The principle of proportionality and the fundamental right to personal data protection: The biometric data processing". In: *Lex Electronica* 17 (2012), p. 1. url: https://www.lex-electronica.org/en/s/159; Anne Peters. "Proportionality as a global constitutional principle". In: *Handbook on Global Constitutionalism*. Cheltenham: Edward Elgar Publishing, 2023, pp. 346–362. doi: https://doi.org/10.4337/9781783477357.00028.

examples of case law from the CJEU, which have relevance for the processing of personal data to develop an AI model.

As stated in the previous paragraph, the essence requirement as a condition for interference does not have a direct equivalent in the wording of Article 8 ECHR. There are, however, some minor traces of the "essence" requirement in the case law from the ECtHR.[37] Case law from the ECtHR regarding the essence requirement has not related to personal data processing, and as noted by the advocate general in Case 311/18 from 2019 "[the ECtHR] has not had recourse, in its case-law relating to Article 8 of the ECHR, to the concept of violation of the essential content, or the very essence, of the right to respect for private life".[38]

Since the requirement for essence, thus, is a condition for interference in fundamental rights without a direct equivalent in the wording of the ECHR, it is pivotal to analyse the case law from the CJEU regarding the essence requirement. The purpose of this analysis is to assess whether the requirement for respecting the "essence" of the fundamental rights in the Charter would require some specific measures to process personal data when developing an AI system.

There are especially two relevant judgements from the CJEU with regard to the requirement for respect for "the essence" of the right under Article 8 of the Charter, namely the judgement of 8 April 2014 in joined cases C-293/12 and C-594/12 Digital Rights Ireland[39] and the judgement of 21 June 2022 in the case C-817/19 Ligue des droits humains.[40]

The judgement of 8 April 2014 in joined cases C-293/12 and C-594/12 Digital Rights Ireland concerned the validity of Directive 2006/24/EC.[41] The

---

[37] Robert Spano. "Forword". In: *Proportionality in Crime Control and Criminal Justice*. Ed. by Emmanouil Billis, Nandor Knust, and Jon Petter Rui. London: Bloomsbury Publishing, 2021. url: https://papers.ssrn.com/sol3/papers.cfm?abstract_id=3979696.

[38] Opinion of Advocate General Saugmandsgaard Øe in Case C-311/18 paragraph 82.

[39] Judgement of the Court (Grand Chamber) of 8 April 2014 in Joined Cases C-293/12 and C-594/12, Digital Rights Ireland Ltd (C-293/12) v Minister for Communications, Marine and Natural Resources, Minister for Justice, Equality and Law Reform, Commissioner of the Garda Síochána, Ireland, The Attorney General ECLI:EU:C:2014:238 paragraph 40.

[40] Judgement of the Court (Grand Chamber) 21 June 2022 in the Case C-817/19 Ligue des droits humains v Conseil des ministers ECLI:EU:C:2022:491.

[41] Directive 2006/24/EC of the European Parliament and of the Council of 15 March 2006 on the retention of data generated or processed in connection with the provision of publicly available electronic communications services or of public communications networks and amending Directive 2002/58/EC OJ L L 105/54.

directive laid down requirements for the general and indiscriminate retention of data generated by telecommunications services for future law enforcement purposes. The CJEU adjudged that the directive was disproportionate and thus invalid. Paragraph (40) of the judgement is especially relevant with regard to the potential obligation under primary law to implement measures when processing personal data to respect the essence of the right to data protection.

The CJEU concluded in paragraph (40) that Directive 2006/24/EC did not adversely affect the essence of the right to data protection in Article 8 of the Charter, because:

> Article 7 of Directive 2006/24 provides, in relation to data protection and data security, that, without prejudice to the provisions adopted pursuant to Directives 95/46 and 2002/58, certain principles of data protection and data security must be respected by providers of publicly available electronic communications services or of public communications networks. According to those principles, Member States are to ensure that appropriate technical and organisational measures are adopted against accidental or unlawful destruction, accidental loss or alteration of the data.

The CJEU's conclusion was that a legal requirement to ensure the adoption of appropriate technical and organisational measures was one of the reasons that the interference did not violate the essence of the right to data protection in Article 8 of the Charter. Conversely, technical and organisational measures to ensure the integrity, confidentiality, and availability of personal data might be a part of the essence of the fundamental right to protection of personal data in Article 8 of the Charter.

The understanding of the essence of the right to personal data protection in the Digital Rights Ireland judgement has been upheld in later Opinions of the Advocate General of the CJEU. See, for instance, the Opinion of Advocate General Pitruzzella of 27 January 2022 in case C-817/19 Ligue des droits humains v Conseil des ministres paragraph (94), where the AG held that:

> As regards the fundamental right to the protection of personal data, the Court appears to find the essence of that right to be preserved when the measure providing for the interference limits the purpose of the processing and establish rules ensuring that the data in question will be secure, in particular from accidental or unlawful destruction, or accidental loss or alteration.

This later opinion from the AG strongly supports that purpose limitation is also a part of the essence of the right to personal data protection in Article 8 of the Charter.

The judgement of 21 June 2022 in the case C-817/19 Ligue des droits humains concerned the validity of the processing of Passenger Name Records

(PNR) data under Article 8 of the Charter.[42] The Court assessed whether the processing of personal data in relation to PNR breached the essence of the right to personal data protection in Article 8 of the Charter. In paragraph (120) of the judgement, the CJEU held that:

> Article 1(2) thereof read in conjunction with Article 3(8) and (9) thereof, as well as Annex II thereto, circumscribes the purposes for which those data are to be processed. Lastly, that same directive, in Articles 4 to 15 thereof, lays down the rules governing the transfer, processing and retention of those data as well as the rules intended to ensure, inter alia, the security, confidentiality and integrity of those data, and to protect them against unlawful access and processing. In those circumstances, the interferences which the PNR Directive entails do not adversely affect the essence of the fundamental rights enshrined in Articles 7 and 8 of the Charter.

Both the Digital Rights Ireland judgement from 2014, subsequent opinions of the advocate general, and the Ligue des droits humains judgement from 2022 suggest that the following aspects of personal data processing form part of the essence of the fundamental right to personal data protection in Article 8 of the Charter:

1. Clearly defined purposes of the processing of personal data. *The purpose limitation principle.*
2. Rules intended to ensure the security, confidentiality, availability, and integrity of personal data and protect the personal data from unlawful access and further processing. *Data protection and cybersecurity by design.*[43]

The two aspects listed above are part of the essence of personal data protection in Article 8 of the Charter, according to the interpretations of the judgements and AG opinions cited above. A violation of the essence of the right in Article 8 through a legislative act would entail that the legislative act is automatically invalid, and there is no room for a balancing exercise; see, for example, the judgement of 6 October 2015 in the case C-362/15 *Schrems* paragraphs 94 to

---

[42] Judgement of the Court (Grand Chamber) 21 June 2022 in the Case C-817/19 Ligue des droits humains v Conseil des ministers ECLI:EU:C:2022:491.

[43] Gloria Gonzáles Fuster. *Study on the Essence of the Fundamental Right to Privacy and to Protection of Personal Data*. Tech. rep. Vrije Universiteit Burssel (VUB) and EDPS, 2022. url: https://www.edps.europa.eu/system/files/2023-11/edps-vub-study_on_the_essence_of_fundamental_rights_to_privacy_and_to_protection_of_personal_data_en.pdf. Last accessed: 26.08.2024.

98.[44] An interference with Article 8 of the Charter not in breach of the essence of the right could still be invalid according to the proportionality test under Articles 8 (2) and 52 (1) of the Charter. Therefore, even though a legislative act or a technological solution allows for interference, has clearly defined purposes, and has implemented technical and organisational measures to ensure the security of the processing of personal data and cybersecurity, such measures could be deemed ineffective. Such ineffectiveness could potentially lead to the interference being disproportionate and thus invalid.

To recapitulate, the processing of personal data is an interference with both the right to personal data protection and the right to a private life. The CJEU has held that the principle of purpose limitation and data protection by design is a part of the essence of the right to data protection. In terms of processing personal data to train and develop AI systems, it is, therefore, crucial to implement purpose limitation and data protection by design measures in order not to breach the essence of the Charter Article 8.

3.2.6 The Fundamental Rights Structure and Processing of Personal Data for AI System Development

One underlying rationale of the GDPR is that the processing of personal data should be proportionate to the legitimate aim pursued with the processing.[45] The wording "proportionality" appears 26 times in the GDPR, and especially relevant Articles include Articles 5, 6, 9, 12–22, 23, 24, 34, 35, 44–50, 83–85, and 90. The principle of proportionality is an underlying rationale of the fundamental principles in Article 5 of the GDPR, especially the lawfulness, purpose limitation, and data minimisation principles. The principle of proportionality is a significant part of balancing the societal need for processing personal data with the interference the processing entails on the right to data protection in the GDPR.

The overall purpose of analysing the principle of proportionality when processing personal data for AI development is to assess whether the principle could function as a guiding principle when processing personal data for AI system development.

Before the processing of personal data in AI development can be analysed, the relationship between the fundamental principles in Article 5 of the GDPR

---

44 Judgement of the Court (Grand Chamber) of 6 October 2015 in case C-362/14 Maximillian Schrems v Data Protection Commissioner, joined party: Digital Rights Ireland Ltd ECLI:EU:C:2015:650.

45 Lee A Bygrave. "Core principles of data privacy law". In: *Data Privacy Law: An International Perspective.* Oxford: Oxford University Press, 2014), pp. 145–168. doi: https://doi.org/10.1093/acprof:oso/9780199675555.003.0005.

and primary law in the Charter needs to be established. The fundamental principles of processing are listed in Article 5 of the GDPR. The principles of data processing are, according to Article 5 (1) (a–f) of the GDPR:

(a) Lawfulness, fairness and transparency.
(b) Purpose limitation.
(c) Data minimisation.
(d) Accuracy.
(e) Storage limitation.
(f) Integrity and confidentiality.

Although the rules in Article 5 (1) (a–f) are titled "Principles", they should be regarded as hard law rules.[46] Infringements with these principles are considered more severe than interference with other Articles in the GDPR. Data protection authorities have, for instance, the authority to issue higher fines under Article 83 (5) (a) for infringement of the fundamental principles, compared to infringement of other requirements of the GDPR.

Processing of personal data for AI model development constitutes an interference with the Charter Article 8. If the processing enters the scope of the GDPR, the controller processing personal data would need to comply with both the fundamental principles of the GDPR and the requirements for lawful interference in the Charter. In the preceding sections and subsections, the primary law in the Charter and the fundamental principles of processing in Article 5 of the GDPR are analysed together, where the fundamental rights structure – the legality and the subtests of the principle of proportionality – function as a guiding structure of the analysis.

The focus of the current chapter will be on the fundamental principles related to data collection, data preprocessing, and personal data processing for model training when developing an AI system. Therefore, the focus will be on GDPR Article 5 (1) (a), (b), (c), the lawfulness principle, the purpose limitation principle, and the data minimisation principle. All the fundamental principles in Article 5 of the GDPR are relevant for processing personal data, but these specific principles are especially relevant for personal data processing during AI system development. The principle of accuracy is addressed in Chapter 4, while storage limitation, integrity, and confidentiality are the focus of Chapter 5. Chapter 4 will also address the purpose limitation principle and

[46] Lee A Bygrave. "Security by design: Aspirations and realities in a regulatory context". In: *Oslo Law Review* 8.3 (2021), pp. 126–177. doi: https://doi.org/10.18261/olr.8.3.2; Armin von Bogdandy. "Founding principles of EU law: A theoretical and doctrinal sketch". In: *European Law Journal* 16 (2 2010), pp. 95–111. doi: https://doi.org/10.1111/j.1468-0386.2009.00500.x.

the data minimisation principle when personal data is processed in deployed AI systems.

3.2.7 Lawfulness and AI System Development

3.2.7.1 Introduction

According to Article 8 (2) of the Charter, personal data "must be processed fairly for specified purposes and on the basis of the consent of the person concerned or some other basis laid down by law". Personal data processed to train and develop an AI model must, in order to be a lawful interference in Article 8 of the Charter, be processed in line with a lawful legal basis. Within the EU, the GDPR contains specific rules that operationalise Article 8 of the Charter, according to recital 1 of the GDPR. The next paragraphs will examine which legal basis in the GDPR can be used for processing personal data to develop AI models. Pursuing the analysis of legal basis, the exemptions for processing special categories of personal data under Article 9 of the GDPR are analysed in an AI system development context.

The lawfulness principle, as outlined in Article 5 (1) (a) of the GDPR, requires the controller to have a valid legal basis for the processing of personal data before the processing and throughout the processing lifecycle. The legal basis must be interpreted in conjunction with the processing to determine whether the processing of personal data is in line with the legal basis. Additionally, measures and means should be introduced to ensure that the processing conforms and complies with the requirements of the chosen legal basis, in accordance with both Articles 25 (1) and 5 (2) of the GDPR.

The appropriate legal bases for processing personal data to develop an AI system, as well as lawful exemptions to process special categories of personal data, are analysed in the following paragraphs. If the processing conforms and complies with the requirements of the legal basis during the processing during AI system development, the lawfulness principle under Article 5 (1) (a) of the GDPR and Article 8 of the Charter will – most likely – be fulfilled.

According to Article 6 (1) of the GDPR, the processing of personal data is lawful only if and to the extent that the conditions under at least one of the alternative legal bases in Article 6 (1) are fulfilled. The legal bases for the processing of personal data in Article 6 (1) GDPR are:

(a) Consent, which needs to be freely given, unambiguous, and purpose-specific.
(b) Performance of a contract. The controller, referring to the natural or legal person determining the purpose and means of the processing, might

process personal data strictly necessary for the performance of the main purpose of a contract where the data subject is a party.

(c) Legal obligations. If the processing of personal data is necessary for compliance with a legal obligation to which the controller is subject, it might constitute a valid legal basis. According to recital 41, the reference to legal obligations or a legislative measure in the GDPR does not necessarily require a legislative act adopted by a parliament. Such legal basis or legislative measures should nevertheless be clear and precise, and their application should be foreseeable for the persons subjected to the processing based on the legal obligation, according to recital 41.

(d) If processing is necessary to protect vital interests, for instance, the life, health, or crucial financial interests closely related to the survival and well-being of an individual, of the data subject, or another natural person, it might constitute a legal basis for processing personal data. Recital 46 of the GDPR describes vital interests as those which are "essential for the life of an individual". The legal basis in Article 6 (1) (d) is a consequence of the right to data protection not being absolute, and that the right to life justifies interferences with the right to data protection.[47]

(e) Processing of personal data (I) necessary for the performance of a task carried out in the public interest, e.g., cybersecurity of software systems or pandemic disease monitoring, or (II) exercise of public authority vested in the controller might constitute a valid legal basis. Both alternatives require a basis for the processing of personal data laid down in Union law or member state law to which the controller is subject, according to Article 6 (3) of the GDPR.

(f) The last legal basis is if processing personal data is if such processing is necessary for the purposes of legitimate interests pursued by the controller. Article 6 (1) (f) cannot be applied where such interests are outweighed by the fundamental rights and freedoms of the data subject in a proportionality assessment. Article 6 (1) (f), thus, requires (I) that the interest pursued by the processing of personal data by the controller is legitimate, (II) that the processing is necessary to achieve these interests, and (III) that the processing is proportionate in relation to the data subject's right to data protection.

---

[47] Waltraut Kotschy. "Article 6: Lawfulness of processing". In: *The EU General Data Protection Regulation (GDPR): A Commentary.* Ed. by Christopher Kuner, Lee A Bygrave, and Christopher Docksey. Oxford: Oxford University Press, 2020, p. 333.

With specific regard to personal data applied to train, test, and validate an AI model, one important question is which one of the legal bases in Article 6 (1) of the GDPR the controller could rely on. The most relevant legal basis for processing personal data to train, test, and validate an AI model is Articles 6 (1) (a), (b), and (f). For controllers under the scope of public law exercising public authority, Article 6 (1) (e) is the most relevant legal basis provided that there is a basis for such processing in member state law or Union law. The preceding paragraphs will – in order to ensure context and oversight – analyse all the legal bases under Article 6 (1) in relation to the processing of personal data to develop an AI system.

3.2.7.2 Consent

According to Article 6 (1) (a), processing shall be lawful if the data subject has given consent to the processing of his or her personal data for one or more specific purposes. The conditions for consent as a legal basis for processing are further elaborated under Article 7 of the GDPR. According to Article 7, the controller shall be able to demonstrate that the data subject has consented. Moreover, according to Article 7, the data subject shall have the possibility to withdraw his or her consent at any time.

In order for the controller to process personal data based on consent to develop an AI system, the controller needs to have a direct relationship with each data subject in order to lawfully gain consent. The controller must carefully explain the processing operations involved in training, testing, and validating the AI model and get free and unambiguous approval from the data subjects to process their personal data for that purpose. Relying on consent under Article 6 (1) (a) as the legal basis for training an AI model, therefore, presupposes that the controller has a direct interaction with the data subject that forms part of the training dataset.

The data subjects must have a genuine free choice, and refusal to consent must not lead to negative consequences for the data subject, according to recital 42 of the GDPR. The power balance or potential power imbalance between the controller and the data subject is especially relevant in the assessment of whether the consent is freely given, according to recital 43. A system for gaining consent where the data subject must opt out in order to not consent to processing of personal data for AI model training is not in line with Article 6 (1) (a) and Article 7 (1) of the GDPR because it is not an unambiguous and freely given indication of the data subject's wish.

If the data subject withdraws consent to the processing, the controller needs to stop processing the data subject's personal data. Withdrawal of consent does not entail that the processing of personal data before the withdrawal has been unlawful, according to Article 7 (3) of the GDPR. With specific regard to consent as the legal basis in order to train an AI model, withdrawal of consent makes further processing complicated. According to Article 17 (1) (a) of the GDPR, the controller shall have the obligation to erase personal data without undue delay if the data subject withdraws consent on which the processing is based according to point (a) of Article 6 (1). When personal data is applied to train an ML model and a data subject withdraws the consent, the controller might, in some instances, be required to retrain the ML model without the data subject's personal data.[48]

To summarise, consent as a legal basis under Article 6 (1) (a) for training and developing an AI system must be an unambiguous, freely given, and informed indication of the data subjects' wishes for the processing to be lawful. The controller must inform the data subject about the purpose of the processing and the legal basis at the time of collecting the personal data from the data subject. Developing and training an AI system is a complex and potentially opaque endeavour. The inherent complexity and lack of transparency of developing an AI system from algorithms and data will most likely make consent a questionable legal basis for processing the personal data required for the development of the AI system. However, depending on the facts of the case, the conclusion may differ. In cases where the controller has a direct relationship with each of the data subjects that form part of the training dataset, consent might be a lawful legal basis for obtaining personal data for AI system development.

3.2.7.3 Performance of a contract

According to Article 6 (1) (b), a valid legal basis for processing personal data is if the processing is necessary for the performance of a contract to with the data subject is party or in order to take steps at the request of the data subject prior to entering into a contract. The CJEU has elaborated on the legal basis in Article 6 (1) (b) in the Meta Platforms Inc. judgement from 2023.[49] The case concerned many different referred questions about, for instance, the relationship between competition law and data protection law. One referred question was whether Meta Platforms Inc., the parent company of i.a. Facebook, Instagram, and WhatsApp, could rely on the performance of a contract to process personal data for reasons of advertising and offer personalised content, network security, product improvement, and seamless use of all group products. The Meta Platform Inc. judgement does not have any reference to AI or ML. However, the processing of personal data for the purposes outlined above

---

48 Bjørn Aslak Juliussen, Jon Petter Rui, and Dag Johansen. "Algorithms that forget: Machine unlearning and the right to erasure". In: *Computer Law & Security Review* 51 (2023), p. 105885. doi: https://doi.org/10.1016/j.clsr.2023.105885.

49 Judgement of the Court (Grand Chamber) in Case C-252/21 Meta Platforms Inc., Meta Platforms Ireland Ltd, Facebook Deutschland GmbH v Budeskartellamt ECLI:EU:C:2023:537.

– behavioural advertising, personalised content, and product improvement – is most likely conducted through some form of ML models on Meta's platforms. In paragraphs 98–99 of the judgement the Court held:

> [I]n order for the processing of personal data to be regarded as necessary for the performance of a contract, within the meaning of that provision, it must be objectively indispensable for a purpose that is integral to the contractual obligation intended for the data subject. The controller must therefore be able to demonstrate how the main subject matter of the contract cannot be achieved if the processing in question does not occur.
>
> The fact that such processing may be referred to in the contract or is merely useful for the performance of the contract is, in itself, irrelevant in that regard. The decisive factor for the purposes of applying the justification set out in point (b) of the first subparagraph of Article 6(1) of the GDPR is rather that the processing of personal data by the controller must be essential for the proper performance of the contract concluded between the controller and the data subject and, therefore, that there are no workable, less intrusive alternatives.

The contract under Article 6 (1) (b) must therefore be a contract between the controller training the AI model and the data subject whose personal data forms part of the training data. The processing of personal data needs to be "objectively indispensable" for the proper performance of the contract, meaning that the subject matter of the contract cannot be achieved if the processing does not occur, according to the CJEU in the Meta Platforms Inc. judgement.[50]

ML models are often developed, trained, tested, and validated on very large datasets comprising personal data from an undefined number of individual data subjects. Because of the vast amount of personal data, it might be challenging to argue that one of these data subjects' personal data is "objectively indispensable" in order to develop the AI model. If it is possible to develop the AI system without the specific personal data from one data subject, the performance of a contract is not dependent on such processing of personal data, and the conditions under Article 6 (1) (b) are thus not fulfilled.

However, some European data protection authorities (DPAs) have opened for Article 6 (1) (b) to be a relevant legal basis for processing personal data to develop AI models. One example is the Danish DPA, which published guidance on this specific topic in February 2024.[51] The case the Danish DPA published guidance about concerned model training from a speech dataset in order to develop a Danish speech-to-text synthesis AI model. Each of the data subjects recorded their voices, and the voice recordings were used to train

50 Ibid.

51 Datatilsynet. *Etablering og dealing av datasæt.* url: https://www.datatilsynet.dk/afgoerelser/afgoerelser/2024/jan/etablering-og-deling-af-datasaet#_ftn1. Last accessed: 01.08.2025.

speech-to-text ML algorithms. The data subjects received remuneration in the form of gift cards. The Danish DPA concluded that Article 6 (1) (b) could be applied as a lawful legal basis in such a situation. The DPA concluded that the contractual objective – reading different Danish voices into recordings – could not be fulfilled without the processing of personal data.

The case from the Danish DPA concerned data subjects who had explicitly entered into a contract where the data subjects' contractual obligation was to provide personal data in the form of speech samples to be applied as a part of a training dataset of an AI model. The DPA's decision could, therefore, not be directly transferred to other cases where the personal data processing to develop an AI model appears more as a side-effect of the core contractual obligation between the controller and the data subject. In such instances, the processing of personal data in order to train an AI model would not be "objectively indispensable" for the performance of a contract.

Could the other alternative under Article 6 (1) (b), "processing is necessary (...) in order to take steps at the request of the data subject prior to entering into a contract", be applied to lawfully process personal data in order to train and develop an AI model? In such a case, it must be objectively indispensable for the performance of the subject matter of the contract that the data subject intends to enter into to process the data subject's personal data to train and develop an AI system. It could, for instance, be objectively indispensable to process the data subject's personal data to train an AI system if the controller is delivering a personalised AI system specially tailored to the data subject. However, in such a case, the data subject will most likely already have entered into the contract and will not be at a pre-contractual stage. Therefore, the first alternative of Article 6 (1) (b) would be the relevant legal basis, and not the pre-contractual alternative.

To summarise, Article 6 (1) (b) requires that it is objectively indispensable to process personal data for the main subject of a contract between the controller and the data subject in order to develop an AI system for the legal basis to be lawful. The legal basis could be applied in cases where the controller has a direct relationship with the data subject and where the subject matter of the contract is to deliver an AI system, i.e., where the data subject's contractual obligation is to deliver personal data in order to develop such a system. However, the contract alternative could not be lawfully applied to process personal data where the development of the AI system is not the specific purpose matter of the contract, e.g., in cases where personal data is processed to develop an AI system in order to "develop our services", "product improvement", or similar vague purposes within a larger, overall contract, terms of service, or as a part of a large contract related to, e.g., a software system delivery or a social media platform.

3.2.7.4 Legal obligation

According to Article 6 (1) (c), a lawful legal basis for processing personal data is if the processing is necessary for compliance with a legal obligation to which the controller is subjected. According to Article 6 (3) of the GDPR, the basis for the processing referred to in point (c) of Article 6 should be laid down in Union law or member state law to which the controller is subject. Could Article 6 (1) (c) be applied to process personal data to develop and train an AI system?

One example of legal obligation functioning as a legal basis for processing personal data in the development phase of an AI system is related to testing and auditing the developed models. One example is Article 10 (5) of the AI Act. According to Article 10 (5) of the AI Act, to the extent strictly necessary for the purposes of ensuring bias detection and correction concerning high-risk AI systems, the providers of such systems might exceptionally process personal data and special categories of personal data. When relying on Article 6 (1) (c) and Article 10 (5) of the AI Act for processing personal data for bias detection, auditing, and testing during the development phase of an AI system, it is important to note that the legal basis covers only the processing for bias detection, auditing, and testing, and not general processing of personal data to develop the AI system.[52] The general processing to develop the AI system, thus, needs to rely on another legal basis in Union or member state law.

3.2.7.5 Vital interest

Article 6 (1) (d) permits the processing of personal data if processing is necessary in order to protect the vital interests of the data subject or another person. It is difficult to imagine how Article 6 (1) (d) could be applied to develop and train an AI system to protect the vital interests of a natural person. It could be conceivable that Article 6 (1) (d) could be applied to process personal data in a case where a finished developed AI system is deployed. Instances where personal data could be processed under Article 6 (1) (d) in a deployed or finished trained AI system could be the case where a patient is unconscious and, thus, unable to consent, and a deployed AI diagnosis system is available in a hospital. In such a case, the hospital could rely on Article 6 (1) (d) to process the unconscious patient's personal data in the deployed AI system. However, training and developing an AI system is a time-consuming process, and Article 6 (1) (d) is, thus, not a relevant legal basis in the development phase.

---

[52] Marvin Van Bekkum. "Using sensitive data to de-bias AI systems: Article 10 (5) of the EU AI act". In: *Computer Law & Security Review* 56 (2025), p. 106115. doi: https://doi.org/10.1016/j.clsr.2025.106115.

3.2.7.6 Public interest and exercise of public authority

Under Article 6 (1) (e), there are two alternative legal bases for processing personal data. The first alternative is that the processing is necessary for the performance of a task carried out in the public interest, and the second alternative is that the processing of personal data is necessary for the exercise of public authority. The two different alternatives in the legal basis in Article 6 (1) (e) are a consequence of the development where several typical governmental purposes are carried out by private or quasi-private parties.

According to Article 6 (3) of the GDPR, Article 6 (1) (e) requires a supplementary legal basis in Union law or member state law to which the controller is subject. The supplementary legal basis must determine the purpose of the processing and establish that the processing is necessary for the exercise of public authority or tasks carried out in the public interest. The supplementary legal basis must, moreover, meet an objective of public interest and be proportionate to the legitimate aim pursued.

Article 6 (1) (e) could most likely be applied by public authorities to process data to train and develop an AI system applied to delivering public services, private authorities delivering services in the public interest, or private authorities pursuing public interests, if there exists a sufficient supplementary legal basis in EU or member state law that permits such processing.

An example where a national DPA concluded that a supplementary legal basis was not sufficient to process personal data to develop an AI system based on Article 6 (1) (e) is from the Norwegian DPA.[53] The Norwegian Public Welfare Authority wanted to process historical personal data to develop an AI system predicting how long a reported sick leave would last, depending on factors such as diagnosis, occupation, age, and address. The supplementary legal basis allowed for the processing of personal data to assess the necessity of having a physical meeting to discuss the patients' sick leave. The Norwegian DPA concluded that the specific supplementary legal basis was too unclear, general, and ambiguous to be applied to develop an AI system based on the processing of historical personal data on sick leave.

A similar case to the Norwegian case is one from the Danish DPA.[54] The City of Copenhagen intended to develop an AI system to detect inhabitants

---

53 Datatilsynet. *NAV – sluttrapport*. url: https://www.datatilsynet.no/regelverk-og-verktoy/sandkasse-for-kunstig-intelligens/ferdige-prosjekter-og-rapporter/nav-sluttrapport/rettslig-grunnlag/. Last accessed: 01.08.2025.

54 Datatilsynet. *Uttalelse om behandlingsgrunnlag til utvikling av AI løsning*. url: https://www.datatilsynet.dk/afgoerelser/afgoerelser/2023/nov/udtalelse-om-behandlingsgrundlag-til-udvikling-og-drift-af-ai-loesning-inden-for-sundheds-og-omsorgsomraadet. Last accessed: 01.08.2025.

in need of rehabilitation, with the overall purpose of making rehabilitation services available for a wider demographic than those requesting the rehabilitation services. The AI tool relied on national patient health records and individual data points such as age, address, social security number, and date of birth. The City of Copenhagen wanted to rely on Article 6 (1) (e) as the legal basis, more specifically, section 86 of the Danish Social Services Act, which requires local Danish councils to offer rehabilitation services. The Danish DPA concluded that the supplementary legal basis was neither sufficiently unambiguous nor sufficiently clear to be applied as a supplementary legal basis for the development of the AI system.[55]

As a general conclusion, Article 6 (1) (e) requires a supplementary legal basis in EU or member state law to which the controller is subject to process personal data to develop an AI system. The specific supplementary legal basis needs to be clear and give unambiguous provisions for processing personal data for specific purposes. Most likely, the supplementary legal basis also needs to clarify that the processing of personal data could be applied to develop an AI system.

3.2.7.7 Legitimate interests

A highly relevant legal basis for processing personal data for training and developing an AI system is Article 6 (1) (f).[56] In order for all the requirements under Article 6 (1) (f) to be fulfilled and the legal basis to be lawfully applied for processing, (I) the processing must pursue a legitimate interest, (II) the processing must be necessary for the purposes of legitimate interests pursued by the controller or by a third party, and (III) the interests in protecting the personal data for the data subject must not override the interest pursued by the processing. The subtests of Article 6 (1) (f) resemble the overall structure of interfering with the right to data protection in Articles 8 (2) and 52 (3) of the Charter.

Public authorities cannot rely on Article 6 (1) (f) where the processing of personal data for developing and training an AI system is related to the performance of the public authorities' tasks, i.e., exercise of public authority, according to the second paragraph of Article 6 (1) of the GDPR.

According to recital 47 of the GDPR, one relevant assessment when assessing whether the interests are legitimate is the reasonable expectations the data subject has, based on the relationship with the controller. Taking into account

55 Ibid.

56 Taner Kuru. "Lawfulness of the mass processing of publicly accessible online data to train large language models". In: *International Data Privacy Law* 14.4 (2024), pp. 326–351. doi: https://doi.org/10.1093/idpl/ipae013.

the context of the collection of personal data, could the data subject reasonably expect that the personal data would be applied to train and develop an AI system? If the data subject cannot reasonably expect such processing, the interests of the controller to process the data are most likely not legitimate, and the interests of the data subject could override the alleged legitimate interests under Article 6 (1) (f). Marketing purposes, fraud prevention, and processing personal data for the purpose of network and information security are mentioned as examples of legitimate interests under Article 6 (1) (f), according to recitals 46–47 of the GDPR.

Several commercial AI developers base the processing of personal data to develop the AI system on legitimate interests, namely, the AI developers' commercial interests in the development.[57] The question of whether purely commercial interests may constitute legitimate interests under Article 6 (1) (f) of the GDPR was referred to the CJEU for a preliminary ruling in the C-621/22 case.[58] The overall subject matter of the referred question in the C-621/22 case was whether Article 6 (1) (f) covers only interests enshrined in law (a positive test) or any interest as long as it is not contrary to the law (a negative test). The facts of the case concern a controller that had sold personal data to third parties without the consent of the data subject, relying on legitimate interests, namely, the commercial interest in selling the data. Such business models are very present in the AI field, where datasets containing personal data are sold to train and develop AI systems.[59] An understanding of Article 6 (1) (f) where the commercial interests of the controller in selling the personal data could constitute a legitimate interest is not necessarily in alignment with recital 47 of the GDPR and the wording of Article 6 (1) (f) where the data has to be processed in a manner that the data subject could reasonably expect. The CJEU held that the objective pursued by the GDPR is to ensure a high level of protection for the fundamental rights and freedoms of natural persons. Moreover, the CJEU held that a wide range of interests is capable of constituting legitimate interests in Article 6 (1) (f). However, the interests pursued must be lawful; the interests cannot be achieved just as efficiently by other less intrusive means of

57 Pablo Trigo Kramcsák. "Can legitimate interest be an appropriate lawful basis for processing artificial intelligence training datasets?" In: *Computer Law & Security Review* 48 (2023), p. 105765. ISSN: 0267-3649. doi: https://doi.org/10.1016/j.clsr.2022.105765. url: https://www.sciencedirect.com/science/article/pii/S026736492200108X.

58 Judgement of the Court (Ninth Chamber) of 4 October 2024 in case C-621/22 Koninklijke Nederlandse Lawn Tennisbond v Autoriteit Persoonsgegevens, ECLI:EU:C:2024:858.

59 Datatrade. *Explore AI ML Training Datasets and Providers*. url: https://datarade.ai/data-categories/ai-ml-training-data. Last accessed: 01.08.2025.

processing, and the need for processing must be examined in conjunction with the data minimisation principle.

The judgement in the C-621/22 case does not rule out the processing of personal data for training and an AI system based on Article 6 (1) (f) and the commercial interests of the AI provider. However, the judgement makes it clear that Article 6 (1) (f) needs the be interpreted restrictively if the data subject has not consented. Moreover, the judgement emphasises that the interest cannot be achieved with less intrusive means, and that the processing must be within the reasonable expectations of the data subject.

To recapitulate, if a controller is developing an AI system and processing personal data in order to train an AI model, all the following conditions would need to be fulfilled for the processing of personal data to be lawful under Article 6 (1) (f) of the GDPR.

First, the controller must assess whether the purpose of processing the personal data to train the AI model pursues a legitimate interest. Such legitimate interests will most likely be fulfilled if the processing is reasonably expected by the data subject, taking into account the information given to the data subject and the relationship between the controller and the data subject.

Second, it must be assessed whether such processing is necessary to achieve the purpose and the legitimate interests. When assessing necessity, a relevant assessment is whether less intrusive means of processing would fulfil the processing purpose. If this assessment is answered in the affirmative, the processing would most likely not be necessary, and Article 6 (1) (f) would not constitute a lawful legal basis for the processing.

Finally, the controller must assess whether the data subjects' interests override the legitimate interests of the controller. In the specific proportionality assessment, the nature of the personal data processed (e.g., whether special categories of personal data will be processed), the relationship between the controller and the data subject, the data subject's reasonable expectations about the processing, and measures to lower the risk of the processing, e.g., pseudonymisation and encryption, are aspects with general relevance in the assessment. Moreover, a specific case-to-case assessment of the processing needs to be conducted, and the proportionality *stricto sensu* (the proportionality in the strict case, i.e., of the specific case under question) needs to be assessed and concluded.

When training an ML model, the controller processing the personal data makes several choices. These choices span from the choice of the ML algorithms applied, the data applied for training, and the variables – i.e., a feature or attribute used as input for training and making predictions – applied in the

ML model.[60] In terms of all the legal bases discussed above, Article 6 (1) (f) (legitimate interest) will afford the controller the most flexibility within these different choices. However, if Article 6 (1) (f) is chosen as the legal basis, the controller has to document that all these choices – the personal data processed, the ML algorithms used, and the variables in the model – are within the reasonable expectations of the data subject, in order for the processing to be lawful, according to Article 6 (1) (f) interpreted in line with recital 47 of the GDPR.

To conclude on the lawfulness of the interference in the right to data protection when processing personal data to develop an AI model, all processing of personal data under the scope of the GDPR must fulfil the conditions under one of the legal bases in Article 6 (1) (a–f) to be lawful. In the absence of the data subject's consent, the other legal bases in Article 6 (1) (b–f) need to be interpreted restrictively, according to the settled case law of the CJEU. The processing of personal data in order to train and develop an ML model is a complex and opaque form of processing. The most relevant legal basis for such processing is a contract under Article 6 (1) (b), where training an ML model is the core contractual obligation for the data subject and legitimate interests in Article 6 (1) (f). For public sector controllers, Article 6 (1) (e) is the most relevant legal basis, presupposing there is an additional legal basis in EU or member state law. For all the legal bases, the information given to the data subject about the processing must be clear at the time of collection of the personal data. Moreover, it is crucial for the controller to document that the conditions under the chosen legal basis were fulfilled at the time of collection and processing, under the accountability principle in Article 5 (2) of the GDPR.

3.2.7.8 Exemptions for processing of special categories of personal data for AI system development

The GDPR differentiates between personal data and special categories of personal data. The latter is personal data closely linked to sensitive attributes about an individual, e.g., religion, sexual orientation, or health. As a general rule, it is prohibited to process special categories of personal data, according to Article 9 (1) of the GDPR. The following paragraphs will focus on the lawful processing of special categories of personal data to develop an AI

[60] Towards Data Science. *Categorical Variables for Machine Learning Algorithms*. url: https://towardsdatascience.com/categorical-variables-for-machine-learning-algorithms-d2768d587ab6. Last accessed: 01.08.2025.

model, according to the derogations from the prohibition in Article 9 (2) of the GDPR.

Special categories of personal data are defined in Article 9 (1) of the GDPR as personal data "revealing racial or ethnic origin, political opinions, religious or philosophical beliefs, or trade union membership, and the processing of genetic data, biometric data for the purpose of uniquely identifying a natural person, data concerning health or data concerning a natural person's sex life or sexual orientation".

A judgement from the CJEU in 2022[61] describes when personal data under Article 4 also could be regarded as special categories of personal data under Article 9. After analysing the legal sources, the CJEU concluded in paragraph (127) of the judgement that:

> Personal data that are liable indirectly to reveal sensitive information concerning a natural person should not be excluded from the strengthened protection regime of Article 9 GDPR.[62]

In the Meta Platform Inc. judgement, the CJEU also analysed the link between personal data and special categories of personal data under Article 9. The CJEU was referred the question of whether Article 9 (1) of the GDPR must be interpreted as it constitutes the processing of special categories of personal data when a data subject visits a website or an app to which one or more of the categories in Article 9 relate, and the controller links the data of the website with the users' social network account. The CJEU answered the question in the affirmative, provided that the information on the website or the app related to the categories of Article 9 allows such information protected under Article 9 of the GDPR to be revealed.[63]

The two judgements cited above have led to a somewhat new understanding of the distinction between personal data and special categories of personal data, where personal data that could reveal special categories through, e.g., deduction or by cross-referencing sources, could be regarded as special categories of personal data under the scope of Article 9 GDPR.

---

[61] Judgement of the Court (Grand Chamber) 1 August 2022 in case C-184/20 OT v Vyriausioji tarnybinės etikos komisija, third party: Fondas 'Nevyriausybini organizacij informacijos ir paramos centras ECLI:EU:C:2022:601.

[62] Ibid.

[63] Judgement of the Court (Grand Chamber) in Case C-252/21 Meta Platforms Inc., Meta Platforms Ireland Ltd, Facebook Deutschland GmbH v Budeskartellamt ECLI:EU:C:2023:537.

When developing and training an AI model, the AI system provider is dependent on extensive amounts of data. In cases where the training dataset does not contain explicit information protected under Article 9 (1) GDPR, but the combination of the variables of information about a natural person makes it possible to infer or deduce special categories of personal data, the judgement from the CJEU from 2022 is an argument for offering that data the specific protection regime under Article 9.[64]

However, according to the facts of the case referred to the CJEU from a Lithuanian court in the OT v Vyriausioji tarnybinės etikos komisija judgement, the personal data that made it possible to deduce special categories of personal data was published on a publicly available website. The case concerned a Lithuanian Ethics Commission reviewing declarations of private interests from public officers. Under Lithuanian law, public officers were mandated to disclose information about themselves and their partners, which was published publicly online. The information published in the case referred to the CJEU did not directly contain special categories of personal data. However, it was possible to deduce sexual orientation – a special category of personal data – from the name of the partner. Since the data was published on a website, one needs to be cautious to establish a general rule that all personal data that can be applied to deduce and infer special categories of personal data should be afforded the protection regime under Article 9. Nevertheless, in cases where datasets used to train ML algorithms are made publicly available and the information in the dataset could be applied to infer special categories of personal data concerning a specific natural person, the judgement in case C- 184/20 supports that the personal data publicly available in the dataset used for training should be regarded as protected under Article 9 of the GDPR.

As a general rule, it is prohibited to process special categories of personal data under Article 9, according to Article 9 (1). To process special categories of personal data, the controller would need to fulfil a lawful derogation under Article 9 (2) of the GDPR.

Special categories of personal data are still personal data; therefore, the controller needs both a legal basis for the processing under Article 6 and a lawful exemption under Article 9 (2) of the GDPR in order for the processing

64 Judgement of the Court (Grand Chamber) 1 August 2022 in case C-184/20 OT v Vyriausioji tarnybinės etikos komisija, third party: Fondas 'Nevyriausybini organizacij informacijos ir paramos centras ECLI:EU:C:2022:601.

to be lawful, according to recital 51 of the GDPR.[65] All the exemptions under Article 9 (2) are to be interpreted restrictively.[66]

3.2.7.9 Explicit consent as an exemption to process special categories of personal data to develop AI systems

The first exemption from the general prohibition of processing special categories of personal data in Article 9 (2) is explicit consent in Article 9 (2) (a). The prohibition does not apply if the data subject has given explicit consent to the processing of those special categories of personal data for one or more specific purposes. Could Article 9 (2) (a) be applied to process special categories of personal data to train and develop an AI system?

The requirements for consent elaborated in Chapter 3.2.7.2 would still apply for explicit consent, as well as the requirement that the consent should be explicit in Article 9 (2) (a). The GDPR does not define the difference between "consent" and "explicit consent" under Article 9 (2) (a). According to the EDPB, the term "explicit" in Article 9 (2) (a) refers to the data subject's expressive statement, which in most cases would be required to be given in writing or, if oral, would require a confirmation from the data subject in some manner.[67] An explicit consent, thus, requires that the consent cannot be implied, as well as a high degree of precision when gaining the consent and when defining

65 Midas Nouwens et al. "Dark patterns after the GDPR: Scraping consent pop-ups and demonstrating their influence". In: *Proceedings of the 2020 CHI Conference on Human Factors in Computing Systems*. New York: Association for Computing Machinery, 2020, pp. 1–13. doi: https://doi.org/10.1145/3313831.3376321; EDPB. *European Data Protection Board, Guidelines 3/2019 on Processing of Personal Data through Video Devices v2.0, (EDPB Guidelines, 2020)*. Page 68. url: https://edpb.europa.eu/our-work-tools/our-documents/guidelines/guidelines-32019-processing-personal-data-through-video_en. Last accessed: 01.08.2025.

66 Marvin van Bekkum and Frederik Zuiderveen Borgesius. "Using sensitive data to prevent discrimination by artificial intelligence: Does the GDPR need a new exception?" In: *Computer Law & Security Review* 48 (2023), p. 105770. ISSN: 0267-3649. doi: https://doi.org/10.1016/j.clsr.2022.105770. url: https://www.sciencedirect.com/science/article/pii/S0267364922001133; Ludmila Georgieva and Christopher Kuner. "Article 9 processing of special categories of personal data". In: *The EU General Data Protection Regulation (GDPR): A Commentary*. Oxford: Oxford University Press, Feb. 2020. isbn: 9780198826491. doi: 10.1093/oso/9780198826491.003.0038. eprint: https://academic.oup.com/book/0/chapter/352296960/chapter-pdf/52771138/isbn-9780198826491-book-part-38.pdf. url: https://doi.org/10.1093/oso/9780198826491.003.0038.

67 EDPB. *Guidelines 05/2020 on Consent under Regulation 2016/679*. url: https://edpb.europa.eu/sites/default/files/files/file1/edpb_guidelines_202005_consent_en.pdf. Last accessed: 01.08.2025.

the processing purposes. An explicit consent, in contrast to consent, would, most likely, be required to be in a written or oral form and cannot be interpreted from the situation, as consent under Article 6 (1) (a) could be in some instances.

If Article 9 (2) (a) would be applied to process special categories of personal data to train an AI model, the conditions for consent elaborated in Chapter 3.2.7.2 must first be fulfilled, meaning that there is no power imbalance between the data subject and the controller, that it is as easy to give consent as to revoke it, and that refusal of consent will not adversely affect the data subject or lead to any detriment for the data subject. Moreover, the controller must be able to document that the consent was explicit. In cases without any such power imbalance, the processing of special categories of personal data for AI development might rely on explicit consent. However, in relation to the vast amount of personal data required to train and develop an AI model and thus also the vast amount of data subjects, explicit consent might not be a very practical exemption, and the consent-gaining scheme might be problematic to operate with a lot of data subjects. Nevertheless, if there is no power imbalance and the data subjects are given clear and intelligible information about what they are explicitly consenting to, Article 9 (2) (a) might be a lawful exemption to process special categories of personal data to train the AI model.

3.2.7.10 Vital interests and exemptions requiring a supplementary legal basis

Article 9 (2) (c) (vital interests) closely resembles the legal basis in Article 6 (1) (d), protection of vital interests. In the exemption under Article 9, the controller furthermore needs to identify that the data subject is "physically or legally incapable of giving consent". As in Article 6 (1) (d), the vital interests are interests "essential for the life of the data subject", according to recital 46, "including physical integrity of life", according to recital 112.

Article 9 (2) (c) is not a relevant exemption for processing special categories of personal data to develop and train an AI model. The exemption might be relevant for processing special categories of personal data when using a finished trained AI system, similar to the legal basis in Article 6 (1) (d), e.g., to process health data in a diagnosis system where the data subject is unconscious.

Under Article 9 (2) (b), a lawful exemption for processing special categories of personal data is that the processing is necessary for the purposes of carrying out the obligations and exercising specific rights of the controller or of the data subject in the field of employment, social security, and social protection law. The exemption under Article 9 (2) (b) needs to be authorised by EU or member state law, and such a secondary legal basis needs to provide appropriate safeguards for the fundamental rights and the interests of the data subject.

Examples of where the processing of special categories of personal data in order to train and develop an AI model in the field of employment would be relevant include, e.g., biometric identification of employees in the workplace or an AI system applied for recruitment, workers management, or similar. Such AI systems are regarded as high-risk AI systems under the AI Act, Article 6 and Annex III (4). However, a relevant question is whether processing special categories of personal data to develop such systems is lawful under the GDPR.

In order for Article 9 (2) (b) to be a relevant exemption for training and developing an AI system on special categories of personal data, there needs to be a legal basis authorising such processing in EU or member state law in the field of employment, social security, and social protection law. No EU legislation provides such a legal basis as of Q3 2025. In order for the controller to rely on Article 9 (2) (b) to process special categories of personal data to develop an AI system, the purpose of the AI system must be within the purpose of employment, social security, and social protection law, and the controller must identify a relevant secondary EU or member state legal basis providing for such processing of special categories of personal data.

Similarly to the exemption for employment, social security, and social protection, the exemptions in Article 9 (2) (g) "substantial public interest", (h) "preventive and occupational medicine", (i) "public interests in the area of public health", and (j) "archiving purposes" requires an additional legal basis in EU or member state law to be lawful. Such a legal basis needs to be clear and also provide suitable and specific measures to safeguard the data subjects.

3.2.7.11 Legitimate interests of a foundation

According to Article 9 (2) (d), an exemption for processing special categories of personal data is if the processing is carried out by an association or not-for-profit body with a political, religious, or trade union aim. The processing must not be disclosed outside such an organisation and relate to members of the organisation. The exemption is not very relevant for developing and training an AI system based on special categories of personal data. Such a system is required to be developed by the different organisations mentioned in Article 9 (2) (d) and relate to the specific special categories of data relevant to the organisation, i.e., trade union membership for trade unions and religion for religious organisations. Thus, the exemption is not a practical exemption relevant to processing special categories of personal data for developing AI systems.

3.2.7.12 Establishment, exercise, or defence of legal claims

Under Article 9 (2) (f), an exemption from the prohibition of processing of special categories of personal data is if the processing "is necessary for the establishment, exercise or defence of legal claims or whenever courts are acting in their judicial capacity". The exemptions have two different alternatives, and the next paragraphs will examine whether the exemption could be applied to process special categories of personal data in order to train and develop an AI system.

Starting with the first alternative – processing is necessary for the establishment, exercise, or defence of legal claims – could special categories of personal data be lawfully processed under the GDPR to train and develop an AI system under the exemption? Article 9 (2) (f) is intended to protect the right to an effective remedy and a fair trial by not hindering the processing of special categories of personal data related to legal claims in court, administrative proceedings, and private tribunals.[68] The second alternative – when courts are acting in their judicial capacity – refers to the courts adjudicating the specific claims put forth by a plaintiff.

As with all the other exemptions under Article 9 (2), the legal claims exemption is to be interpreted restrictively.[69] A restrictive interpretation entails that the controller processing special categories of personal data under the exemption needs to have a concrete and specific intention to make a claim, in the case of the plaintiff, or the case of the defendant, defending themselves against an actual claim.[70] The exemption can, therefore, not be lawfully applied in anticipation of a potential future legal claim. The GDPR does not apply to

---

68 Ludmila Georgieva and Christopher Kuner. "Article 9 processing of special categories of personal data". In: *The EU General Data Protection Regulation (GDPR): A Commentary.* Oxford: Oxford University Press, Feb. 2020. isbn: 9780198826491. doi: 10.1093/oso/9780198826491.003.0038. eprint: https://academic.oup.com/book/0/chapter/352296960/chapter-pdf/52771138/isbn-9780198826491-book-part-38.pdf. url: https://doi.org/10.1093/oso/9780198826491.003.0038.

69 Marvin van Bekkum and Frederik Zuiderveen Borgesius. "Using sensitive data to prevent discrimination by artificial intelligence: Does the GDPR need a new exception?" In: *Computer Law & Security Review* 48 (2023), p. 105770. ISSN: 0267-3649. doi: https://doi.org/10.1016/j.clsr.2022.105770. url: https://www.sciencedirect.com/science/article/pii/S0267364922001133; Ludmila Georgieva and Christopher Kuner. "Article 9 processing of special categories of personal data". In: *The EU General Data Protection Regulation (GDPR): A Commentary.* Oxford: Oxford University Press, Feb. 2020. isbn: 9780198826491. doi: 10.1093/oso/9780198826491.003.0038. eprint: https://academic.oup.com/book/0/chapter/352296960/chapter-pdf/52771138/isbn-9780198826491-book-part-38.pdf. url: https://doi.org/10.1093/oso/9780198826491.003.0038.

70 Ludmila Georgieva and Christopher Kuner. "Article 9 processing of special categories of personal data". In: *The EU General Data Protection Regulation (GDPR): A Commentary.* Oxford: Oxford University Press, Feb. 2020. isbn: 9780198826491. doi: 10.1093/oso/9780198826491.003.0038. eprint: https://academic.oup.com/book/0/chapter/352296960/chapter-pdf/52771138/isbn

the processing of law enforcement authorities, and the exemption cannot be applied to AI systems used for predictive policing or similar. Processing of personal data by competent authorities for preventing crime is under the scope of the Law Enforcement Directive.[71] In case the data is processed by a controller under the scope of the GDPR for purposes related to identifying legal claims, for instance, by a public authority to detect social security fraud or similar, the exemption is not relevant either. The reason is that the restrictive interpretation of Article 9 (2) (f) calls for the controller to have a concrete and specific intention to make a claim in the near future and cannot, therefore, rely on the exemption in Article 9 (2) (f) to identify potential legal claims.

The derogation in Article 9 (2) (f) is, thus, not a relevant exemption for the processing of special categories of personal data to develop an AI model.

3.2.7.13 Data manifestly made public by the data subject and the lawfulness of web crawling

The business models of several commercial companies developing large language models and pre-trained generative transfer models are to crawl and scrape the Internet for data to train the algorithms applied to develop a model.[72] The data crawled is often multimodal, meaning it comprises different formats and types. If the data could identify or be used to identify a natural person, it is regarded as personal data under Article 4 (1) of the GDPR. Under Article 9 (2) (e) of the GDPR, special categories of personal data could lawfully be processed if the data subject has made their personal data manifestly public. Several of the commercial AI model providers base the lawfulness of scraping data on the fact that the personal data is publicly available online.[73] The next paragraphs will address the lawfulness of web crawling personal data

-9780198826491-book-part-38.pdf. url: https://doi.org/10.1093/oso/9780198826491.003.0038.

71 Directive (EU) 2016/680 of the European Parliament and of the Council of 27 April 2016 on the protection of natural persons with regard to the processing of personal data by competent authorities for the purposes of the prevention, investigation, detection or prosecution of criminal offences or the execution of criminal penalties, and on the free movement of such data, and repealing Council Framework Decision 2008/977/JHA [2016] OJ L 119/89.

72 Midas Nouwens et al. "Dark patterns after the GDPR: Scraping consent pop-ups and demonstrating their influence". In: *Proceedings of the 2020 CHI Conference on Human Factors in Computing Systems*. 2020, pp. 1–13. doi: https://doi.org/10.1145/3313831.3376321.

73 Bloomberg Law. *OpenAI's Legal Woes Driven by Unclear Mesh of Web-Scraping Laws*. url: https://news.bloomberglaw.com/ip-law/openais-legal-woes-driven-by-unclear-mesh-of-web-scraping-laws. Last accessed: 01.08.2025.

under the exemption in Article 9 (2) (e) – special categories of personal data manifestly made public.

Before analysing web crawling and the “manifestly made public” exemption in Article 9 (2), it is necessary to elaborate on some aspects of web crawling. The overall idea with web crawling is to extract data of interest from the web, copy it, and store the data in a repository.[74] The purpose of such crawling is to collect data for a database that is used, e.g., to train AI models. A web crawling scheme comprises a web crawler and a data extractor. The web crawler, also known as a bot or a web robot, browses the Internet for relevant data and sends requests to relevant pages, extracting the data on the webpages in an HTML (Hyper Text Markup Language) format. After fetching the data in the HTML format, the data extractor retrieves the relevant information in the HTML format. Lastly, the relevant extracted data is converted into a structured format in a database.[75] One efficient manner for a webpage to protect the public data on the webpage from scraping is through the webpage’s Robot.txt. The Robot.txt includes instructions for web crawling bots, and such instructions can include which data the web crawler bots are allowed and not allowed to scrape from the page.

Even though web scraping is commonly used, a crucial question is whether such data processing is lawful under the GDPR. As a starting point, information scraped online that allows for the identification of a natural person would be defined as personal data. The scraping process would be regarded as processing, and the entity responsible for the web scraping would be the controller under the GDPR.

As previously elaborated, recital 51 requires that both a legal basis under Article 6 (1) and a lawful exemption under Article 9 (2) are fulfilled in order for the processing of special categories of personal data to be lawful. Article 9 (2) (e) is therefore not a *lex specialis* exemption where the processing of personal data is lawful just because the data subject has made his or her personal data publicly available online.[76]

---

[74] Catherine Altobelli et al. “To scrape or not to scrape? The lawfulness of social media crawling under the GDPR”. In: *Deep Diving into Data Protection*. Ed. by J. Herveg. Namur: Larcier, p. 6. ISSN: 9782807926493; Moaiad Ahmad Khder. “Web scraping or web crawling: State of art, techniques, approaches and application”. In: *International Journal of Advances in Soft Computing & Its Applications* 13.3 (2021), pp. 145–168.

[75] Moaiad Ahmad Khder. “Web scraping or web crawling: State of art, techniques, approaches and application”. In: *International Journal of Advances in Soft Computing & Its Applications* 13.3 (2021), pp. 145–168.

[76] Maarten Truyens and Patrick Van Eecke. “Legal aspects of text mining”. In: *Computer Law & Security Review* 30.2 (2014), pp. 153–170. ISSN: 0267-3649.

The entity responsible for the web scraping – the controller – therefore needs to fulfil one of the legal bases in Article 6 (1) (a–f) and, if the personal data scraped is regarded as special categories of personal data, the controller also needs to fulfil one of the exemptions under Article 9 (2). The legal bases are elaborated in subsection 3.2.7, and the most relevant would be Article 6 (1) (a), consent, (b) performance of a contract, and 6 (1) (f) legitimate interests. The controller cannot, therefore, freely scrape personal data based on it being made public by the data subject.

In the manifestly made public alternative, special categories of personal data must be made available to an indeterminate number of users for the exemption to be lawfully applied. Moreover, the data subject has to deliberately make the special categories public. The wording "manifestly" made public in Article 9 (2) (e) requires an affirmative act from the data subject itself.

The CJEU adjudged the question of whether a "like" or comment from the data subject on a webpage related to special categories of Article 9 made the data manifestly made public, in the Meta Platforms Inc. judgement.[77] The CJEU held that the following conditions must be fulfilled to rely on the derogation to process special categories of personal data.

- The special categories of personal data have to be made public by the data subject themselves. The derogation is not relevant for data concerning persons other than the person who made that data public.
- The data subject must have intended, explicitly and by a clear affirmative action, to make the personal data accessible to the general public.
- Merely visiting a website or app is not an example of such a clear, explicit, and affirmative action.
- If the data subjects interact with a website or an app with a "like" or similar, the manifestly made public alternative may be lawfully applied only when the data subject has in their individual settings selected with full knowledge of the fact and where the data subject has clearly made the choice to have the data made accessible to an unlimited number of persons, according to paragraphs 74–85 of the Meta Platforms Inc. judgement.[78]

---

doi: https://doi.org/10.1016/j.clsr.2014.01.009. url: https://www.sciencedirect.com/science/article/pii/S0267364914000260.

[77] Judgement of the Court (Grand Chamber) in Case C-252/21 Meta Platforms Inc., Meta Platforms Ireland Ltd, Facebook Deutschland GmbH v Budeskartellamt ECLI:EU:C:2023:537.

[78] Judgement of the Court (Grand Chamber) in Case C-252/21 Meta Platforms Inc., Meta Platforms Ireland Ltd, Facebook Deutschland GmbH v Budeskartellamt ECLI:EU:C:2023:537.

In order for a web crawler to process special categories of personal data based on Article 9 (2) (e), the controller needs to be certain that the data published on openly available web pages or social media sites is made manifestly public by the data subject, and not a third party. Article 9 (2) (e) is – as with the other exemptions under Article 9 – to be interpreted restrictively.[79] If the controller is uncertain and cannot document that the special categories of personal data are published by the data subject, the controller cannot lawfully rely on the "manifestly made public" derogation. Even though, for instance, the crawled data stems from a social media with user verification, the controller needs to document that the crawled special category of personal data concerns the verified data subject. A verified user could, e.g., share special categories of personal data about other users. Moreover, the controller needs to ascertain that the user has, in their individual settings, through a clear and affirmative act, chosen to make the special categories of personal data available to an unlimited number of persons.

One related guidance on the term "manifestly made public" from the EDPB is guidance 3/2019 on processing personal data through video devices.[80] The EDPB states that the exemption in Article 9 (2) (e) cannot be applied to further process special categories of personal data from publicly available places because the entering of the camera sphere by the data subject does not constitute a sufficient affirmative act of the data subject.

To conclude, in order to process publicly available special categories of personal data in web crawlers to collect a dataset used to develop AI models, the controller needs to rely on a legal basis and a relevant derogation under Article 9 (2). The exemption in Article 9 (2) (e) "manifestly made public" is not regarded as *lex specialis* for the overall processing and cannot be relied on to process personal data in web crawlers from a perspective that the greater (processing of special categories of personal data) includes the lesser (processing of personal data), according to recital 51 of the GDPR.

---

[79] Ludmila Georgieva and Christopher Kuner. "Article 9 processing of special categories of personal data". In: *The EU General Data Protection Regulation (GDPR): A Commentary.* Oxford: Oxford University Press, Feb. 2020. isbn: 9780198826491. doi: 10.1093/oso/9780198826491.003.0038. eprint: https://academic.oup.com/book/0/chapter/352296960/chapter-pdf/52771138/isbn-9780198826491-book-part-38.pdf. url: https://doi.org/10.1093/oso/9780198826491.003.0038.

[80] EDPB. *European Data Protection Board, Guidelines 3/2019 on Processing of Personal Data through Video Devices v2.0 (EDPB Guidelines, 2020).* Page 68. url: https://edpb.europa.eu/our-work-tools/our-documents/guidelines/guidelines-32019-processing-personal-data-through-video_en. Last accessed: 01.08.2025.

In order to lawfully rely on the exemption in Article 9 (2) (e), the controller needs to document that the data crawled relates to a specific data subject who has made the data public with a clear affirmative act. The exemption under Article 9 (2) (e) in a web crawling setting has various complexities, which make it less relevant. Therefore, it is advisable to avoid processing special categories of personal data based on the exemption through web crawling practices.

The subsections above have focused on the lawfulness of the interference that personal data processing constitutes in developing an AI model. The focus of analysis has been on both the legal basis in Article 6 (1) of the GDPR and exemptions for processing special categories of personal data. To conclude, although AI model development is a complex and potentially opaque form of processing, it is feasible to process personal data lawfully on the basis of consent, performance of a contract, legitimate interests, or public interest, if the processing is in accordance with a legal basis in Union or member state law. The most practical legal bases for processing personal data for AI system development are the performance of a contract and legitimate interests.

3.2.8 Legitimate Aim and AI System Development

3.2.8.1 Introduction to the legitimate aim subtest

While the former subsection focused on the lawfulness of the interference, the current subsection (3.2.8) focuses on the next subtest under the criteria for interfering with the fundamental right to data protection under the Charter, the legitimate aim subtest. In the context of AI system development, the relevant question under the subtest would be whether the processing of personal data to develop an AI model pursues an aim that is regarded as legitimate. The legitimate aim subtest and the lawfulness of the processing of personal data elaborated in the former subsection are closely related. For example, under Article 6 (1) (f) of the GDPR, the controller needs to clarify the legitimate interests pursued with the processing. This assessment will closely resemble the legitimate aim subtest.

The legitimate aim subtest has ties to both legality and proportionality. In relation to legality, the legitimate aim of interfering with a fundamental right will often – explicitly or implicitly – be a part of the legal basis that justifies the interference. In relation to proportionality, the legitimate aim is guiding both the suitability and the necessity subtests elaborated below.

The purpose of analysing the legitimate aim subtest as a specific assessment in AI systems development is particularly to address cases where the development is not covered by the scope of the GDPR, but the processing still falls under the scope of the Charter. An example of the relevance of the legitimate aim subtest is if an AI system is developed for a purpose outside the scope of the GDPR, such as law enforcement or public security purposes. In such a case, the legitimate aim subtest would not be activated under secondary law. However, the subtest should still need to be assessed to ensure compliance with the fundamental right to data protection, both under the Charter and according to the ECHR.

The test of whether the purpose of the interference – in this context, the processing of personal data – is regarded as legitimate has internal and external dimensions.[81] The correlation between the specific aim pursued and the means applied to reach the aim is referred to as the internal dimension of the legitimate aim test. When assessing the internal dimension of legitimate aim in a proportionality assessment, the object under scrutiny is the connection between the aim pursued and the means applied.[82] The external dimension of the legitimate purpose test refers to the aims achieved by the interference. In such an external dimension, the means pursued to reach a certain external purpose could be regarded as the cause of the realisation of the purpose.

Some aims of an interference would never be regarded as legitimate in the Union acquis; for instance, if an AI system provider processes personal data to develop an AI system intended to unlawfully discriminate against vulnerable groups in society. In such an instance, the interference cannot be justified because the overall aim of the interference – unlawful discrimination – is not regarded as legitimate, according to the external dimension of the legitimate aim subtest.

3.2.8.2 Purpose limitation in AI system development

As concluded in subsection 3.2.5, purpose limitation forms part of the "essence" of the right to data protection in Article 8 of the Charter. In its wording, Article 8 (1) of the Charter also requires that personal data is processed fairly for "specified purposes". It is, therefore, pivotal to ensure purpose limitation when processing personal data in AI system development, to comply with both Article 5 (1) (b) in the GDPR and Article 8 of the Charter – including the respect for the essence of the right and the legitimate aim subtest.

The purpose limitation principle in Article 5 (1) (b) requires controllers to collect and process personal data only for specified, explicit, and legitimate purposes. The purpose limitation principle has two primary implications for the processing of personal data.

First, before collecting and processing personal data, the controller must establish the purpose of the processing.

---

[81] Humberto Ávila. *Theory of Legal Principles.* Dordrecht: Springer, 2007, p. 114.

[82] Ibid.

Second, once the purpose is specified, and the processing of personal data has commenced, the general rule is that the personal data cannot be further processed for purposes other than the original one, according to Article 5 (1) (b). There are, however, some exemptions for processing for archiving purposes in the public interest, for scientific or historical research purposes, for statistical purposes, and for purposes compatible with the original processing purpose.

The processing purpose should be explicit and specific. Therefore, the development of AI systems should ensure that personal data is processed only for the original purpose and that any further processing for another purpose is assessed according to the criteria and requirements for repurposing in Article 6 (4) of the GDPR.

In relation to the processing of personal data to develop AI systems, the purpose limitation principle will be fulfilled if the original purpose of the collection of personal data is to develop an AI system. AI systems often serve multiple purposes, or the purposes of the finished trained system could be defined only after the system has been developed. Such AI systems are known as general-purpose AI systems. To illustrate, assume that an organisation intends to collect a dataset containing video data of natural persons – personal data – and to develop an AI model based on the training dataset. During the development process, the organisation noticed that the developed AI model detected sudden physical movements in the training data. The organisation develops the model further into a fall-detection AI system. The AI system is later applied by others for fall detection in welfare technology to prevent injuries. This is an example of an AI project where the purpose of the processing is decided during the development process and not when the personal data is collected.

Generative AI – AI models used to generate content such as text, audio, images, or videos – could be considered as a form of general-purpose AI model that raises issues under the purpose limitation principle. In the development of generative AI models, a core model is often developed. This core model could, e.g., be further trained and fine-tuned within an organisation for various purposes, often through a method known as Retrieval Augmented Generation (RAG).[83] When personal data is trained to develop the core model, the organisation responsible for this training might not know what the purpose of the fine-tuned model is going to be. The original training of the core model and the fine-tuning would be regarded as constituting different purposes, and

---

[83] Medium. *Fine-Tuning versus RAG in Generative AI Applications*. url: https://harsha-srivatsa.medium.com/fine-tuning-versus-rag-in-generative-ai-applications-architecture-d54ca6d2acb8. Last accessed: 01.08.2025.

in case both the original training and the fine-tuning are done by the same or different controllers, the purposes need to be specified and explained to the data subject.[84]

The specified purpose of the processing forms the basis for the assessment of the data minimisation, lawfulness, transparency, and fairness principles in Article 5 (1). A clearly defined purpose of the processing of personal data at both the time of development of the core generative AI model and the fine-tuning is, therefore, a prerequisite for the assessment of the other fundamental principles of processing in Article 5 of the GDPR.

In order for the development of a general-purpose AI system to be in line with the purpose limitation principle in Article 5 (1) (b), some guidance is to be found from the French Data Protection Authority, Commission Nationale de l'informatique et des Libertés (CNIL).[85] According to CNIL, the purpose cannot be defined in too general terms and needs to be defined in a precise and explicit manner. A relevant question is whether, e.g., "the development of an AI system" would be a sufficiently explicit and precise purpose, or if the specific purpose of what the AI system is intended to predict, infer, or generate also needs to be specified. According to the guidance from the French DPA, the first alternative would be a sufficiently defined purpose, if both the "type" of AI system developed is defined by the controller and the intended technical functionalities and capabilities of the finished developed AI system are defined and communicated to the data subject.[86] However, the answer would depend on the type of personal data processed and the risks involved with the personal data processing. The final conclusion on the purpose limitation principle and the development of general-purpose AI models would need to be defined by a recommendation from the EDPB or in a judgement from the CJEU.

Frequently, personal data is collected for one original purpose and repurposed to develop AI systems; for instance, data is often collected in line with Article 6 (1) (b) to deliver a service – e.g., a software platform or a social media site – and further processed to deliver various AI functionalities or to develop AI functionalities within the services. Is such repurposing of personal data processing in line with the purpose limitation principle?

The purpose limitation principle prevents controllers from processing the data further when the secondary processing is incompatible with the original

---

[84] ICO. *Generative AI Second Call for Evidence: Purpose Limitation in the Generative AI Lifecycle*. url: https://ico.org.uk/about-the-ico/what-we-do/our-work-on-artificial-intelligence/generative-ai-second-call-for-evidence/. Last accessed: 01.08.2025.

[85] CNIL. *Defining a Purpose*. url: https://www.cnil.fr/en/defining-purpose. Last accessed: 01.08.2025.

[86] Ibid.

purpose. The question of repurposing the processing of personal data for AI system development is a highly debated topic and, currently, the only authoritative legal sources on the question include the wording of the GDPR and guidance from various DPAs.

According to Article 5 (1) (b), further processing "incompatible" with the initial processing purpose is not in line with the purpose limitation principle. Article 5 (1) (b) lists "statistical purposes" as not incompatible with the original purpose. ML could be described as similar to and building on statistical models.[87] Could further processing for AI development purposes rely on the statistics exemption?

The meaning of the statistics exemption in Article 5 (1) (b) of the GDPR is elaborated in the Commission Recommendation under the Data Protection Directive from 1997.[88] The exemption has remained unchanged under the GDPR. According to the Recommendation, statistical purposes refer to "the elaboration of statistical surveys or the production of statistical, aggregated results. Statistics aim at analysing and characterising mass or collective phenomena in a considered population", according to the Recommendation's appendix, point 1.[89]

In order for the statistical exemption to come into effect, the purpose of further processing needs to be the production of statistical surveys or results in analysing a phenomenon in a considered population. Even though the method used resembles a traditional statistical method – e.g., ML – the exemption cannot be lawfully applied for further processing to develop an AI system, unless in cases where the purpose of the AI system is to produce statistics.

Furthermore, it needs to be assessed in which cases further processing for AI development would be in line with Article 5 (1) (b). According to Article 6 (4) of the GDPR, the following aspects are relevant when assessing whether the new purpose is "compatible" with the original processing purpose, in cases where the further processing is not based on consent or Union or member state law:

---

87 Matthew Stewart. *The Actual Difference between Statistics and Machine Learning*. url: https://towardsdatascience.com/the-actual-difference-between-statistics-and-machine-learning-64b49f07ea3. Last accessed: 26.08.2024.

88 Committee of Ministers of the Council of Europe Council of Europe. *Recommendation Concerning the Protection of Personal Data Collected and Processed for Statistical Purposes (Rec(1997)18, 30 September 1997)*. url: https://rm.coe.int/cmrec-97-18-concerning-the-protection-of-personal-data-collected-and-p/1680a43b63. Last accessed: 01.08.202.

89 Ibid.

a) Any link between the purposes for which the personal data have been collected and the purposes of the intended further processing.
b) The context in which the personal data has been collected, in particular regarding the relationship between data subjects and the controller.
c) The nature of the personal data, in particular whether special categories of personal data are processed, pursuant to Article 9, or whether personal data related to criminal convictions and offences are processed, pursuant to Article 10.
d) The possible consequences of the intended further processing for data subjects.
e) The existence of appropriate safeguards, which may include encryption or pseudonymisation.

According to the CJEU, the aim of the requirements above is to establish a specific, logical, and sufficiently close link between the purposes for which the personal data was initially collected and the further processing of that data, and ensure such further processing does not deviate from the legitimate expectations of the data subjects. The criteria limit the possibility of reuse of personal data by ensuring a balance between the need for predictability and legal certainty regarding the processing purposes and the recognition of a degree of flexibility for the controller in the management of that data.[90]

In cases where a controller wishes to repurpose personal data processing to develop an AI system, the new purpose needs to be compatible with reference to the aspects elaborated above. The relevance of the question and some complicating factors could be illustrated with an example. A controller collects the personal data of their employees in line with Article 6 (1) (b) "performance of a contract". The processing is conducted by a processor with which the controller has a data processing agreement. The processor wants to develop an AI system and decides to process the personal employee data to develop such a system. Is such further processing for a new purpose in line with the GDPR?

First, the controller-processor relationship under the GDPR does not fit well with a processor repurposing the data for their own purpose. Under Article 28 (10) of the GDPR, a processor that processes personal data in breach of the controller's instructions becomes the controller in their own right for the processing. A lawful processing operation in such an example, therefore, presupposes the original controller's instruction, or at least consent, according to Article 28 (10) of the GDPR. Furthermore, the conditions for compatibility

[90] Judgement of the Court (First Chamber) of 20 October 2022 in case C-77/21 Digi Távközlési és Szolgáltató Kft. v Nemzeti Adatvédelmi és Információszabadság Hatóság ECLI:EU:C:2022:805 paragraph 36.

under Article 6 (4) need to be fulfilled for the processing by the processor for a new purpose under the processor's own interest for the processing to be in line with the purpose limitation principle. According to Article 13 (3), the original controller also needs to inform the data subjects about the repurposing of the processing to develop an AI system in such a case.

To summarise, in the current landscape, many actors repurpose personal data processing for training and developing AI systems. Such actors are frequently the processors under the GDPR of the personal data that was originally collected for a different purpose. For such a processing operation to be in line with the GDPR interpreted in accordance with the Charter, the following requirements must be fulfilled:

1. The original controller must instruct the processor to repurpose the processing, or at the very least consent to such repurposing, in accordance with Article 28 (10) of the GDPR.
2. The new purpose needs to be compatible with the original purpose, according to the requirements under Article 6 (4) of the GDPR.
3. The controller originally collecting the personal data needs to inform the data subject about the repurposing, according to Articles 13 (3) and 14 (4) of the GDPR.
4. The new purpose needs to be suitable, necessary, and a proportionate interference in the right to data protection.

3.2.9 Suitability and AI System Development

An important aspect of the suitability subtest under the principle of proportionality is determining whether the AI system under development is an appropriate means for the legitimate aim pursued. The suitability test is oriented towards the goal of the interference and the relationship between the aim pursued and the means applied.[91]

In the CJEU, the suitability often forms part of the Court's test of whether an interference is "manifestly inappropriate".[92] In the ECtHR, the suitability test is more hidden in the Court's reasoning under the principle of proportionality.

---

[91] Tor-Inge Harbo. "The function of proportionality analysis in European law". In: *The Function of Proportionality Analysis in European Law*. Leiden: Brill Nijhoff, 2015, p. 201.

[92] Ibid., p. 72; Takis Tridimas. "The general principles of EU law and the Europeanisation of national laws". In: *Review of European Administrative Law* 13.2 (2020), pp. 5–31. doi: 10.7590/187479820X15930701852193.

However, suitability often forms part of both the necessity and proportionality *stricto sensu* test in the reasoning of the ECtHR.[93]

When determining whether a highly advanced technological system, such as an AI system, is a suitable means to reach the aim pursued, the outcome of the suitability test would be highly dependent on the effect and the margin of error of the AI system. When evaluating the proportionality of the PNR directive, the CJEU, for instance, assessed false positive outputs of the ML model used to screen flight passengers for security threats. The efficiency and the error rate in the AI system would therefore be part of the suitability test under the principle of proportionality.[94]

When evaluating and testing an AI system, it is possible to calculate the margin of error of the system in uncertainty quantification by comparing the outputs from the ML algorithms with traditional statistical analytical tools.[95] An acceptable margin of error is dependent on the purpose of the AI system. If the AI system is used, for instance, by a law enforcement authority to draw inferences about a natural person, a lower margin of error is acceptable compared to a less critical application, due to the potential negative effects a false positive output would have.

The European Parliament adopted a resolution on AI in criminal law and its use by the police and judicial authorities in criminal matters in October 2021.[96] A Parliament resolution is non-binding for EU institutions and member states, but it is a statement from the Parliament that it considers a topic to be of particular importance. The Parliament expresses the following statement in section M. of the resolution: "whereas the routine deployment of algorithms, even with a low false positive rate, can result in false alerts outnumbering correct alerts by far".[97] The cited excerpt of the resolution makes it evident that false positive results in an AI system deployed for law enforcement purposes could confront the suitability of the system. The cited excerpt also illustrates that suitability is not solely an assessment of the appropriateness of the intro-

---

[93] Handyside v the United Kingdom, 7 December 1976 Series A no. 24 paragraph 52.

[94] Judgement of the Court (Grand Chamber) 21 June 2022 in the Case C-817/19 Ligue des droits humains v Conseil des ministers ECLI:EU:C:2022:491.

[95] Niclas Ståhl et al. "Evaluation of uncertainty quantification in deep learning". In: *International Conference on Information Processing and Management of Uncertainty in Knowledge-Based Systems.* Cham: Springer Nature, 2020, pp. 556–568. doi: https://doi.org/10.1007/978-3-030-50146-4_41.

[96] European Parliament resolution of 6 October 2021 on artificial intelligence and criminal law and its use by the police and judicial authorities in criminal matters [2021] OJ C 132.

[97] Ibid.

duced measures. Suitability also takes into account the effect an inappropriate interference would have on the natural persons affected.

To summarise, the result of the suitability test when assessing the proportionality of an AI system interfering with fundamental rights would depend on the effect and uncertainty of the output and the intended purpose of the AI system under development. In a practical and consequential sense, the quality of the outputs of the AI system would relate to the suitability as a subtest of the principle of proportionality. An AI system that produces erroneous outputs to a large extent would not be an efficient solution to the problem the AI system is applied to solve. However, in a fundamental rights context, the suitability subtest requires that personal data is not processed if the results of the processing are not suitable to achieve the legitimate aim of the processing. A fundamental right should not be interfered with if it is unsuitable.

The suitability subtest, in a narrow sense, is an assessment of the relevance and irrelevance of the outputs of the AI system. In addition, the suitability of the system is integral to the proportionality *stricto sensu* subtest. A system deemed less suitable will detrimentally impact the weight given to the aim of the interference when evaluated against the fundamental right being interfered with.

3.2.10 Necessity and AI System Development

3.2.10.1 Introduction

The necessity subtest of the principle of proportionality is a goal-oriented test. The purpose of the test is to review whether the interference constitutes the least restrictive measure that fulfils the objective pursued.

Through a consistent body of case law from the CJEU, the Court has set the threshold for measures that interfere with the right to data protection to be "strictly necessary" in light of the objective pursued with the processing of personal data.[98]

A core part of the necessity assessment under the principle of proportionality is the legitimate aim of the interference, in this context, the processing of

98 Joined Cases C-203/15 and C-698/15 Tele2 Sverige AB v Post- och telestyrelsen and others, Judgement of 21 December 2016 (Grand Chamber) (ECLI:EU:C:2016:970) para 115; Case C-2017/16 Ministerio Fiscal, Judgement of 2 October 2018 (Grand Chamber) (ECLI:EU:2018:788) para 52; Joined Cases C-511/18, C-512/18 and C-520/18 La Quadrature du Net and Others v Premier minister and Others, Judgement of 6 October 2020 (Grand Chamber) (ECLI:EU:C:2020:791) para 112.

personal data.[99] The interference and the assessment of the interference would, thus, be assessed differently if the purpose is to protect the vital interests of the state, compared to if the purpose is behavioural advertising.

The necessity and strict necessity test in relation to the processing of personal data to train and develop an AI system is intrinsically linked to the purpose limitation and data minimisation principle in Article 5 of the GDPR. The necessity of the processing must be reviewed in line with the processing purpose, and there, thus, needs to be strict criteria for lawful repurposing of personal data processing.

Moreover, if more personal data than is strictly necessary for the processing purpose is processed to train an AI system, the processing of personal data is not in line with the necessity subtest under the principle of proportionality. The next paragraphs will analyse the data minimisation principle in AI system development.

3.2.10.2 Data minimisation and AI system development

The data minimisation principle in Article 5 (1) (c) requires that personal data is adequate, relevant, and limited to what is necessary in relation to the purposes for which it is processed. Concerning the fundamental rights in Articles 7 and 8 of the Charter and Article 8 of the ECHR, the principle of data minimisation could be viewed as an operationalisation of the requirement that interferences in these rights must be necessary to be lawful.

If more data than required is processed, the interference with the right to data protection is not necessary, according to Article 8 (2) of the ECHR and Article 52 of the Charter. The core of the data minimisation principle is that controllers should not collect and process more personal data than is required for the processing purpose. As a part of the assessment of the amount of personal data necessary for the purpose, it is essential to assess whether the processing purpose necessitates the processing of personal data at all, according to recital 39 of the GDPR. The data minimisation principle possesses both a qualitative and a quantitative aspect.[100] The quantitative aspect relates to the amount of personal data processed and the number of data subjects, while the

---

99 Lorenzo Dalla Corte. "On proportionality in the data protection jurisprudence of the CJEU". In: *International Data Privacy Law* 12.4 (July 2022), pp. 259–275. ISSN: 2044-3994. doi: 10.1093/idpl/ipac014. eprint: https://academic.oup.com/idpl/article-pdf/12/4/259/47703258/ipac014.pdf. url: https://doi.org/10.1093/idpl/ipac014.

100 Cécile de Terwagne. "Article 5. Principles Relating to processing of personal data". In: *The EU General Data Protection (GDPR): A Commentary*. Ed. by Christopher Kuner et al. Oxford: Oxford University Press, 2020, p. 317.

qualitative part pertains to the sensitivity of the personal data processed, e.g., whether or not special categories of personal data are processed.[101]

The data minimisation principle in AI system development is closely related to the data preprocessing steps frequently conducted in AI system development before training the algorithms to develop an AI model. These preprocessing steps are elaborated in subsection 2.5.1 in Chapter 2 of the book. Before typical preprocessing steps are conducted, such as cleaning the data and removing outliers and missing values, it is crucial to define the selection and collection criteria to collect only the relevant personal data to develop the AI system and to comply with the data minimisation principle.

If the data collection procedure is not automated, it is important to delete irrelevant data that does not align with the collection criteria after such data has been identified by the controller developing the AI system.

After these steps have been carried out, it is again crucial to perform the preprocessing steps to assess whether the training data is relevant, aligning with the selected collection criteria, and that irrelevant personal data is removed and erased. If such steps are performed in the data collection and training phase, there is a higher likelihood of complying with the data minimisation principle in Article 5 (1) (c) of the GDPR and, thereby, also the necessity subtest under the principle of proportionality.

Another method to achieve data minimisation during AI model training is Federated Learning (FL). FL is applied when multiple actors collaborate in training an AI model but do not want to share the training data.[102] In federated learning, the participants share the model and the partially trained model, but not the training data. Each time, a participant receives the partially trained model from another participant, uses their training data to further train the model, and then sends the result to the next participant.[103] This procedure continues until the resulting trained model satisfies some optimisation criteria.

Employing federated learning offers high utility since the AI model is trained on the entire training data, even if this data is split among different participants. Hence, the data processing is potentially minimised for each of

---

101 Ibid.

102 David Enthoven and Zaid Al-Ars. "Fidel: Reconstructing private training samples from weight updates in federated learning". In: *2022 9th International Conference on Internet of Things: Systems, Management and Security (IOTSMS)*. New York: IEEE, 2022, pp. 1–8. doi: 10.1109/IOTSMS58070.2022.10062088.

103 David Enthoven and Zaid Al-Ars. "Fidel: Reconstructing private training samples from weight updates in federated learning". In: *2022 9th International Conference on Internet of Things: Systems, Management and Security (IOTSMS)*. New York: IEEE, 2022, pp. 1–8. doi: 10.1109/IOTSMS58070.2022.10062088.

the participants by not processing the other participant's data in the model training process.

Other technical methods that might be applied to minimise the personal data processed during model training might be through the use of synthetic training data, i.e., data that resembles the real data used through proxies but does not make it possible to identify a natural person. However, experimental evaluation has revealed that it might be possible to infer or deduce data subjects from synthetic data.[104] Synthetic data should therefore be viewed as a potential method for data minimisation in model training and not a panacea.

3.2.11 Proportionality *Stricto Sensu* and AI System Development

3.2.11.1 Introduction

The aim of the proportionality *stricto sensu* test is to balance the interference to determine whether pursuing the purpose outweighs the interference in the fundamental right.[105]

The last part of the proportionality principle, the proportionality *stricto sensu* test, could be identified through a systematic reading of the case law from the ECtHR.[106] In the EU legal order, the CJEU has applied the suitability and necessity test and concluded that an interference was in breach of the fundamental rights in Articles 7 and 8 of the Charter in several cases. Since all the subtests of the proportionality principle are sequential and all subtests have to be passed for an interference not to breach the fundamental right, there are fewer traces of proportionality *stricto sensu* in the case law from the CJEU.[107]

---

[104] Felix Hermsen and Avikarsha Mandal. "Privacy and utility evaluation of synthetic tabular data for machine learning". In: *Privacy and Identity Management. Sharing in a Digital World.* Ed. by Felix Bieker et al. Cham: Springer Nature, 2024, pp. 265–281. isbn: 978-3-031-57978-3.

[105] Aharon Barak. *Proportionality: Constitutional Rights and Their Limitations.* Cambridge, UK: Cambridge University Press, 2012, p. 342.

[106] Jeremy McBride. "Proportionality and the European Convention on Human Rights". In: *The Principle of Proportionality in the Laws of Europe.* Ed. by Evelyn Ellis. Oxford: Hart Publishing, 1999, p. 23; Aharon Barak. *Proportionality: Constitutional Rights and Their Limitations.* Cambridge, UK: Cambridge University Press, 2012, p. 342; Eva Brems and Laurens Lavrysen. "'Don't use a sledgehammer to crack a nut': Less restrictive means in the case law of the European Court of Human Rights". In: *Human Rights Law Review* 15.1 (2015), pp. 139–168. doi: https://doi.org/10.1093/hrlr/ngu040.

[107] Valsamis Mitsilegas and Emmanouil Billis. "Article 49 – Principles of legality and proportionality of criminal offences and penalties". In: *The EU Charter of Fundamental Rights: A Commentary.* Ed. by Steve Peers et al. London: Bloomsbury Publishing, 2021; Lorenzo Dalla Corte. "On proportionality in the

Even though the proportionality *stricto sensu* test is not that apparent in CJEU case law, there are still some traces of the subtest. Some legal scholars claim that traces of proportionality *stricto sensu* could be identified as part of the necessity subtest in the case law from the CJEU.[108]

In the words of the ECtHR, the proportionality *stricto sensu* test aims to assess "whether a fair balance was struck between the demands of the general interests of the community and the requirements of the protection of the individual's fundamental rights (...) The search for this balance is inherent in the whole of the convention".[109]

Some legal scholars have criticised the proportionality *stricto sensu* test for depriving fundamental rights of their normative power. Habermas claims that by balancing fundamental rights, rights are downgraded to the level of goals, policies, and values.[110] In order to avoid an irrational and arbitrary *stricto sensu* balancing test, several scholars have argued that the proportionality *stricto sensu* test must have an analytical structure.[111]

The benefit of the interference and the harm caused by limiting the fundamental right are the focus of the *stricto sensu* test.[112] The balancing test considers, on the first end of the scale, the purpose of the interference, the likelihood of achieving the purpose, and the benefit achieved by fulfilling the purpose. The other end of the scale holds the interference with the fundamental right. The interference with the fundamental right could be analysed by examining the harm the interference would entail and the probability of the harm occurring. A problem with such an approach to the *stricto sensu* subtest relates to the incommensurability of comparing an interference in a fundamental right with the fundamental right.[113] The problem of incommensurability could be countered with the fact that when balancing an interference in a fundamental

data protection jurisprudence of the CJEU". In: *International Data Privacy Law* 12.4 (2022), pp. 259–275. doi: https://doi.org/10.1093/idpl/ipac014.

108 Lorenzo Dalla Corte. "On proportionality in the data protection jurisprudence of the CJEU". In: *International Data Privacy Law* 12.4 (2022), pp. 259–275. doi: https://doi.org/10.1093/idpl/ipac014; Takis Tridimas. "Proportionality in European Community law: Searching for the appropriate standard of scrutiny". In: *The Principle of Proportionality in the Laws of Europe*. Ed. by Evelyn Ellis. Oxford: Hart Publishing, 1999, pp. 65–84.

109 Sporrong and Lönnroth v Sweden, 23 September 1982, Series A no. 52 paragraph 69.

110 Jürgen Habermas. *Between Facts and Norms: Contributions to a Discourse Theory of Law and Democracy*. Cambridge, MA: MIT Press, 1998, p. 259.

111 Aharon Barak. *Proportionality: Constitutional Rights and Their Limitations*. Cambridge, UK: Cambridge University Press, 2012, p. 342.

112 Ibid., p. 340.

113 Ibid., p. 482.

right with the social importance of the interference, the common denominator in such a balancing act is the relativity necessary to achieve balance.

The last step of the proportionality *stricto sensu* test balances these two ends against one another. Such a balancing exercise may appear abstract. However, some techniques are applied by international courts and tribunals. One technique compares the situation of the pursued purpose before and after the interference in question occurred. The situation of the aim pursued is balanced against the situation of the fundamental right before and after the interference. The weight of the social importance of the interference is compared to the weight of the importance of preventing harm.[114] In the development phase of an AI system, such an effect would need to be prognosticated.

In relation to the interference, the processing of personal data developing an AI system constitutes the fundamental right to data protection, some relevant aspects in the balancing exercise under the proportionality *stricto sensu* subtest are technical and organisational measures to lower the interference and the compliance with the data subjects' rights under the GDPR. Compliance with data subjects' rights during the AI development process is especially relevant when assessing and balancing interference with fundamental rights. The next paragraphs will address some specific rights in Chapter III of the GDPR in relation to AI system development.

3.2.11.2 Data subjects' rights and AI system development

The following paragraphs will analyse the rights of the data subjects under the GDPR in the context of AI system development under the lens of the proportionality *stricto sensu* subtest. These rights of the data subjects are analysed under the proportionality *stricto sensu* subsection below because compliance with these rights could potentially have a considerable significance in the balancing exercise under the proportionality *stricto sensu* subtest.

The reference to the rights and freedoms of the data subjects in the GDPR encompasses both the specific rights in Articles 12 to 22 of the GDPR, the rights to information, access, rectification, erasure, restriction of processing, and the right not to be subject to automatic decision-making under Article 22, and the fundamental freedoms – including other freedoms than privacy and data protection – in the Charter, according to recital 4 to the GDPR.

The rights under Articles 12 to 22 of the GDPR have exemptions and are not absolute. The non-absolute nature of the rights entails that they often have to be interpreted on a case-by-case basis. The current paragraphs will address some overarching aspects of some specific rights under Chapter III of the GDPR during the processing of personal data during AI system development.

---

114 Ibid., p. 482.

A relevant decision from a DPA regarding the relationship between the rights of the data subject and AI system development is from the Hungarian DPA.[115] A Hungarian bank had developed and installed an AI-based voice recognition system to detect the emotional state of customers calling the bank's customer service line. If a customer "sounded" angry, emotional, or upset, the AI system would detect such a state in order for upset customers to be prioritised in the phone queue. The Hungarian DPA concluded that the AI-based system that detected emotional states from voice breached a plethora of GDPR articles, including Article 5 and the principle of lawfulness, transparency, and purpose limitation, the requirement to inform data subjects under Article 12, the right to object, and data protection by design in Article 25. The DPA concluded that the bank breached Article 25 (1) and the requirement to inform under Article 12 because more advanced forms of processing require more advanced and transparent information to be given to the data subjects. The bank had not offered the data subject such information and did not inform the callers about the use of the emotional AI system. The controllers had thus not sufficiently balanced the high risk of data subjects' rights and freedoms concerning the use of the system under the GDPR. This balance further highlights the relationships between the rights in Chapter III of the GDPR and the proportionality *stricto sensu* subtest. An AI-based voice recognition system, such as the one used in the Hungarian bank, is most likely under the scope of the general prohibition under the AI Act Article 5 (1) (f) if such an AI system is used to infer emotions in the area of workplaces and educational institutions.

The DPA decision cited above concerned the processing of personal data in a deployed AI system. However, there are some aspects also relevant to the processing of personal data during AI system development and data subjects' rights. First, an advanced form of processing personal data, such as AI development, would, generally, entail more advanced information to be given to the data subjects, in line with Articles 12–14 of the GDPR. Second, the controller processing the data needs to implement measures to ensure the right to object, the right to erasure, and other specific rights in Chapter III of the GDPR when personal data is processed during AI development. The rights in Chapter III of the GDPR will be further addressed in Chapters 4 and 5 of the book.

3.2.11.3 Fairness and transparency in AI system development

According to Article 5 (1) (a) of the GDPR, the fairness principle requires controllers to process personal data fairly with respect to the data subject.

---

115 Hungarian National Authority for Data Protection and Freedom of Information. *Case No NAIH-85 – 3/2022 Budapest Bank*. url: https://naih.hu//hatarozatok-vegzesek?download=517:mesterseges-intelligencia-alkalmazasanak-adatvedelmi-kerdesei?. Last accessed: 01.08.2025.

The processing of personal data to develop an AI model constitutes an interference with both the fundamental right to privacy and the right to data protection in Articles 7 and 8 of the Charter and Article 8 of the ECHR.[116] For an interference in these rights to be lawful, the interference needs to have a basis in law, pursue a legitimate aim, and be necessary and proportionate, *stricto sensu*. The fairness principle in Article 5 (1) (a) of the GDPR relates to the principle of proportionality outlined in Articles 7, 8, and 52 in the Charter and in Article 8 (2) ECHR and could be viewed as an operationalisation of the *stricto sensu* subtest. If the processing of personal data is discriminatory against the data subjects, the processing would not be fair, would not pursue a legitimate aim, and would, therefore, not be proportionate.[117]

The processing of personal data should be conducted in a manner not disproportionately detrimental, not discriminatory to an extent violating discriminatory legislation, or unexpected for the data subject, nor should it manipulate or mislead the data subject.[118] Key measures when developing an AI system in line with the fairness principle include granting the data subject as much autonomy as possible in deciding how their personal data is processed and the scope of the processing operations. The processing must comply with the information communicated to the data subject and not be discriminatory, misleading, or exploitative. The controller has varying degrees of power over the data subject, and this power should not be used to lock the data subject to specific services during the AI development process.

The fairness principle in Article 5 (1) (a) also relates to the right not to be subject to an automated individual decision in Article 22 GDPR. The controller must implement some measures and means to ensure human oversight over automated processing and countermeasures to ensure that algorithms do not exhibit discriminatory biases. The principle in Article 5 (1) (a) of the GDPR requires that the controller processing personal data to develop an AI system audits and tests the training process for algorithmic biases. Biases could potentially lead to discriminatory and, thus, unfair results of the processing and thereby lead to the processing of personal data not pursuing a legitimate aim.

---

116 Joined Cases C-92/09 and C-93/09 Volker and Markus Schecke GbR, Hartmut Eifert v Land Hessen, joined party Bundesanstalt für Landwirtschaft und Ernährung ECLI:EU:C:2010:662 paragraph 47 and Amman v Switzerland app. no 27798/95 paragraph 30.

117 Lee A Bygrave. "Machine learning, cognitive sovereignty and data protection rights with respect to automated decisions". In: *The Cambridge Handbook of Information Technology, Life Sciences and Human Rights*. Ed. by Marcello Ienca et al. Cambridge, UK: Cambridge University Press, 2022, pp. 166–188. doi: https://doi.org/10.1017/9781108775038.016.

118 Ibid.

Bias detection must therefore be addressed in the development phase. Article 22 of the GDPR will be further analysed in Chapter 4 of the book.

Moreover, Article 5 (1) (a) requires the processing of personal data to be transparent. The reference to transparency in Article 5 (1) (a) is further elaborated in recital 58:

> The principle of transparency requires that any information addressed to the public or to the data subject be concise, easily accessible and easy to understand, and that clear and plain language and, additionally, where appropriate, visualisation be used.

In relation to the processing of personal data during the development of an AI system, the transparency principle requires the controller to give the data subject that forms part of the training dataset appropriate, intelligible, and understandable information about the processing. AI system development is a complex form of processing, and the controller needs to make the information on how data subjects' personal data is processed understandable to lay people, not just experts, to comply with the transparency principle. The principle is closely linked to the right to information in Article 12 of the GDPR.

The transparency principle in Article 5 (1) (a) could be required as a necessary step in order for the data subject to understand the processing of personal data. A non-transparent, opaque, and potentially explorative form of processing personal data in AI system development could be viewed as potentially unfair and thereby not proportionate. The transparency and fairness principle in Article 5 (1) (a) is thus closely connected to the *stricto sensu* subtest under the principle of proportionality.

3.2.12 Summary

The current section has focused on data protection regulation during AI system development, more specifically on collecting and processing personal data to develop AI models in line with the GDPR and Article 8 of the Charter. The chapter has identified that both the purpose limitation principle and measures to ensure the confidentiality and integrity of the personal data processed are, potentially, a part of the essence of the right in Article 8, according to the analysed case law. These specific parts of the processing of personal data could therefore be described as constitutional limits across Europe regarding personal data processing. Data processed during model training and AI system development, therefore, needs to be purpose-oriented and to have data protection by design measures to ensure the confidentiality and integrity of the personal data processed.

Moreover, a key focus of the chapter has been on the legal basis for processing personal data for AI development and lawful exemptions for processing special categories of personal data. The legal analysis has identified that Article 6 (1) (a) (consent), (b) (performance of a contract), and (f) (legitimate interests) are the most relevant legal bases for processing personal data to develop AI models. There are specific conditions that need to be fulfilled for all these legal bases. For special categories of personal data, explicit consent and the exemptions that require a supplementary legal basis in EU or member state law are the most relevant exemptions for processing special categories of personal data during AI model development.

Another focus of the subsections above has been on the connections between the principle of proportionality and the specific requirements for the lawful processing of personal data under the GDPR. The subsections have identified several relevant connections between the subtest of the principle of proportionality and the principles and requirements under the GDPR. The connections include the following: The connection between the legitimate aim subtest and the purpose limitation principle, the link between the accuracy of an AI system and the suitability subtest, and the link between necessity and data minimisation. A guiding structure for the processing of personal data to develop an AI system is of little value if it breaches primary law in the EU acquis. The subsections above have been an attempt to bridge both primary and secondary law and to map and identify relevant legal issues related to processing personal data for AI model development.

The legal analysis performed in the chapter may seem unquestionable. However, in current commercial AI development practices, personal data is crawled, scraped, stored, and further processed to develop AI systems on the basis that they are publicly available online. The above analysis concluded that such practices are not in line with the GDPR, interpreted in line with Article 8 of the Charter. New technology should not come with a fundamental right of infringement as an expense. The focus at the end of the chapter will, therefore, be on how the conclusions from the current legal analysis could – potentially – be implemented in the MLOps framework for more efficient compliance during AI model development.

3.3 THE DATA COMPONENT AND SPECIFIC REQUIREMENTS IN THE AI ACT

3.3.1 Introduction

The current section (3.3) will focus on the specific data governance requirements in the AI Act and how providers could comply with these data governance requirements when developing and training an AI model.

The AI Act was adopted by the European Parliament in March 2024, and various requirements will enter into force from 9 to 36 months after the Act has been published in the *Official Journal of the European Union*.[119] The AI Act was published in the *Official Journal* on 12 July 2024.[120] The AI Act is a new regulation, and traditional legal sources such as case law, guidance from supervisory authorities, enforcement decisions, and legal literature are therefore lacking or sparse. The subsections on the AI Act in the current and next chapters of the book will, therefore, mainly interpret the Articles of the AI Act in line with the recitals.

In order to get a comprehensive overview of the data governance requirements, it is first necessary to provide a general introduction to the scope, structure, and definitions of the AI Act in subsection 3.3.2. Subsection 3.3.3 interprets the purpose of the AI Act by analysing the legal history, legal basis, and scope of the Act. In subsection 3.3.4, the focus is on the specific data governance requirements in the AI Act and how to comply with them during the development process of an AI system.

3.3.2 General Introduction to the AI Act

The AI Act has the character of being a product safety regulation combined with requirements to protect fundamental rights. Such a regulatory mix of purposes is not common in the EU acquis. Traditional product safety regulations, such as regulations regarding medical devices[121] or machinery,[122] regulate risks mainly to the health and safety of natural persons and not fundamental rights. Traditional product safety regulations also impose obligations on the manufacturers and providers of the products and not the users of the product. The AI Act, however, regulates the risks to health, safety, and fundamental

---

119 European Parliament. *Artificial Intelligence Act: MEPs Adopt Landmark Law*. url: https://www.europarl.europa.eu/news/en/press-room/20240308IPR19015/artificial-intelligence-act-meps-adopt-landmark-law. Last accessed: 26.08.2024.

120 Regulation (EU) 2024/1689 of the European Parliament and of the Council of 13 June 2024 laying down harmonised rules on artificial intelligence and amending Regulations (EC) No 300/2008, (EU) No 167/2013, (EU) No 168/2013, (EU) 2018/858, (EU) 2018/1139 and (EU) 2019/2144 and Directives 2014/90/EU, (EU) 2016/797 and (EU) 2020/1828 (Artificial Intelligence Act) [2024] OJ L 2024/1689.

121 Regulation (EU) 2017/746 of the European Parliament and of the Council of 5 April 2017 on in vitro diagnostic medical devices and repealing Directive 98/79/EC and Commission Decision 2010/227/EU [2017] OJ L 117/176.

122 Directive 2006/42/EC of the European Parliament and of the Council of 17 May 2006 on machinery, and amending Directive 95/16/EC [2006] OJ L 157/24 [as repealed by the Machinery Regulation].

rights, according to Article 1 of the AI Act. Moreover, the AI Act also imposes requirements for the users of the AI system, referred to as the deployer. It is, thus, important to interpret the AI Act in line with two different types of potentially overlapping regulations.

- A core fundamental right regulation: the GDPR.
- A more traditional risk regulation: cybersecurity regulations.

According to recital 10 of the AI Act, the AI Act "does not seek to affect the application of existing Union law governing the processing of personal data". In Article 2 (7) of the AI Act, it is specified that the GDPR apply to personal data processed in connection with the rights and obligations laid down in the AI Act. Only Article 10 (5) of the AI Act regarding the processing of special categories of personal data for the debiasing of AI systems and Article 59 regarding further processing of personal data for developing certain AI systems in the public interest in the AI regulatory sandbox derogate from the GDPR under the AI Act, according to Article 2 (7) of the AI Act.

The focus of the current chapter of the book is on data used to develop an AI model or an AI system. The current subsection will therefore focus on data-relevant requirements in the AI Act. In order to get a full and comprehensive overview of the requirements for data governance in the AI Act, it is first necessary to define some of the terms used in the Act. Under Article 2 (1), the AI Act applies to "providers placing on the market or putting into service AI systems or placing on the market general-purpose AI models in the Union, irrespective of whether those providers are established or located within the Union or in a third country". Moreover, the Act relates to "deployers of AI systems that have their place of establishment or who are located within the Union".

Providers of AI systems are defined in Article 3 (2) as a "natural or legal person, public authority, agency or other body that develops an AI system or a general purpose AI model or that has an AI system or general purpose AI model developed and places them on the market or puts the system into service under its own name or trademark, whether for payment or free of charge". Deployers are further defined in Article 3 (4) of the Act as "any natural or legal person, public authority, agency or other body using an AI system under its authority except where the AI system is used in the course of a personal non-professional activity". The market is defined in Article 3 (9) as the market within the EU.

Furthermore, there are some definitions in the AI Act especially relevant to the current chapter of the book regarding data processed in AI system development. The AI Act Article 3 (29-32) defines training data, validation data, testing data, and input data. In many ways, these definitions are equivalent to how they are used in the AI field.

Article 3 (33) of the AI Act defines biometric data. The definition of biometric data is almost identical to the definition of biometric data in Article 3 (14) of the GDPR. However, the definition of biometric data in the GDPR contains the requirement that the data "allow or confirm the unique identification of that natural person". This specific requirement is not present in the same definition in the AI Act. Nevertheless, the inclusion of the definitions of biometric identification and biometric verification in the AI Act Articles 3 (35) and (36) includes the specific requirement in the GDPR, such that the two definitions in the two different rule sets remain similar.

The definition of special categories of personal data in Article 3 (50) of the AI Act is equivalent to the same definition under the GDPR. Personal data in the AI Act article 3 (50) is also the equivalent of the same term applied under the GDPR. The AI Act defines "sensitive operational data" as "operational data related to the activities of prevention, detection, investigation and prosecution of criminal offences, the disclosure of which can jeopardise the integrity of criminal proceedings", in Article 3 (38) of the AI Act.

Before entering into the specific data governance and other specific requirements in the AI Act relevant to data processed for AI system development, it is necessary to specify the scope of the Act and the scope of the requirements for high-risk AI systems. The overall scope of the AI Act, according to Article 2, encompasses the following circumstances and roles:

- Providers placing or putting AI systems into service in the Union.
- Deployers of AI systems that have their place of establishment within the Union.
- Providers or deployers placed within a third country where the output produced by the AI system is used in the Union.
- Importers and distributors of AI systems.
- Product manufacturer placing on the market or putting into service an AI system together with their product.
- Authorised representatives of providers, who are not established in the Union.
- Affected persons who are located in the Union.

The AI Act shall not apply to areas outside the scope of EU law and should not affect the member states' competencies concerning national security, defence, or military, according to Article 2 (3) of the AI Act. The AI Act shall not apply to AI systems and models, including their output, that are specifically developed and put into service for the sole purpose of scientific research and development, according to the AI Act Article 2 (6).

According to recital 11 of the AI Act, certain AI systems may fall under the scope of the AI Act even if they are neither placed on the market nor put into service nor used in the Union. An example is if an operator established in the Union contracts certain services to an operator established outside the Union in relation to an activity to be performed by an AI system that would qualify as high risk. To prevent the Act from being circumvented by operators in the Union collecting data, transferring the data outside the Union to process it in a high-risk AI system, and then importing the outputs, the AI Act would also enter into effect in such instances, under recital 11. The requirement in such instances is that the output is intended to be used within the Union.

The scope of the AI Act under Article 2 is illustrated in the flowchart in Figure 3.1.

Most of the requirements in the AI Act are imposed on high-risk AI systems. Besides describing the overall scope of the AI Act under Article 2 of the Act, it is important to analyse the scope of high-risk AI systems under the AI Act. High-risk AI systems should be placed on the Union market, put into service, or used only if they comply with certain mandatory requirements in Chapter III of the AI Act, according to recital 27. High-risk AI systems are classified according to Article 6 of the AI Act.

Under Article 6 (1) of the AI Act, an AI system should be classified as a high-risk AI system if it is intended to be used as a safety component of a product or if the AI system itself is a product, and if this product is covered by Union product safety legislation listed in Annex II and the product is required to undergo a third-party conformity assessment according to the product safety legislation in Annex II. Annex II Section I lists 12 different product safety regulations and directives, e.g., regulations on the safety of machinery,[123] toys,[124] recreational personal watercraft,[125] and in vitro diagnostic medical devices.[126] The product safety regulation referred to in Annex I to the AI Act defines

123 Directive 2006/42/EC of the European Parliament and of the Council of 17 May 2006 on machinery, and amending Directive 95/16/EC [2006] OJ L 157/24 [as repealed by the Machinery Regulation].

124 Directive 2009/48/EC of the European Parliament and of the Council of 18 June 2009 on the safety of toys [2009] OJ L 170/1.

125 Directive (EU) 2013/53 of the European Parliament and of the Council of 20 November 2013 on recreational craft and personal watercraft and repealing Directive 94/25/EC [2013] OJ L 354/90.

126 Regulation (EU) 2017/746 of the European Parliament and of the Council of 5 April 2017 on in vitro diagnostic medical devices and repealing Directive 98/79/EC and Commission Decision 2010/227/EU [2017] OJ L 117/176.

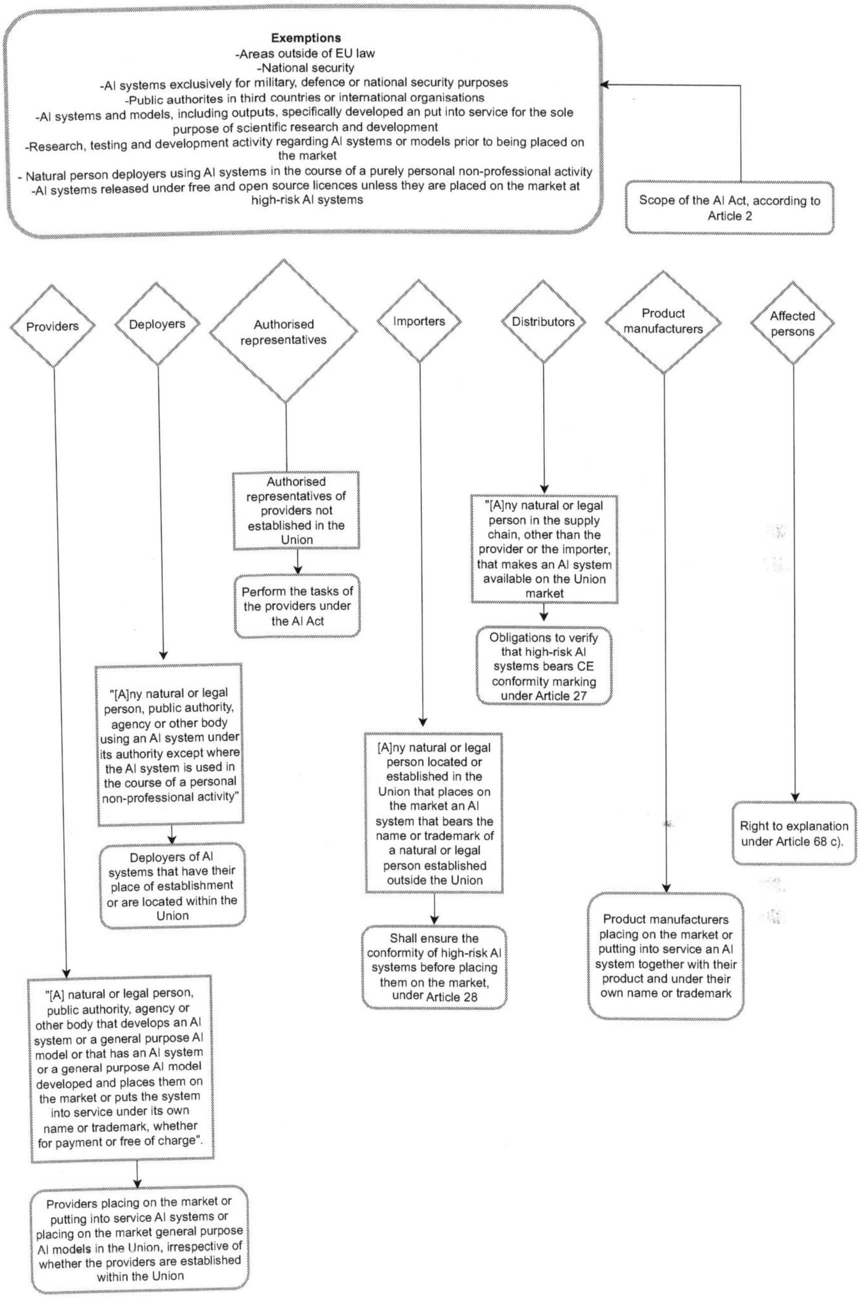

Figure 3.1 Flowchart of the scope of the AI Act under Article 2

whether the specific product's medical third-party conformity assessment, and thereby enters the scope of high-risk AI systems. To use the medical device regulation[127] as an example, an invasive medical device with respect to body orifices intended for transient use does not require a third-party conformity assessment, while a short-term use device expected to be used in the ear canal requires a third-party conformity assessment, according to Rule 5.1 of the medical device regulation. Accordingly, a hearing aid with AI functionality will be a high-risk AI system, while a hearing aid expected to be used for less than 60 minutes will not be a high-risk AI system, according to the AI Act Article 6 (1), Annex I (11) and the medical device regulation rule 5.1.

Article 6 (1) of the AI Act covers AI systems that form part of a product or are themselves a product under EU product safety regulation. The first category of high-risk AI systems, thus, covers the overall purpose of the AI Act related to the mitigation of risks to the health and safety of natural persons. In Article 6 (2), some AI systems might pose a high risk not just to the health and safety of natural persons, but also to their fundamental rights according to the Charter. In accordance with Article 5 (2), AI systems referred to in Annex III should be regarded as high risk. Annex III lists the following areas as areas with high-risk AI systems.

- Biometrics, insofar far their use is permitted under relevant Union law.
- Critical infrastructure.
- Education and vocational training.
- Employment, workers management, and access to self-employment.
- Access to and enjoyment of essential private services and essential public services, and benefits.
- Law enforcement, insofar as their use is permitted under relevant Union or national law.
- Migration, asylum, and border control management, insofar as their use is permitted under relevant Union or national law.
- Administration of justice and democratic processes.

127 Regulation (EU) 2017/745 of the European Parliament and of the Council of 5 April 2017 on medical devices, amending Directive 2001/83/EC, Regulation (EC) No 178/2002 and Regulation (EC) No 1223/2009 and repealing Council Directives 90/385/EEC and 93/42/EEC [2017] OJ L 117/1.

3.3.3 Establishing the Purpose of the AI Act

3.3.3.1 Introduction

The AI Act has been described as a mix between a product safety regulation and a fundamental rights instrument.[128]

The overall aim of the book is to develop a compliance by design approach to AI system development and deployment. In order to develop such an approach, it is crucial to have an understanding of the object and purpose of the AI Act. Which "risks" is the AI Act intended to mitigate, and how do these risks relate to fundamental rights, particularly the fundamental rights to privacy and data protection?

The next paragraphs will analyse and distil the overall purpose of the AI Act by analysing the legal history and predecessors of the Act (3.3.3.2), the legal bases of the Act in the Treaty of the Functioning of the European Union (TFEU) (3.3.3.3), and how the legal bases relate to the overarching scope of the Charter, with a particular focus on how the purpose of the AI Act shines through the fundamental rights lens in 3.3.3.4.

3.3.3.2 Predecessors of the AI Act: ethical frameworks

The history of the AI Act dates back to the European Commission's high-level expert group on AI, which was established in 2018.[129] The high-level expert group delivered an ethics guideline for trustworthy AI, policy and investment recommendations, an assessment list for trustworthy AI, and sectoral policy recommendations.[130]

The term "trustworthy" is an inherently ambiguous and opaque term that offers minimal insight into the overall purpose of the AI Act. However, the high-level expert group's operationalisation of the term "trustworthy" could shed some more light on the work of the high-level expert group and, thus, also indirectly the AI Act. The seven key requirements for trustworthy AI include:

1. Human agency and oversight.
2. Technical robustness and safety.

---

128 Marco Almada and Nicolas Petit. "The EU AI Act: A medley of product safety and fundamental rights?" In: *Robert Schuman Centre for Advanced Studies Research Paper* 2023/59 (2023). doi: http://dx.doi.org/10.2139/ssrn.4308072.

129 European Commission. *High-Level Expert Group on Artificial Intelligence.* url: https://digital-strategy.ec.europa.eu/en/policies/expert-group-ai. Last accessed: 26.08.2024.

130 European Commission. *High-Level Expert Group on Artificial Intelligence.* url: https://digital-strategy.ec.europa.eu/en/policies/expert-group-ai. Last accessed: 26.08.2024.

Table 3.1 Overview of the link between "trustworthy" AI and data protection

Requirement in the assessment list for trustworthy AI	Data protection equivalent
Human agency and oversight	Article 22 (3) GDPR
Technical robustness	Article 32 GDPR
Privacy and data governance	Charter Article 8, GDPR
Transparency	Article 5 (1) (a) GDPR
Non-discrimination	Article 22, 5 (1) (a) GDPR
Fairness	Article 5 (1) (a) GDPR
Environmental and societal well-being	-
Accountability	Article 5 (2) GDPR

3. Privacy and data governance.
4. Transparency.
5. Diversity, non-discrimination, and fairness.
6. Environmental and societal well-being.
7. Accountability.[131]

Several of the seven key requirements for trustworthy AI are closely interlinked with the fundamental right to privacy and data protection. The third requirement is directly linked. The links between the other key requirements and the fundamental right to data protection and the GDPR are summarised in Table 3.1.

As evident from Table 3.1, several of the requirements from the high-level expert group are similar to requirements in the GDPR. However, even though both the GDPR and the requirements in the high-level expert group's report, e.g., require transparency, it is important to keep in mind that the GDPR regulates data in a technology-neutral manner while the AI Act is technology-specific. Transparency in relation to the processing of personal data and transparency in relation to a system are closely related, but not interchangeable. Transparency in data protection shall enable data subjects to understand how their personal data is processed and thereby assess the lawfulness of the processing. Transparency in technology-specific regulation, such as the AI Act, is a requirement countering the inherent opaqueness in AI systems.

131 European Commission. *Assessment List for Trustworthy Artificial Intelligence (ALTAI) for Self-Assessment.* url: https://digital-strategy.ec.europa.eu/en/library/assessment-list-trustworthy-artificial-intelligence-altai-self-assessment. Last accessed: 26.08.2024.

It is important to note that the aforementioned list of requirements originates from a soft law framework preceding the enactment of the AI Act. Moreover, when the high-level expert group delivered their policy recommendations in 2019, AI use cases were less widespread in society. Given that the GDPR had recently come into effect when the high-level expert group's recommendations were delivered, it stands to reason that the expert group would draw inspiration from the provisions and requirements of the GDPR.

Both the high-level expert groups' report and the AI Act are examples of a policy and governance approach known as digital constitutionalism.[132] Digital constitutionalism is a policy intended to limit the exercise of power in a networked society and protect fundamental rights.[133] Similar to constitutions limiting the exercise of public powers, digital constitutionalism intends to limit the exercise of power by private companies developing technology. The purpose of the high-level expert group was not, first and foremost, to contribute to how AI systems could be developed without legal or regulatory hurdles. The purpose was to contribute to protecting natural persons from the known, foreseeable, and unknown risks related to the widespread deployment of AI systems in society. When the work by the high-level expert group is read through a digital constitutional lens, it becomes evident that the purpose of the predecessors of the AI Act was to protect natural persons and society from risk and harm, and not, first and foremost, to contribute to innovation in AI development.

The work of the high-level expert group is not formally part of the legislative process and does not have the status as *travaux préparatoires* to the AI Act. Even if the high-level expert group's report had the status of preparatory work, the report would not be a representation of the intention of the legislator of the AI Act due to the collective body nature of the EU legislator, shared across the Commission, the Council, and the European Parliament. However,

132 Nicola Palladino. "The role of epistemic communities in the 'constitutionalization;' of Internet governance: The example of the European Commission High-Level Expert Group on Artificial Intelligence". In: *Telecommunications Policy* 45.6 (2021). Norm entrepreneurship in Internet Governance, p. 102149. ISSN: 0308-5961. doi: https://doi.org/10.1016/j.telpol.2021.102149. url: https://www.sciencedirect.com/science/article/pii/S0308596121000537.

133 Edoardo Celeste. "Digital constitutionalism: A new systematic theorisation". In: *International Review of Law, Computers & Technology* 33.1 (2019), pp. 76–99. doi: 10.1080/13600869.2019.1562604; Giovanni De Gregorio. "The rise of digital constitutionalism in the European Union". In: *International Journal of Constitutional Law* 19.1 (Apr. 2021), pp. 41–70. ISSN: 1474-2640. doi: 10.1093/icon/moab001. eprint: https://academic.oup.com/icon/article-pdf/19/1/41/38501964/moab001.pdf. url: https://doi.org/10.1093/icon/moab001.

given the technical and complex nature of the AI Act, the high-level expert group's report might be applied to shed some light on the AI Act.

The work by the expert group resulted in legislative action from the EU, the AI Act, which was adopted in 2024. The high-level expert group can be viewed as necessary background material for understanding the AI Act. However, it is also important to keep in mind that the AI Act has been subject to extensive rounds of trialogue negotiations in the EU, including substantial lobbying.[134] Although the core tenets of the high-level expert group's work are included in the AI Act, the Act has been substantially changed throughout the legislative process.

To get one step closer to the purposes of the AI Act, the legal basis of the Act will be interpreted in the next paragraphs.

3.3.3.3 The legal bases of the AI Act

The legal basis of a regulation is an important starting point when interpreting and deciding the overall purpose of a rule set.

According to recital 3 of the AI Act, Article 114 of the Treaty on the Functioning of the European Union (TFEU) is the main legal basis of the AI Act. Article 114 of the TFEU has the following wording:

> The European Parliament and the Council shall, acting in accordance with the ordinary legislative procedure (...), adopt the measures for the approximation of the provisions laid down by law, regulation or administrative action in the Member States which have as their object the establishment and functioning of the internal market.

The main purpose of the legal basis of the AI Act is, thus, the functioning of the internal market. According to recital 3 of the AI Act, the need for the AI Act is due to the member states adopting their own AI regulations. Diverging AI regulations across Europe may decrease legal certainty and lead to fragmentation of the internal market, according to recital 3. Uniform regulations across the EU member states would contribute to the free circulation, innovation, deployment, and uptake of AI systems across the EU member states.

TFEU Article 114 is not the only legal basis of the AI Act. Specific rules in the AI Act concerning restrictions for AI systems for remote biometric identification for the purpose of law enforcement, the use of AI systems for risk assessments of natural persons for the purpose of law enforcement, and the use of AI systems for the biometric categorisation for the purpose of law enforcement is based on Article 16 of the TFEU, according to recital 3 of the AI Act.

---

134 Jascha Bareis. *BigTech's Efforts to Derail the AI Act*. url: https://verfassungsblog.de/bigtechs-efforts-to-derail-the-ai-act/. Last accessed: 26.08.2024.

Article 16 of the TFEU allows for the EU legislator to lay down rules relating to the protection of individuals with regard to the processing of personal data.

Article 16 of the TFEU is probably chosen as the legal basis for the regulations on AI systems employed in law enforcement because it is challenging to justify that the requirements for these AI systems pertain to the internal market, given that law enforcement is typically recognised as a competence of the member states. Article 16 of the TFEU is traditionally applied to lay down rules relating to the protection of personal data, typically regulations and directives such as the GDPR and the Law Enforcement Directive (LED).[135] In the AI Act, Article 16 TFEU is applied as a legal basis for rules potentially infringing the fundamental rights to privacy and data protection. Given that Article 16 of the TFEU serves as the legal basis for the rules relating to data processed in AI systems for law enforcement purposes, and recognising that the primary purpose of Article 16 is to protect personal data, it logically follows that the rules within the AI Act based on Article 16 should be interpreted and applied in a manner that enhances the right to data protection.

Hence, the legal bases of the AI Act are both Articles in the TFEU relating to the functioning of the internal market and personal data protection. However, the Charter – an example of the primary law of the EU – will apply regardless of the legal basis that secondary law is based on, due to the *lex superior* nature of the Charter. The next paragraphs will, therefore, analyse the relationship between the AI Act and primary law further.

3.3.3.4 The purpose of the AI Act through a fundamental rights lens

The purpose of the AI Act is to ensure a high level of protection of health, safety, and fundamental rights enshrined in the Charter of Fundamental Rights of the European Union, according to recital 1 of the AI Act. Moreover, recital 2 of the AI Act requires the Act to be applied in accordance with the values of the Union enshrined in the Charter. Furthermore, according to recitals 5 and 6 of the AI Act, "AI may cause harm to public interest and fundamental rights", and it is therefore "vital for AI and its regulatory framework to be developed in accordance with Union values as enshrined in Article 2 of the Treaty of the European Union (TEU), the fundamental rights and freedoms enshrined in the Treaties and, pursuant to Article 6 TEU, the Charter".

---

135 Directive (EU) 2016/680 of the European Parliament and of the Council of 27 April 2016 on the protection of natural persons with regard to the processing of personal data by competent authorities for the purposes of the prevention, investigation, detection or prosecution of criminal offences or the execution of criminal penalties, and on the free movement of such data, and repealing Council Framework Decision 2008/977/JHA [2016] OJ L 119/89.

According to recital 7 of the AI Act, the rules of the AI Act shall be "consistent with the Charter". Since the Charter has the status of primary EU law, the provision that the AI Act needs to be consistent with the Charter is essentially unnecessary. Nevertheless, the inclusion of this specific recital in the AI Act emphasises that part of the purpose of the AI Act is to ensure fundamental rights protection during the development and use of AI systems.

According to the recitals of the AI Act, the purpose of the Regulation is to ensure fundamental rights protection during the development and use of AI systems. Moreover, the recitals to the AI Act establish that the material and procedural rules of the AI Act need to be interpreted and applied pursuant to the requirements in the Charter.

The Charter has many rights potentially relevant to the development and use of AI systems. The rights in Articles 7 (right to a private life), Article 8 (right to data protection), Article 10 (freedom of thought), Article 11 (freedom of expression and information), and Article 21 (right to non-discrimination) are all relevant for the development and the use of AI systems. The book, in both the current chapter and in Chapter 6, will, for the sake of relevance to the GDPR, limit its scope to Articles 7 and 8 of the Charter.

Fundamental rights protection, including Articles 7 and 8 of the Charter, is only one of many purposes of the AI Act. The AI Act should also contribute to other public interests such as health and safety, democracy, the rule of law, and environmental protection, according to recital 8. The AI Act functions as a uniform legal framework to ensure a single EU market for AI systems, while at the same time ensuring fundamental rights protection – including the right to a private life and data protection. Privacy and data protection are, thus, one of several purposes being operationalised through the material and procedural rules of the Act.

The subsections above have identified that privacy and data protection were one of the foundational tenets behind the work of the high-level expert group on AI, that the AI Act is partly grounded in a development known as digital constitutionalism, and that data protection and privacy are one of the purposes of the AI Act. As an overall conclusion, it is possible to contend that data protection and privacy are one of the core purposes of the AI Act.

The next subsection of the book will return to the overall purpose of the current chapter, to identify data-relevant requirements in the development phase of AI systems in the AI Act.

3.3.4 Data Governance Requirements for High-Risk AI Systems

The current chapter of the book focuses on the requirements specifically relevant to the data applied for training an AI system. Compliant processing of data in a deployed AI system is the focus of the next chapter of the book.

Specific relevant requirements for the inference part of an AI system will be analysed in Chapters 4 and 5. A general overview of the requirements for high-risk AI systems, however, will be provided in the following subsection.

In cases where a high-risk AI system is also a product under the product safety regulation listed in Annex II, Section A to the AI Act, the provider has the choice to implement the appropriate testing and reporting processes under the AI Act in addition to the product safety regulation, according to Article 8 (2) of the AI Act. Providers of high-risk AI systems must establish, implement, document, and maintain a risk management system under Article 9 of the AI Act. Moreover, there are requirements to draw up technical documentation for high-risk AI systems under Article 11; to allow for the automatic recording of events (logs) over the duration of the lifetime of the system, according to Article 12; there are transparency and provisions on information to deployers in Article 13; human oversight in Article 14; and accuracy, robustness, and cybersecurity in Article 15. A high-risk AI system also needs to receive the CE mark and be registered in an EU database before being placed on the market or put into service, according to Articles 17, 50, and 51 of the AI Act. The main requirements for high-risk AI systems and their interrelationships are summarised in in the flowchart in Figure 3.2.

A requirement for high-risk AI systems, especially relevant in relation to the processing of data during the development process of AI systems, is the data governance requirements in Article 10 of the AI Act. The data governance requirements establish specific quality criteria for training, validation, and testing datasets for high-risk AI systems, according to Article 10 (1). Article 10 sets out minimum requirements for a data governance system that providers of high-risk AI systems must implement.

- The mandatory practices in such a data governance system under Article 10 of the AI Act include relevant design choices, data collection processes, and the origin of data. If the data is personal data, the provider must also include the original purpose of the data collection.
- Relevant data preparation processing, e.g., annotation, labelling, cleaning, updating, enrichment, and aggregation.
- Assumptions about the information that the data are supposed to measure and represent.
- Assessments of the availability, quantity, and suitability of the required datasets.
- Examination of possible biases that are likely to affect health and safety, negatively impact fundamental rights, or lead to prohibited discrimination.
- Appropriate measures to prevent and mitigate such biases and the identification of relevant data gaps.

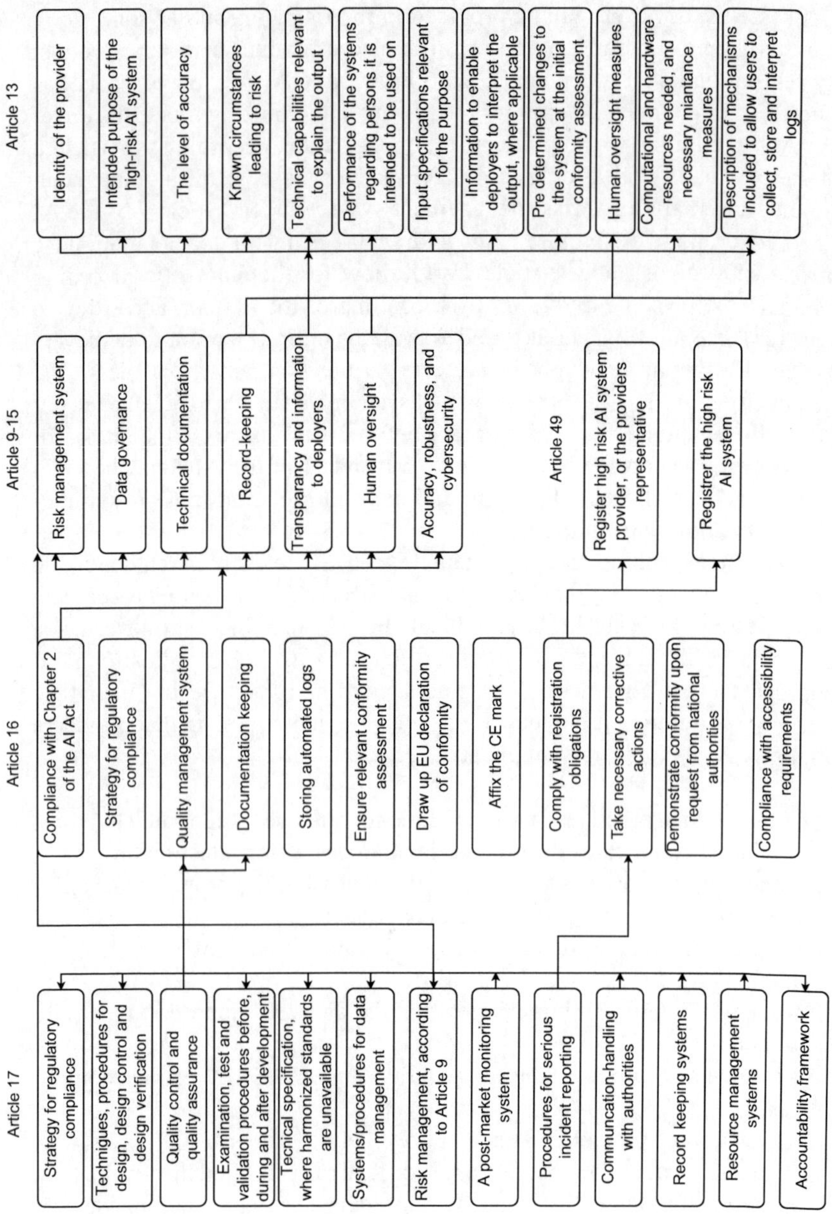

Figure 3.2 Requirements for providers of high-risk AI systems under the AI Act

According to Article 10 (3) of the AI Act, training datasets shall be relevant, sufficiently representative, and, to the best extent possible, free of errors, and complete in view of the intended purpose of the high-risk AI system. The statistical properties of datasets must be relevant to the intended use of high-risk AI systems, including the persons the AI system is intended to be applied.

In order to mitigate the risk of potential inherent bias in high-risk AI systems, the characteristics or elements that are particular to the specific geographical, contextual, behavioural, or functional setting where the AI system is intended to be used shall be taken into account in the datasets, according to the AI Act Article 10 (4).

Article 10 (5) sets out the specific requirements for processing special categories of personal data under Article 9 of the GDPR in order to ensure bias detection and correction. The processing needs to be strictly necessary and under the subject of appropriate safeguards for the data subject. Article 10 (5) (a–f) lists the specific conditions for such bias detection. As elaborated in 3.2.7.4, the AI Act Article 10 (5) might be a lawful legal basis for processing personal data for bias detection and correction, according to the GDPR Article 6 (1) (c).

While the current subsection has focused on describing the data-relevant requirements for high-risk AI systems in the AI Act, the last subsection of the chapter will focus on whether and how such requirements could be embedded in MLOps when developing a high-risk AI system.

3.4 THE DATA COMPONENT AND CYBERSECURITY REGULATION

3.4.1 Introduction

The current subsection will address some relevant cybersecurity regulation requirements for data processing during AI system development. The key focus of the subsection will be on some specific requirements in the CRA.[136]

While data protection is a fundamental right according to the Charter Article 8, cybersecurity is an emerging and prioritised policy area in the EU acquis. The security of the processing of personal data and the cybersecurity of a system are closely related. Scholars argue that cybersecurity is gradually becoming such a prioritised policy area that there are reasons to believe that

136 Regulation (EU) 2024/2847 of the European Parliament and of the Council of 23 October 2024 on horizontal cybersecurity requirements for products with digital elements and amending Regulations (EU) No 168/2013 and (EU) 2019/1020 and Directive (EU) 2020/1828 (Cyber Resilience Act) OJ/L 2024/2847.

cybersecurity will eventually evolve into a fundamental right in the EU, either through inclusion in the Charter or through interpretations by the CJEU.[137]

Data protection regulation is a traditional rights-based form of regulation, while cybersecurity regulation is more characterised as a form of risk regulation. In a risk-based approach, relevant actors are required to identify risks, assess the risks, and introduce risk-mitigating measures. When training an AI system on openly available personal data, there is a risk that the data collection not only breaches data protection regulations but also potentially poses a cybersecurity risk for the overall finished trained AI system. The next paragraphs will address how these risks associated with the data processed in high-risk AI systems are addressed in the CRA.

The relevance of the question discussed could be illustrated with an example. A data poisoning attack happens when an adversary attacker poisons the training data of an AI system under development.[138] The objective of the adversary in data poisoning attacks is to get the AI system to misclassify objects or data. Such misclassifications are accomplished by substituting the training data with the adversary's data to achieve misclassification and weaken the model's accuracy. Data poisoning can occur either at the data collecting stage, i.e., in the original data source or in the database of the AI system provider.[139] Mitigating measures for data poisoning attacks during AI development and whether current cybersecurity regulations address such risk will be the focus in the following.

---

[137] Luca Tosoni. *The Fundamental Right to Cybersecurity.* Oslo: University of Oslo, 2023. url: http://urn.nb.no/URN:NBN:no-nb_digibok_2023033148096; Pier Giorgio Chiara. "Towards a right to cybersecurity in EU law? The challenges ahead". In: *Computer Law & Security Review* 53 (2024), p. 105961. ISSN: 0267-3649. doi: https://doi.org/10.1016/j.clsr.2024.105961. url: https://www.sciencedirect.com/science/article/pii/S0267364924000281.

[138] Raghvinder S Sangwan, Youakim Badr, and Satish M Srinivasan. "Cybersecurity for AI systems: A survey". In: *Journal of Cybersecurity and Privacy* 3.2 (2023), pp. 166–190. ISSN: 2624-800X. doi: 10.3390/jcp3020010. url: https://www.mdpi.com/2624-800X/3/2/10.

[139] Raghvinder S Sangwan, Youakim Badr, and Satish M Srinivasan. "Cybersecurity for AI systems: A survey". In: *Journal of Cybersecurity and Privacy* 3.2 (2023), pp. 166–190. ISSN: 2624-800X. doi: 10.3390/jcp3020010. url: https://www.mdpi.com/2624-800X/3/2/10.

3.4.2 Establishing the Purpose of the CRA and the NIS 2 Directive

3.4.2.1 Introduction

The current subsection will examine the purpose of cybersecurity regulation, more specifically the NIS 2 Directive[140] and the CRA,[141] in relation to the purpose of the GDPR and the AI Act. The current subsection will function as a necessary prerequisite for understanding the cybersecurity regulations, the relationships and interconnections between cybersecurity regulations, the AI Act, and the GDPR. Moreover, the current subsection will function as a prerequisite for the proportionality by design concept developed in Chapter 6 of the book.[142]

As highlighted in the introduction to the book, cybersecurity is a relatively new policy goal in EU law, and cybersecurity as a policy ideal is more recent than privacy and data protection, which have a legislative history in the EU dating back to the Data Protection Directive from 1995.[143] Cyberspace and the Internet have a borderless nature surpassing national jurisdictions, traditional diplomacy, and traditional international collaborations. The international and national threats to information systems, such as electoral interference, cyberattacks, and other threats, have led to regulations and directives that attempt to mitigate these threats.

The next paragraphs will analyse the overall purpose and policy ideal of these directives and regulations, particularly the NIS 2 Directive and the CRA. The focus will especially be on attempting to reconcile these purposes with the purposes of the GDPR and the AI Act. Are data protection, AI Regulation, and cybersecurity regulations attempting to achieve the same policy ideal through different approaches? One manner to answer this research question is to

140 2022/2555 of the European Parliament and of the Council of 14 December 2022 on measures for a high common level of cybersecurity across the Union, amending Regulation (EU) No 910/2014 and Directive (EU) 2018/1972, and repealing Directive (EU) 2016/1148 (NIS 2 Directive) [2022] OJ L 333/80.

141 Regulation (EU) 2024/2847 of the European Parliament and of the Council of 23 October 2024 on horizontal cybersecurity requirements for products with digital elements and amending Regulations (EU) No 168/2013 and (EU) 2019/1020 and Directive (EU) 2020/1828 (Cyber Resilience Act) OJ/L 2024/2847.

142 Subsection 3.4.2 is a rewritten part of Bjørn Aslak Juliussen, Jon Petter Rui, and Dag Johansen. "Developing with compliance in mind: Addressing data protection law, cybersecurity regulation, and AI regulation during software development". In: *IFIP International Summer School on Privacy and Identity Management*. Springer, 2023, pp. 81–96

143 Directive 95/46/EC of the European Parliament and of the Council of 24 October 1995 on the protection of individuals with regard to the processing of personal data and of the free movement of such data [1995] OJ L 281/31.

analyse the differences in assessing risk to data protection, cybersecurity, and the risks associated with AI systems across the NIS 2 Directive, the GDPR, and the AI Act. If the analysis identifies similar risk assessment methodologies and similar interests pursued in the rule sets, the research question could be answered in the affirmative. However, if both the risk assessment methodologies and the risk(s) mitigated through the regulations differ, this supports that the purposes of the regulations are different.

3.4.2.2 Risk management in the NIS 2 Directive and the GDPR: risks to public interests vs. risks to rights?

The NIS 2 Directive requires that operators of essential services for society – e.g., health-care providers, energy sector entities, and food distributors – must conduct risk analyses of their networks and information systems, and have measures for incident handling and crisis management.[144] If an essential entity is non-compliant with the NIS 2 Directive, it risks fines of up to 10,000,000 euros or 2% of total worldwide annual turnover, under the NIS 2 Directive Article 31 (4).[145]

Are the risks managed under cybersecurity regulations such as the NIS 2 Directive and the risks managed under Article 32 of the GDPR inherently different? In order to answer this question, the risk management requirements of both the NIS 2 Directive and the GDPR must be analysed.

The risk management in the NIS 2 Directive consists of three main pillars: (I) Governance, (II) Risk-management measures, and (III) Reporting obligations. The cybersecurity risk-management measures in the NIS 2 Directive Article 21 shall ensure appropriate and proportionate technical, operational, and organisational measures to manage the risk of cybersecurity incidents. The relevant risks are both risks posed to the security of network and information systems, and risks due to the impact on the recipients of the service, according to Article 21 (1), second paragraph. Downtime in a health-care system may, for instance, pose a risk both to the functioning of that specific system and to the health care and well-being of patients.

---

144 Directive (EU) 2022/2555 of the European Parliament and of the Council of 14 December 2022 on measures for a high common level of cybersecurity across the Union, amending Regulation (EU) No 910/2014 and Directive (EU) 2018/1972, and repealing Directive (EU) 2016/1148 (NIS 2 Directive) [2022] OJ L 333/80.

145 Section 3.4.2.2 is a rewritten part of Bjørn Aslak Juliussen, Jon Petter Rui, and Dag Johansen. "Developing with compliance in mind: Addressing data protection law, cybersecurity regulation, and AI regulation during software development". In: *IFIP International Summer School on Privacy and Identity Management*. Cham: Springer Nature, 2023, pp. 81–96.

In the assessment of which technical, operational, and organisational measures are appropriate to mitigate identified risks, the state of the art, European and international standards, and the cost of implementation should be taken into account, according to Article 21 (2) of the NIS 2 Directive. In the overall assessment of the proportionality of the risk-management measure, due account should be taken of the entity's exposure to risk, the size of the entity, the likelihood of occurrence and the severity of potential cybersecurity incidents, and the societal and economic impact of cybersecurity incidents, pursuant to Article 21 (2). Proportionality under Article 21 (2) is an application of the principle of proportionality as a general EU principle, and not directly related to fundamental rights. In the NIS 2 Directive, the "interference" to which the proportionality is applied to assess the appropriateness of is, thus, the regulatory impact of the regulation on the entities, and not the fundamental rights impact on affected natural persons. This entails that, although there is a reference to proportionality in the NIS 2 Directive, the purpose of the NIS 2 Directive is to protect the internal market from dissolution and negative impact and not first and foremost to protect the fundamental rights of natural persons.

In line with NIS 2 being a directive and that the member states, therefore, have more autonomy and choice in implementing the requirements in national law, Article 21 (2) (a)–(d) lists the minimum requirements for cybersecurity incident risk-management measures. The measures should have an all-hazard approach and should include policies on risk analysis and information system security, incident handling, and business continuity. The business continuity measures include strategies for backup management, supply chain security, security in the acquisition of network and information systems, policies on the effectiveness of cybersecurity risk management, cybersecurity hygiene and training, procedures on encryption and cryptography, human resources security, access controls and asset management, and the use of authentication solutions.

Article 24 of the GDPR mandates that controllers pursue the rights and obligations in the regulation through a risk-based approach. The requirements in Article 24 must be interpreted together with Article 32 regarding the security of the processing of personal data and Article 25 regarding data protection by design and by default. The controller, taking into account the state of the art, the costs of implementation, and the nature, scope, context, and purposes of the processing of personal data, as well as the risk of varying severity and likelihood, must implement appropriate technical and organisational measures to ensure appropriate security of the processing of personal data. Such technical and organisational measures could include pseudonymisation and encryption of personal data. Moreover, the ability to ensure confidentiality, integrity, availability, and resilience in the systems and services, the ability to restore the availability and access to personal data in the event of an incident, and processes for testing, assessing, and evaluating the security of processing must be in place.

When assessing risk to the security of the processing of personal data under Article 32 of the GDPR, recital 76 of the regulation requires that risks are evaluated on the basis of an objective assessment, where it is established whether data processing operations involve a risk or a high risk. The GDPR does not contain a risk assessment methodology for assessing such risks. However, the principle of accountability in Article 5 (2) requires that such a risk assessment is systematic and that future audits are possible to conduct from the risk assessment. Several European data protection authorities recommend the use of international standards – such as ISO/IEC 27001 from the International Organization for Standardization (ISO) and the International Electrotechnical Commission (IEC)[146] – when risk-assessing under Article 32 of the GDPR.[147] Originally, ISO/IEC 27001 is a standard for information security and not specifically data protection.

The main purpose of the GDPR, as expressed in Article 1 of the regulation, is both to protect natural persons with regard to the processing of personal data and to ensure the free movement of personal data within the Union. Natural persons cannot be efficiently protected with regard to the processing of personal data without efficient cybersecurity measures and risk management of cybersecurity incidents, as expressed in Article 32 of the GDPR. The risks managed through Articles 24, 25, and 32 of the GDPR are risks both to the security of the processing of personal data and to the rights and freedoms of the data subjects, according to 32 (1). The relevant rights for the data subjects are the right to privacy and data protection, and the specific rights in Articles 12 to 22 of the GDPR. The fundamental freedoms cover respect for private and family life; home and communications; the protection of personal data; freedom of thought, conscience, and religion; freedom of expression and information; freedom to conduct a business; the right to an effective remedy and a fair trial; and cultural, religious, and linguistic diversity, according to recital 4 of the GDPR.

---

146 ISO. *ISO/IEC 27001 and Related Standards*. url: https://www.iso.org/isoiec-27001-information-security.html. Last accessed 01.08.2025.

147 Norwegian Data Protection Authority. *ISO/IEC 27001*. url: https://www.datatilsynet.no/rettigheter-og-plikter/virksomhetenes-plikter/informasjonssikkerhet-internkontroll/etablere-internkontroll/iverksette-styringssystem-for-informasjonssikkerhet/. Last accessed: 01.08.2025. Danish Data Protection Authority. *ISO/IEC 27001*. url: https://www.datatilsynet.dk/hvad-siger-reglerne/vejledning/sikkerhed/katalog-over-foranstaltninger. Last accessed: 01.08.2025. ICO. *ISO/IEC 27001*. url: https://ico.org.uk/for-organisations/the-guide-to-nis/security-requirements/. Last accessed: 01.08.2025.

Assessing the risks to the security of a software system, or an AI system, in a critical or important sector entity under the NIS 2 Directive and the risks to the security of personal data processing might initially seem like two similar risk assessments. However, when keeping in mind that the risk assessments under the NIS 2 Directive shall identify and mitigate risks to systems in critical sector entities to reduce negative societal effects and that the risk assessments under the GDPR shall identify and mitigate risks of adverse impact on the rights and fundamental freedoms of data subjects, the assessments seem different. First, the public interests pursued in the NIS 2 Directive and the individual rights and freedoms pursued under the GDPR are inherently distinctive. Second, a risk to an information system and a risk to a right are also unique in relation to the risk assessment methodology typically applied.[148] While a risk to the security of a system could be measured by the likelihood and severity of the risk materialising, a risk to a right is more value-embodied and harder to quantify in metrics.

To conclude, security aspects are a crucial part of an assessment of the security of processing personal data under the GDPR. However, the risk assessments under the NIS 2 Directive and the GDPR have different purposes and do not coincide.

3.4.2.3 Differences in risk management across cybersecurity regulation and the AI Act

> Cybersecurity plays a crucial role in ensuring that AI systems are resilient against attempts to alter their use, behaviour, performance or compromise their security properties by malicious third parties exploiting the system's vulnerabilities. Cyberattacks against AI systems can leverage AI-specific assets, such as training data sets (e.g., data poisoning) or trained models (e.g., adversarial attacks), or exploit vulnerabilities in the AI system's digital assets or the underlying ICT infrastructure. To ensure a level of cybersecurity appropriate to the risks, suitable measures should therefore be taken by the providers of high-risk AI systems.[149]

The cited excerpt from recital 76 of the AI Act highlights the critical role and importance of cybersecurity in AI systems. AI systems might, due to their

---

[148] Niels van Dijk, Raphaël Gellert, and Kjetil Rommetveit. "A risk to a right? Beyond data protection risk assessments". In: *Computer Law & Security Review* 32.2 (2016), pp. 286–306. ISSN: 0267-3649. doi: https://doi.org/10.1016/j.clsr.2015.12.017. url: https://www.sciencedirect.com/science/article/pii/S026736491500182X.

[149] Regulation (EU) 2024/1689 of the European Parliament and of the Council of 13 June 2024 laying down harmonised rules on artificial intelligence and amending Regulations (EC) No 300/2008, (EU) No 167/2013, (EU) No 168/2013, (EU) 2018/858, (EU) 2018/1139 and (EU) 2019/2144 and Directives 2014/90/EU, (EU) 2016/797 and (EU) 2020/1828 (Artificial Intelligence Act) [2024] OJ L 2024/1689.

internal opaqueness, pose risks to cybersecurity, but AI systems also show significant potential to be used to improve the cybersecurity of systems and networks.[150] Recitals 51 and 89 of the NIS 2 Directive emphasise that both the EU member states and the critical sector entities should pursue the use of cybersecurity-enhancing technologies, such as AI and ML systems, to enhance their capabilities and the security of networks and information systems.

What is the role of cybersecurity in the AI Act, and how might the future interplay between the AI Act and the NIS 2 Directive take form? High-risk AI systems in the AI Act include the management and operation of critical infrastructures, according to Annex III of the act. Annex III Section 2 to the AI Act lists AI systems applied in the management of critical digital infrastructure, road traffic, and supply of water, gas, heating, and electricity as high-risk AI systems, as their failure might put at risk the life and health of persons on a large scale. The reference to critical infrastructure in the AI Act is not coherent with the concept of critical entities in the NIS 2 Directive. The lack of a cross-reference between the two legislations could lead to an inconsistent interpretation of critical entities and infrastructures across the NIS 2 Directive and the AI Act.

The interplay between a cybersecurity regulation, such as the NIS 2 Directive, and the AI Act is best illustrated by the use of an example. Suppose that a road traffic authority makes use of a video-based AI system to manage traffic in a city region. Such a road traffic entity must comply with the requirements for entities in the sector of high criticality pursuant to the NIS 2 Directive Article 2 (1) and Annex 1 Section 2 (d). Furthermore, if an AI system is used in such a critical entity, the proposed AI Act comes into effect.

First of all, the requirements in the AI Act differ between providers and deployers of AI systems. As a starting point, suppose that the public road traffic agency, a critical entity under the NIS 2 Directive, is the provider of the AI system. A provider of an AI system is defined in Article 3 (1) of the AI Act as "a natural or legal person, public authority, agency or other body that develops an AI system or that has an AI system developed with a view of placing it on the market or putting in into service under its own name or trademark". If the public road traffic management agency internally develops an AI system for road traffic management, it will fulfil the definition of a provider in the AI Act.

Among the AI Act provisions, Article 15 (4) has significant similarities with the NIS 2 Directive, requiring that high-risk AI systems shall "be resilient as

---

150 Iqbal H Sarker, Md Hasan Furhad, and Raza Nowrozy. "AI-driven cybersecurity: An overview, security intelligence modeling and research directions". In: *SN Computer Science* 2.3 (2021), p. 173. doi: 10.1007/s42979-021-00557-0.

regards attempts by unauthorised third parties to alter their use or performance by exploiting the system vulnerabilities".

Now, suppose that the public road traffic management entity is a deployer and not the provider of a high-risk AI system. A deployer of an AI system is defined in Article 3 (4) of the AI Act as "any natural or legal person, public authority, agency or other body using an AI system under its authority". The requirements for deployers of high-risk AI systems, pursuant to Article 28 (2–5) AI Act, are that the deployer shall use the systems in accordance with the instructions, the deployer shall ensure that the input data is relevant for the application of the high-risk AI system, and the deployer shall monitor the operation of the high-risk AI system based on the instructions of use.

The examination of the interplay between the cybersecurity provisions of the AI Act and the NIS 2 Directive requires an interpretation of the different purposes of the two legal frameworks. A high-risk AI system – for instance, the road traffic management system – is high risk due to the inherent risk such an AI system may pose to the health and safety of natural persons. At the same time, road traffic management is regarded as a critical sector entity under the NIS 2 Directive due to the importance such an entity has at a societal level. The cybersecurity requirements in the AI Act, therefore, primarily aim to protect the natural person's health, safety, and fundamental rights from harm and interference. The cybersecurity requirements in the NIS 2 Directive first and foremost aim to increase cyber resilience and thereby reduce the negative societal impact a cyber incident could have on society and the economy in the internal market.

How do the risk management measures identified under the NIS 2 Directive above – where the overall objective of the risk assessment under the cybersecurity regulations is to mitigate risks to systems in a critical sector to reduce negative social effects – relate to the risk management measures under the AI Act?

As identified in subsection 3.3.3, the risks managed under the risk management system in Article 9 (1) of the AI Act are the risk to health and safety and the risk to fundamental rights. Similar to the risk management measures under the GDPR, the AI Act also has an individual or group focus on how the high-risk systems might affect natural persons. Cybersecurity regulations, such as the NIS 2 Directive, have a more societal focus where cyberattacks represent a matter of public interest. The risks managed across cybersecurity regulations are thus more related to the economy, democracy, and health, rather than individual fundamental rights on an individual or aggregated group level.

The risk management across the AI Act, where fundamental right protection is one of the purposes of the AI Act, and cybersecurity regulations, such as the NIS 2 Directive and the CRA, are inherently different. Therefore, as a general conclusion, there is no room for convergence between the AI Act and the cybersecurity regulations in relation to the risk management procedures.

Even though the two different legal frameworks have different objectives, backgrounds, and scopes, several positive synergies could be made by working together and including, for instance, aspects of the risk management process in the NIS 2 Directive in risk and quality management under the AI Act and vice versa in cases where both the AI Act and the NIS 2 Directive come into effect. If aspects of the risk of cyber incidents are included in the quality and risk management of AI systems, there are reasons to believe that the overall security, trust, confidence, and resilience of AI systems might increase.

The current subsection concluded that the differences in the risks managed under cybersecurity regulations, on the one hand, and the GDPR and the AI Act, on the other hand, are inherently different and that cybersecurity regulation, although it is a focus of the compliance by design concept being analysed throughout the book, needs to be assessed side by side with the other rule sets and that it is not possible to merge the risk management measures across the regulations and directives.

3.4.3 Data Relevant Requirements in the CRA

The former subsections analysed the NIS 2 Directive as an example of a cybersecurity framework. The NIS 2 Directive applies to networks and information systems in sectors of high criticality and therefore puts more focus on governance and risk management measures. The CRA is an example of a cybersecurity regulation with more substantial technology-related demands for products. The CRA will therefore be put under scrutiny as part of the data component of the compliance by design concept in the following subsection.

The CRA is a Regulation that applies to products with digital elements whose intended or reasonably foreseeable use includes a direct or indirect logical or physical data connection to a device or a network, according to Article 2 of the CRA.

In November 2023, the co-legislators in the EU, the Council and the Parliament, agreed on the CRA.[151] The Regulation applies from 11 December 2027. The overall aim of the Act is to shift some of the responsibilities for cyber vulnerabilities in software and high-risk AI systems from the users to the software and AI developers, according to the explanatory memorandum of the CRA section 1.

---

[151] European Commission. *Commission Welcomes Political Agreement on Cyber Resilience Act.* url: https://ec.europa.eu/commission/presscorner/detail/en/ip_23_6168. Last accessed: 26.08.2024.

The CRA aims to both strengthen the obligations of software and hardware developers to mitigate inherent vulnerabilities in the products when they are detected and to inform users about the risk of inherent vulnerabilities, preventing users from choosing products with inadequate cybersecurity properties. The CRA inhibits requirements for the design, development, production,

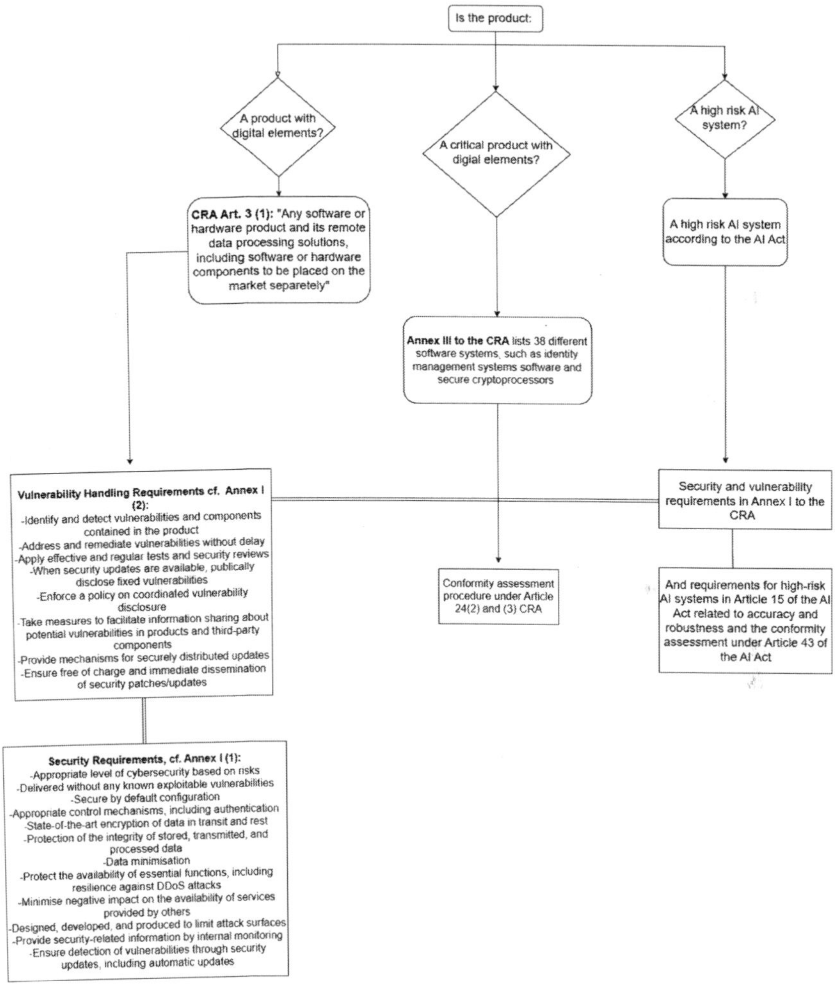

Figure 3.3 *Flowchart of the requirements for digital products, critical digital products, and high-risk AI systems under the scope of the CRA*

and making available in the market for hardware and software products. The requirements under the CRA for products with digital elements and crucial products with digital elements are listed in the flowchart in Figure 3.3.

High-risk AI systems, according to the AI Act, must comply with the requirements for accuracy and cybersecurity in the AI Act and the requirements in Section 1 to Annex 1 to the CRA, according to CRA Article 12 (1).

In relation to the data applied when training and developing a high-risk AI system, the requirements in Section 1 (3) (d–h) are especially relevant:

According to section 1 (2) (d–h) in Annex 1 to the CRA, the provider of the high-risk AI system must protect the integrity of stored, transmitted, or otherwise processed data, against manipulation, modification, or corruption; process only relevant data limited to what is necessary; protect essential functions against denial of service attacks; limit external attack surfaces; and minimise their negative impact on the availability of services provided by others.

The requirements in Annex I to the CRA pursue a risk-based approach, meaning that the providers need to assess potential risk and introduce relevant risk-mitigating measures. If the provider of a high-risk AI system identifies that there is a risk of a data poisoning attack on the training dataset, the provider needs to lessen such a risk by introducing relevant risk mitigating measures to lower the attack vector, according to the CRA Annex I Section 1 (2) (j).

To summarise, there are cybersecurity requirements for high-risk AI systems in both the AI Act Article 15 and the CRA. Providers of high-risk AI systems also entering the scope of the CRA must comply with both Annex 1 Section 1 of the CRA and the AI Act, according to Article 12 (1) of the CRA. There are some requirements in the CRA that are relevant for data processed during AI system development, especially requirements intended to lower the risk of data poisoning attacks against training datasets.

3.5 IMPLEMENTING THE IDENTIFIED LEGAL REQUIREMENTS IN MLOPS

3.5.1 Introduction

As elaborated in Chapter 2 of the book, **M**achine **L**earning **Op**eration**S** (MLOps) is a practice and a methodology where DevOps – methodologies for constant updates of deployed software – are adapted to ML. MLOps could contribute to updating a deployed ML model to avoid the model being outdated by a statistical phenomenon known as concept drift. MLOps contributes to such an objective by having automatic pipelines that continuously train the ML model in a deployed setting.

The overall aim of section 3.5 is to address whether some of the identified data-related legal requirements in data protection law, the AI Act, and the

CRA could be implemented in the MLOps framework to contribute to compliance with these regulations.

The next subsections will especially focus on compliance with the purpose limitation principle, data minimisation and accuracy in data protection law, data governance requirements under the AI Act, and data poisoning detection of training data under cybersecurity regulation.

3.5.2 Implementing Data Protection Requirements in MLOps

The analysis of the data protection requirements during data collection and model training, especially focused on the legal basis relevant to AI system development and the purpose limitation principle.

While the MLOps framework could include regulatory requirements – and frequently more often includes regulatory requirements – the legal requirements under the GDPR still need to be analysed and concluded before the personal data is collected and processed. The potential for implementing legal and specific regulatory requirements in the MLOps framework will, therefore, be more pertinent for AI regulations and in other phases of the AI system development and lifecycle, for instance, during the inference stage, as will be the focus in Chapter 4.

A reason behind the difficulty of implementing and potentially automating compliance with some of the fundamental principles of the GDPR, e.g., the purpose limitation principle, is that some of the principles have more procedural than substantial or material content. For instance, through legal rigour in the data protection policy and written documentation, it is possible to comply with the purpose limitation principle without altering the processing operations. Therefore, one of the main principles elaborated above, the purpose limitation principle, does not have the potential to be implemented in MLOps through CI/CD/CT.

MLOps practices should still include references to the GDPR and data protection regulations. However, due to the case-by-case need for interpretation and the specifics of each AI project, the potential positive effects of such inclusion in MLOps through continuous training are not so evident in the data protection aspects related to data collection and processing during AI system development.

3.5.3 Implementing AI Act Requirements in MLOps

The current subsection will address whether the specific data governance requirements for high-risk AI systems – including requirements for data governance – could be implemented within the MLOps framework.

MLOps – as elaborated in Chapter 2 – is characterised by pipelines for continuous training for deployed ML models to avoid the ML model being outdated due to discrepancies between the data the ML model has been trained on and the data processed in the deployed ML model, referred to as concept drift.

A relevant question is whether continuous training within MLOps could be applied to comply with the data governance requirements for high-risk AI systems under the AI Act.

The data governance requirements in Article 10 of the AI Act especially focus on the training, validation, and testing of datasets that should meet specific quality criteria. Article 10 especially focuses on data governance practices appropriate for the intended purpose of the high-risk AI system. Such practices should include, among others, relevant data-preparation practices, formulation of assumptions, and examination in view of possible biases.

MLOps could – potentially – cater for a harmonised approach to data governance practices of high-risk AI systems under data collection, preprocessing, and model training of high-risk AI systems. By standardising and harmonising a common approach to data bias detection; identification of data gaps; formulation of assumptions; and practices of annotation, labelling, cleaning, updating, enriching, and aggregating the data used to develop high-risk AI systems, there is a potential for both more efficient compliance with the AI Act and to cross-fertilise and gain experience from different high-risk AI system projects.

MLOps is a concept in the developing phase, and standardisation and regulatory issues are becoming more and more relevant within MLOps. After the entry into force of the AI Act, one potential for more efficient compliance is to implement the specific regulatory requirements in the AI Act into the MLOps framework. It is worth noting that the inclusion of regulatory aspects in MLOps should not be viewed as a convenient solution to meet the requirements of the AI Act on paper, without actually implementing them within the AI systems in practice.

3.5.4 Implementing Cybersecurity Requirements in MLOps

One cybersecurity attack type relevant to data used to develop AI systems is the risk of data poisoning of the training data. One relevant question is whether MLOps practices could be applied to detect when adversaries attempt to poison the training data to lower the ML model's performance.

MLOps is a paradigm that comprises best practices. The practices intended to avoid and mitigate data poisoning attacks will relate most to practices on how data is stored and processed securely during model training and model deployment.

Zhang et al.[152] have presented security patterns for ML development. In their work, they present templates to lower attack vectors in ML model development to protect data in transit, rest, and during processing from – among other factors – data poisoning attacks.

These templates include methods for secure data collection; how to store such data securely, including managing access to the data used to train ML models; how to clean and label the training data without known security risks; and how to transmit the data between entities in the ML value chain without known security risks.[153]

With regard to cybersecurity threats during data collection for ML model training, potential mitigating measures could include authentication mechanisms to verify the data sources, a logging function to monitor the data, access control for the collected data, and a secure data transmission pattern if data is collected from sensors and physical devices. If data is collected from physical sensors, a potential mitigating measure against cybersecurity attacks could be to keep the devices in a protected and controlled area.[154]

In relation to the secure storage of the training data, mitigating measures include encryption and authentication mechanisms, access control, a secure data transmission pattern, and security logging with data version control.[155]

With regard to data cleaning and labelling, a known risk is data poisoning. A mitigating measure to counter the risk of data poisoning is a poisoned data filtering mechanism. Further mitigating measures specific to this phase include secure data storage, authentication, access control, security logging with version control, and data transmission patterns.[156]

The former paragraphs have exemplified that there are instances from the literature on mitigating measures to lower the related cybersecurity risks of data processing in ML model development. When the requirements in the CRA apply in the EU, the providers are required to assess such known risks and to implement relevant mitigating measures. The CRA is a part of the new legislative framework and will have several harmonised standards and technical standards, according to Article 18 of the CRA. A viable future approach is to implement such regulatory and technical mitigating measures in the MLOps framework.

---

152 Xinrui Zhang and Jason Jaskolka. "Security patterns for machine learning: The data-oriented stages". In: *Proceedings of the 27th European Conference on Pattern Languages of Programs*. New York: association for Computing Machinery, 2022, pp. 1–12. doi: https://doi.org/10.1145/3551902.3565070.

153 Ibid.

154 Ibid.

155 Ibid.

156 Ibid.

A trained ML model is only as accurate as the data it is trained on. If the model is trained on low-quality data, the model will also, most likely, have low quality in the form of the model's performance and accuracy, known as the garbage-in-garbage-out problem.[157] Developing a common MLOps framework where known cybersecurity attacks are mitigated to an acceptable level could contribute to both CRA compliance and more accurate ML models with a lower inherent risk of data poisoning.

3.6 SUMMARY

This chapter's most important findings are summarised as follows:

- The collection and processing of (personal) data for AI system development could enter the scope of data protection regulation, cybersecurity regulation, and the AI Act.
- Purpose limitation and data protection by design is part of the "essence" of Article 8 of the Charter, and the lack of such measures during AI model development could potentially be a violation of Article 8 of the Charter.
- Consent, performance of a contract, and legitimate interests are the most relevant legal bases for processing personal data for AI model development.
- Repurposing of personal data for AI system development requires that the new purpose is compatible with the original collection purpose, that the processor that repurposes gathers the consent of the original controller, and that the original controller informs the data subjects.
- Data poisoning of training data is a cybersecurity risk that is partially covered in the CRA.
- The data governance requirements under the AI Act, as well as relevant cybersecurity requirements for high-risk AI systems under the CRA, could potentially be included in the MLOps framework.

157 Monique F Kilkenny and Kerin M Robinson. "Data quality: 'Garbage in–garbage out.'" In: *Health Information Management Journal* 47.3 (2018), pp. 103–105. doi: https://doi.org/10.1177/1833358318774357.

4. The model component: accurate and secure inference

4.1 INTRODUCTION

The former chapter focused on compliance in the development phase of AI systems. This chapter focuses on relevant legal requirements under data protection regulation, cybersecurity regulation, and the AI Act for developed and deployed AI models applied to draw inferences. The current chapter is titled *The model component*, referring to a finished-trained and deployed AI model that is being used in an operational setting to draw inferences about natural persons. The overall focus of the chapter is on identifying specific legal requirements relevant to a deployed model within data protection regulation – the GDPR interpreted in line with the Charter – the CRA, and the AI Act. Specific relevant requirements for drawing inferences from a deployed AI model are analysed and identified under these three different rule sets. As in the former chapter, the overall objective of the current chapter is also to suggest a compliance by design approach for the identified legal requirements. Similarly to the previous chapter, this approach is presented by analysing whether some of the identified legal requirements could be implemented in the MLOps framework.

In order to place the legal analysis in a context, it is first necessary to recapitulate some details from the former chapter and provide some additional technical background information. Chapter 3 focused on data set collection and the training of an algorithm to develop a finished AI model. The collection and processing of the datasets applied for training would enter the scope of the GDPR if the data fulfils the definition of personal data. However, as elaborated in Chapter 3 (3.2.7.13), industry practices for collecting training data often include data scraping, where personal data and non-personal data are collected together by crawling the Internet.

The finished trained AI model also constitutes data and would qualify as "any information" under the definition of personal data in Article 4 (1) of the GDPR. This data is a representation of the trained model. For example, a trained ML model consists of a matrix of different numbers from the parameters of the internal structures of the model and the weights and parameters from the neurons and synapses, in the case of neural networks, of the model.[1] The model data would constitute personal data if it is possible to identify a natural person and such identification is a reasonable means; for instance, if the model leaks training data about a specific individual data subject.

The focus of the current chapter and the scope of the GDPR are related to personal data being processed in the finished trained and deployed AI model to draw inferences about data subjects; for instance, if an AI model is used to make predictions about a person as part of a decision-making process. The relevance of the GDPR – in the current context – is a result of personal data being processed in an AI model. This is because the input and output data of the model are linked to a natural person, and not specifically because the model was trained on personal data, as was highlighted in Chapter 3.

The sections of Chapter 4 are organised as follows:

Section 4.2 analyses specific relevant data protection regulation requirements for the processing of personal data in deployed AI models, including the fundamental principles of accuracy, purpose limitation, data minimisation, and requirements for individual automated decision-making producing legal or similar effects according to Article 22 of the GDPR.

In section 4.3, specific relevant requirements for deployed AI models in the CRA are identified and analysed.

Section 4.4 focuses on identifying requirements for deployed high-risk AI models in the AI Act, with a specific focus on the responsibilities of deployers and the relationship between requirements for deployed AI models and requirements for the design and development of the AI model.

Section 4.5 analyses the scope of the right to an explanation of individual decisions under Articles 13–15 of the GDPR and Article 86 (1) of the AI Act. These two different rights to an explanation are analysed together because they have close interrelations. The objective of the analysis is to establish the scope of the right to explanation under the rule sets. Building on the identified scopes, section 4.5 assesses various methods of explainable AI (XAI) to determine which XAI methods comply with the right to receive an explanation.

As in the former chapter, an objective of the current chapter is to assess whether some of the identified legal requirements could be implemented in MLOps both through the inclusion of regulatory requirements in the MLOps methodology and through CI/CD/CT, referring to Continuous Integration, Continuous Delivery, and Continuous Training (section 4.6).

Finally, section 4.7 summarises the overall findings of the chapter.

---

1 Christoph Molnar. *Interpretable Machine Learning*. Lulu.com, 2020.

4.2 THE MODEL COMPONENT AND DATA PROTECTION REGULATION

4.2.1 Introduction

The former chapter of the book analysed data protection requirements under the Charter and the GDPR when collecting training data, constituting personal data and processing personal data to develop and train an AI model. The focus in the next subsections will be on data protection regulation requirements, in the GDPR interpreted in light of the Charter, when personal data is processed in a deployed and finished trained AI model to draw inferences.

Chapter 3 analysed the lawfulness of personal data processing during training data collection and model training, and the principles of purpose limitation and data minimisation. Concerning the legal bases applied to process personal data in deployed AI models, some specific nuances might differentiate from dataset collection and model training to the inference stage. However, these nuances are of relatively small significance. For the sake of avoiding repeating the legal analysis of the legal basis for processing, the legal bases will not be analysed again in a deployed AI model context in the following sections.

The next sections will analyse the fundamental principle of accuracy, purpose limitation, and data minimisation when personal data is processed in deployed AI models (section 4.2.2). Section 4.2.3 analyses Article 22 of the GDPR (the right not to be subject to individual automated decision-making) and its significance for personal data processing in a deployed AI model. Article 22 is interpreted in line with a recent judgement from the CJEU in the Schufa Holding AG case.[2] Finally, section 4.2.4 summarises the findings of the chapter.

4.2.2 Fundamental Principles of Processing

4.2.2.1 Introduction

The subsequent paragraphs will analyse the fundamental principles of accuracy (4.2.2.2), purpose limitation (4.2.2.3), and data minimisation (4.2.2.4) when personal data is processed in deployed AI models.

4.2.2.2 Accuracy

A deployed AI model consists of an algorithm trained on training data that is used on previously unseen data to draw inferences. In a deployed setting,

---

2 Judgement of the Court (First Chamber) in Case C-634/21 OQ v Land Hessen and Schufa Holding AG ECLI:EU:C:2023:957.

the operational data is processed in the AI model and used to draw inferences or as the first part of an automated decision-making process. An AI model is an approximation of the statistical correlations in the training data, and the deployed AI model does not, therefore, have 100% accuracy when unseen data is processed.[3] The question analysed in the next paragraphs focuses on the material content of the fundamental principle of accuracy in the GDPR in a deployed AI model context. More specifically, the question analysed addresses how to achieve compliance with the principle of accuracy when processing personal data in a deployed AI model.

According to Article 5 (1) (d) of the GDPR, personal data shall be "accurate, and where necessary, kept up to date; every reasonable step must be taken to ensure that personal data that are inaccurate, having regard to the purposes for which they are processed, are erased or rectified without delay ('accuracy')". An equivalent to the principle of accuracy in the GDPR under the Charter is the subtest of suitability under the principle of proportionality. The relationship between secondary law in the GDPR and primary law under the Charter is further addressed in Chapter 6 of the book.

"Accuracy" is not defined in the recitals or the Articles of the GDPR. The principle of accuracy in data protection regulation has been described as a principle with little attention in the data protection scholarly field.[4] The relatively unexplored nature of the accuracy principle in the academic literature, combined with the possibility of testing and quantifying accuracy in AI models, makes the combination of the accuracy principle and processing of personal data in deployed AI models a timely subject of analysis.

It is a relatively straightforward task to identify and rectify inaccurate personal data when the data concerned is objectively incorrect and in a tabular

---

3 Ming Yin, Jennifer Wortman Vaughan, and Hanna Wallach. "Understanding the effect of accuracy on trust in machine learning models". In: *Proceedings of the 2019 Chi Conference on Human Factors in Computing Systems*. 2019, pp. 1–12. doi: https://doi.org/10.1145/3290605.3300509.

4 Diana Dimitrova. "The rise of the personal data quality principle. Is it legal and does it have an impact on the right to rectification?" In: *EJLT European Journal of Law and Technology* 12 (3 2021). doi: http://dx.doi.org/10.2139/ssrn.3790602; Elisabetta Biasin. "Why accuracy needs further exploration in data protection". In: *CAIP 2021: Proceedings of the 1st International Conference on AI for People: Towards Sustainable AI, CAIP 2021, 20–24 November 2021, Bologna, Italy*. European Alliance for Innovation. 2021, p. 96. doi: http://dx.doi.org/10.4108/eai.20-11-2021.2314205; Dara Hallinan and Frederik Zuiderveen Borgesius. "Opinions can be incorrect (in our opinion)! On data protection law's accuracy principle". In: *International Data Privacy Law* 10.1 (Jan. 2020), pp. 1–10. ISSN: 2044-3994. doi: 10.1093/idpl/ipz025. eprint: https://academic.oup.com/idpl/article-pdf/10/1/1/33151826/ipz025.pdf. url: https://doi.org/10.1093/idpl/ipz025.

form – e.g., a wrong name, age, or similar of a natural person – processed in a traditional software system. It is a more challenging task to identify and rectify an inaccurate inference from a deployed AI model. As elaborated in Chapter 3, personal data is defined in a broad manner in Article 4 (1) of the GDPR, interpreted in line with case law from the CJEU. This broad definition will make outputs of AI models personal data when the outputs are related to a natural person or, e.g., applied to draw inferences about a natural person. A diagnosis about a natural person inferred from a deployed AI system or a prediction of the value of a property will, for instance, be regarded as personal data as long as the property value relates to a natural person. In order to analyse the principle of accuracy in a deployed AI context, it is necessary to first consider the wording of Article 5 (1) (d) in line with the relevant recitals and other principles of the GDPR and to identify and analyse the relatively scarce legal literature concerning the accuracy principle.

The principle of accuracy is a part of Convention 108[5] Article 5 (d) and was included in the predecessor of the GDPR, the Data Protection Directive[6] Article 6 (1) (d). In addition to Article 5 (1) (d), the principle of accuracy is also mentioned in Articles 15 and 18 of the GDPR in relation to the data subjects' rights to rectification and the right to restriction of processing in Article 18 (1) (a) of the GDPR. According to recital 39 of the GDPR, the controller shall take "[e]very reasonable step" to ensure that "personal data which are inaccurate is rectified or deleted".

In legal literature, the accuracy principle has been described as a fundamental principle with a dual role.[7] First, the principle functions as a substantive norm requiring that personal data processed by controllers is correct, reliable, and updated. Second, the principle acts as a functional prerequisite for data subjects' rights, such as the right to rectification and the right to object to

---

5 Council of Europe. *Convention for the Protection of Individuals with Regard to the Automatic Processing of Individual Data, 28 January 1981, ETS 108.*

6 Directive 95/46/EC of the European Parliament and of the Council of 24 October 1995 on the protection of individuals with regard to the processing of personal data and of the free movement of such data [1995] OJ L 281/31.

7 Elisabetta Biasin. "Why accuracy needs further exploration in data protection". In: *CAIP 2021: Proceedings of the 1st International Conference on AI for People: Towards Sustainable AI, CAIP 2021, 20–24 November 2021, Bologna, Italy*. European Alliance for Innovation. 2021, p. 96. doi: http://dx.doi.org/10.4108/eai.20-11-2021.2314205; Dara Hallinan and Frederik Zuiderveen Borgesius. "Opinions can be incorrect (in our opinion)! On data protection law's accuracy principle". In: *International Data Privacy Law* 10.1 (Jan. 2020), pp. 1–10. ISSN: 2044-3994. doi: 10.1093/idpl/ipz025. eprint: https://academic.oup.com/idpl/article-pdf/10/1/1/33151826/ipz025.pdf. url: https://doi.org/10.1093/idpl/ipz025.

further processing of inaccurate personal data in Articles 15 and 18 of the GDPR.[8]

Legal literature also highlights the close interrelation between the principle of accuracy and other fundamental principles of processing in Article 5. This relationship can be illustrated with an example. Assume that inaccurate personal data is collected and further processed, and the processing operations culminate in the personal data being applied to make a decision concerning a data subject. In such a case, the principle of accuracy is not complied with by the controller processing the personal data. Moreover, such a processing operation – where clearly erroneous personal data is used to make a decision about a data subject – could also be described as unfair and thus in breach of the fairness principle in Article 5 (1) (a).

According to Article 5 (1) (d), personal data should be accurate "having regard to the purposes for which they are processed". The processing purpose is thus relevant when assessing whether the personal data should be rectified and erased, and the means necessary to be conducted by the controller in identifying inaccurate personal data.

As previously stated, the output of a deployed AI system could range from categories such as a prediction, a classification, or generated content. When such outputs fulfil the definition of personal data, it is not an easy task to classify outputs as binary correct or incorrect. Since the accuracy of personal data, especially outputs of AI systems, needs to be interpreted contextually and in line with the processing purpose, the terms under- and over-accuracy have been introduced in the literature.[9]

Under-accuracy occurs when the output from the AI system is not accurate enough for the data subject involved because the training data of the AI system differs too much from the operational data and the generated output. The outputs, therefore, lead to various adverse consequences for the data subject. Consider a case where a credit risk model is not trained on data concerning individual contractors or sole proprietors with varying paychecks from one month to another. In such an incident, the output of the AI system could be inaccurate since the data it has been trained on is not representative enough, an example of under-accuracy.[10]

Over-accuracy in a deployed AI model is when the model is trained on so much and so detailed data that the outputs potentially have adverse effects and consequences for the data subject. For instance, consider if a credit risk

---

8 Ibid.

9 Gloria González Fuster. "Inaccuracy as a privacy-enhancing tool". In: *Ethics and Information Technology* 12 (2010), pp. 87–95. doi: https://doi.org/10.1007/s10676-009-9212-z.

10 Ibid.

AI model is trained on so detailed and accurate data – e.g., all social media preferences from 10 years back – that the manoeuvre space of the data subject is limited. In such a case, the over-accuracy of the personal data potentially places the AI system in breach of both the purpose limitation and the data minimisation principle.[11]

The examples above illustrate the correlation between an AI system's accuracy and the principle of accuracy in data protection regulation. It is important to note that accuracy under the GDPR is not completely the same as the accuracy of an AI system, referring to the system's statistical accuracy. The latter refers to metrics on how the AI model performs on previously unseen data. If an AI model has a measured accuracy of 78%, the system classifies 78% of the test data correctly compared to the ground truth, i.e., the correct classification.

According to the principle of accuracy, accuracy is both contextual and dependent on the processing purpose. Hence, the statistical accuracy of an AI model does not need to reach 100% to comply with the principle. However, the controller needs to take reasonable steps to ensure that the AI system is accurate enough for its intended context and with regard to the purposes for which the personal data are processed. Since the controllers need to take reasonable measures to ensure that personal data that is inaccurate is rectified, one first step to achieve such rectification could be to disclose the statistical accuracy of the AI systems to their users and to mark the output of a statistical prediction from an AI system as a prediction and not a factually correct statement.

In order to further examine the relationship between the principle of accuracy and the statistical accuracy of a deployed AI system, consider a pet image AI system used to classify pictures of animals as either pets or wild animals. A measure of the AI system's accuracy is how many images are correctly classified out of all classified images. Such an accuracy measure could, however, be unreliable. Suppose that 70% of the images were images of pet animals. In such an instance, an AI system classifying every image as a pet would have 70% statistical accuracy. A measure of correct predictions in proportion to all predictions of the system is, thus, potentially misleading.

In order to have a more accurate measure of an AI system's performance, it is necessary to categorise its outputs as either false positives (an image classified as a pet that is actually a wild animal) or false negatives (an image classified as a wild animal that is actually an image of a pet).

The positive predictive value of an AI system is the proportion of positive identifications that are true positives. In other words, a measure of the number

[11] Ibid.

of cases identified as a positive (a pet in the example) that is a true positive.[12] If 80 out of 100 images classified as pets are indeed pets, the positive predictive value is 80%. In other words, when the AI image classifier classifies an image as a pet, it is correct 80% of the time.

Sensitivity is a measure of the number of cases that are positive (pets in the example) that are correctly classified.[13] If the data contains 10 pets out of 100 images, and the AI system classifies 7 images of the pet images correctly, the sensitivity is 7 out of 10, 70%. Sensitivity is an accuracy measure of how well the AI system classifies the pet images. When the sensitivity is 70%, the AI system correctly identifies 70% of the pet images.

Generally, there is a trade-off between the positive predictive value and the sensitivity, meaning that maximising positive predictive value might lead to fewer false positives but could result in more false negatives, potentially lowering sensitivity. Conversely, maximising sensitivity might increase the number of false positives, impacting the positive predictive value.[14] In other words, if the AI system is stricter in identifying images of pets, only classifying images that reach a certain threshold, the positive predictive value might increase due to fewer false positives. However, some of the photos of pets will be missed, reducing sensitivity. If more images of pets are classified as positive, if the AI system is more lenient, fewer pet images are missed, increasing the sensitivity. However, the positive predictive value might decrease due to more false-positive predictions.

When assessing the trade-off between the positive predictive value and the sensitivity of an AI system in the example above, it is relatively easy to find the ground truth, whether an image depicts a pet or a wild animal. However, the output of the AI system might be more difficult to test against ground truth in other instances because the classification is not a binary yes or no or due to the lack of high-quality test data.

For the purpose of determining acceptable statistical accuracy under the accuracy principle in the GDPR, it is important to assess the purpose of the deployed AI system and the potential negative effects the outputs could have on the data subject. Generally, it is associated with a higher risk for the data subject if the output is used, for instance, to diagnose or for triage in a hospital, compared to whether the output is applied to classify emails as spam or not.

---

12 Haiying Wang and Huiru Zheng. "Positive predictive value". In: *Encyclopedia of Systems Biology*. Ed. by Werner Dubitzky et al. New York: Springer, 2013, pp. 1723–1724. isbn: 978-1-4419-9863-7. doi: 10.1007/978-1-4419-9863-7_256. url: https://doi.org/10.1007/978-1-4419-9863-7_256.

13 Ibid.

14 Ibid.

In the current context, accuracy is addressed under the GDPR and the right to data protection in Article 8 of the Charter. It is, however, important to note that the principle of accuracy also has connections to the right to a private life under Article 8 of the ECHR. One example of this connection is the case Romet v. The Netherlands from the ECtHR.[15] The case concerned an applicant who had his driving licence stolen. After he reported the license stolen, the Dutch Road Transport Agency registered 1737 different motor vehicles in the applicant's name due to misuse of the driving license. Moreover, Dutch authorities issued several motor vehicle tax assessments and fines due to the various motor vehicles not being insured. The applicant was also held liable for damages caused by vehicles registered in his name. Dutch authorities refused to rectify or annul the incorrect vehicle registrations in the applicant's name. The applicant questioned these refusals to annul the registrations in the Dutch court system and eventually complained to the ECtHR.

The ECtHR held that the failure of the Dutch authorities to annul the driving license when it was reported stolen constituted an interference in Article 8 of the ECHR. The Court further held that the failure of the authorities to correct the 1737 incorrect vehicle registrations in the applicant's name constituted a violation of Article 8 of the ECHR. Failure to correct incorrect personal data might therefore also be a violation of the right to a private life under Article 8 of the ECHR, in addition to a violation of the right to data protection. The Romet v. The Netherlands case is an example that if CoE states do not have sufficient safeguards against erroneous personal data processed in a deployed AI model to draw an inference against natural persons, it might constitute a violation of Article 8 of the ECHR.

Chapter 3 elaborated on concept drift in deployed AI models. It is important to assess the accuracy of an AI system throughout the system's lifecycle since the operational data of the deployed AI system might change over time. The last subsection of Chapter 4 will address whether and how the accuracy principle could be complied with through the MLOps framework by detecting and mitigating concept drift.

To recapitulate, the accuracy principle under Article 5 (1) (d) of the GDPR is closely linked to the purpose limitation, data minimisation, and fairness principles. The accuracy of outputs of deployed AI models also has a connection to the right to a private life under Article 8 of the ECHR. The accuracy principle relates to the purpose of the processing and sets limits to the outputs of AI systems if the output relates to a natural person and fulfils the definition in Article 4 (1) of the GDPR. Moreover, the principle of accuracy also relates

---

15 Judgement of the Court (Third Section) 14 February 2012 App NO 7094/06 in the Case of Romet v The Netherlands.

to the suitability and proportionality *stricto sensu* subtests under the principle of proportionality in Article 52 of the Charter. Lower accuracy would, for instance, be part of the overall proportionality in the interference with the right to data protection. Lastly, it is important to recapitulate that the statistical accuracy of an AI system is not completely interchangeable with accuracy under the GDPR.

4.2.2.3 Purpose limitation in deployed AI models

Chapter 3 interpreted the purpose limitation principle in Article 5 of the GDPR in an AI model training context. The next paragraphs will interpret the principle of purpose limitation in the GDPR when personal data is processed in a deployed AI model.

The purpose limitation principle in Article 5 (1) (b) requires that personal data is processed for specific, explicit, and legitimate purposes. One risk in relation to the purpose limitation principle is that an AI model is trained and developed for a specific purpose and used for another purpose in a deployed context. For instance, consider if an AI model trained and developed to identify the risk of schizophrenia or other mental illnesses[16] is used by a recruiter for decision support. Other examples include if an AI model developed as a predictive policing tool for serious crimes is used to identify potential administrative offences such as minor tax evasion, or if an AI model developed to predict the correct dosage of medicines from various demographic parameters is used by a health insurer to predict and calculate an insurance premium.

In the examples above, personal data is processed in finished trained AI models to draw inferences in a manner not intended when developing the AI model. The next paragraphs will analyse such practices to assess whether they are aligned with the requirement that personal data should be processed for "legitimate" purposes in Article 5 (1) (b) of the GDPR. The requirement that the purpose of the processing needs to be legitimate is both a reference to the lawfulness requirement in the GDPR – i.e., that the processing needs to fulfil a legal basis – and a reference to legitimacy in a broader manner, i.e., a more comprehensive reference to the legal system as such.[17] In order to analyse compliance with the purpose limitation principle in deployed AI models further, it is necessary to distinguish between purpose limitation in deployed AI models

---

16 Alberto Parola et al. "Voice patterns in schizophrenia: A systematic review and Bayesian meta-analysis". In: *Schizophrenia Research* 216 (2020), pp. 24–40. doi: https://doi.org/10.1016/j.schres.2019.11.031.

17 Michèle Finck and Asia Biega. "Reviving purpose limitation and data minimisation in data-driven systems technology and regulation," in: *Techreg* (2021). doi: https://doi.org/10.26116/techreg.2021.004.

that have been developed for a specific purpose during the development process and general purpose AI models, also referred to as generative AI models.

When personal data is processed in a deployed AI model that is developed for an explicit purpose, the purpose limitation principle in Article 5 (1) (b) requires that the processing of personal data is specific (sufficiently precise), explicit, and in line with the data subjects reasonable expectations, according to Article 5 (1) (b) and recital 50 of the GDPR. In the examples in the introduction, where an AI model developed to detect mental illness in a clinical setting is applied in a recruitment context, the processing might contravene the data subjects' reasonable expectations and thus also the purpose limitation principle. It is not reasonable to expect, from the job applicants' perspective, that an AI model processes the data collected during a recruitment process to predict whether or not the applicant has or is at risk of having a mental illness. In such a situation, the principle of purpose limitation might be breached because the purpose of the finished trained AI model does not align with the reasonable expectations of the data subject, in line with the overall processing purpose. In other terms, the processing of personal data in an AI model to detect mental illness is not compatible with the overall processing purpose, recruitment, under Article 6 (4) GDPR.[18]

Furthermore, the processing of personal data in a deployed AI model needs to be legitimate, referring to both the lawfulness requirement under the GDPR and other examples of Union and member state law, such as criminal law, employment law, non-discrimination law, or intellectual property law.[19] In this regard, it is important to interpret the legitimacy requirement in line with case law from the CJEU and ECtHR about processing practices, e.g., case law about facial recognition technology.[20] As elaborated in Chapter 1 of the book, a solution in compliance with the GDPR but in breach of primary law or the ECHR could not be regarded as a compliance by design approach.

Moreover, it has to be analysed how to comply with the purpose limitation principle under Article 5 (1) (b) when processing personal data in deployed general-purpose AI models. Unlike the deployed AI models analysed in the former paragraph, general-purpose AI models are not necessarily developed

---

18 Ibid; Rainer Mühlhoff and Hannah Ruschemeier. "Updating purpose limitation for AI: A normative approach from law and philosophy". In: Available at SSRN 4711621 (2024).

19 Michèle Finck and Asia Biega. "Reviving purpose limitation and data minimisation in data-driven systems technology and regulation," in: *Techreg* (2021). doi: https://doi.org/10.26116/techreg.2021.004.

20 Glukhin v Russia, 4 July 2023 App No 11419/20 ECLI:CE:ECHR:2023:0704JUD001151920.

with a specific purpose in mind.[21] In Chapter 3, the granularity and specificity when defining the purpose of a general-purpose AI model in the development phase were analysed. As concluded in 3.2.8.2, purposes such as "the development of an AI system" might be specific enough, according to the French DPA, provided that both the "type" of AI system developed is defined by the controller and the intended technical functionalities and capabilities of the finished developed AI system are defined and communicated to the data subject.[22] However, when personal data is processed not to develop an AI system but to draw inferences in a deployed AI system, the purpose must, most likely, be specified and have more granularity than in the development phase.

When defining the purpose and deciding the level of specificity and granularity needed in a deployed AI model, it could be relevant to interpret the level of specificity in line with the objective of the purpose limitation principle. The main objectives of the purpose limitation principle are that the data subject should understand how and for what reasons their personal data is processed, the controller should define the purpose to ensure and bind themselves to the processing purpose, and supervisory authorities should be able to assess the compliance of the processing and whether the processing is in line with the specified and pre-defined purpose.[23] Therefore, e.g., processing purposes for deployed AI models such as "to provide, administrate, maintain, and/or analyse the [s]ervices" or "[t]o communicate with you"[24] are so vague, open-ended, and general that they do not fulfil the overall objectives of defining and specifying the purpose. Therefore, as a general conclusion, the processing purposes of deployed general-purpose AI models must be defined in a more specific manner than the examples above when used in an organisation to draw inferences about natural persons.

---

21 ICO. *Generative AI Second Call for Evidence: Purpose Limitation in the Generative AI Lifecycle*. url: https://ico.org.uk/about-the-ico/what-we-do/our-work-on-artificial-intelligence/generative-ai-second-call-for-evidence/. Last accessed: 01.08.2025.

22 CNIL. *Defining a purpose*. url: https://www.cnil.fr/en/defining-purpose. Last accessed: 01.08.2025.

23 ICO. *Generative AI Second Call for Evidence: Purpose Limitation in the Generative AI Lifecycle*. url: https://ico.org.uk/about-the-ico/what-we-do/our-work-on-artificial-intelligence/generative-ai-second-call-for-evidence/. Last accessed: 01.08.2025. Michèle Finck and Asia Biega. "Reviving purpose limitation and data minimisation in data-driven systems technology and regulation," in: *Techreg* (2021). doi: https://doi.org/10.26116/techreg.2021.004.

24 LLC OpenAI OpCO. *Privacy Policy*. url: https://openai.com/policies/privacy-policy. Last accessed: 26.08.2024.

To conclude, for AI models developed for a specific purpose, the requirement that a purpose must be legitimate could limit the processing of such AI models for other purposes than intended during the development phase, when the AI models are applied in a deployed setting. For general-purpose AI models, it is relevant to interpret the purpose limitation principle for deployed general-purpose AI models in line with the objective of the purpose limitation principle. The objective of the purpose limitation principle for the controller, data subject, and supervisory authorities is to understand how the processing is conducted and what consequences the processing of personal data could have. The specificity and granularity of the purpose of processing personal data in a deployed general-purpose AI model need to be defined in a manner that makes it possible to achieve these aims.

4.2.2.4 Data minimisation in deployed AI models

As also elaborated in Chapter 3, in relation to the processing of personal data in AI system development, the data minimisation principle is a necessary consequence of the purpose limitation principle. When personal data shall be processed for explicit and clearly defined purposes that need to be defined before collecting the personal data, it is a necessary consequence to only process personal data required in relation to the processing purpose, according to Article 5 (1) (c) of the GDPR. In order to adhere to the data minimisation principle, personal data cannot be collected and processed for the sole purpose of collecting personal data. Personal data processing constitutes a risk for the data subject. This risk relates, among other things, to potential misuse of the data, and the data minimisation principle aims to lower this inherent risk associated with personal data processing.

According to Article 25 (1) of the GDPR – titled "Data protection by design and by default" – the controller – both before the collection of the personal data and throughout the processing lifecycle – shall "implement appropriate technical and organisational measures (...) which are designed to implement data protection principle, such as *data minimisation*, in an effective manner (...)". Moreover, according to Article 25 (2), the controller shall implement appropriate technical and organisational measures to ensure that, by default, only personal data necessary for each specific purpose of the processing is processed. The data minimisation principle is explicitly mentioned as an example in Article 25 (1) concerning data protection by design and in Article 25 (2) in relation to data protection by default. A reason behind this exemplification is that data minimisation, in opposition to, e.g., the fairness or the purpose limitation principle, could be described as a principle with a more substantial, material, and technical character that might be more feasible to implement through technical measures.

The next paragraphs will analyse examples of technical measures to comply with the data minimisation principle when processing personal data to draw inferences in a deployed AI model.

According to Article 5 (1) (c), personal data shall be adequate, relevant, and limited to what is necessary for the processing purpose. The assessments of adequacy, relevance, and necessity are closely interrelated when personal data is processed in deployed AI models to draw inferences. The assessments of adequacy, relevance, and necessity are required to be conducted in a holistic manner on a case-by-case basis, and they cannot, therefore, be reduced to simple assessments of quantity and metrics of personal data.

Consider a scenario where a credit default model has been developed, but the dataset on which it was trained does not have a broad enough inclusion of the variety of data subjects in the real world. In such cases, the model may make predictions about an individual based on demographics that were not adequately represented in the training data. To ensure that the model provides relevant and accurate predictions about a natural person, it may be necessary to include more and additional data about that individual in the deployed model. This inclusion of more data will ensure an adequate and more relevant inference. Hence, relevance, adequacy, and necessity might deviate between different data subjects in a deployed AI model. This example also illustrates that the principle of accuracy and the data minimisation principle are closely related.

In Article 25 (1) of the GDPR, pseudonymisation is mentioned as one technical measure to implement the data minimisation principle. Pseudonymisation entails replacing identifiers with a pseudonym that is kept separately. For instance, to replace the name of a data subject with an alphanumerical code and to keep the additional information that attributes the alphanumeric code to the name separate and in a secure manner. Pseudonymised personal data is still regarded as personal data, according to the definition in Article 4 (5) of the GDPR. Even though pseudonymised data is still regarded as personal data, it is a technical means that potentially enhances the data minimisation principle because the inherent risk of the processing is reduced when the personal data undergoes pseudonymisation. The next paragraphs will address other technical measures that potentially have the same effect when personal data is processed in deployed AI models.

One approach similar to pseudonymisation that would lower the risk of personal data processing in deployed AI models is to make personal data less readable for natural persons. For instance, consider a deployed facial recognition system. Limiting the data processed in the deployed AI system from fully identifiable identifiers of natural persons to data only the model is dependent to identify a face – e.g., the biometric measures of a face – could potentially lower the inherent risk of the processing. The reason behind the potential decrease in this possible risk is that an eventual leak of the data processed in a model could not, in itself, identify a natural person. The biometric identifiers would still be regarded as personal data, but the risk would potentially be lower since the data is not identifiable for natural persons.[25]

Another technical means that could lower the risk of the processing of personal data and thereby also enhance the data minimisation principle in deployed AI models is to run the model locally and not on a centralised platform.[26] By keeping the personal data on a local device and not sharing it on a platform together with data of numerous other data subjects, the overall personal data processed in the deployed AI model is minimised. For instance, several commercial actors have started to run voice recognition ML models locally on the user's devices.[27] The processing would still need to comply with the GDPR, and the AI model would need to efficiently compute on a local device, but such a local processing operation could minimise the overall data processed and the risk of misuse of personal data in deployed AI models.

Federated learning (FL) is also an example of a potential technical means that could contribute to the data minimisation principle. The overall idea behind FL is to train a deployed AI model on various datasets by not sharing the training or deployed data between entities, but by sharing the partly trained model.[28] One of the participants in training or fine-tuning a deployed model trains or fine-tunes the model on their data, shares the trained or fine-tuned model with the other participants, uses their data to further develop the model, and then sends the model further on in the chain.

In a deployed setting, consider, for instance, a consortium of insurance providers that wants to develop an LLM-based predictor of whether an insurance claim is fraudulent.[29] The companies do not have enough data by themselves to fine-tune the LLM-based fraud detector and therefore want to collaborate

---

25 Information Commissioner's Office. *How Should We Assess Security and Data Minimisation in AI?* url: https://ico.org.uk/for-organisations/uk-gdpr-guidance-and-resources/artificial-intelligence/guidance-on-ai-and-data-protection/how-should-we-assess-security-and-data-minimisation-in-ai/. Last accessed: 01.08.2025.

26 Robin Staab et al. "From principle to practice: Vertical data minimization for machine learning". In: *arXiv preprint arXiv:2311.10500* (2023). doi: https://doi.org/10.48550/arXiv.2311.10500.

27 Apple Machine Learning Research. *Hey Siri: An On-Device DNN-Powered Voice Trigger for Apple's Personal Assistant.* url: https://machinelearning.apple.com/research/hey-siri. Last accessed: 01.08.2025.

28 Li Li et al. "A review of applications in federated learning". In: *Computers & Industrial Engineering* 149 (2020), p. 106854. doi: https://doi.org/10.1016/j.cie.2020.106854.

29 Medium. *Fraud Detection via LLM.* url: https://medium.com/@aevalone/fraud-detection-via-llm-9c88a6a9f0dc. Last accessed: 01.08.2025.

to fine-tune the model in an operational setting. The different collaborators do not want to share their customer data outside their organisation, for both data protection and trade secret concerns. The collaborators, therefore, train the LLM-based fraud detector on claims and share the partially fine-tuned model.

Even though raw data is not shared when utilising FL, experimental evaluations have revealed that it is possible that the parameters of the trained model could reveal information about the data the model has been trained on.[30] The sharing of a partially trained AI model between parties in FL will therefore still be regarded as the processing of personal data, given that the AI model has been trained on personal data, and it is possible to identify natural persons from the leaks. Nevertheless, FL might be a technical measure to comply with the data minimisation principle during both the development phase of an AI model and the deployment phase.

To summarise, in a deployed AI model setting, the data minimisation principle needs to be interpreted together with the other fundamental principles of processing – including the purpose limitation and accuracy principle – to process the relevant, adequate, and necessary personal data. Moreover, Articles 25 (1) and (2) require the controller to introduce technical and organisational measures to enhance the fundamental principles, where the data minimisation principle is explicitly mentioned. Such technical measures could be to pseudonymise the personal data, to make it readable and understandable for the AI models but not to natural persons, to process it locally and not on a centralised platform such as in the cloud, or to use Federated Learning (FL).

4.2.3 Automated Decision-Making, Profiling, and the Use of AI Systems

4.2.3.1 Introduction

Deployed AI models that process personal data often do so to draw inferences, and such inference is frequently applied as part of a decision-making process. Automated individual decision-making inhibits an inherent risk of discriminatory effects based on biases in the data, according to recital 71 of the GDPR. To reduce the inherent risk of negative effects from such biases, automated individual decision-making is regulated in Article 22 of the GDPR. According to Article 22 (1), "the data subject shall have the right not to be subject to a decision based solely on automated processing, including profiling, which

[30] David Enthoven and Zaid Al-Ars. "Fidel: Reconstructing private training samples from weight updates in federated learning". In: *2022 9th International Conference on Internet of Things: Systems, Management and Security (IOTSMS)*. New York: IEEE, 2022, pp. 1–8. doi: https://doi.org/10.1109/IOTSMS58070.2022.10062088.

produces legal effects concerning him or her or similarly significantly affects him or her".

Profiling is defined in Article 4 (4) of the GDPR as "any form of automated processing of personal data consisting of the use of personal data to evaluate certain personal aspects relating to a natural person, in particular, to analyse or predict aspects concerning that natural person's performance at work, economic situation, health, personal preferences, interests, reliability, behaviour, location or movements".

When the output from a deployed AI system is used as part of a decision-making process concerning natural persons – either a public decision such as profiling used to detect tax evasion or a private decision such as automatic loan assessments in a bank – Article 22 of the GDPR most likely enters into effect, provided that the processing of personal data enters the territorial and material scope of the regulation.

The next paragraphs will identify the legal requirements in Article 22 by analysing recent case law from the CJEU. After the scope of Article 22 (1) of the GDPR has been established, the exemptions under Article 22 (2) are put under scrutiny.

4.2.3.2 Article 22 of the GDPR interpreted in line with the Schufa Holding AG case

The overall scope of the GDPR concerns the automatic processing of personal data, according to Article 1 of the regulation. The scope of Article 22 of the regulation enters into force when such automatic processing is solely applied further to make a decision that produces a legal effect for a data subject or similarly significantly affects him or her. The rationale and the purpose of Article 22 of the GDPR are to ensure human dignity in automated decisions and to ensure that natural persons maintain the ultimate control over decisions that affect other natural persons.[31] The right also addresses the risk of errors and unfair discrimination from ML models and other forms of automated decision-making, according to recital 71.

Recital 71 of the GDPR lists credit scoring or e-recruitment as typical examples of such automated decisions. In European Data Protection Board (EDPB)–endorsed guidance from the predecessor of the EDPB, Working Party number 29 (WP29), another example is dynamic pricing of products, i.e., individual pricing of products in e-commerce, where the price decision is based solely on

---

[31] Lee A Bygrave. "Minding the machine v2. 0: The EU general data protection regulation and automated decision making". In: *Algorithmic Regulation*. Oxford: Oxford University Press, 2019, Forthcoming, University of Oslo Faculty of Law Research Paper No. 2019-01 (2019). doi: https://doi.org/10.1093/oso/9780198838494.003.0011.

automated processing of personal data and the price excludes certain people from buying the product.[32]

The decision must be based "solely" on the automated processing of personal data. Article 22, thus, regulates solely automated decisions, solely automated profiling, and solely automated decisions based on profiling. It is, therefore, not a prerequisite for the entry into force of Article 22 (1) that the individual decision is based on profiling.

Since the coming into effect of the GDPR, a scholarly debate and legal uncertainty have existed on whether Article 22 is a reactive right for the data subject or a proactive ban that the controller should implement. The CJEU's judgement of 7 December 2023 in the Schufa Holding AG case is – to some extent – settling this debate.[33] The judgement especially concerned the question of the requirement that the decision must be "solely" based on automated processing and the question of whether Article 22 is a right for the data subject or a prohibition for the controller.

The case concerned Schufa Holding AG, a private German credit scoring company that provided credit scores to financial institutions concerning third parties, particularly consumers, based on ML. These credit scores were further used by banks and financial institutions to either refuse or accept credit applications. A credit score is a prognosis on the probability of future economic behaviour of a natural person, for instance, the probability that the person will default on their credit. This score is based on certain characteristics of the person that place the person in a group. The group placement is based on an assumption that when assigning a person to a group with similar characteristics, similar behaviour to the behaviour of the majority of the group participants can be predicted, according to the Schufa judgement paragraph 14.

Schufa had contractual arrangements with various financial institutions where Schufa transmitted the credit score to the financial institutions, and the institutions decided whether or not to approve the credit applications. One natural person who got their credit application rejected requested an explanation and erasure of their personal data from Schufa. The case entered the German court system, and the question of whether or not Schufa was under the scope of Article 22 of the GDPR was referred to the CJEU by the German court. Schufa argued that they did not enter the scope of Article 22 because the Article concerned "solely" automated decisions and further argued that the decision (the approval or refusal of the credit application) was made by the

32 EDPB. *Guidelines on Automated Individual Decision-Making and Profiling for the Purposes of Regulation 2016/679 (wp251rev.01)*. url: https://ec.europa.eu/newsroom/article29/items/612053. Last accessed: 01.08.2025.

33 Judgement of the Court (First Chamber) in Case C-634/21 OQ v Land Hessen and Schufa Holding AG ECLI:EU:C:2023:957.

financial institution and not Schufa. The credit score, therefore, according to Schufa, merely acted as a prerequisite for the final decision and could not by itself be regarded as a decision.

The German court referred the question of whether a credit score could constitute a decision under Article 22 of the GDPR to the CJEU based on both a factual and a legal argument. As for the factual argument, although credit scores and probability values are simply a basis when deciding whether to approve or deny a credit application, such scores and probability values are often very influential in the credit application. The legal argument considered that the referring court had doubts whether the objectives of Article 22, especially the right to an explanation, would be circumvented if Article 22 were interpreted not to apply to the processing of personal data for credit scoring.

The CJEU interpreted Article 22 in a wide manner in line with the context and objective, and not solely the wording of the Article. The CJEU held that the applicability of Article 22 is dependent on (I) that there must be a decision, (II) that the decision must be based solely on the automated processing of personal data, and (III) that the decision must produce legal effects concerning the interested party or similarly significantly affect him or her.

A "decision" is not defined in the GDPR, but the CJEU interpreted the concept as capable of including a number of acts which may affect the data subject in many ways, and that concept is broad enough to encompass the result of calculating a person's creditworthiness. Moreover, the CJEU held that the processing of personal data to calculate a credit score would also fulfil the definition of profiling in the GDPR. The credit scoring would thus also enter the scope of Article 22 (1) since profiling is especially mentioned in the Article.

In relation to the third condition, that the decision must produce legal effect or similarly affect the data subject, the CJEU held that when a credit score is produced, the market standard is that the third party to whom the score is transmitted draws strongly on the value. An insufficient probability value, therefore, almost in all cases, leads to a refusal of a credit application. The CJEU concluded that when a credit score produced by a credit scoring company plays a determining role in the granting of credit, the establishment of that value must be qualified in itself as a decision producing a legal effect or producing a similarly significant factual effect for the data subject, under the scope of Article 22.

In accordance with the competence of the CJEU, the referring court must define the factual context of the question it is asking.[34] In the Schufa Holding

[34] Judgement of the Court (Second Chamber) of 13 July 2017 In Case C-76/16 Ingsteel spol. s r. o., Metrostav a.s. v Úrad pre verejné obstarávanie, ECLI:EU:C:2017:549 paragraph 50.

AG case, the referring court had defined the question as the financial institution "drawing strongly" on the credit score for its decision on the contractual relationship with the data subject. The understanding of "decision" under Article 22 (1) to include a preliminary basis conducted by another party than the controller making the decision is, therefore, only relevant where the initial profiling by another party has "a determining role" in the final decision.

In cases where a third party draws strongly on such automated decisions – the first initial decision, in this case, the credit score – would also be regarded as automated decision-making under the scope of Article 22. The Schufa Holding AG judgement also establishes that Article 22 is a proactive prohibition and not a right the data subject needs to invoke in order for the requirements to enter into effect.

The Schufa case entails that automated individual decisions producing legal effects or significantly affecting a data subject are prohibited, even without the data subject enforcing the prohibition. For controllers processing personal data in deployed AI systems, the understanding of Article 22 (1) in the Schufa Holding AG case would entail that more profiling conducted will be included in the scope of Article 22 than previously expected and that the controllers must map out if the profiling is used by third parties to make decisions. If so, the controllers need to rely on the derogations under Article 22 (2). Article 22 (2) establishes the exemptions from the prohibition, and the next paragraphs will analyse when such automated individual decisions are lawful under the GDPR.

4.2.3.3 Exemptions from the prohibition of individual automated decision-making producing legal or similar effect

According to Article 22 (2), the prohibition in Article 22 (1) does not apply if the individual automated decision is necessary for entering into, or the performance of, a contract between the data subject and a controller; if the individual automated decision is authorised by Union or member state law to which the controller is subject and which also lays down suitable measures; or if the individual automated decision is based on the data subjects' explicit consent.

In order to achieve a consistent level of data protection across the requirements of the GDPR, the requirement for explicit consent, the performance of a contract, and supplementary legal basis should be interpreted in line with how these conditions function in other requirements in the GDPR. Explicit consent should therefore be interpreted in line with how this condition is understood in Article 9 (1), the performance of a contract, should be understood in line with Article 6 (1) (b), and the supplementary legal basis should be clear and unambiguous, as the requirements under Article 6 (3) of the GDPR.

Special categories of personal data under Article 9 of the GDPR can only be processed under the data subject's explicit consent or if the processing is necessary for the substantial public interest on the basis of Union or member state law, according to Article 22 (4). Such processing of special categories of personal data for individual automated decision-making also requires suitable measures to safeguard the data subject's rights, freedoms, and legitimate interests, according to Article 22 (4).

Processing of personal data in an AI system that enters the scope of Article 22 is still processing of personal data under the scope of the remainder of the requirements of the GDPR. The processing, thus, needs to comply with the fundamental principles in Article 5, satisfy the conditions for a lawful legal basis in Article 6 (1), and the controller needs to demonstrate compliance with those principles, under the accountability principle in Article 5 (2) of the GDPR.

There are several examples from national DPAs of deployed AI systems breaching the prohibition on individual automated decision-making in Article 22 of the GDPR. One example where the Italian DPA concluded that an individual automated decision-making process was not in line with Article 22 relates to a food delivery platform.[35] A delivery platform offered delivery of food and other goods on an app. The DPA's inspection considered the processing of personal data of staff delivering the food and goods based on orders in the app. In essence, an automated individual decision-making system in the online platform decided whether or not drivers received new shifts. The input data in the deployed AI model included data on how quickly the drivers previously had accepted shifts, how fast they had delivered previous deliveries, and customer evaluations. The DPA held that the processing constituted individual automated decision-making within the scope of Article 22 and that the contract between the drivers and the online platform constituted a lawful exemption for the processing. However, the Italian DPA further held that the technical and organisational measures introduced to lower the risk of discriminatory effects for the data subjects were not sufficient. The controller had implemented periodical reviews to ensure the accuracy of the personal data. However, the DPA found that such reviews were not sufficient to lower the inherent risk of bias and discrimination with the individual automated decision-making procedure in the deployed AI model in the online delivery platform.[36]

As elaborated in the Italian delivery case, a controller processing personal data as part of an individual automated decision-making process is required

---

35 The Italian Data Protection Authority. *Garante per la protezione dei dati personali (Italy) – 9685994*. url: https://gdprhub.eu/index.php?title=Garante_per_la_protezione_dei_dati_personali_(Italy)_-_9685994. Last accessed: 01.08.2025.

36 The Italian Data Protection Authority. *Garante per la protezione dei dati personali (Italy) – 9685994*. url: https://gdprhub.eu/index.php?title=Garante_per_la_protezione_dei_dati_personali_(Italy)_-_9685994. Last accessed: 01.08.2025.

to implement appropriate and suitable measures to safeguard the data subjects' rights, freedoms, and legitimate interests, under Article 22 (3). Such suitable measures should, as a minimum requirement, include the right to obtain human intervention, to express the view of the data subject, and to contest the individual automated decision, according to Article 22 (3). Recital 71 of the GDPR lists the use of appropriate mathematical or statistical procedures for the profiling and the implementation of technical and organisational measures appropriate to ensure that the risk of errors is minimised, as examples of suitable measures.

The next paragraphs will address some other examples of technically suitable measures in a deployed AI system that enter the scope of Article 22.

The guidance from WP29, endorsed by the EDPB, lists examples of technical measures potentially constituting sufficient safeguards under Article 22.[37] These technical measures include:

- Regular quality assurance checks. Such checks should ensure that the deployed AI system does not discriminate against the data subjects it draws automated decisions about and that the data subjects are treated fairly.
- Algorithmic auditing. Such auditing processes should ensure that the AI models are performing as intended, that they have not developed concept drifts, and that the outputs are not erroneous.
- Third-party auditing. In cases where the individual automated decision has a high impact on the data subject's rights and freedoms, the algorithmic auditing could potentially be conducted by an independent third party to ensure impartiality.
- Contractual assurance for third-party AI models. Such assurance should include that the AI model has been sufficiently tested in the development phase by the AI system provider.
- Data minimisation.
- Anonymisation and pseudonymisation techniques.
- Mechanisms for human intervention and the possibility for contesting the decision.[38]

Natural persons subjected to an individual automated decision have the right to receive meaningful information about the logic involved, under Articles 13

[37] EDPB. *Guidelines on Automated Individual Decision-Making and Profiling for the Purposes of Regulation 2016/679 (wp251rev.01)*. url: https://ec.europa.eu/newsroom/article29/items/612053. Last accessed: 01.08.2025.

[38] EDPB. *Guidelines on Automated Individual Decision-Making and Profiling for the Purposes of Regulation 2016/679 (wp251rev.01)*. url: https://ec.europa.eu/newsroom/article29/items/612053. Last accessed: 01.08.2025.

(2) (f), 14 (2) (g), and 15 (1) (h). These requirements will be analysed together with the right to an explanation under the AI Act in section 4.5 of the book.

To summarise, individual automated decisions which have legal or similar effects on data subjects are prohibited in Article 22 (1) of the GDPR. The CJEU has interpreted "decisions" widely to also include profiling conducted by a third party that forms the basis of a decision made by another party. The prohibition has three exemptions in Article 22 (2), and the controller needs to implement additional safeguards to mitigate the negative effects and risks that such automated decisions have on the data subjects.

4.3 THE MODEL COMPONENT AND CYBERSECURITY REGULATION

4.3.1 Introduction

While the former sections have focused on data protection requirements for a deployed AI model, the next subsections will address some specific requirements for deployed AI models under the CRA.[39]

One of the overall objectives of the CRA is to set boundary conditions for the development of secure products with digital elements, and that manufacturers take security seriously throughout a product's lifecycle, according to recital 2 of the CRA. According to recital 1 to the CRA, the overall purpose of the regulation is to address the critical impact cyberattacks have on the Union economy, democracy, consumer safety, and health, address cyber resilience at the Union level, and improve the functioning of the internal market.

Since the CRA sets out boundaries for the lifecycle of a product with digital elements, the CRA is also relevant for deployed AI models. An AI system also enters the scope of the CRA if it is regarded as a product with digital elements. It is therefore relevant to identify and assess requirements for operational AI models under the CRA.

The next subsections will identify requirements for deployed high-risk AI systems under the CRA and analyse how common cybersecurity attacks on deployed AI models and other AI-specific cybersecurity vulnerabilities are addressed in the CRA.

[39] Regulation (EU) 2024/2847 of the European Parliament and of the Council of 23 October 2024 on horizontal cybersecurity requirements for products with digital elements and amending Regulations (EU) No 168/2013 and (EU) 2019/1020 and Directive (EU) 2020/1828 (Cyber Resilience Act) OJ/L 2024/2847.

4.3.2 Requirements for Deployed AI Models under the CRA

The CRA sets out objective-oriented and technology-neutral essential cybersecurity requirements for products with digital elements to apply horizontally for such products sold on the Union market, according to the CRA recital 8. The technology-neutral nature of such requirements entails that the requirements also apply to AI systems that are part of a product with digital elements.

The CRA intends to lower the inherent risk of digital products posing cybersecurity risks to organisations and individuals through essential requirements for such products. These essential requirements include the data-relevant requirement elaborated in subsection 3.4.4. The essential requirements are included in section 1 of Annex 1 of the CRA, according to Article 6 (1) of the CRA. These requirements include vulnerability management and handling management – i.e., requirements for deployed and operational digital products that either have an identified cybersecurity risk or where a cybersecurity attack occurs. The focus in the next paragraphs will be on cybersecurity requirements for handling cybersecurity risks and vulnerabilities of deployed AI models and operational high-risk AI systems under the scope of the CRA.

According to Article 12 of the CRA, products with digital elements classified as high-risk AI systems according to Article 6 of the AI Act should comply with the essential requirements for products with digital elements under the CRA. In the assessment of cybersecurity risks for products with digital elements that are also high-risk AI systems, the cyber resilience of such a system shall also be considered. The risk to cyber resilience should especially take into account the attempts by third parties to alter the use, behaviour, or performance of the AI system, including AI-specific vulnerabilities such as data poisoning or adversarial attacks or risk to fundamental rights, according to recital 51 to the CRA.

According to recital 51 to the CRA, risk to deployed high-risk AI systems should take into account AI-specific vulnerabilities to the AI system's cyber resilience, including risk to fundamental rights. What are some of the common attack vectors, i.e., a manner for an adversary to enter into a network or a software system, for deployed AI models, and how do they relate to the risk to fundamental rights?

A vulnerability is defined in the CRA Article 3 (40) as "a weakness, susceptibility or flaw of a product with digital elements that can be exploited by a cyber threat". The legal definition in the CRA closely resembles commonly used definitions in the security field, e.g., the definition of a cybersecurity vulnerability by the US-CERT Coordination Centre: as "a set of conditions or behaviours that allows the violation of an explicit or implicit security policy".[40]

AI-specific vulnerabilities for an operational AI model would be weaknesses in the AI model that can be exploited by an adversary. The major focus of the current scholarly field and systematic literature reviews is on cybersecurity vulnerability exposure during model training, referred to as data poisoning.[41] Mitigating measures for data poisoning attacks was the focus in Chapter 3, the focus of the current chapter is on AI-specific vulnerabilities and vulnerability management of deployed and operational AI models.

AI-specific vulnerabilities differ depending on how much access the adversarial attacker has to the AI model. When the adversary has full access to the AI model, the attack is easier than if the attacker has access to only its inputs and outputs.[42] In situations where the adversary has full access and can transfer the AI model to its environment and modify the internal components, both the attack surface and the potential negative consequences of the attack are more severe, compared to where the attacker has access to only the inputs and outputs of the AI model. However, there are examples of adversaries re-creating the model from input-output access and thereby creating a situation similar to an attacker with full access to the model.[43]

In order to analyse existing vulnerabilities within AI systems, one possible approach is to begin with examples of known attacks on deployed AI models.

---

40 Allen D Householder et al. *The Cert Guide to Coordinated Vulnerability Disclosure*. 2017. url: https://insights.sei.cmu.edu/documents/1945/2017_003_001_503340.pdf.

41 Jonathan M Spring et al. "On managing vulnerabilities in AI/ML systems". In: *Proceedings of the New Security Paradigms Workshop 2020*. 2020, pp. 111–126. doi: https://doi.org/10.1145/3442167.3442177; Battista Biggio and Fabio Roli. "Wild patterns: Ten years after the rise of adversarial machine learning". In: *Proceedings of the 2018 ACM SIGSAC Conference on Computer and Communications Security*. New York: Association for Computing Machinery, 2018, pp. 2154–2156. doi: https://doi.org/10.48550/arXiv.1712.03141; Nicolas Papernot et al. "Sok: Security and privacy in machine learning". In: *2018 IEEE European Symposium on Security and Privacy (EuroS&P)*. New York: IEEE, 2018, pp. 399–414. doi: 10.1109/EuroSP.2018.00035.

42 Jonathan M Spring et al. "On managing vulnerabilities in AI/ML systems". In: *Proceedings of the New Security Paradigms Workshop 2020*. 2020, pp. 111–126. doi: https://doi.org/10.1145/3442167.3442177.

43 Microsoft Learn. *Security Engineering Threat Modeling Aim*. url: https://learn.microsoft.com/en-us/security/engineering/threat-modeling-aiml. Last accessed: 26.08.2024.

In a systematic literature review, Kumar et al.[44] have identified different types of attacks on deployed AI models:

1. **Perturbation attack.** In a perturbation attack, adversaries change the input data of an AI model in order to get the desired output. The aim of the attacker is to attack the integrity of the deployed AI system in order to lower the performance of the system.

   Examples include manipulating pixels in an image recognition system to misclassify an image or manipulating text to get lower performance from a LLM. When a deployed self-learning model is fed with enough manipulated input data, the overall performance of the model will be lower over time. The adversary attacker does not need to misuse the AI system and does not need to illegally enter the AI system; the perturbation is done on the input data that is fed to the system.[45]

   Mitigation measures for perturbation attacks on deployed AI models include more adversarial training, i.e., including perturbation in the AI model training to make the model more robust.
2. **Poisoning attack.** Data poisoning attacks are often conducted on AI models in the training phase. However, also deployed AI models might have a risk of being subjected to data poisoning attacks. A targeted data poisoning attack might take place where the goal is to misclassify a specific data point for a deployed model.

   An example is when Microsoft launched the conversation chatbot Tay in 2016. The bot was able to communicate with Twitter users, and a portion of the live conversations was applied as feedback to train the chatbot further. Twitter users asked the bot to repeat inappropriate content, and after 16 hours of live use, the bot was generating such offensive content that Microsoft had to take it down.[46]

   Mitigating measures for data poisoning attacks in deployed AI models include various monitoring techniques to detect data poisoning and other anomalies, or to continuously train the deployed ML model to keep it updated.
3. **Model inversion attack.** In a model inversion attack, the adversary reconstructs the training data the AI model has been trained on from the output

---

44 Ram Shankar Siva Kumar et al. "Failure modes in machine learning systems". In: *arXiv preprint arXiv:1911.11034* (2019). doi: https://doi.org/10.48550/arXiv.1911.11034.

45 Ibid.

46 Tomáš Zemčık. "Failure of chatbot Tay was evil, ugliness and uselessness in its nature or do we judge it through cognitive shortcuts and biases?" In: *AI & Society* 36 (2021), pp. 361–367. doi: https://doi.org/10.1007/s00146-020-01053-4.

of a deployed model. The adversary attacker reconstructs the training data by training a separate ML model on the outputs, where the objective of the separate ML model is to infer the input from the output of the original model.

Examples of successful model inversion attacks include the reconstruction of faces from a facial recognition model[47] and patients' health data from an AI system used to guide medical treatments from the patient's genotype and background.[48] The attacker needs access to only the model output to perform a model inversion attack and does not need any specific privileged access.

Mitigating measures for model inversion attacks on deployed AI models include adding noise to the output to make it more difficult to infer information from the output, limiting the number of queries and inputs a user can submit to the model, adversarial training, and access control and authentication.

4. **Membership inference attack.** A membership inference attack is somewhat similar to a model inversion attack. However, in a membership inference attack, the objective of the attacker is to discover whether a specific data point, e.g., the name of a specific data subject, was part of the training dataset of the AI model or not.

   A membership inference attack is possible because a trained ML model – generally – performs better on the trained data than on unseen data, known as overfitting. Based on the confidence score a finished trained model gives on various data points, it is possible to build a separate ML model that infers whether a specific data point is part of the original training dataset or not.

   Mitigating measures for membership inversion attacks can include differential privacy, where noise is added to provide a theoretical privacy guarantee and to distil knowledge in the model, i.e., to distil the knowledge of a large ML model in a smaller model where it is difficult to infer sensitive data from.

---

47 Yuheng Zhang et al. "The secret revealer: Generative model-inversion attacks against deep neural networks". In: *Proceedings of the IEEE/CVF Conference on Computer Vision and Pattern Recognition*. 2020, pp. 253–261. doi: 10.1109/CVPR42600.2020.00033.

48 Matthew Fredrikson et al. "Privacy in pharmacogenetics: An end-to-end case study of personalized warfarin dosing". In: *23rd USENIX Security Symposium (USENIX Security 14)*. 2014, pp. 17–32. url: https://www.usenix.org/system/files/conference/usenixsecurity14/sec14-paper-fredrikson-privacy.pdf.

5. **Model stealing.** In model stealing or model extraction attacks, an adversary attacker re-creates the whole underlying AI model from the model's output.

   The attackers query the model and use the outputs from the queries to train a new model with the same underlying functionality as the original AI model.

   The motivation for a model-stealing attack could be to use the model either for the attacker's purposes or as a first step in a membership inference attack.

   Mitigation measures for model stealing attacks include limiting the number of queries from individual users or IP addresses.
6. **Reprogramming ML systems.** By specifically designing a specific prompt, query, or input for an AI model, a successful adversary might reprogram the AI model to perform a task that deviates from the original purpose of the AI system provider. One example of such an attack is when adversaries successfully retrieved training data from a LLM, including sensitive data and personal data, by having the model repeat the prompt several times and thereby detecting an unknown vulnerability.[49]
7. **Adversarial example in the physical domain.** This attack type includes changes to the physical domain to make the AI model misclassify or misinterpret inputs. Examples include adding stickers to a stop sign to make an image recognition model in a self-driving car in order to misinterpret the stop sign as another sign.[50]
8. **Malicious ML provider recovering training data.** The attack types include where the AI system provider of a deployed AI model is malicious and extracts the deployer's data from the deployed AI model.

In accordance with recital 51 to the CRA, the assessments of the AI-specific vulnerabilities should include an assessment of how they might affect fundamental rights. The most relevant fundamental rights in relation to the attack types elaborated above are the risk of interference with the right to private life in Article 7 of the Charter and the risk of interference with the fundamental right to data protection in Article 8 of the Charter. These interferences might take place in the attack types because personal data from the training datasets

[49] Milad Nasr et al. "Scalable extraction of training data from (production) language models". In: *arXiv preprint arXiv:2311.17035* (2023). doi: https://doi.org/10.48550/arXiv.2311.17035.

[50] Katherine R Garcia et al. "Drivers' understanding of artificial intelligence in automated driving systems: A study of a malicious stop sign". In: *Journal of Cognitive Engineering and Decision Making* 16.4 (2022), pp. 237–251. doi: https://doi.org/10.1177/15553434221117001.

is disclosed and breached. Potentially, the fundamental right to life might also be affected, e.g., in the stop sign example under point number 7 above.

According to the CRA Article 12, Annex 1 Section 1 and recital 51, the provider of a product with digital elements that is – at the same time – a high-risk AI system shall assess the risk to the cyber resilience of such a product, including AI-specific vulnerabilities. The examples of AI-specific vulnerabilities listed above are examples of risks to the cyber resilience of a high-risk AI system. According to sections 1 and 2 of Annex 1 to the CRA, the provider shall have essential cybersecurity requirements implemented. Moreover, the provider needs to have implemented vulnerability handling requirements within their organisation. Such vulnerability handling includes requirements to share and disclose information about a cyber incident that has taken place.

Annex I to the CRA does not give any specific guidance on how to manage identified vulnerabilities in a product with digital elements that are also a high-risk AI system. The CRA does not give any specific guidance on how to, e.g., handle a data poisoning attack or a membership inference attack on a deployed AI model. Specific guidance on such vulnerability handling will most likely be given in the harmonised standards and technical standards under Article 27 of the CRA. However, in order to prognosticate how such vulnerability handling of identified AI-specific vulnerabilities in deployed AI models could take place in the future, a natural starting point is in the technical literature.

One example of such literature on vulnerability handling of AI-specific cybersecurity vulnerabilities is the work of Spring et al.[51] The approach for vulnerability handling of deployed AI models of Spring et al. is to build on existing practices for vulnerability handling – Common Vulnerabilities and Exposures (CVE) Identifiers, CVE ID – and to implement the approach in the AI field on deployed AI models. CVE ID is a system for assigning a name and reference to common cybersecurity vulnerabilities. Identifying an attack and assigning it a CVE ID is a common approach in vulnerability management. Vulnerability management is a practice where a vulnerability or an exposure is identified and managed through a structured process consisting of phases: discovery, report intake, analysis, coordination, disclosure, and response.

With AI systems being more and more applied in various fields of society, the attack types described above and new, current unknown attack types will – most likely – be more and more common. The vulnerability management requirements under Annex 1 to the CRA and according to the harmonised standards under the CRA Article 27 will most likely build on existing methods

---

[51] Jonathan M Spring et al. "On managing vulnerabilities in AI/ML systems". In: *Proceedings of the New Security Paradigms Workshop 2020*. 2020, pp. 111–126. doi: https://doi.org/10.1145/3442167.3442177.

for vulnerability management. An important research path is to develop effective vulnerability-handling procedures for deployed AI models. Such procedures will – in all likelihood – build on existing procedures such as the phases of vulnerability management outlined above. Section 4.6 will return to how MLOps might potentially offer some common procedures for vulnerability management of deployed AI models.

To summarise, the CRA requires that providers of products with digital elements that are – simultaneously – a high-risk AI system under the AI Act identify specific risks to the cyber resilience of such AI systems. The current subsection has identified some AI-specific attack types on deployed AI models and also identified examples of how such AI-specific risk could be mitigated.

4.4 THE MODEL COMPONENT AND REQUIREMENTS IN THE AI ACT

4.4.1 Introduction

> Whilst risks related to AI systems can result from the way such systems are designed, risks can also stem from how such AI systems are used. Deployers of high-risk AI systems therefore play a critical role in ensuring that fundamental rights are protected, complementing the obligations of the provider when developing the AI system.
>
> (AI Act recital (93))

The quoted excerpt illustrates that while most of the requirements in the AI Act are put on providers of high-risk AI systems, several requirements in the AI Act are also imposed on deployers of deployed high-risk AI systems. The AI Act is an example of product safety regulation. By placing requirements on the users – deployers – of high-risk AI systems, the AI Act differs from more traditional product safety regulations. The Medical Device Regulation[52] or the Toys Safety Directive[53] does not contain requirements on how the products should be used, only how they should be produced. The next subsections will identify legal requirements for finished trained and deployed AI models under the AI Act. In order to move towards a compliance by design approach to the development and use of AI systems, it is first necessary to identify and interpret the relevant requirements for AI systems under the AI Act. This mapping exercise is a necessary prerequisite for the potential inclusion of the identified

---

[52] Regulation (EU) 2017/745 of the European Parliament and of the Council of 5 April 2017 on medical devices, amending Directive 2001/83/EC, Regulation (EC) No 178/2002 and Regulation (EC) No 1223/2009 and repealing Council Directives 90/385/EEC and 93/42/EEC [2017] OJ L 117/1.

[53] Directive 2009/48/EC of the European Parliament and of the Council of 18 June 2009 on the safety of toys [2009] OJ L 170/1.

legal requirements in the AI Act into the MLOps framework, which is the focus of section 4.6.

The definitions of the AI Act and the scope of the AI Act, including the scope of the requirements for high-risk AI systems, are elaborated in subsection 3.3.2 in Chapter 3 of the book. Similar to Chapter 3, the current chapter will also focus on high-risk AI systems, with some additional focus on legal requirements for deployed general-purpose AI models and general-purpose AI models with systemic risk. Before the requirements for deployed high-risk AI systems and general-purpose AI models can be elaborated, it is necessary to analyse the scope of the prohibited AI systems under the AI Act Article 5.

4.4.2 Prohibited Use of AI Systems under the AI Act

The AI Act inhibits a use-case-centric approach to AI systems, meaning that deployed high-risk AI models are regulated through their proposed use. A consequence of this use-case-centric approach is that the use of some deployed AI systems is prohibited, to place on the market, put into service, or use because their intended application poses too high a risk to the health and safety of natural persons and their fundamental rights. The following AI systems are prohibited from being deployed in the EU, according to Article 5 of the AI Act:

- The use of an AI system that "deploys subliminal techniques or deceptive techniques, with the objective of, or the effect of, materially distorting the behaviour of a person or a group of persons by appreciably impairing their ability to make an informed decision, thereby causing a person to take a decision that that person would not have taken in a manner that causes or is likely to cause that person, another person or group of persons significant harm", according to Article 5 (1) (a).

  Recital 28 of the AI Act elaborates that AI systems used for manipulative, exploitative, and social control practices are particularly harmful and contradict Union values of human dignity, freedom, equality, democracy, the rule of law, and fundamental rights in the Charter. Recital 29 exemplifies AI systems that nudge persons into decisions in a way that subverts or impairs their autonomy, decision-making, and free choices, as an example of prohibited AI systems under Article 5 (1) (a).

  The techniques employed by the AI system need to be "subliminal or deceptive", according to Article 5 (1) (a). Recital 29 lists audio, image, or video stimuli beyond human perception that subvert or impair natural persons in ways that people are not consciously aware of, as examples. Machine-brain interfaces and virtual reality (VR) are explicitly mentioned as examples in the recital.

The use of AI systems in lawful medical treatment or physical rehabilitation carried out in accordance with the applicable law and medical standards is not subject to the prohibition in Article 5 (1) (a), according to recital 29. Neither is – in itself – the use of AI systems for legitimate commercial practices, e.g., for the purpose of advertising.

The prohibition in Article 5 (1) (a) functions side by side with the prohibitions for unfair commercial practices leading to financial harm under Directive 2005/29/EC.[54]

It is hard to conceive how an AI system could be described as deploying "subliminal techniques or deceptive techniques, with the objective of, or the effect of, materially distorting the behaviour of a person or a group" without the AI system having been proven to have such an effect on natural persons. In other words, how could the market surveillance authority prove that an AI system will have such an effect without it being placed on the market first? When the prohibition of AI systems enters into force in the EU member states, one manner to enforce the prohibition is to remove existing systems already placed on the market producing such a manipulative effect or to review how AI systems of a similar nature function in jurisdictions outside the EU.

- The use of an AI system that exploits vulnerabilities of a person or a specific group of persons due to their age, disability, or a specific social or economic situation, with the objective, or the effect, of materially distorting the behaviour of that person or a person belonging to that group in a manner that causes or is reasonably likely to cause that person or another person significant harm, is prohibited in Article 5 (1) (b).

  Recital 29 of the AI Act contains a reference to Directive 2019/882 for the definition of disability.[55] The prohibition in Article 5 (1) (b) does not require intent from the AI system provider. The negative effects and harms of exploitative systems might be accumulated over time or be caused by factors outside the control of the provider or deployer, for instance, biases caused by proxies. An example of biases caused by proxies is when data in the dataset does not in itself relate to a social or economic situation

---

[54] Directive 2005/29/EC of the European Parliament and of the Council of 11 May 2005 concerning unfair business-to-consumer commercial practices in the internal market and amending Council Directive 84/450/EEC, Directives 97/7/EC, 98/27/EC and 2002/65/EC of the European Parliament and of the Council and Regulation (EC) No 2006/2004 of the European Parliament and of the Council ('Unfair Commercial Practices Directive') [2005] OJ L 149/22.

[55] Directive (EU) 2019/882 of the European Parliament and of the Council of 17 April 2019 on the accessibility requirements for products and services [2019] OJ L 151/70.

of a natural person, but the data might be a proxy for such a relation, for example, a zip code may represent specific aspects of a natural person's socioeconomic situation, leading to discrimination in a deployed AI system. The prohibition in Article 5 (1) (b) also enters into effect where the harm is caused by such an accumulated effect or due to external factors, according to recital 29.

- In Article 5 (1) (c), social scoring systems are prohibited from use in the EU. Deployed AI systems that evaluate or classify natural persons or groups of natural persons over a certain time based on their social behaviour or known, inferred, or predicted personal or personality characteristics are prohibited. The scope of the prohibition includes such systems that lead to detrimental or unfavourable treatment of certain people or whole groups in social contexts that are unrelated to the contexts in which the data was originally collected or generated. Moreover, the prohibition enters into effect when the social score causes detrimental or unfavourable treatment of certain natural persons or groups that is unjustified or disproportionate to their social behaviour or its gravity.

  According to recital 31 of the AI Act, social scoring practices are prohibited both for private and for public actors because of the potential discriminatory outcomes and exclusion of certain groups, and because data unrelated to the context in which it was originally generated or collected is used for detrimental treatment of natural persons or groups. The prohibition should not affect lawful evaluation practices of natural persons that are carried out for a specific purpose in accordance with Union or national law, according to recital 31.
- Article 5 (1) (d) prohibits the use of AI systems that make risk assessments of natural persons to assess the likelihood of a natural person committing a criminal offence. Such AI systems are prohibited from use when the input of the AI system consists of personality traits and characteristics that are profiled. The prohibition does not apply to the use of such AI systems for decision support when the system is used to support the human assessment of the involvement of a person in a criminal activity, which is already based on objective and verifiable facts directly linked to a criminal activity.

  In line with the presumption of innocence, recital 42 holds that natural persons should always be judged on their actual behaviour and not on outputs from AI systems based solely on profiling personality traits. However, an AI system producing risk assessments in a law enforcement context could be applied in the Union when the analytics is not based on the personality traits of individuals, according to recital 42. Recital 42 exemplifies such risk analytics systems as AI systems applied to assess the risk of financial fraud based on suspicious transactions and the localisation of illegal goods based on known trafficking routes.

- Article 5 (1) (e) contains a specific prohibition of AI systems, which is more linked to the data applied to develop the system. In the article, the placing on the market, the putting into service for this specific purpose, or the use of AI systems that create or expand facial recognition databases through the untargeted scraping of facial images from the Internet or CCTV footage.

  The prohibition of untargeted scraping of facial photos has several connections to the lawfulness of data scraping under the GDPR, elaborated in 3.2.7.13. One example of an AI system using facial recognition from untargeted scraping is Clearview AI.[56] The reasoning behind the prohibition is, according to recital 44, to avoid feelings of mass surveillance and to avoid "gross violations of fundamental rights, including the right to privacy".
- Under Article 5 (1) (f), AI systems used to "infer emotions" of a natural person in the area of workplace and educational institutions, except for the use for medical and safety reasons, are prohibited. "Emotions" are defined in recital 18 of the AI Act as feelings such as "happiness, sadness, anger, surprise, disgust, embarrassment, excitement, shame, contempt, satisfaction and amusement". Physical states, such as pain or fatigue, are not included in the notion of emotions, according to recital 18. An AI system used to detect fatigue or tiredness in safety-critical operations, such as for pilots or truck drivers, is, therefore, not included in the prohibition in Article 5 (1) (f).

  The reasoning behind the prohibition of the use of AI systems to infer emotions in the workplace or educational institutions is based on the uncertain scientific basis of inferring emotions, the cultural variety of emotions, and the potential for discriminatory outcomes of such AI systems, according to recital 44. The risk of such discrimination is especially evident in the field of workplace and education due to the imbalance of power between the entity using the system – in this context, an employer or an educational institution – and the natural person subjected to the emotion inferring AI system, according to recital 44.
- Article 5 (1) (g) prohibits the use of AI systems for biometric categorisation of natural persons based on their biometric data to deduce or infer their race, political opinions, trade union membership, religious or philosophical beliefs, and sex life or sexual orientation. The prohibition in Article 5 (1) (g) does not include any labelling or filtering of lawfully acquired biometric datasets, such as images, based on biometric data or categorising of biometric data in the area of law enforcement.

[56] Clearview AI. *Privacy policy.* url: https://www.clearview.ai/privacy-policy. Last accessed: 26.08.2024.

A biometric AI system used to infer the information above is processing both special categories of personal data under Article 9 of the GDPR in the form of biometric data and special categories of personal data in the form of the inferred outputs regarding race, political opinions, trade union membership, religious or philosophical beliefs, and sex life and sexual orientation. Even though such processing is prohibited under Article 9 (1) of the GDPR – with the exemptions in Article 9 (2) – Article 5 (1) (g) of the AI Act prohibits the use of the AI system, even in situations where one of the exemptions in Article 9 (2) of the GDPR for processing of special categories of personal data is fulfilled.

- Finally, Article 5 (1) (h) prohibits the use of "real-time" remote biometric identification systems in publicly accessible spaces for the purpose of law enforcement. "Real-time remote biometric identification system" is defined in Article 3 (42) as "a remote biometric system whereby the capturing of biometric data, the comparison and the identification all occur without a significant delay, comprising not only instant identification, but also limited short delays in order to avoid circumvention". An example of such an AI system is facial recognition systems in publicly available spaces, or similar systems to detect a natural person from sensors collecting audio, video, or other sensory inputs in real time.

The use of such systems is particularly intrusive to the rights and freedoms of concerned persons and could "evoke a feeling of constant surveillance and indirectly dissuade the exercise of the freedom of assembly and other fundamental rights", according to recital 32 to the AI Act. Moreover, if the AI systems have technical inaccuracies, the outputs of the deployed AI model could lead to biased results and discriminatory effects. Especially, such discriminatory results may be linked to age, ethnicity, race, sex, or disabilities. When the AI system operates in real time, the opportunity for corrections and audits is limited. The real-time operation of the AI system further increases the risk to the rights and freedoms of the persons subjected to real-time remote biometric identification systems.

The prohibition has several exemptions that will be identified in the following. When the real-time remote biometric AI system is used for specific substantial public interests, the importance of using the system outweighs the risk in a proportionality assessment conducted by the EU lawmaker *ex-ante* in the AI Act.

First, the prohibition does not apply if the use is strictly necessary for the targeted search of victims of abduction, trafficking, sexual exploitation of human beings, and searches for missing people, according to Article 5 (1) (h) (i).

Second, under Article 5 (1) (h) (ii), the use of real-time biometric identification systems for publicly accessible spaces for the purpose of law enforcement is not prohibited when it is strictly necessary for the prevention of a specific, substantial threat to life or physical safety of natural persons. Moreover, the prohibition does not cover the use of such real-time biometric identification systems when it is strictly necessary to prevent a genuine and present or a genuine or foreseeable threat of a terrorist attack. The wording "genuine and present or genuine or foreseeable" threat is somewhat similar to the conditions established by the CJEU for the lawful use of bulk surveillance capabilities of collected and stored metadata from electronic communications.[57]

Third, a real-time remote biometric identification system might be used to localise or identify a person suspected of having committed the specific criminal offences listed in the next paragraph. The use needs to be conducted as a part of a criminal investigation, prosecution, or execution of a criminal penalty, according to Article 5 (1) (h) (iii). Moreover, the specifically listed criminal offences need to be punishable with at least four years of a custodial sentence in member state law. The criminal offences, according to Annex II to the AI Act, are the following:

1. Terrorism.
2. Trafficking in human beings.
3. Sexual exploration of children and crimes related to child sexual abuse material.
4. Illicit trafficking of narcotics.
5. Illicit trafficking of weapons, munitions, or explosives.
6. Murder, grievous bodily injury.
7. Illicit trade in human organs or tissues.
8. Illicit trafficking in nuclear or radioactive materials.
9. Kidnapping, illegal restraint, or hostage-taking.
10. Crimes within the jurisdiction of the International Criminal Court (ICC).

[57] Judgement of the Court (Grand Chamber) of 6 October 2020 In Joined Cases C-511/18, C-512/18, and C-520/18, La Quadrature du Net (C-511/18 and C-512/18), French Data Network (C-511/18 and C-512/18), Fédération des fournisseurs d'accès à Internet associatifs (C-511/18 and C-512/18), Igwan.net (C-511/18) v Premier ministre (C-511/18 and C-512/18), Garde des Sceaux, ministre de la Justice (C-511/18 and C-512/18), Ministre de l'Intérieur (C-511/18), Ministre des Armées (C-511/18),ECLI:EU:C:2020:791; Judgement of the Court (Grand Chamber) of 21 December 2016 in Joined Cases C-203/15 and C-698/15, Tele2 Sverige AB (C-203/15) v Post- och telestyrelsen, and Secretary of State for the Home Department (C-698/15) v Tom Watson, Peter Brice, Geoffrey Lewis, ECLI:EU:C:2016:970.

11. Unlawful seizure of aircraft and ships.
12. Rape.
13. Environmental crime.
14. Organised or armed robbery.
15. Sabotage.
16. Participation in a criminal organisation involved in one or more of the offences listed in the list above.

The EU lawmaker recognises the criminal offences listed above as both offences that might justify the interference in various fundamental rights that the use of remote real-time identification systems would entail and offences where the use of such system could be a practical pursuit, meaning that a real-time remote biometric AI system might be useful to identify a person suspected of committing the various listed criminal offences.

Article 5 (1) (h) concerns real-time identification in publicly accessible spaces. Hence, the use by the police, border control, or customs of biometric systems to identify a natural person crossing a border or similar would not be under the scope of the prohibition, according to recital 33. The rationale behind this clarification in the recital is presumably that when a person is crossing a border, there is a reasonable expectation to be subject to surveillance and, thus, also remote biometric identification.

The use of the AI systems for the exemptions listed above would entail that the system is deployed; for instance, that the sensors such as cameras are in place and that the system is in standby mode and ready to identify an individual suspected of committing terrorism, kidnapping, or some of the other criminal offences listed. The use of the exemptions in the AI Act, therefore, carries a risk of the high level of protection of fundamental rights in the general prohibition being undermined. In order to avoid this effect, the exemptions would need to be interpreted restrictively. In accordance with recital 34, the use of remote biometric identification systems should only be deployed to confirm a targeted individual's identity and should be limited to what is strictly necessary concerning the time, personal scope, and geographical scope.

National law enforcement authorities need to conduct a fundamental rights impact assessment before the use of remote real-time biometric identification systems is deployed and are required to register the system in a database, according to Article 5 (2).

The relevant AI authority and national data protection authorities need to be notified after each use of the remote real-time AI system, according to Article 5 (4) and recital 36.

The use of a real-time AI system for biometric identification also needs to be authorised in member state law, according to Article 5 (5) and recital 36.

Moreover, according to Article 5 (3) and recital 35, such use should be subject to an express and specific authorisation by a judicial authority whose decision is binding for the member state prior to the use of the system with a view to identifying a person or persons. As an exception, under urgency, the law enforcement authority itself could authorise the use. In such situations, the law enforcement authority should seek authorisation from the judicial authority without undue delay and at the latest within 24 hours. If such an *ex-post* authorisation is rejected, the use of real-time biometric identification systems linked to that authorisation should cease with immediate effect and all the data related to such use should be discarded and deleted, according to Article 5 (3) and recital 35 of the AI Act.

According to Article 5 (3), no decision that produces an adverse effect on a person may be taken solely on the outputs of the "real-time" remote biometric identification system.

The use of a deployed real-time biometric identification system would entail the processing of biometric data. In a law enforcement context, the processing of biometric data is regarded as the processing of special categories of personal data, according to Article 10 of the Law Enforcement Directive (LED).[58] According to both Article 5 of the AI Act and recital 38, the exemption for the use of a real-time AI system for biometric identification under the AI Act is *lex specialis* of the processing of special categories of personal data. However, the AI Act does not provide a legal basis for such processing under the exemptions under Article 5. The legal basis under Article 8 of the Law Enforcement Directive, therefore, has to be included in national law in the member states, according to recital 38 of the AI Act.

Ireland and Denmark are not covered by the requirements in Article 5 (3)–(8) of the AI Act, according to recitals 40 and 41. These two countries, thus, do not need prior authorisation to use real-time remote biometric identification systems; they do not need to notify relevant authorities after the use, and Ireland and Denmark do not need to comply with some of the other procedural requirements for the use of such systems.

The overarching focus of the current chapter in the book is on the requirement for the use of AI models in a deployed context. The paragraphs above have analysed which AI systems are prohibited under the AI Act and the corresponding exemptions from the prohibitions. AI systems are dynamic and often

58 Directive (EU) 2016/680 of the European Parliament and of the Council of 27 April 2016 on the protection of natural persons with regard to the processing of personal data by competent authorities for the purposes of the prevention, investigation, detection or prosecution of criminal offences or the execution of criminal penalties, and on the free movement of such data, and repealing Council Framework Decision 2008/977/JHA [2016] OJ L 119/89.

evolve into new use cases or purposes. The regulatory approach of listing AI systems after purpose, where some purposes are prohibited, could be criticised for being static. The Commission, therefore, has competence under Article 112 of the AI Act to evaluate and review the listed prohibitions under Article 5 once a year and for a period of five years from the entry into force of the AI Act. If the Commission identifies a need for inclusion in the list of prohibited practices, it would need to reenter the legislative process with the European Parliament and the Council.

The next subsection will analyse requirements for deployed high-risk AI systems under the AI Act.

4.4.3 Requirements for Deployed High-Risk AI Systems

4.4.3.1 Important definitions

The AI Act contains requirements for providers, deployers, authorised representatives, importers, distributors, and product manufacturers. The focus in the next paragraphs is mainly on requirements for deployers of high-risk AI systems.

A deployer is defined in the AI Act as "any natural or legal person, public authority, agency or other body using an AI system under its authority except where the AI system is used in the course of a personal non-professional activity", according to the AI Act Article 3 (4).

Since the definition of deployer relates to the use of an AI system, the focus in the following will be on legal requirements for finished-trained and developed AI systems. Legal requirements for developing AI systems, including data governance requirements, are analysed in Chapter 3. The main focus of the current chapter will first be on high-risk AI systems. The scope of such systems is elaborated in subsection 3.3.2 in Chapter 3.

A high-risk AI system must comply with the requirements in Section 2 of the AI Act, according to Article 8 (1). Most of these requirements relate to data governance and the development phase of an AI system, covered in Chapter 3. However, some requirements are also relevant for a deployed AI system.

4.4.3.2 The deployer's role in the risk management and post-market monitoring system

Under Article 9 (1), a high-risk AI system shall have a corresponding risk management system. A risk management system not only relates to the operational phase of the system but also shall be established in the development phase and implemented and maintained under the entire lifecycle of the AI system, according to Article 9 (1) and (2) of the AI Act. Such a risk management system would require systematic review and updating, also during the deployment phase of the system. According to Article 9 (2), the risk management system should consist of a continuous iterative process focusing on the identification and analysis of known and foreseeable risks that the AI system can pose for the health, safety, and fundamental rights of natural persons. Moreover, the risk management system shall estimate and evaluate the risk that may emerge when the AI system is used for its intended purpose and under reasonably foreseeable misuse, and the adoption of targeted and appropriate risk management measures, according to Article 9 (2) (a–d). When identifying the appropriate risk management measures, the technical feasibility of eliminating or reducing the risk, the control measures addressing risks that cannot be eliminated, and information and training to the deployers are relevant, according to Article 9 (5) (a–c).

The relevance of risk management under Article 9 of the AI Act for deployed AI systems is best illustrated with an example. In order to give an example in the next paragraph, it is important to provide some clarification about the risk management system. First, it is important to keep in mind that the risk managed in the system is the risk to health and safety and adverse interferences with fundamental rights, according to Article 9 (1) interpreted in line with Article 9 (2) (a). The relevant risks under Article 9 are "only those which may be reasonably mitigated" or eliminated through the development or design of the high-risk AI system. The wording of Article 9 presupposes that risk identification and risk mitigation are conducted solely in the development phase. How should the deployer of an AI system that detects a risk while the system is in use react and potentially mitigate such a risk? Since the risk mitigation measures include the risks that might be mitigated through the development or design, one approach to mitigate such risks is to reenter the development phase when a risk is detected in a deployed AI system. Such reentry into the development phase is the essence of methodologies such as DevOps and MLOps. The applicability of such an approach could be illustrated in the following example.

Suppose that a high-risk AI system is deployed in the field of educational training to monitor and detect prohibited behaviour of students during tests and exams, under Annex III section 3 (d) of the AI Act. The AI system uses GPT-detecting technology[59] to monitor whether or not students have applied LLMs to write the text for them. In GPT-detector training, patterns of words are detected that are often used by LLMs, but not by humans. Suppose that the high-risk AI system has not taken into account that when LLMs are increasingly used by students, the detected word patterns can also be incorporated by human writers through the inspiration they receive from reading more and

[59] Eric Mitchell et al. "Detectgpt: Zero-shot machine-generated text detection using probability curvature". In: *International Conference on Machine Learning*. PMLR. 2023, pp. 24950–24962.

more GPT-generated text. Therefore, if the deployed AI system does not have these effects implemented through retraining of the deployed AI system, there is a risk of an increasing level of false positives. Such false positives could pose a risk to the fundamental rights of the students. A relevant question is how these risks could be mitigated when the AI system is deployed. First, according to Article 9 (4), the risk-mitigating measures should minimise the risk while achieving a balance in implementing the measures. Moreover, according to Article 9 (3), the risk shall concern only the risk that can be reasonably mitigated or eliminated through the development, design, or provision of adequate technical information. In the example above, if the deployer detects an increasing number of false positives, the deployer could either request the provider to retrain the AI model to include continuous training through MLOps (elaborated in section 4.6) or communicate to the natural persons using the system that there is an increasing risk of false positive outputs. The specific risk-mitigating measures in such a situation would be dependent on the specifics of the case under question and would need to be decided on a case-by-case basis.

Testing is an important part of the risk-management system under Article 9 of the AI Act. Testing is, however, frequently conducted in the development phase of an AI system. In situations where a developed AI system is intended to be deployed in a specific setting, the providers might test the AI systems in real-world conditions, under Article 9 (6). Such testing must take place before the high-risk AI system enters the market. Even though the testing in real-world conditions takes place before the high-risk AI system enters the market, real-world testing could be described as part of the deployment phase. Real-world testing shall be conducted to identify the most relevant risk management measures to ensure that the system performs consistently. When testing in real-world conditions, the provider needs to comply with the requirements in Article 60 of the AI Act. These requirements include drawing up a real-world testing plan that is submitted to the AI market surveillance authority, getting the testing plan approved by the market surveillance authority, and registering the real-world testing in a specific EU database. Moreover, the provider conducting real-world testing needs to be established in the Union or have appointed a legal representative established in the Union, and data can be transferred to third countries only where applicable and appropriate safeguards are implemented. Real-world testing can not last longer than necessary and in any case not longer than six months, vulnerable persons subjected to the real-world testing need to be appropriately protected, the deployers cooperating need to be informed about all aspects of the testing, the subjects of the testing need to give their informed consent to be subject to the real-world testing, the provider or prospective provider must effectively oversee the real-world testing, and, lastly, the predictions of the AI system under testing must have the possibility to be effectively reversed and disregarded, according to Article 60 (4) (a–k).

The risk management system under Article 9 (1) is closely related to the post-market monitoring system of deployed AI systems under Article 72 of the AI Act. According to Article 9 (2) (d), the risk management system shall comprise the evaluation of risks possibly arising based on the analysis of data gathered from the post-market monitoring system. The purpose of the post-market monitoring system is for the high-risk AI system provider to actively collect, document, and analyse relevant data, which may be provided by deployers or which may be collected by other sources. These data shall make it possible to assess the performance of high-risk AI systems throughout their lifetime and to evaluate the continuous compliance of AI systems, according to Article 72 (2). When high-risk AI systems interact with other AI systems, the post-market monitoring shall include an analysis of this interaction, where relevant.

Law enforcement is one area covered by the high-risk AI system definition in the AI Act. Operational data from high-risk AI systems used for law enforcement is regarded as very sensitive. If the confidentiality or integrity of such data is breached, it may cause severe risks to the fundamental rights of natural persons as well as risks of compromising ongoing law enforcement operations. The requirement for providers of high-risk AI systems to collect data in the post-market monitoring system does, therefore, not cover sensitive operational data, defined in Article 3 (38) as "operational data related to activities of prevention, detection, investigation or prosecution of criminal offences, the disclosure of which could jeopardise the integrity of criminal proceedings".

If the post-market monitoring system for high-risk AI systems detects a risk to health, safety, or fundamental rights of natural persons through the data collected in the deployed AI systems, the risk should be included in the risk management system in Article 9. What kind of risk could the post-marked monitoring system detect? One example is concept drift, where the data the AI model is trained on during the development process no longer matches the data in the deployed AI model. This aspect of post-market monitoring is mentioned in recital 155. In this recital, the importance of a post-market monitoring system is to "ensure that the possible risk emerging from AI systems which continue to 'learn' after being placed on the market or put into service can be more efficiently and timely addressed". The post-marked monitoring system is therefore especially important in covering concept drifts in the data and situations where the AI model continues to learn, and thereby potentially develops in a manner where it could pose a risk to health and safety and fundamental rights of natural persons, e.g., due to the model developing biases in a deployed setting.

The post-marked monitoring system for high-risk AI systems and the risk management system are also closely related to the requirement for record-keeping under Article 12. The obligation for record-keeping relates to both providers and deployers of high-risk AI systems. According to Article 12 (1), record-keeping is defined as the technical automatic recording of events ("logs") in an AI system's lifetime. The purpose of such logs is to ensure a level of traceability of the functioning of a high-risk AI system that is appropriate for the intended purpose. Moreover, according to Article 12 (2), the logging capabilities shall enable the identification of situations that may result in high-risk AI systems presenting a risk, to facilitate the post-market monitoring system under Article 72, and to facilitate the deployer's obligation to keep the logs under Article 26 (6) of the AI Act.

4.4.3.3 The deployer role in record-keeping and serious incident reporting

Under the AI Act, both providers and deployers of high-risk AI systems are required to keep logs of the processing of the system (record-keeping) and to report serious incidents to relevant authorities. The next paragraphs will analyse the requirements for record-keeping and serious incident reporting.

Record-keeping capabilities for high-risk AI systems used for biometric identification under Annex III point (1) (a) have specific requirements. According to Article 12 (3), such a high-risk AI system shall provide a recording of the period of each use of the system (start date and time and end date and time of each use), the reference database used for identifying a natural person by the biometric identification system, the input data that has led to a search match, and the identification of the natural person involved in the verification. The last requirement refers to the fact that, under Article 14 (5), the deployer of the high-risk AI system used for biometric identification needs to ensure that no action is taken by the deployer based on the identification resulting from the high-risk AI system unless the identification has been confirmed by at least two natural persons with the necessary competence, training, and authority. National member state law might provide a derogation from the verification requirement under Article 14 (5) for high-risk AI systems used for law enforcement, migration, or border control.

Post-market monitoring of deployed AI systems is closely linked to the requirement to report serious incidents to relevant authorities. When a provider or, if applicable, the deployer becomes aware that the deployed AI system has caused a serious incident – i.e., a malfunctioning of the AI system that directly or indirectly leads to the death of a person, serious harm to a person's health, a serious, and irreversible disruption of the management of critical infrastructure, the infringement of obligations under Union law intended to protect fundamental rights, or serious harm to property or the environment, according to Article 3 (49) (a–d) – the provider or the deployer needs to report it, according to Article 73. Such reports need to be made to the market surveillance authorities of the member states where the incident occurred, according to Article 73 (1). These types of serious incidents will most likely be detected either through the risk management system under Article 9 or through the post-market monitoring system under Article 72.

Article 73 further contains several procedural requirements for serious incident reporting, including deadlines for reporting, further reporting to other national authorities by the AI market surveillance authority, and requirements for the market surveillance authority to take appropriate measures to reduce the risk of further serious incidents in other deployed high-risk AI systems.

4.4.3.4 The deployer role in the requirement for human oversight

Human oversight is a key requirement for high-risk AI systems, according to Article 14 of the AI Act. The requirements for human oversight relate to both the development phase, where human oversight interfaces need to be included in the design of the system, and the deployment phase. The human oversight measures need to be developed in a manner commensurate with the risks identified in the risk management system.

These measures need to be built into the system by the provider or identified by the provider in the development phase and then implemented by the deployer in the deployed AI system. When the high-risk AI system is deployed and operational, the deployer needs to understand the capacities and limitations of the system. Only when understanding these capabilities and limitations, the deployer is able to detect anomalies, dysfunctions, and unexpected performance by the high-risk AI system.

Automatisation bias, i.e., the tendency to automatically rely on the output of an automated system without taking into account any contravening information, is especially relevant in AI systems.[60] In high-risk AI systems, such automation bias carries a risk to the health and safety of natural persons and their fundamental rights. The classification of an AI system as high risk entails that it is used in areas or as part of products where it is a high risk to health and safety and fundamental rights interference. Thus, automation bias is a concern in such deployed AI systems and in accordance with Article 14 (4) (b), the deployer needs to remain aware of the risk of automation bias, especially for high-risk AI systems used for decision support.

The deployer, or the natural person within the deployer responsible for the human oversight component of high-risk AI systems under Article 14, also needs to correctly interpret the output in accordance with any available

---

[60] Kathleen L Mosier and Linda J Skitka. "Automation use and automation bias". In: *Proceedings of the human factors and Ergonomics Society Annual Meeting*. Vol. 43. 3. SAGE Publications Sage CA: Los Angeles, CA. 1999, pp. 344–348. doi: https://doi.org/10.1177/154193129904300346.

interpretation tools and methods, to decide in which situations where the output or the high-risk AI system should not be applied or to override or reverse a specific output, and to intervene in the operation of the AI system if it is an unacceptable risk to health and safety and fundamental rights in the form of a stop button or a similar procedure, according to Article 14 (4) (a–e).

The idea of human oversight is also referred to as a human-in-the-loop, and has been part of the AI Act from the start of the process, the first proposal from the European Commission in April 2021. Article 14 of the AI Act requires human oversight of high-risk AI systems but has vague and ambiguous requirements for "who, how, and when", referring *who* within the deployer that should conduct the oversight, *how* this oversight should be conducted, and *when* in the lifecycle of an output from a high-risk AI system the human oversights should be conducted.[61]

Since the "who, how, and when" of human oversight under Article 14 of the AI Act has uncertain wording, the choices made by the high-risk AI system provider in designing the interpretability methods and the human-machine interface will have a significant impact. This impact could be illustrated with an example. Under Article 14 (1) of the AI Act, it is the responsibility of the provider to design the human-machine interfaces such that the natural persons in the deployer responsible for the human oversight could carry out their requirement for human oversight.

Suppose that the provider is developing a high-risk AI system intended to be used to make decisions affecting terms of work-related relationships, according to Annex III (4) (a). The system shall evaluate office workers' performance based on metrics such as how often they take breaks, how many cases they resolve in a given timeframe, and feedback from external end-users. Suppose that the providers design the human-machine interface on an aggregated group level and not on an individual output level. It is, thus, possible to understand the inner workings of the high-risk AI system, but not how an individual decision is made. In such a case, there is a risk that the human-machine interface could represent a false sense of control. Although the human-machine interface is supposed to be carried out by natural persons in the deployer during the deployment of a high-risk AI system, the human-in-the-loop of a deployed AI system is highly dependent on choices made by the provider in the development phase.

[61] Lena Enqvist. "'Human oversight' in the EU artificial intelligence act: What, when and by whom?" In: *Law, Innovation and Technology* 15.2 (2023), pp. 508–535. doi: 10.1080/17579961.2023.2245683.

4.4.3.5 Accuracy and cybersecurity in deployed high-risk AI systems

Cybersecurity risks, data breaches, and breaches of the security of the processing of personal data are – potentially – more likely to occur when a high-risk AI system is deployed, compared to the development phase. Article 15 (1) of the AI Act, therefore, requires that high-risk AI systems are to be developed with an appropriate level of accuracy, robustness, and cybersecurity and perform consistently with respect to these metrics throughout the high-risk AI systems' lifecycle.

Cybersecurity is a dynamic, changing, and evolving field. A secure practice, such as an encryption protocol or system in 2020, might be regarded as insecure today due to the detection of inherent zero-day vulnerabilities or the development of cyberattacks and intrusion methods. Hence, the technical aspects of how to measure the appropriate level of cybersecurity, robustness, and accuracy could be difficult to implement in a regulation. The technical measurements and metrics should therefore be developed by the Commission in cooperation with relevant stakeholders, according to Article 15 (2).

How should the deployer of a high-risk AI system assess and mitigate risks related to accuracy, cybersecurity, and robustness? Article 15 supposes that a cybersecurity incident, data breach, or other accuracy incident will occur. Therefore, high-risk AI systems need to be developed as resilient as possible for inconsistencies that may occur when the system is deployed. Such resilience could be reached through implementing technical means in the systems themselves, but also through drafting instructions for use and drawing up backup and fail-safe plans to guide the process when an inconsistency occurs, according to Article 15 (4) of the AI Act.

A feedback loop is a situation where the outputs from the AI system are fed into the system as input. When a high-risk AI system continues to learn after being deployed, there is a risk of potential biases in the data reinforcing themselves through the output being used as input for future operations. Article 15 (4) requires that the provider develop high-risk AI systems in a manner where such a risk is reduced or eliminated as far as possible with appropriate mitigating measures.

The deployer has a role in reducing the risk of negative consequences of cybersecurity, robustness, and accuracy inconsistencies. This role includes acting in accordance with the instructions for use from the provider as well as following the instructions in the drawn-up backup and fail-safe plans when an inconsistency, cybersecurity breach, or robustness flaw is detected.

4.4.3.6 The provider–deployer relationship and responsibilities in deployed high-risk AI systems

As indicated above, many of the requirements for high-risk AI systems in the AI Act pertain to the provider of the system in the development phase.

Testing, risk management, quality management, and procedural requirements, such as including the system in a database and affixing the CE mark, must be conducted before the high-risk AI system enters the market. The main focus of the current chapter is on high-risk AI systems that have been developed and deployed in an operational setting. The next paragraphs will address the provider-deployer relationship for such AI systems, relating to which requirements the provider has to comply with and the requirements that the deployer needs to adhere to.

The relationship between the provider and the deployer can often be a dynamic relationship where the provider initially deploys a high-risk AI system and then gradually gives the deployer more and more control before the deployer assumes overall control over the high-risk AI system towards the end of the development process. The requirement for automatic logs and record-keeping of the high-risk system is a requirement regardless of whether the provider or deployer has assumed control over the high-risk AI system. Under Article 16 (1) (e), the provider is responsible for the logs and the requirement for record-keeping under Article 19 when the high-risk AI system is deployed under the provider's control. In addition to the automatic logs, the providers are required to keep technical documentation and other specific documentation mentioned for 10 years after the high-risk AI system has been placed on the market, according to Article 18 (1) of the AI Act.

Under Article 16 (1) (j) of the AI Act, providers of high-risk AI systems shall also take necessary corrective actions and provide information as required under Article 20. Article 20 of the AI Act concerns the responsibilities of providers that have placed a high-risk AI system on the market – i.e., a deployed high-risk AI system – and have reason to consider that the deployed system is not in conformity with the requirements for high-risk AI systems. When a provider has such a suspicion, the provider must bring the system into conformity, withdraw it, disable it, or recall it, according to Article 20 (1). Moreover, when the provider of a deployed high-risk AI system becomes aware of the high-risk AI system presenting a risk, the provider shall investigate the cause of the risk in collaboration with the deployer, inform the market surveillance authority in the member state, and, where applicable, also notify any relevant certification bodies under Article 44 of the AI Act, according to Article 20 (2).

Some specific procedural requirements for providers for deployed high-risk AI systems and cooperation with competent member state authorities, and requirements to appoint authority representatives for providers established in third countries are regulated in Articles 21 and 22 of the AI Act.

The responsibility for deployers of high-risk AI systems is regulated in Article 26 of the AI Act. The deployers are responsible for ensuring that they use the system in accordance with the instructions for use from the provider, assign human oversight to natural persons in accordance with Article 12, and ensure that the input data is relevant and sufficiently representative. Article 25 regulates the situations where the deployers themselves assume responsibility as providers. If the deployers put their name or trademark on a high-risk AI system already on the market in breach of contractual arrangements, the deployer itself assumes responsibility as the provider. Moreover, the deployer assumes responsibility as a provider if they make a substantial modification to the high-risk AI system or if they modify the intended purpose of an AI system in such a way that a system initially not developed as a high-risk AI system becomes a high-risk AI system.

A specific requirement for deployers of some high-risk AI systems is the requirement for a fundamental right impact assessment under Article 27. As elaborated in Chapter 3 and further elaborated in Chapter 6, Article 8 of the Charter has a horizontal scope, meaning that it can be invoked internally between private parties, and not just vertically between a natural person and the contracting state. The fundamental right impact assessment is a necessary prerequisite to ensure an acceptable level of fundamental rights impact. The requirement to assess the fundamental rights impact *ex-ante* makes the protection of fundamental rights more proactive. The requirement to conduct a fundamental rights impact assessment is placed on deployers that are governed by public law, private entities providing public services, and deployers of high-risk AI systems intended to be used to assess the creditworthiness of natural persons and uses for risk assessment and pricing of life and health insurance offered to natural persons, according to the AI Act Article 27 (1) and Annex III (5) (b) and (c). The fundamental rights impact assessment shall, as a minimum, include the following components, according to Article 27 (1):

- A description of the processes that the high-risk AI system will be used for, and how the AI system will be used for its intended purpose.
- A description of the time period of the use of the deployed AI system, including the frequency of use.
- The categories of natural persons and groups affected by the use of the high-risk AI system in its intended context of use.
- The risk of harm to these categories of natural persons.
- A description of the human rights oversight measures implemented.
- The planned measures taken when such risks materialise, for instance, governance mechanisms and the possibility of complaining.

A fundamental rights impact assessment shares some similarities with a Data Protection Impact Assessment (DPIA). According to Article 27 (4) of the AI Act, a DPIA under the GDPR or the LED could complement a fundamental rights impact assessment. A DPIA and a fundamental rights impact assessment differ, however, in one core aspect. A fundamental right impact assessment under Article 27 of the AI Act shall include the planned measures when a risk to a fundamental right materialises. A DPIA, however, shall include "the measures envisaged to address the risks, including safeguards, security measures and mechanisms to ensure the protection of personal data and to demonstrate compliance with this Regulation taking into account the rights and legitimate interests of data subjects and other persons concerned", according to Article 35 (7) (d) of the GDPR.

The impact assessment under the AI Act has the character of presupposing that a risk to a right will occur and shall contain the measures when such a risk occurs, while a DPIA shall include safeguards to address the risk to an acceptable level. The risk assessment of the AI Act could be described as a plan for when the risks to fundamental rights emerge, while the DPIA has more of the character of planning how to address the risks before they emerge. The relationship between the DPIA and the fundamental rights impact assessment will, most likely, be further clarified once the AI Act enters into effect and the template from the AI office referred to in Article 27 (5) of the AI Act for impact assessments becomes available.

As a general conclusion on the requirements for deployed high-risk AI systems, the most substantial and material requirements are allocated to providers in the development phase. However, there are some relevant requirements for deployed high-risk AI systems, including post-market monitoring, record-keeping, risk management, serious incident reporting, and the requirement to conduct fundamental rights impact assessments before using some specific high-risk AI systems.

4.4.3.7 Requirements for deployed general-purpose AI models and general-purpose AI models with systemic risk

Overall, the most comprehensive requirements for deployed AI systems in the AI Act are put on high-risk AI systems. The AI Act was first proposed by the European Commission in April 2021. At that time, general-purpose AI models were not commonly deployed. At the end of 2022, ChatGPT and other commercial pre-trained transformer models became publicly available.[62] To ensure that these general – and not purpose-specific – AI models were not left unregulated, the EU legislator included requirements for general-purpose AI models and general-purpose AI models with systemic risk in the AI Act. The next paragraphs will define the scope of these requirements and analyse the legal requirements for general-purpose AI models and general-purpose AI models with systemic risk.

---

62 OpenAI. *ChatGPT.* url: https://chat.openai.com/. Last accessed: 01.08.2025.

General-purpose AI models are regulated in Chapter V of the AI Act. General-purpose AI models are defined in Article 3 (63) as "an AI model, including where such an AI model is trained with a large amount of data using self-supervision at scale, that displays significant generality and is capable of competently performing a wide range of distinct tasks regardless of the way the model is placed on the market and that can be integrated into a variety of downstream systems or applications". The definition does not include general-purpose AI modes used for research before the models are placed on the market.

General-purpose AI models with systemic risks are the subject of most of the requirements for general-purpose AI models. Systemic risk is defined in Article 3 (65) as a risk specific to the general-purpose AI model that is "having a significant impact on the Union market due to their reach, or due to actual or reasonably foreseeable effects on public health, safety, public security, fundamental rights, or society as a whole, that can be propagated at scale across the value chain".

The classification of a general-purpose AI model with systemic risk – according to Article 51 of the AI Act – is an assessment of the impact capabilities of the AI system. A general-purpose AI model needs to have high-impact capabilities to be defined as a general-purpose AI model with systemic risk. High-impact capabilities are defined in Article 3 (64) as "capabilities that match or exceed the capabilities recorded in the most advanced general-purpose AI models". Under Article 51 (1) (a), the high-impact capabilities need to be evaluated on the basis of appropriate technical tools and methodologies, such as indicators and benchmarks. The benchmark and indicators are further elaborated in Annex XIII to the AI Act and in delegated acts adopted by the Commission. If the cumulative amount of computation used for the training of the general-purpose AI model measured in FLOPs is greater than 10^{25}, there is a presumption of high-impact capabilities and thus also a systemic risk, according to Article 51 (2). FLOPs – Floating Point Operations – is a measure of the processing speed and capability of the AI algorithm and model.[63]

When a provider develops a general-purpose AI model and has reason to believe that it might be a general-purpose AI model with systemic risk, e.g., because the cumulative amount of computation used for the training of the general-purpose AI model measured in FLOPs is greater than 10^{25}, the provider has an obligation to inform the Commission under Article 52 (2). The providers of a general-purpose AI model need to comply with the obligations

63 Knowledge Base. *Understand measures of supercomputer performance and storage system capacity.* url: https://kb.iu.edu/d/apeq. Last accessed: 01.08.2025. Jeff Johnson. "Rethinking floating point for deep learning". In: *arXiv preprint arXiv:1811.01721* (2018). doi: https://doi.org/10.48550/arXiv.1811.01721.

in Article 53 (1). These include technical documentation, information to the deployers that shall enable the deployers to understand the capabilities of the general-purpose AI model, put in place a policy to comply with copyright law, and disclose the data used to train the model in a specific template, according to Article 53 (1) (a–d).

Providers of general-purpose AI models with systemic risk shall comply with the obligations in the former paragraph and the requirements in Article 55 (1). These requirements include model evaluation in accordance with a standardised state-of-the-art evaluation tool, adversarial testing, assessing and mitigating possible systemic risk at a Union level, reporting serious incidents to the AI office and national authorities, and ensuring an adequate level of cybersecurity protection, under Article 55 (1) (a–d).

To summarise, general-purpose AI models, such as LLMs, were released to the public in the middle of the legislative process of the AI Act. The requirements for these models were, therefore, not included from the start and were implemented mid-process. The requirements for general-purpose AI models may not seem that strict, and, at first glance, they may seem ineffective in reducing the risk to health and safety and fundamental rights. However, these requirements must be viewed holistically in relation to the requirements for high-risk AI models. The requirements elaborated above require specific measures only for the general-purpose model. When such a general model is used for a high-risk purpose, the requirements for general-purpose AI models and high-risk AI models must be complied with concurrently.

The next section will progress from analysing the requirements that the deployers need to comply with when using a deployed AI model to analysing the right to an explanation of a decision inferred by the use of an AI system under the GDPR and the AI Act.

4.5 RIGHT TO AN EXPLANATION OF A DECISION FROM A DEPLOYED AI SYSTEM

4.5.1 Introduction

Imagine these two scenarios: You receive a warning that your current employment contract is going to be terminated due to poor work performance, or you get a notification from the tax authority that they will be conducting a manual inspection of your tax returns for the last 10 years. A natural response to either of these two notifications is to ask: Why? In both scenarios, the majority of people would most likely view it as unacceptable to receive a response that only states that an AI system recommended terminating the contract and manually reviewing the tax returns.[64]

The next subsections will analyse whether the affected data subject has a right to receive a meaningful explanation in scenarios such as the two scenarios above, where a deployed AI system has inferred a decision about a natural person. Both the right to an explanation of individual automated decision-making under the GDPR (in subsection 4.5.2) and the right to an explanation of individual decision-making under the AI Act (in subsection 4.5.3) are analysed. These two different rights to an explanation are analysed together because the right to an explanation under these two rule sets has close interrelations. The objective of the legal analyses is to establish the scope of the right to explanation under the different rule sets. In the next section, building on the identified scopes of the right to an explanation under the GDPR and the AI Act, various XAI methods are assessed in order to determine which of these methods could be implemented in the AI systems to comply with the right to explanation under the GDPR and the AI Act (in subsection 4.5.4). Lastly, subsection 4.5.5 summarises the overall findings of section 4.5.

4.5.2 The Right to an Explanation of Automated Decision-Making under the GDPR

The right to an explanation of automated decision-making in the GDPR presupposes that the overall scope of the GDPR – the territorial and material scope – enters into effect and that processing falls under the scope of Article 22 of the GDPR. Article 22 of the GDPR is analysed in subsection 4.2.3 above, where it is concluded that it contains a right with a corresponding prohibition that the controller needs to implement regardless of it being invoked by the data subject.

The right to an explanation of an individual automated decision made in accordance with Article 22 of the GDPR is not part of the wording of Article 22. The right to an explanation of such a decision is part of Article 13–15 of the GDPR. The right to be informed of the reasons behind an automated decision is, thus, separated from the right not to be subject to such a decision.

Article 13 of the GDPR regulates the information the controller processing personal data needs to give to the data subject when the personal data is collected from the data subject itself. Typically where the data subject itself provides their personal data to the controller.

64 Section 4.5 is a rewritten version of Bjørn Aslak Juliussen. The right to an explanation under the GDPR and the AI Act. In: *International Conference on Multimedia Modeling*. Singapore: Springer Nature, 2025. pp. 184–197.

Article 14 of the GDPR concerns the information the controller is required to inform the data subject about when the personal data has not been obtained from the data subject, e.g., from other data subjects, other controllers, where personal data is collected from sensors, or similar.

Both Articles 13 and 14 regulate the information that needs to be given to the data subject by the controller. The data subject is not required to perform any action, such as making a request, to obtain the information covered in Articles 13 and 14. Article 15, however, provides the right to access information for the data subject and regulates the information that the controller is required to provide when requested by the data subject.

Articles 13 and 14 require the controller to provide the data subject with the information at the time of collection of the personal data, while Article 15 requires the controller to provide the information at the time of the request for information, and no later than one month after the request has been submitted, under Article 12 (3).

Article 13 (1) (f), Article 14 (2) (g), and Article 15 (1) (h) all have the same wording regarding automated decision-making under Article 22:

> [The controller shall provide the data subject with information about] the existence of automated decision-making, including profiling, referred to in Article 22 (1) and (4) and, at least in those cases, *meaningful information about the logic involved*, as well as the significance and the envisaged consequences of such processing for the data subject. (my emphasis)

The term "meaningful information about the logic involved" is highly debated in the scholarly literature. Some interpret the right to information in Articles 13, 14, and 15 as a right to an explanation of automated decision-making.[65] Some of the literature argues that the right in question is very limited, to the point where it is almost non-existent.[66] Other legal scholars place themselves

---

[65] Bryce Goodman and Seth Flaxman. "EU regulations on algorithmic decision-making and a 'right to explanation.'" In: *ICML Workshop on Human Interpretability in Machine Learning (WHI 2016), New York, NY.* http://arxiv. *org/abs/1606.08813 v1.* 2016. doi: https://doi.org/10.1609/aimag.v38i3.2741.

[66] Sandra Wachter, Brent Mittelstadt, and Luciano Floridi. "Why a right to explanation of automated decision-making does not exist in the General Data Protection Regulation". In: *International Data Privacy Law* 7.2 (June 2017), pp. 76–99. ISSN: 2044-3994. doi: 10.1093/idpl/ipx005. eprint: https://academic.oup.com/idpl/article-pdf/7/2/76/17932196/ipx005.pdf. url: https://doi.org/10.1093/idpl/ipx005.

in a moderate position and argue that the right needs to be interpreted contextually.[67]

The analysis of Article 22 in subsection 4.2.3 concluded that Article 22 – interpreted in light of recent case law from the CJEU, the Schufa Holding AG case[68] – is a right with a corresponding prohibition the controller needs to implement and not a reactive right for the data subject. The controller, therefore, needs to map out their processing operations and have control over whether or not they have individual automated decision-making processes implemented. The obligation for the controller to inform the data subject whether the controller has automated decision-making processes implemented, according to Articles 13 (1) (f), 14 (2) (g), and 15 (1) (h), is therefore not a complicated right to comply with for the controller. The complicating factor of the right to an explanation is the requirement to provide the data subject with "meaningful information about the logic involved" in automated decision-making.

What does "meaningful information about the logic involved" entail when a deployed AI system is used for automated individual decision-making? The right to meaningful information about the logic involved was not included in the predecessor of the GDPR, the data protection directive,[69] although Articles 12 (a) and 15 (1) of the Directive contained some traces of a right to explanation. The right to receive meaningful information about the logic involved will be interpreted in line with the existing legal sources in the following paragraphs. The existing legal sources are mostly the wording of the GDPR, including the wording of the different official language versions, and legal literature. The next subsections will also analyse some technical literature on XAI methods to shed light on the content and scope of the right to receive meaningful information about the logic involved.

A question that first needs to be resolved is whether the wording "meaningful information about the logic involved" should be interpreted differently across Articles 13, 14, and 15 of the GDPR, despite the identical wording in the different Articles.

In order to answer this question, it is necessary to interpret the different Articles not just according to their wording, but also in light of their objectives

---

67 Andrew D Selbst and Julia Powles. "Meaningful information and the right to explanation". In: *International Data Privacy Law* 7.4 (Dec. 2017), pp. 233–242. ISSN: 2044-3994. doi: 10.1093/idpl/ipx022. eprint: https://academic.oup.com/idpl/article-pdf/7/4/233/22923065/ipx022.pdf. url: https://doi.org/10.1093/idpl/ipx022.

68 Judgement of the Court (First Chamber) in Case C-634/21 OQ v Land Hessen and Schufa Holding AG ECLI:EU:C:2023:957.

69 Directive 95/46/EC of the European Parliament and of the Council of 24 October 1995 on the protection of individuals with regard to the processing of personal data and of the free movement of such data [1995] OJ L 281/31.

and context. Articles 13 and 14 of the GDPR regulate the information the controller needs to give to the data subject when collecting personal data, typically through the information provided to the data subject in a privacy policy. The objective of providing this information is to make the data subject aware of how his or her personal data is going to be processed. Since the information is given at the time of collection, before the actual processing by the use of automated individual decision-making has taken place, the "meaningful" criterion needs to be interpreted in this context.

The information given to the data subject about the intended automated processing at the time of collection under Articles 13 and 14 needs to be meaningful to enable the data subject to decide whether or not to consent to the processing – if the processing relies on Article 6 (1) (a). Moreover, the information provided to the data subjects should enable the data subjects to assess whether or not they should invoke specific rights when the processing of personal data has commenced.

Since the processing of personal data in the automated decision-making process has not commenced when the personal data is collected, meaningful information about the logic involved under Articles 13 and 14 would entail a general description of the overall AI system intended to be used in the automated decision-making process. Such a description could include information about how the AI model is trained, i.e., the training data and the type of AI algorithm used; typical outputs of the AI model, i.e., if the output is a prediction, classification, or generated content; and the sensitivity and the positive predictive value of the finished trained AI model, if possible. These various types of information would be examples of information given that would enable the data subject to invoke their rights at the time of collecting the personal data and throughout the processing lifecycle.

The right to meaningful information about automated decision-making under Article 15 – on the other hand – is part of a reactive right after the processing of personal data has taken place. According to recital 63 of the GDPR, the purpose of the right to access in Article 15 is to enable the data subject to "verify the lawfulness of the processing". When the data subject submits an access request, personal data has been processed, and the data subject wants to receive information about the actual processing and the processing of personal data as part of an automated individual decision.

"Meaningful information about the logic involved" will, thus, differ under Articles 13 and 14 – on the one hand – and Article 15 – on the other hand. What constitutes meaningful information will differ when the information is general information about the overall processing in an AI system, prior to the processing, compared to information about the actual processing of personal data that has taken place within a system pursuing an access request from the data subject.

To illustrate with an example, when a data subject has had their loan application rejected due to profiling in an automated credit scoring process and thus submits an access request, the data subject does not – most likely – have a general curiosity about the credit scoring processing, but is enquiring about the individual decision that has taken place and why it was rejected. The right to access in Article 15 of the GDPR could also be viewed as a necessary prerequisite to enable and invoke the other rights in Chapter III of the GDPR, including the rights to erasure, rectification, and restriction of profiling in Articles 16, 17, and 18 of the GDPR.

What does it entail that the information about the logic in the automated decision-making process must be "meaningful" under Article 15 (1) (h)? In order to shed more light on this term, one starting point could be to also look into other official language versions of the GDPR than the English one. All the different language versions of an EU regulation are equally authentic and – in line with settled case law from the CJEU – the different language versions require a uniform interpretation on the basis of the real intention of its author and in light of the versions in all other languages.[70]

The term "meaningful" in the English version of the GDPR is "aussagekräftige informationen" in the German version, "information utiles" in the French, "nuttige informative" in the Dutch, and "meningsfulde" in the Danish language versions of the GDPR. Some nuances are present in each of these language versions. The French wording "information utiles" and the Dutch wording "nuttige informative" entail that the information should be understandable, helpful, and useful for the data subject. The German "aussagekräftige" entails that the information given should be sound and reliable. The information explaining the logic involved in the automatic decision-making process, therefore, needs to be an actual and reliable representation of the automated processing. Lastly, the German wording "aussagekräftige" also supports the utility of the information, meaning that the information given should be capable of reaching the purpose of Article 15. The information provided under an access request should thus enable the data subject to assess the lawfulness of the processing.[71] The "*meaningful* information" condition under Article 15 of the GDPR, therefore, carries elements of understandability, usefulness, reliability, and utility.

---

70 European Parliament. *Legal Aspects of EU Multilingualism*. url: https://www.europarl.europa.eu/RegData/etudes/BRIE/2017/595914/EPRS_BRI%282017%29595914_EN.pdf. Last accessed: 01.08.2025.

71 Bart Custers and Anne-Sophie Heijne. "The right of access in automated decision-making: The scope of article 15(1)(h) GDPR in theory and practice". In: *Computer Law & Security Review* 46 (2022), p. 105727. ISSN: 0267-3649. doi: https://doi.org/10.1016/j.clsr.2022.105727. url: https://www.sciencedirect.com/science/article/pii/S026736492200070X.

The meaningful information should be about the "logic" involved in the automated decision-making process. The wording of Article 15 concerns the "logic" of the automated processing and not the specific technology applied. Hence, the data subject does not have the right to obtain the name of the AI system or the AI system providers' name under an access request per Article 15.

According to recital 63 of the GDPR, the right to receive meaningful information about the logic involved in automated decision-making should not "adversely affect the rights or freedoms of others, including trade secrets or intellectual property and in particular the copyright protecting the software. However, the result of those considerations should not be a refusal to provide all information to the data subject". The controller could therefore refuse to give information about trade secrets and copyright-protected material under the access request, but could not refuse an overall request for meaningful information about the logic involved by reference to recital 63. In line with recital 63, the controller could refuse, e.g., to disclose the specific algorithm used or the name of the AI system provider under reference to trade secret or copyright law, provided the requirements in the trade secret directive[72] are fulfilled and that the conditions for copyright protection are met. However, trade secret protection and copyright law could not be the sole reason behind the refusal of an access request under Article 15, meaning that only the trade secret and copyright-protected material could be left undisclosed.

The information about the logic involved must be meaningful to the data subject. The explanation of the logic could be descriptive and at a high level. However, the level of abstraction in the explanation must be interpreted in line with the purpose of Article 15, to enable the data subject to assess the lawfulness of the processing, according to recital 63. This needs to be assessed contextually and on a case-by-case basis. However, two examples can be given that do not allow data subjects to assess the lawfulness of the processing for automated decision-making. An explanation of the logic, such as that the automated decision-making process "applies machine learning" or "applies AI", is too abstract for the data subject to assess lawfulness. Another example is the following: "The automated decision-making processes use a support vector machine to assess whether individual data points are placed on the maximum-margin hyperplane during the perceptron of optional stability". The latter description is too advanced for it to be meaningful for the data subject, and the

[72] Directive (EU) 2016/943 of the European Parliament and of the Council of 8 June 2016 on the protection of undisclosed know-how and business information (trade secrets) against their unlawful acquisition, use and disclosure [2016] OJ/L 157/1.

description does not make it possible for them to assess the lawfulness of the processing either.

One relevant judgement concerning the right to receive meaningful information about the logic involved in deployed AI systems is the Dun and Bradstreet Austria judgement from the CJEU.[73] The case concerned which information the controller needs to disclose to data subjects when ML models are applied for automated decision-making in the form of credit scoring. The CJEU interpreted Article 15 (1) (h) of the GDPR concerning the requirement that the information needs to be meaningful. After interpreting different language versions of the GDPR, the CJEU concluded that the wording of Article 15 (1) (h) covers "all relevant information concerning the procedure and principles relating to the use, by automated means, of personal data with a view to obtaining a specific result". Moreover, the CJEU also held that this information, in line with the obligation of transparency in Article 12, must be provided in a concise, transparent, intelligible, and easily accessible form.

Furthermore, the CJEU held that the requirements of Article 15 (1) (h) of the GDPR cannot be satisfied by "the mere communication of a complex mathematical formula", since such information is not intelligible to the data subjects. According to the CJEU, the controller should find a manner to tell the data subjects about the rationale behind, or the criteria relied on, to reach the automated decision that relies on the output of an AI system. Various types of explainable AI (XAI) provide more meaningful explanations for the data subject than others. The book will return to the requirement for a meaningful explanation of the logic involved while explaining the XAI methods in subsection 4.5.4 below.

To recapitulate, both Articles 13, 14, and 15 contain a right to receive meaningful information about the logic involved when processing personal data as part of automated decision-making under Article 22 of the GDPR. However, Articles 13 and 14 of the GDPR apply to the collection of personal data, while Article 15 contains reactive rights that are dependent on requests from the data subject. Hence, Articles 13 and 14, on the one hand, and Article 15, on the other hand, will provide different types of explanations where the former is more general *ex-ante* AI system descriptions and the latter is *ex-post* explanations of a specific decision.

Article 15 requires the controller to provide "meaningful" information. By interpreting more language versions of the GDPR, it is possible to argue that the meaningful condition requires the information to be understandable,

---

73 Judgement of the Court (First Chamber) of 27 February 2025 in case C-203/22 CK v Magistrat der Stadt Wien, other party: Dun and Bradstreet Austria GmbH ECLI:EU:C:2025:117.

useful, reliable, and have utility for assessing the lawfulness of the processing for the data subject. The meaningful criterion needs to be further assessed contextually on a case-by-case basis.

4.5.3 The Right to an Explanation under the AI Act

An affected person has a right to an explanation of individual decision-making under the AI Act. According to Article 86 (1) of the AI Act:

> [a]ny affected person subject to a decision which is taken by the deployer on the basis from the high-risk AI systems listed in Annex III (...), which produces legal effects or similarly significantly affects that person in a way that they consider to have adverse impact on their health, safety or fundamental rights shall have the right to obtain from the deployer clear and meaningful explanations of the role of the AI system in the decision-making procedure and the main elements of the decision taken.

High-risk AI systems in Annex III point 2 – critical infrastructure such as safety components in the management of critical digital infrastructure, road traffic, or in the supply of water, gas, heating, and electricity – is not covered by the right to an explanation of an individual decision-making process under Article 86, according to Article 86 (1). Each member state may also derogate from the right to an explanation in Article 86 (1) in member state law, according to Article 86 (2).

The right to an explanation is part of the remedies subsection in the enforcement section of the AI Act. The purpose of the right to explanations is, thus, to act as a prerequisite for the providers and the deployers to comply with the AI Act through affected persons requesting information. When the conditions under Article 86 – elaborated below – are fulfilled, the activating criterion for the scope of the right to an explanation is that the affected persons "consider" that the output from the AI system has an adverse impact on their health, safety, or fundamental rights.

One relevant question is whether the deployer is required to explain the role of the output of the AI system only in the later decision process or whether the logic of the AI system needs to be explained. The wording of Article 86 (1) requires explaining the role of the AI system only in the decision-making process. However, if Article 86 (1) is interpreted in line with recital 171 of the AI Act, it becomes apparent that the explanation should be "clear and meaningful" and provide "a basis on which the affected persons are able to exercise their rights". The right to an explanation under Article 86 (1) does, thus, not only cover the simple role the output from the AI system had in the decision process but also – as far as it is feasible – the data, algorithm type, and other relevant aspects of the inferred output from the AI system.

Moreover, the right to an explanation under the AI Act "shall apply only to the extent" that the right is not covered under Union law, according to the AI Act Article 86 (3). If a data subject under the GDPR has the right to meaningful information about the logic involved in automated individual decision-making under Article 15 (1) (h) of the GDPR, the right to an explanation under Article 86 does not apply, according to Article 86 (3). The former subsection concluded that Article 15 (1) (h) of the GDPR contains a right to meaningful information about the logic involved in automated decisions and that this right contains a right to an *ex-post* explanation of individual decisions. The remainder of the legal analysis will presuppose that Article 15 (1) (h) of the GDPR provides a right similar to Article 86 (1) of the AI Act.

In which cases could affected persons rely on Article 86 (1) of the AI Act because their right to an explanation is not covered by the GDPR? The wording of Article 86 of the AI Act and the wording of Article 22 of the GDPR are not completely interchangeable. While Article 22 (1) of the GDPR covers a "decision based solely on automated processing", Article 86 (1) of the AI Act has a broader scope and covers decisions which are taken "on the basis of the output from a high-risk AI system". In the Schufa Holding AG case, analysed in 4.2.3.2, the CJEU has included profiling conducted by another entity as a decision under Article 22 (1) where the controller draws strongly on the conducted profiling. The wording of the GDPR "decision based solely" on automated processing could, thus, not be interpreted strictly by its wording and also covers situations where it is a market standard to draw strongly on a profiled or automated decision, even though the first decision is conducted by another entity. The AI Act Article 86 covers only decisions taken on the basis of a high-risk AI system. To illustrate the relationships between the right to meaningful information about the logic involved under the GDPR and the right to an explanation under the AI Act, consider these scenarios:

- Imagine that an AI system is used for recruitment to filter applications and to analyse and evaluate job candidates. Such an AI system is classified as a high-risk AI system according to Annex III Section 4 (a). The system is fully automated, and decisions to reject applications or accept them for interviews are based solely on the AI system. In this instance, the job selection process is based solely on automated decision-making under Article 22 (1) of the GDPR. E-recruitment is also mentioned as an example in recital 71 of the GDPR. Since the data subject has a right to receive meaningful information about the logic involved under Article 15 (1) (h) of the GDPR, the right to explanation under Article 86 (1) could not enter into effect, under Article 86 (3). To conclude, when Article 22 (1) of the GDPR is activated through automated decision-making and the AI system applied is regarded as high risk under the AI Act, the right to information about the logic involved under the GDPR prevails.

- Second, consider that an AI system is used solely to decide prices in an online e-commerce setting. The prices are based on the personal data submitted to the e-commerce site. According to guidance from the EDPB, such price setting could be regarded as a decision with similar effect under Article 22 (1) of the GDPR if the pricing discriminates against certain people and groups from buying the product.[74] If such automated decision-making enters the scope of the GDPR Article 22 (1), the data subject can request an explanation about the logic involved under Article 15 (1) (h). However, the affected person does not have a right to an explanation under Article 86 (1) of the AI Act since the AI system used for price setting is not regarded as high risk in accordance with Annex III of the AI Act. Hence, when automated decision-making enters the scope of the GDPR, but the AI system applied is not high risk under the AI Act, the affected person has a right to an explanation about the logic involved under the GDPR and not under the AI Act.
- Suppose that an AI system is used to influence the outcome of a local referendum. Such an AI system is regarded as high risk, according to Annex III 8 (b) of the AI Act. If such an AI system processes personal data, it could be argued that the automated decision-making does not legally or significantly factually affect a data subject, since the decision is a referendum and not a decision directed towards the data subject. Hence, the high-risk AI system in this specific use case does not enter the scope of Article 22 (1) of the GDPR. In this example, the affected person has a right to an explanation under Article 86 (1) of the AI Act, but not under Article 15 (1) (h) interpreted in line with Article 22 (1) of the GDPR.
- Consider an AI system that is high risk under the AI Act, but not entering the scope of the GDPR. One example could include high-risk AI systems used for law enforcement purposes outside the scope of the GDPR. Another example could include high-risk AI systems not processing personal data. However, it is highly unlikely that, e.g., a triage system under Annex III 5 (d) of the AI Act or AI systems used to grant, reduce, revoke, or reclaim public benefits under Annex III 5 (a) do not process personal data. One example is if an AI system is used by a judicial authority to interpret the law, under Annex III 8 (a) and does not process personal data. In such an

74 EDPB. *Guidelines on Automated Individual Decision-Making and Profiling for the Purposes of Regulation 2016/679 (wp251rev.01)*. url: https://ec.europa.eu/newsroom/article29/items/612053. Last accessed: 01.08.2025.

instance, the affected person has a right to an explanation under the AI Act Article 86 (1) of the AI Act and not under the GDPR.

- If an AI system infers a decision while not entering GDPR Article 22 (1) and is not regarded as a high-risk AI system under Annex III of the AI Act, the affected person does not have a right to explanation under either rule set. For instance, if a tax authority has a profiling system that flags individuals who are subject to manual inspection. It is possible to argue that the manual inspection is not a legal decision or a decision similarly affecting the individual, under Article 22 (1) of the GDPR. At the same time, the Schufa judgement is not completely transferable since it is not certain whether the authority "draws strongly" on the flag. Annex III does not list such an AI system as high risk, meaning the affected person may not have a right to an explanation under the GDPR or the AI Act.

To conclude, the right to an explanation under Article 86 (1) of the AI Act covers outputs from high-risk AI systems in Annex III when the output forms the basis for a decision affecting natural persons. Such a right applies only to the extent that the right to an explanation is not otherwise provided in Union law, for instance, in Article 15 (1) (h) of the GDPR. The examples in the list above have covered situations where both the AI Act and the GDPR come into effect, and what this overlap in scope signifies for the right to an explanation. The next subsection will address how the right to an explanation in the GDPR and AI Act relates to various methods of XAI.

4.5.4 Explainable AI (XAI) Methods and the Right to Explanation

4.5.4.1 Introduction

Based on the above legal analyses, subsection 4.5.4 will examine XAI methods in light of the right to meaningful information about the logic involved in automated decision-making under Article 15 (1) (h) of the GDPR and the right to an explanation of individual decisions under Article 86 (1) of the AI Act. The results of the above analyses will be interpreted together with various methods for interpretable AI and XAI in order to examine the technical feasibility of explaining individual decisions from various AI systems.

4.5.4.2 XAI methods

XAI is an expanding and evolving research field.[75] One motivation behind the development of methods explaining the outputs of AI systems is to comply with regulations such as the GDPR and the AI Act.[76]

In subsection 4.5.3, it was established that an explanation under Article 15 (1) (h) is required to provide useful, reliable, and understandable information about the logic involved in automated decision-making. This explanation should provide the data subject with enough information to enable the data subject to assess the lawfulness of the processing of personal data in the automated decision-making process. An explanation under Article 86 (1) of the AI Act should be a "meaningful explanation of the role of the AI system in the decision-making procedure and the main elements of the decision taken".

---

75 Christoph Molnar. *Interpretable Machine Learning*. Lulu.com, 2020; Tim Miller. "Explanation in artificial intelligence: Insights from the social sciences". In: *Artificial Intelligence* 267 (2018), pp. 1–38. doi: https://doi.org/10.48550/arXiv.1706.07269. arXiv: 1706.07269 [cs.AI]; David Gunning et al. "XAI—Explainable artificial intelligence". In: *Science Robotics* 4.37 (2019), eaay7120. doi: https://doi.org/10.1126/scirobotics.aay7120; Timo Speith. "A review of taxonomies of explainable artificial intelligence (XAI) methods". In: *Proceedings of the 2022 ACM Conference on Fairness, Accountability, and Transparency*. New York: Association for Computing Machinery, 2022, pp. 2239–2250. doi: https://doi.org/10.1145/3531146.3534639; Ahmed Shihab Albahri et al. "A systematic review of trustworthy and explainable artificial intelligence in healthcare: Assessment of quality, bias risk, and data fusion". In: *Information Fusion* (2023). doi: https://doi.org/10.1016/j.inffus.2023.03.008; Rudresh Dwivedi et al. "Explainable AI (XAI): Core ideas, techniques, and solutions". In: *ACM Computing Surveys* 55.9 (2023), pp. 1–33. doi: https://doi.org/10.1145/3561048; Sajid Ali et al. "Explainable Artificial Intelligence (XAI): What we know and what is left to attain trustworthy artificial intelligence". In: *Information Fusion* 99 (2023), p. 101805. doi: https://doi.org/10.1016/j.inffus.2023.101805; Mir Riyanul Islam et al. "A systematic review of explainable artificial intelligence in terms of different application domains and tasks". In: *Applied Sciences* 12.3 (2022), p. 1353. doi: https://doi.org/10.3390/app12031353; Pantelis Linardatos, Vasilis Papastefanopoulos, and Sotiris Kotsiantis. "Explainable AI: A review of machine learning interpretability methods". In: *Entropy* 23.1 (2020), p. 18. doi: https://doi.org/10.3390/e23010018.

76 Cecilia Panigutti et al. "The role of explainable AI in the context of the AI Act". In: *Proceedings of the 2023 ACM Conference on Fairness, Accountability, and Transparency*. New York: Association for Computing Machinery, 2023, pp. 1139–1150. doi: https://doi.org/10.1145/3593013.3594069; Lars Ole Hjelkrem and Petter Eilif de Lange. "Explaining deep learning models for credit scoring with SHAP: A case study using open banking data". In: *Journal of Risk and Financial Management* 16.4 (2023), p. 221. doi: https://doi.org/10.3390/jrfm16040221.

Which XAI methods could provide such meaningful explanations under Article 15 (1) (h) of the GDPR and Article 86 (1) of the AI Act?

XAI is a term used for methods and ML models used for making ML models and their outputs understandable to natural persons.[77] In the XAI field, the terms "interpretable" and "explainable" are sometimes used interchangeably and sometimes used to denote different notions. In the next paragraphs, the term "interpretable" will be used in line with the definition from Miller as "[t]he degree to which a human can understand the cause of a decision".[78] "Explainability" will be applied as a term that relates to the interpretability of individual outputs from an AI system.[79] Hence, in the following paragraphs, interpretability refers to the AI model as such, while explainability refers to the individual outputs from the AI system.

There are various methods to achieve XAI. Generally, it is possible to divide current XAI methods into intrinsic or post-hoc XAI methods.[80] Intrinsic methods are interpretable on their own, due to their "simple" structure and self-explainable structure. Post-hoc methods apply such intrinsic methods on top of an uninterpretable AI method or utilise other methods to explain AI models that are not interpretable. In other words, in *post-hoc* XAI, a white box explainable model is put on top of a black box model to explain the outputs of the black box model.

4.5.4.3 Instrinsic XAI methods

Another typical manner to distinguish XAI methods is between XAI methods that make the whole trained AI model interpretable and XAI methods that make the model output explainable. Since both Article 15 (1) (h) of the GDPR and Article 86 (1) of the AI Act revolve around the explainability of individual decisions, the next paragraphs will focus on XAI models for model output explainability. Both intrinsic and post-hoc methods will be analysed.

An example of a potential intrinsic interpretable XAI method is to use "simple" models that are in themselves interpretable to draw inferences. One

---

77 Christoph Molnar. *Interpretable Machine Learning*. Lulu.com, 2020.

78 Tim Miller. "Explanation in artificial intelligence: Insights from the social sciences". In: *Artificial Intelligence* 267 (2018), pp. 1–38. doi: https://doi.org/10.48550/arXiv.1706.07269. arXiv: 1706.07269 [cs.AI].

79 Christoph Molnar. *Interpretable Machine Learning*. Lulu.com, 2020.

80 Nathan Colaner. "Is explainable artificial intelligence intrinsically valuable?" In: *AI & Society* 37 (2022), pp. 231–238. doi: https://doi.org/10.1007/s00146-021-01184-2; Daniel Vale, Ali El-Sharif, and Muhammed Ali. "Explainable artificial intelligence (XAI) post-hoc explainability methods: Risks and limitations in non-discrimination law". In: *AI and Ethics* 2.4 (2022), pp. 815–826. doi: https://doi.org/10.1007/s43681-022-00142-y.

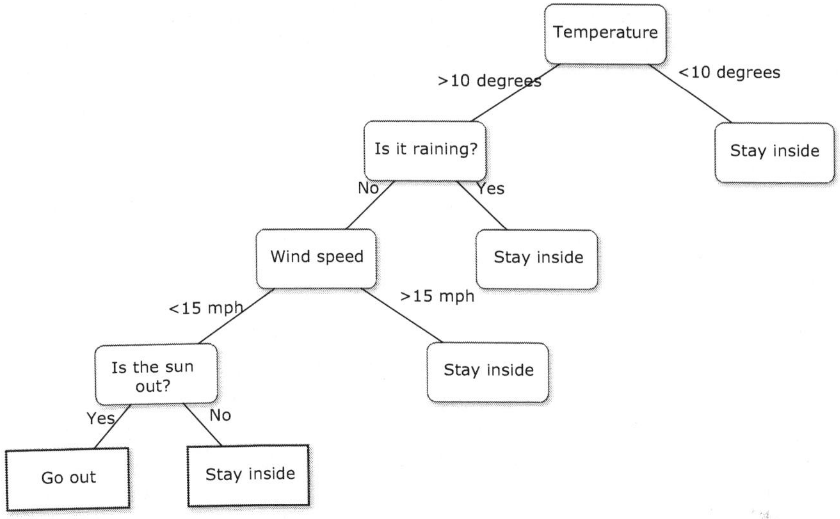

Figure 4.1 *Visual illustration of a decision tree*

example is a type of supervised ML known as decision trees.[81] A decision tree can, e.g., be applied to predict outcomes or classify data. The structure and inner workings of a decision tree could be illustrated with an offline example. Suppose that person A wants to decide whether or not he or she wants to go out and do an outdoor activity. He or she wants to go out and do an outdoor activity if it is above 10 degrees Celsius, not raining, if the current wind speed is below 15 nautical miles per hour (mph), and if the sun is shining. The predicted outcome of the decision tree, whether he or she goes out and does an outdoor activity or stays inside, is referred to as a leaf node.[82] The intermediate subsets – in the example, temperature, rain, wind speed, and whether the sun is shining – are called internal nodes. The deciding factors, above 10 degrees, less than 15 mph wind, and whether or not the sun is shining – are called cut-off values. The decision tree is illustrated in Figure 4.1.

In the example illustrated in Figure 4.1, the intermediate subsets and the cut-off values are decided before the decision tree is made. However, when a decision tree is applied as a supervised ML method, the intermediate subsets and cut-off values are detected and applied by the algorithm in the training data.

81 Christoph Molnar. *Interpretable Machine Learning.* Lulu.com, 2020; Lior Rokach and Oded Maimom. *Data Mining with Decision Trees: Theory and Applications.* Singapore: World Scientific, 2014. doi: https://doi.org/10.1142/9097.
82 Ibid.

The algorithm discovers and represents the relationships between the data in the decision tree model.[83] The tree representation of the model thereby makes the relationships between the different data interpretable and the individual output explainable, as long as the decision tree is not too large. One algorithm typically applied in decision trees is the CART (Classification and Regression Trees) algorithm.[84]

In short, the CART algorithm "builds" the three and the internal nodes by analysing how often a data point occurs in the training data. This is done until a pre-defined stopping criterion is reached. The CART algorithm decides the cut-off values – in the example above, e.g., >< 10 degrees – by splitting the data into clusters of similar data and deciding which splits result in the most homogeneous, "similar", subnodes.[85] To return to the example in Figure 4.1, if the provider has data on the temperature of 100 days and also data on whether or not the person goes out and does an activity, the split on 10 degrees would be made if most of the days with above 10 degrees resulted in going out, and vice versa. The decision on maximising the similarity in each of the two subnodes is made according to an index. In this index, the split on 10 degrees results in the most different data in the two subnodes of the data in the dataset.[86]

When explaining an individual output of a decision tree, the deployer of a tree-based model starts in the inferred decision, for instance, the "go out" leaf node and traverses the tree model through the internal nodes to the start. To provide a textual interpretation, the different intermediate subsets are connected with "and". An example of an individual explanation of the decision tree in Figure 4.1 would be: "The model predicted to 'go out' because the 'sun is out' is positive, the wind speed is < 15 mph, 'it is raining' is negative, and the temperature is > 10 degrees Celsius". An intrinsic interpretable XAI method, such as a decision tree, thus makes it possible to provide an explanation of the specific predicted output.

There are several other examples of intrinsic XAI methods, such as linear and logistic regression, decision rules, Generalised Linear Models (GLM), and

---

83 Lior Rokach and Oded Maimom. *Data Mining with Decision Trees: Theory and Applications*. Singapore: World Scientific, 2014. doi: https://doi.org/10.1142/9097.

84 Stuart L Crawford. "Extensions to the CART algorithm". In: *International Journal of Man-Machine Studies* 31.2 (1989), pp. 197–217. ISSN: 0020-7373. doi: https://doi.org/10.1016/0020-7373(89)90027-8. url: https://www.sciencedirect.com/science/article/pii/0020737389900278.

85 Ibid.

86 Lior Rokach and Oded Maimom. *Data Mining with Decision Trees: Theory and Applications*. Singapore: World Scientific, 2014. doi: https://doi.org/10.1142/9097; Christoph Molnar. *Interpretable Machine Learning*. Lulu.com, 2020.

Generalised Additive Models (GAMs).[87] However, to analyse whether intrinsic XAI methods comply with the identified legal requirements under Article 15 (1) (h) of the GDPR and Article 86 (1) of the AI Act, the logic of intrinsic supervised models established with the decision tree example is sufficient.

The legal analysis of Article 15 (1) (h) of the GDPR established that the purpose of the access right is for the data subject to assess the lawfulness of the processing. Moreover, in order to assess the lawfulness, the explanation of the output of an individual decision-making process needs to be understandable, reliable, and have utility for the data subject.

Intrinsic models, such as decision trees, represent the relationships between the data points in a manner that corresponds to the inference being made. In contrast to post-hoc explanations elaborated below, the explanations are therefore reliable since the explanation is part of the model that is used to draw inferences. Moreover, provided that the decision tree is not too large, it is also a pedagogical and easily understandable explanation that gives the data subject an understanding of how their personal data is being processed. Intrinsic explanations, provided that they are not too advanced, would therefore represent explanations that comply with the objective and purpose of the right to receive meaningful information about the logic involved in individual automated decision-making in Article 15 (1) (h) of the GDPR.

In relation to Article 86 (1) of the AI Act, the purpose of the explanation is to provide a remedy for the affected persons who have been affected by high-risk AI systems in a manner that they consider has had an adverse impact on their health, safety, and fundamental rights. An explanation that should explain the role the AI system has in the decision being inferred by a high-risk AI system, needs to – as long as it is feasible – be an actual representation of how the data is being processed within the AI system. An intrinsic XAI method, such as a decision tree, would thus be a method to explain an individual decision from a high-risk AI system in compliance with Article 86 (1) of the AI Act.

4.5.4.4 Post-hoc XAI methods

The intrinsic XAI methods elaborated above are examples of XAI methods where the model itself is interpretable, and the output from the model, therefore, becomes explainable. Intrinsic interpretable models, such as decision trees, limit the predictive performance of the model since interpretable models are mainly limited to more "simple" forms of processing, and also limit the solving of the ML tasks to a specific model. Post-hoc explanations, also referred to as model-agnostic XAI methods, separate the explanation of

---

87 Christoph Molnar. *Interpretable Machine Learning*. Lulu.com, 2020.

individual decisions from the model that is applied to draw inference.[88] The model that provides the interpretability and the explanations is put on top of the AI model that performs the tasks or inferences. The next paragraphs will address two such methods typically applied, Shapley values and local surrogate models, and examine if a post-hoc XAI method complies with Article 15 (1) (h) of the GDPR and Article 86 (1) of the AI Act. The reason behind the choice of these two methods is that they are local, meaning that they explain the individual decisions made rather than provide for the overall global model to be interpretable, because they have a clear logic, and because they are frequently applied.

Shapley values is a theoretical concept from collaborative game theory used in the XAI field to provide an explanation of how much "influence" each parameter in the AI model has on the output of the model.[89] One approach to explain Shapley values is by way of example. Suppose that a natural person has applied for a loan and therefore has undergone a credit scoring process using ML. The credit score was 100 and negative, and the application was rejected. An average person in the same neighbourhood, at the same age, and with similar income has an average credit score of 200, which will get the application accepted. Applied ML models for credit scoring use many features to calculate the credit risk. One developed credit scoring model based on Natural Language Processing (NLP), e.g., uses 12 016 different features to calculate the credit score and risk of credit default.[90] An individual having their loan rejected would be curious about which of these features are most important for the output, which features they could improve to get their loan accepted, and, as in the example above, why their application was rejected and their neighbours accepted. Shapley values is originally a method to calculate the division of a price between players who have won a game together based on how much each player contributed to winning the game.[91]

[88] Ibid.

[89] Lloyd S Shapley. *A Value for N-Person Game.* Santa Monica: RAND, 1952. url: https://www.rand.org/pubs/papers/P295.html. Last accessed: 01.08.2025. Lars Ole Hjelkrem and Petter Eilif de Lange. "Explaining deep learning models for credit scoring with SHAP: A case study using open banking data". In: *Journal of Risk and Financial Management* 16.4 (2023), p. 221. doi: https://doi.org/10.3390/jrfm16040221.

[90] Lars Ole Hjelkrem and Petter Eilif de Lange. "Explaining deep learning models for credit scoring with SHAP: A case study using open banking data". In: *Journal of Risk and Financial Management* 16.4 (2023), p. 221. doi: https://doi.org/10.3390/jrfm16040221.

[91] Lloyd S Shapley. *A Value for N-Person Game.* Santa Monica: RAND, 1952. url: https://www.rand.org/pubs/papers/P295.html. Last accessed: 01.08.2025.

In a deployed ML setting, the "price" refers to the individual inferred prediction, the "game" refers to the ML model, the gain refers to the actual predicted value minus the average predicted value, and the players are the different features in the ML model that "collaborate" to reach the specific output. The objective of the Shapley values is to explain the discrepancy between the inferred prediction, in the credit score example 100, and the average predicted credit score of 200.[92]

Shapley values – building on collaborative game theory – is the average value of one player in a game, calculated on the performance of the coalition with and without the specific player.[93] In XAI, Shapley values make it possible to evaluate the value or contribution of specific features in the output of an ML model. This evaluation is done by calculating the average marginal contribution of the feature across possible coalitions with other features.

Suppose that years of education is a feature in the credit scoring example. For simplicity, suppose that the credit score depends on three features: net salary, age, and years of education. We want to calculate the contribution of the *education* feature to the output of the credit scoring model. By selecting random data from the dataset, the feature *education* is replaced with random data points and the output is calculated. Then, the output of the model with and without the feature is calculated. However, the various features are interrelated, and it is not as simple as calculating the average of the education feature. The overall credit score would, e.g., be low even with a high education feature but with a low net salary. Thus, the feature *education* needs to be interpreted in various coalitions with the other features, and the outcome of these different coalitions also needs to be averaged to calculate the Shapley value of the feature. This step is repeated, and the average "value" referring to the increase or decrease in the output, the credit score, is repeated across different possible coalitions between features and values for education.

Shapley values are computationally expensive because all the different subsets of features need to be calculated. With three different features in the example above, this makes $2^3 = 8$ different feature subsets. However, with

---

92 Christoph Molnar. *Interpretable Machine Learning*. Lulu.com, 2020; Lars Ole Hjelkrem and Petter Eilif de Lange. "Explaining deep learning models for credit scoring with SHAP: A case study using open banking data". In: *Journal of Risk and Financial Management* 16.4 (2023), p. 221. doi: https://doi.org/10.3390/jrfm16040221.

93 Lloyd S Shapley. *A Value for N-Person Game*. 1952. url: https://www.rand.org/pubs/papers/P295.html. Last accessed: 01.08.2025. Christoph Molnar. *Interpretable Machine Learning*. Lulu.com, 2020.

10 features, it is $2^{10} = 1024$ different coalitions of the features.[94] In terms of explainability, Shapley values are the average contribution of the feature across different coalitions and not the value of the feature if the feature is removed. Shapley values, therefore, offer explainability of individual decisions, but they are computationally expensive and only an approximation of the feature's importance.[95]

Shapley values is an example of an explainability method that calculates feature importance, how important one feature is to reach a specific output of an ML model. Another method to explain individual outputs from black box ML models is local surrogate models. One such surrogate model is LIME (Local Interpretable Model-agnostic Explanations).[96] When it is not possible to interpret an ML model because it is a black box model, LIME makes explanations possible by perturbing the input to the black box model and testing how the model performs around a specific output when the input is changed. This perturbed input data and corresponding output data from the model are used to create a model on top of the black box model that is intrinsically interpretable, for instance, a decision tree.[97] The explanation of the individual decision from the black box model can then be interpreted by the intrinsically interpretable model trained on the input and output data from the uninterpretable black box model.

94 Lloyd S Shapley. *A Value for N-Person Game.* 1952. url: https://www.rand.org/pubs/papers/P295.html. Last accessed: 01.08.2025. Kjell Hausken. "The Shapley value of coalitions to other coalitions". In: *Humanities and Social Sciences Communications* 7.1 (2020), pp. 1–10. doi: https://doi.org/10.1057/s41599-020-00586-9.

95 Christoph Molnar. *Interpretable machine learning.* Lulu.com, 2020; Xuanxiang Huang and Joao Marques-Silva. "On the failings of Shapley values for explainability". In: *International Journal of Approximate Reasoning* (2024), p. 109112. ISSN: 0888-613X. doi: https://doi.org/10.1016/j.ijar.2023.109112. url: https://www.sciencedirect.com/science/article/pii/S0888613X23002438.

96 Christoph Molnar. *Interpretable machine learning.* Lulu.com, 2020; Muhammad Rehman Zafar and Naimul Khan. "Deterministic local interpretable model-agnostic explanations for stable explainability". In: *Machine Learning and Knowledge Extraction* 3.3 (2021), pp. 525–541. doi: https://doi.org/10.3390/make3030027.

97 Muhammad Rehman Zafar and Naimul Khan. "Deterministic local interpretable model-agnostic explanations for stable explainability". In: *Machine Learning and Knowledge Extraction* 3.3 (2021), pp. 525–541. doi: https://doi.org/10.3390/make3030027; Christoph Molnar. *Interpretable Machine Learning.* Lulu.com, 2020.

Are model-agnostic explanation methods acceptable explanations under Article 86 (1) of the AI Act and Article 15 (1) (h) of the GDPR? One aspect when analysing this question is that it was established under the German-language version of Article 15 (1) (h) of the GDPR that the meaningful information about the logic involved must be "reliable". When using a surrogate model to explain another model, there is no guarantee that the explanation "matches" the processing conducted in the underlying black box model. The models on top of the black box model, such as the LIME method and Shapley values, are just approximations of input-output data in LIME and feature importance in Shapley values. However, the wording of both the GDPR and the AI Act in relation to the right to an explanation is open-ended. In the GDPR, only information about the "logic involved" is required, and in the AI Act, information about the role of the AI system in the decision-making is required to be given to affected persons. Therefore, as a general conclusion, both intrinsic explanations and post-hoc explanation methods, such as Shapley values and surrogate models, comply with the right to explanation of decisions under the GDPR and the AI Act.

XAI is an evolving research field, and XAI methods are becoming more and more advanced. As these methods advance and it becomes more technically feasible to explain individual automated decisions, the corresponding rights to receive such explanations, for instance, in the GDPR and the AI Act, should evolve too. Today, these rights are open-ended, reflecting the difficulty in explaining outputs from AI models. However, if such explanations are becoming more and more feasible as the XAI technology improves, a natural response is to specify and strengthen the right of natural persons to receive explanations of outputs inferred from deployed AI models, both under data protection law and in the AI Act.

4.5.5 Summary

Section 4.5 has established the scope of the right to explanation in the GDPR and the AI Act.

The right to receive meaningful information about the logic involved regards decisions under Article 22 (1) of the GDPR. In order to receive such meaningful information, the AI system must process personal data and enter the overall scope of the GDPR. The output of the AI system needs to produce a legal effect or similarly affect the data subject, according to Article 22 (1). The requirements and the scope of Article 22 of the GDPR are further elaborated in subsection 4.2.3.

The "right to an explanation" of an individual automated decision is not a part of Article 22, but Articles 13–15 of the GDPR. Articles 13 and 14 of the GDPR regulate the information the controller needs to give to the data subject prior to the automated decision-making beginning, at the time of data collection. Therefore, the information about the logic involved would entail an *ex-ante* system description. The legal analysis concluded that for such information to be meaningful for the data subject, the "explanation" of the logic involved should involve the data the AI system has been trained on, the type of AI algorithm used, typical outputs of the AI model, and, if possible, the sensitivity and positive predictive value of the trained AI system.

Article 15, on the other hand, is part of the right to access that the data subject can request after the automated decision-making has occurred. The purpose of this information about the logic is to enable the data subject to assess the lawfulness of the processing. By interpreting different language versions, it is possible to contend that the information should be reliable, understandable, and useful for the data subject. The specific information about the logic involved in automated decision-making must be interpreted on a case-by-case basis, but the requirements for understandability, reliability, and usefulness could represent guiding elements in this assessment.

The analysis of the right to an explanation of individual decisions from high-risk AI systems in Article 86 (1) of the AI Act concluded that the right to an explanation is a remedy that should provide a clear and meaningful basis on which affected persons of high-risk AI systems could exercise their rights. The right to explanation in the AI Act only covers situations where the affected persons do not have a similar right according to Union law. Thus, if the data subject can request meaningful information about the logic involved in automated decision-making under Article 15 (1) (h) of the GDPR, the data subject cannot request an explanation under Article 86 (1) of the AI Act simultaneously. The explanation under Article 86 (1) of the AI Act should cover "clear and meaningful explanations of the role of the AI system in the decision-making procedure and the main elements of the decision taken".

The subsection about the various XAI methods examined two main categories of XAI methods, intrinsic methods and post-hoc methods. Intrinsic methods, such as linear and logistic regression and decision trees, are in themselves interpretable and thereby offer explainability for individual outputs. Post-hoc interpretability, such as Shapley values and LIME, offers explainability by putting another model on top of the AI model used to draw inferences.

The different XAI methods were interpreted in line with the established legal requirements for explanations under Article 15 (1) (h) of the GDPR and Article 86 (1) of the AI Act. The legal analysis problematises whether a post-hoc explanation offers reliability because a model is put on top of another model used to draw inferences. It was, however, concluded that both intrinsic and post-hoc XAI methods could be applied to comply with both Article 15 (1) (h) of the GDPR and Article 86 (1) of the AI Act.

4.6 IMPLEMENTING THE LEGAL REQUIREMENTS IN THE MLOps FRAMEWORK

4.6.1 Introduction

In an article published in December 2023, a team of researchers successfully extracted sensitive training data from chatbots known as Generative Pre-trained Transformers (GPTs). The method applied involved the insertion of a prompt, which instructed the chatbot to repeat a word as many times as possible. Unexpectedly, the chatbot began to disclose sensitive personal data from its training dataset in addition to repeating the prompt. The disclosed output data from the training data set included the names and contact information of real natural persons.[98]

This example illustrates the impact of inherent vulnerabilities in operational AI models, where cybersecurity incidents and data protection breaches can – and potentially will – occur. In such scenarios, it is critical to have a framework in place that can identify these vulnerabilities during the operational phase of an AI model and revert to the development phase of the model for rectification. MLOps is an example of such a framework. The subsequent subsections will address how to embed compliance issues in the MLOps process to enhance data protection, cybersecurity, and AI Act compliance that takes place within deployed AI models.

As elaborated in Chapter 2, MLOps is a framework for automatically updating operational ML models through pipelines that connect the continuous updating of the ML model in the development phase with the ML model deployed in an operational setting. The next subsection will suggest how the existing MLOps framework and some of the identified legal requirements in data protection regulation, cybersecurity regulation, and the AI Act have the potential for a natural alignment.

4.6.2 Towards Data Protection Compliance in Deployed AI Models through MLOps

The current subsection will address how MLOps could potentially represent a step to improve compliance with the GDPR when an ML model is deployed. The subsection will focus on how Continuous Integration / Continuous Delivery / Continuous Training (CI/CD/CT) in MLOps might represent a quantitative

[98] Milad Nasr et al. "Scalable Extraction of Training Data from (Production) Language Models". In: *arXiv preprint arXiv:2311.17035* (2023). doi: https://doi.org/10.48550/arXiv.2311.17035.

key performance indicator (KPI) that could be used to document data protection compliance, in accordance with Article 5 (2) of the GDPR. Moreover, the current subsection will also focus on how CI/CD/CT in MLOps might contribute to the explainability of individual decision-making under Article 22 (1) of the GDPR interpreted in line with Article 15 (1) (h).

As elaborated in Chapter 3, the controller needs to document compliance with the GDPR under Article 5 (2). Quantitative key performance indicators (KPIs) are recommended by the EDPB to document compliance with the GDPR under the principle of accountability under Article 5 (2) of the GDPR.[99] A KPI is a metric used to measure something. A quantitative KPI is based on measurable metrics such as statistics, numbers, or data. In case an ML model is applied and processes personal data, does CI/CD/CT under the MLOps framework – specifically automatic testing – have any parallels with KPIs? Could automatic testing in MLOps be applied as a means to document accountability with the fundamental principles for processing personal data in the GDPR?

In ML and MLOps, the testing of the ML model and the automatic testing applied in CI/CD/CT involve testing the features of the ML model, the data, and the infrastructure. When the ML model processes personal data, the validation testing of data and features during development and deployment could potentially be applied to document that the processing of personal data is in line with the fundamental principles in Article 5 (1) of the GDPR.

Some of the fundamental principles in Article 5 (1) GDPR, such as the lawfulness, fairness, transparency, or purpose limitation principle, involve a more procedural and organisational approach rather than a substantial, material, and technical approach to data protection, meaning that the principles are adhered to mainly through legal analysis and specifications rather than technical measures. It is therefore unlikely that current ML techniques and MLOps techniques might be automated in a MLOps pipeline that relates to these specific principles. However, some of the other principles in Article 5, such as the data minimisation principle and the principle of accuracy, might be easier to implement in a MLOps pipeline. These principles relate to aspects of the data that might be tested with metrics within MLOps pipelines.

With regard to the data minimisation principle, is it possible to automatically detect and document compliance with the principle in Article 5 (1) (c) in MLOps? Goldsteen et. al.[100] have performed an experimental evaluation of

---

99 EDPB. *Guidelines 4/2019 on Article 25 Data Protection by Design and by Default Version 2.0 Adopted on 20 October 2020.* url: https://edpb.europa.eu/sites/default/files/files/file1/edpb_guidelines_201904_dataprotection_by_design_and_by_default_v2.0_en.pdf. Last accessed: 01.08.2025.

100 Abigail Goldsteen et al. "Data minimization for GDPR compliance in machine learning models". In: *AI and Ethics* 2.3 (2022), pp. 477–491. doi: https://

the data minimisation principle in ML models. In general, ML models apply significant amounts of (personal) data for training and when the ML model is applied in operational use. In the experimental evaluation, the authors' aim was to reduce the amount of personal data processed at the inference stage, while at the same time not losing too much model accuracy. The data minimisation experiment did not require model retraining, but it was concerned with minimising data at the inference stage, and not the model training stage. The overall approach involved suppressing and generalising personal data in the ML model's operational stage. The methodology applied involved reducing both the amount of data and the granularity of the data applied in the ML model at runtime. An example the authors give is that age might be represented in 10-year ranges rather than exact age. The approach aims to minimise model accuracy loss at the same time as decreasing the data to improve data protection.

The method applied by Goldensteen et. al. involves training a surrogate model to guide the generalisation of the features at runtime. The training of the surrogate model that guides the generalisation of the runtime data is done automatically and could, thus, be part of the MLOps framework. The surrogate model that generalises the data points continues to generalise the features until an accuracy threshold is met. When the features are generalised, these features are implemented in the ML model that draws inference, thereby potentially achieving data minimisation, according to Article 5 (1) (c).

The approach to data minimisation of the data applied in runtime might also relate to the principle of accuracy under Article 5 (1) (d) of the GDPR and, more specifically, concept drift in ML models. Concept drift occurs when a trained ML model becomes less accurate because the data in the operational setting changes or shifts. Concept drift could be illustrated with an example. Suppose that an e-commerce site has developed an ML model to predict which clothes to suggest to customers in an online shopping portal. The ML model does not account for seasonal changes, and a concept drift therefore occurs when winter evolves into spring or spring into summer. The trained ML model does not fit with the changes in the operational data in the e-commerce site, and a concept drift has occurred where the data no longer corresponds to the trained model.

Such a concept drift relates to the principle of accuracy of personal data processing in Article 5 (1). According to Article 5 (1) (d) "personal data shall be accurate and, where necessary, kept up to date; every reasonable step must be taken to ensure that personal data that are inaccurate, having regard to the purposes for which they are processed, are erased or rectified without delay".

---

doi.org/10.48550/arXiv.2008.04113.

The principle of accuracy relates to both personal data that has never been correct and outdated personal data. Concept drift in operational ML models is an example of (personal) data that is no longer kept up to date in relation to the purpose of the processing of the personal data in the ML model.

MLOps have – at a high level – two approaches to detect and prevent concept drift: an active approach or a passive approach.[101] The active approach involves attempting to detect the shift in the data environment during runtime and having mitigating measures in place – such as model retraining – if such drifts are detected. The passive approach involves updating the model continuously without regard to detected shifts in the model during runtime. Several commercial MLOps platforms, such as SageMaker from Amazon Web Services (AWS), have algorithms in place to detect concept drift. SageMaker has data distribution-based drift detectors implemented, an example of an active approach to concept drift.[102] The principle of accuracy under Article 5 (1) (d) GDPR requires "every reasonable step" to be taken to rectify or erase inaccurate personal data. The introduction of concept drift detection and mitigation as part of MLOps might be a potential first step to comply with the fundamental principle of accuracy.

How does Article 22 of the GDPR relate to MLOps practices? Article 22 has several exemptions from the general prohibition in Article 22 (1), according to Article 22 (2). Performance of a contract, explicit consent, and exemptions in member state laws are relevant exemptions from the general prohibition of automated decision-making. In case a controller has an automated decision-making process, the data subject has the right to meaningful information about the logic involved, as well as the significance and the envisaged consequences of such processing for the data subject, under the right to access in Article 15 (1) (h). MLOps practices might be a step towards making it possible to give the data subject such information. The next paragraph will explain how MLOps might contribute to providing this information.

Is it possible that MLOps practices could automate the controllers' obligations under Article 15 (1) (h)? The wording of Article 15 (1) (h) is as follows: "The data subject shall have the right to obtain from the controller (...) the following information (...) the existence of automated decision-making, including profiling, referred to in Article 22 (1) and (4) and, at least in those cases, meaningful information about the logic involved, as well as the significance and the

---

101 Gregory Ditzler et al. "Learning in nonstationary environments: A survey". In: *IEEE Transactions on Knowledge and Data Engineering* 10.4 (2015), pp. 2346–2363. doi: https://doi.org/10.1109/MCI.2015.2471196.

102 Amazon Web Service. *Detecting Data Drift Using Amazon Sagemaker*. url: https://aws.amazon.com/blogs/architecture/detecting-data-drift-using-amazon-sagemaker/. Last accessed: 01.08.2025.

envisaged consequences of such processing for the data subject". The "significance and the envisaged consequences" of automated decision-making will – most likely – be fulfilled only through an organisational measure and not a technical measure such as MLOps. The next paragraph will, therefore, focus on whether MLOps might be a technical measure that can provide "meaningful information about the logic involved" when an ML model is applied as part of an automated decision-making process. Article 15 (1) (h) is a reactive right that the controller processing the personal data needs to comply with after the right has been invoked by the data subject. Article 13 (2) (f) and 14 (2) (g) of the GDPR are obligations that the controllers need to comply with regardless of whether they have been invoked by the data subject. These articles contain notification obligations for controllers concerning data collected from the data subject (Article 13) and data collected from sources other than the data subject (Article 14). According to Article 13 (2) (f) and 14 (2) (g), the controller is obliged to "provide the data subject with the following information necessary to ensure fair and transparent processing (...) the existence of automated decision-making, including profiling, referred to in Article 22 (1) and (4) and, at least in those cases, meaningful information about the logic involved, as well as the significance and the envisaged consequences of such processing for the data subjects".

A relevant question that needs to be answered before the question of whether MLOps practices could be applied to comply with the right to explanation is what is meant by the wording "meaningful information about the logic involved" in automated decision-making under Article 22 of the GDPR. First, an explanation could either be global or individual, i.e., the explanation of the logic involved could either concern the general functionality of the ML system or the reasoning of a specific individual decision. Moreover, the explanation of the decision could also be given at the time the personal data used to infer the decision is made – i.e., before the decision is collected – or after the decision-making process under Article 22 has taken place.[103]

Some scholars have argued that the wording of Articles 13 (2) (f), 14 (2) (g), and Article 15 (1) (h), especially "envisaged consequences", calls for a future-oriented right to explanation and that the right to explanation is a global, *ex-ante* right to the logic typically involved and not an *ex-post* specific

103 Sandra Wachter, Brent Mittelstadt, and Luciano Floridi. "Why a right to explanation of automated decision-making does not exist in the General Data Protection Regulation". In: *International Data Privacy Law* 7.2 (June 2017), pp. 76–99. ISSN: 2044-3994. doi: 10.1093/idpl/ipx005. eprint: https://academic.oup.com/idpl/article-pdf/7/2/76/17932196/ipx005.pdf. url: https://doi.org/10.1093/idpl/ipx005.

right to obtain an explanation of a decision already made.[104] As elaborated in section 4.5, there is some legal uncertainty on whether there exists a right to an explanation of an individual automated decision under the GDPR. The CJEU has interpreted Article 22 in a purpose-oriented manner in relation to other referred questions. A broad interpretation of Articles 13, 14, 15, and 22 could establish such a right to an individual *ex-post* right to explanations of individual decision-making. However, what is certain is that the right to access information about the logic involved in an automated decision-making process needs to be interpreted together with Article 12 of the GDPR, which relates to all information given by the controllers to the data subject. According to Article 12 (1), all information given under Articles 13, 14, and 15 shall be "in a concise, transparent, intelligible and easily accessible form, using clear and plain language". The information about the logic involved, therefore, needs to be intelligible, and it is not sufficient to provide the specific ML algorithm or a piece of computer code to the data subject. Could MLOps practices potentially provide such meaningful information, both globally concerning the overall system making the decision and concerning a specific decision?

There exist ML algorithms that are interpretable "by design", for instance, decision trees. Such XAI methods provide ML models that are possible to interpret. Other XAI approaches add another ML model on top of the models that draw inferences. The purpose of this additional model is to act as an interpretable model that can provide an interpretation of the decision. Another widely adopted XAI method is Shapley values based on game theory. One potential for future research is to provide XAI methods in MLOps in order to have the potential to explain or interpret the automated decisions inferred from personal data. Others, for instance, Baniecki et. al. have provided a Python package that implements a model-agnostic interface for explainability and fairness.[105]

To summarise, MLOps is an emerging concept that has the potential to support several of the fundamental principles of Article 5 (1) GDPR when personal data is processed by ML models. These principles include the principle of accuracy, the purpose limitation principle, and the right to receive information about the logic involved during automatic decision-making. MLOps practices have the potential to include such compliance aspects, and the practical implementation of the GDPR principles in MLOps will – most likely – develop further in the future. If the controller implements MLOps practices intended to automate compliance with the fundamental principles of the GDPR in

---

[104] Ibid.

[105] Hubert Baniecki et al. "Dalex: Responsible machine learning with interactive explainability and fairness in Python". In: *Journal of Machine Learning Research* 22.214 (2021), pp. 1–7. doi: https://doi.org/10.48550/arXiv.2012.14406.

deployed AI models, the outputs of such automation could – potentially – be applied to document the compliance under the principle of accountability in Article 5 (2) of the GDPR.

4.6.3 Towards Cybersecurity Regulation Compliance in MLOps

Section 4.6 started with an example where a cybersecurity vulnerability was detected in a deployed ML model. In such an instance, there needs to be a possibility to revert from the operational setting of the deployed ML model to the training and development phase to rectify the vulnerability. MLOps – building on DevOps philosophy – bridges the operational and development phases of ML models, thereby potentially offering such an opportunity.

Within the MLOps framework, suggestions for cybersecurity build on implementing existing cybersecurity components such as access control, authentication, and authorisation in the systems supporting the ML model.[106]

The cybersecurity of deployed AI models also needs to cater for AI-specific cybersecurity vulnerabilities of deployed AI models. Subsection 4.3.2 elaborated on AI-specific vulnerabilities of deployed AI models and how they could be mitigated with various risk mitigation measures. The next paragraphs will address how MLOps practices in deployed AI models could potentially enhance the cybersecurity of the deployed AI model, and thus also contribute to cybersecurity regulation compliance.

The methods for compliance with data protection regulation above focused on alterations to the data in the form of aggregating the input data used to make an inference, and not processing data on an individual data subject level. The cybersecurity strategies for deployed AI models, however, relate more to the system surrounding the deployed AI model and less to the data processed in it. Overall, potential defence techniques implemented in MLOps for deployed AI models could be separated into cryptography-based and access rights-based strategies.[107]

Cryptography-based strategies guarantee the confidentiality and integrity of the data processed in deployed AI models through encryption. Encryption techniques are applied to prevent access to the deployed AI model through

---

[106] Yann Billeter et al. "MLOps as an enabler of trustworthy AI". In: *11th IEEE Swiss Conference on Data Science (SDS), Zurich, Switzerland, 30–31 May 2024*. ZHAW Zürcher Hochschule für angewandte Wissenschaften. 2024. doi: https://doi.org/10.21256/zhaw-30443.

[107] Alka Luqman, Riya Mahesh, and Anupam Chattopadhyay. "Privacy and security implications of cloud-based AI services: A survey". In: *arXiv preprint arXiv:2402.00896* (2024). doi: https://doi.org/10.48550/arXiv.2402.00896.

cryptographic algorithms.[108] Homomorphic encryption is another example where computations can be made on encrypted data without decrypting the data before the computation.[109] Experimental evaluations have been performed on Fully Homomorphic Encryption (FHE) on deep neural networks.[110] Such computations are costly, and there is a trade-off between the complexity of the computation that can be applied to the encrypted data and the computational performance.[111] However, FHE has been computed in deep neural networks, and it is, therefore, a promising path towards more secure deployment of AI models.

Another cryptography-based strategy to guarantee the integrity and thereby the cybersecurity of the deployed ML model is secure multiparty computation.[112] Secure multiparty computations can potentially secure the deployed model parameters and the data applied to make inferences. In secure multiparty computation, different parties could jointly compute a function without sharing the input data to the function with each other through a cryptographic protocol. When secure multiparty computation is applied in an ML context, the *function* computed between the parties might be a deployed ML model.[113] Applying secure multiparty computation has communication overhead, meaning that the inference from the ML model takes a longer time. However, using secure multiparty computation on deployed ML models might lower the risk of cybersecurity vulnerabilities since the model owner does not get access to the input or output data. The inherent risk of cybersecurity vulnerabilities such as membership inference, model inversion attacks and perturbation attacks elaborated under subsection 4.2.3 might be lowered.

Access right-based strategies related to the cybersecurity of deployed ML models include traditional access strategies such as authorisation,

---

108 Ibid.

109 Bjørn Aslak Juliussen et al. "The third country problem under the GDPR: Enhancing protection of data transfers with technology". In: *International Data Privacy Law* 13.3 (2023), pp. 225–243.

110 Joon-Woo Lee et al. "Privacy-preserving machine learning with fully homomorphic encryption for deep neural network". In: *iEEE Access* 10 (2022), pp. 30039–30054. doi: https://doi.org/10.1109/ACCESS.2022.3159694.

111 Néstor J Hernández Marcano et al. "On fully homomorphic encryption for privacy-preserving deep learning". In: *2019 IEEE Globecom Workshops (GC Wkshps)*. New York: IEEE, 2019, pp. 1–6. doi: https://doi.org/10.1109/GCWkshps45667.2019.9024625.

112 Brian Knott et al. "Crypten: Secure multi-party computation meets machine learning". In: *Advances in Neural Information Processing Systems* 34 (2021), pp. 4961–4973. doi: https://doi.org/10.48550/arXiv.2109.00984.

113 Ibid.

authentication, and access control policies. Other methods involve restricting access to parameters of the ML model and isolating the deployed ML model to trusted enclaves that cannot be accessed, known as Trusted Execution Environments.[114]

To conclude, while data protection compliance issues for deployed AI models include alterations to the data processed in the deployed models to draw inferences, cybersecurity compliance issues encompass methods to protect the confidentiality and integrity of the data processed in the model and the model's parameters. Such methods include both cryptography-based strategies and access-right-based strategies. By including such security methods in the MLOps framework through best practices, it is possible to enhance the overall cybersecurity of deployed AI models, contribute to complying with cybersecurity regulations, and potentially mitigate inherent cybersecurity vulnerabilities in deployed AI models.

4.6.4 Towards AI Act Compliance in MLOps

In relation to the AI Act, concept drift detection and CI/CD/CT have the potential to be included in MLOps for AI Act compliance.

According to the AI Act Article 15 (1), high-risk AI systems shall be designed and developed in such a way that they "achieve an appropriate level of accuracy, robustness, and cybersecurity and that *they perform consistently in those respects throughout their lifecycle*". Moreover, Article 15 (4) requires technical measures to be taken to enhance the resilience regarding errors that may occur when the AI system is deployed. Article 15 (4) further requires appropriate mitigation measures to eliminate or reduce biased outputs from feedback loops. The next paragraph will argue that concept drift detection and CI/CD/CT in MLOps might provide such a technical measure to enhance the resilience towards errors of deployed AI systems.

Subsection 4.6.2 elaborated on the active and passive approach to concept drift detection, where the active approach involves attempting to detect the shift in the data environment during AI model deployment and having mitigating measures in place – such as model retraining – if such shifts are detected. The passive approach involves updating the model continuously without regard to detected shifts in the deployed model. The AI Act Article 15 (4) requires

114 Joon-Woo Lee et al. "Privacy-preserving machine learning with fully homomorphic encryption for deep neural network". In: *iEEE Access* 10 (2022), pp. 30039–30054. doi: https://doi.org/10.1109/ACCESS.2022.3159694; Bjørn Aslak Juliussen et al. "The third country problem under the GDPR: Enhancing protection of data transfers with technology". In: *International Data Privacy Law* 13.3 (2023), pp. 225–243.

only technical measures to ensure that the model is resilient towards errors that might occur during its deployment, such as concept drift. Both active and passive concept drift detection and mitigation measures might, therefore, be implemented to comply with the AI Act Article 15. CI/CD/CT is an example of a passive approach where the deployed AI model is continuously retrained to avoid concept drift. The risk-based approach of the AI Act entails that the choice of an active or passive approach to concept drift detection and mitigation in deployed high-risk AI systems is dependent on the identified risk and type of high-risk AI system.

4.7 SUMMARY

This chapter's important findings are summarised as follows:

- The current chapter has focused on legal requirements for deployed AI systems under the GDPR, the AI Act, and the CRA. Under the GDPR, the focus has been especially on the fundamental principles of accuracy, purpose limitation, and data minimisation. The analysis of the principle of accuracy has established that the overall accuracy of an AI system, often measured with the metrics sensitivity and positive predictive values, does not completely correspond to the principle under the GDPR, where the principle relates to the accuracy in line with the processing purpose.
- The AI Act has the most substantial requirements for the development phase of AI systems. However, the AI Act also contains prohibitions on specific AI systems. For deployed AI systems, the AI Act contains requirements for risk management, post-market monitoring, record-keeping and serious incident reporting, human oversight, accuracy and cybersecurity of high-risk AI systems, and some specific requirements for general-purpose AI models and general-purpose AI models with systemic risk.
- High-risk AI systems entering the scope of the CRA need to assess and mitigate risks to the cyber resilience of the AI system according to the CRA. AI-specific vulnerabilities of deployed AI models include perturbation attacks, poisoning attacks, model inversion attacks, membership inference attacks, model stealing attacks, and attacking the infrastructure surrounding the deployed AI model. Since deployed AI models carry distinct vulnerabilities, the risk-mitigating measures need to be targeted when deployed high-risk AI systems also enter the scope of the CRA.
- By interpreting Article 22 (1) of the GDPR in line with the Schufa Holding AG judgement from the CJEU, it was established that Article 22 (1) establishes a prohibition that the controller needs to implement without it being invoked by the data subject. Moreover, profiling conducted by third parties

could be included in the scope of Article 22 when another party draws strongly on the profiling to produce a decision with legal or similar effect. For controllers processing personal data in deployed AI systems, the understanding of Article 22 (1) would entail that more profiling conducted will be included in the scope of Article 22 than previously expected and that the controllers must map out if the profiling is used by third parties to make decisions. If automated individual decision-making takes place, the controllers need to rely on the derogations under Article 22 (2).

- Article 15 (1) (h) of the GDPR contains a right to receive meaningful information about the logic involved in automated decision-making. By interpreting legal literature and different language versions of the GDPR, the chapter established that the right relates to *ex-post* explanations of individual decisions. The right has to be assessed on a case-by-case basis. Generally, the access right should make it possible for the data subject to assess the lawfulness of the automated decision-making. Thus, the explanation has to be understandable, reliable, and useful for the data subject.
- Article 86 (1) of the AI Act provides a right to an explanation of individual decisions from high-risk AI systems listed in Annex III to the AI Act. The right does not enter into effect where affected persons have a right in other regulations under Union law, such as Article 15 (1) (h) of the GDPR.
- Both intrinsic and post-hoc XAI methods may be used to comply with the right to an explanation under Article 15 (1) (h) of the GDPR and Article 86 (1) of the AI Act.
- MLOps practices can enhance the principle of accuracy and purpose limitation under the GDPR, accuracy and robustness in the AI Act, and cybersecurity requirements for high-risk AI systems under the CRA through embedding compliance issues in the MLOps framework and addressing concept drift through CI/CD/CT.

5. The AIaaS component: legal requirements for AI as a Service

5.1 INTRODUCTION

The two previous chapters have mapped out and analysed legal and compliance requirements for training data collection and model training in Chapter 3 and model inference in Chapter 4. The current chapter shifts focus to the legal requirements relevant when a finished AI system is applied through a widely used business model known as AI as a Service (AIaaS). AIaaS refers to various forms of AI outsourcing where trained AI models are offered by providers through cloud-based interfaces.[1] Many AIaaS providers also have functionalities that facilitate continuous learning throughout the use of the ML model.[2]

The application of ML models through AIaaS could be illustrated with an example. Suppose that a small tour operator wants to offer more effective and improved customer service for their visitors. However, the operator does not have the resources or competencies to develop an AI-driven chatbot using ML from beginning to end. The tour operator has the data needed to develop a customer service chatbot. Therefore, the operator integrates a finished trained ML model, fine-tunes it on their data, and includes ML functionalities through an AIaaS provider. The ML model is accessed on the AIaaS platform through Application Programming Interfaces (APIs).[3]

---

[1] Sebastian Lins et al. "Artificial intelligence as a service: Classification and research directions". In: *Business & Information Systems Engineering* 63 (2021), pp. 441–456. doi: https://doi.org/10.1007/s12599-021-00708-w; Jennifer Cobbe and Jatinder Singh. "Artificial intelligence as a service: Legal responsibilities, liabilities, and policy challenges". In: *Computer Law & Security Review* 42 (2021), p. 105573. ISSN: 0267-3649. doi: https://doi.org/10.1016/j.clsr.2021.105573. url: https://www.sciencedirect.com/science/article/pii/S0267364921000467.

[2] Amazon Web Service. *Detecting Data Drift Using Amazon Sagemaker.* url: https://aws.amazon.com/blogs/architecture/detecting-data-drift-using-amazon-sagemaker/. Last accessed: 01.08.2025.

[3] Sascha Preibisch. *API Development.* Berkeley: Apress, 2018.

The legal requirements for a compliance by design approach to the processing of personal data within AI systems potentially differ substantially when the AI system is independently developed and deployed, and when the AI model is offered as a service and fine-tuned for a specific organisation through an AIaaS platform. Therefore, data protection regulation, cybersecurity regulation, and AI regulation need to be specifically analysed and assessed in an AIaaS setting in the current chapter. The sections of Chapter 5 are organised as follows:

- Section 5.2 provides a substantive overview of AIaaS. Included in the overview are examples of the terms of service from some of the largest AIaaS providers regarding relevant compliance aspects, including data protection.
- In Section 5.3, relevant data protection regulation aspects of AIaaS are analysed, particularly the legal basis for the processing of personal data to develop the ML model on the AIaaS platform further, joint controllership of AIaaS providers, and requirements for third-country transfers in Chapter V of the GDPR in an AIaaS context.
- Section 5.4 addresses cybersecurity regulation compliance in AIaaS, with a specific focus on the security of APIs.[4] APIs are frequently applied to offer AI models on the AIaaS platforms.
- Section 5.5 focuses on relevant requirements for AIaaS in the AI Act, specifically focusing on AI lifecycle management requirements and the provider/deployer relationship on AIaaS platforms.
- Section 5.6 summarises the overall findings of the chapter and provides concluding remarks.

5.2 AI AS A SERVICE (AIAAS)

AIaaS – sometimes also referred to as Machine Learning as a Service (MLaaS)[5] – is a commercially used term and, thus, does not have an authoritative legal or technical definition. One definition from Lins et al. refers to AIaaS as "cloud-based systems providing on-demand services to organisations and individuals to deploy, develop, train, and manage AI models".[6] This broad

4 Ibid.

5 Mauro Ribeiro, Katarina Grolinger, and Miriam AM Capretz. "Mlaas: Machine learning as a service". In: *2015 IEEE 14th International Conference on Machine Learning and Applications (ICMLA)*. New York: IEEE, 2015, pp. 896–902. doi: https://doi.org/10.1109/ICMLA.2015.152.

6 Sebastian Lins et al. "Artificial intelligence as a service: Classification and research directions". In: *Business & Information Systems Engineering* 63 (2021), pp. 441–456. doi: https://doi.org/10.1007/s12599-021-00708-w.

definition, based on how the term AIaaS is used in the industry, covers ready-to-use AI applications, tools assisting developers to implement AI capabilities, and AI infrastructure such as hardware solutions for computational power, network, and storage capacity.[7]

As in the example of the development of an AI-based chatbot in section 5.1, the need for AIaaS stems from several factors, including a lack of expertise and knowledge, few AI professionals, and a lack of budget and expertise required to develop an AI system from start to end. These constraints have fostered a business model that combines ML models with cloud computing, making it possible to use finished trained models to draw inferences and, at the same time, have on-demand access to a "shared pool of configurable computing resources (...) that can be rapidly provisioned".[8]

Cloud technology is the key to AIaaS. In general, cloud computing delivers computing resources over a network, such as the Internet.[9] The computing resources – the hardware – are moved from the local computer to a server park. Cloud computing resources are rented by the operators who use them and are billed according to the actual use of the resources.[10] The renters or tenants of the cloud infrastructure build the infrastructure on their existing platforms. In AIaaS, the cloud infrastructure is implemented into existing or new software, services, or applications. In the example in the introduction where a tour provider would like to implement an AI-based customer service chatbot, the chatbot could be delivered via an existing app that is connected to the AI services delivered on the cloud infrastructure.

AIaaS is offered through cloud services. It is therefore necessary to place AIaaS in context with other service models offered through the cloud: Software as a service (SaaS), Platform as a service, and Infrastructure as a service (IaaS).[11] SaaS makes it possible to use cloud-based applications directly; examples include Office365, where Microsoft Office applications are moved to the cloud. PaaS are more directed towards developers than towards end-users, making it possible to use a development and deployment environment

---

[7] Ibid.

[8] P Mell and T Grance. *The NIST Definition of Cloud Computing*. Tech. rep. Gaithersburg: National Institute of Standards and Technology, 2011.

[9] Nick Antonopoulos and Lee Gillam. *Cloud Computing*. Vol. 51. 7. Cham: Springer, 2010. doi: https://doi.org/10.1007/978-3-319-54645-2.

[10] Google Cloud. *Cloud Billing Overview*. url: https://cloud.google.com/billing/docs/concepts. Last accessed: 26.08.2024.

[11] Farrukh Nadeem. "Evaluating and ranking cloud IaaS, PaaS and SaaS models based on functional and non-functional key performance indicators". In: *IEEE Access* 10 (2022), pp. 63245–63257. doi: https://doi.org/10.1109/ACCESS.2022.3182688.

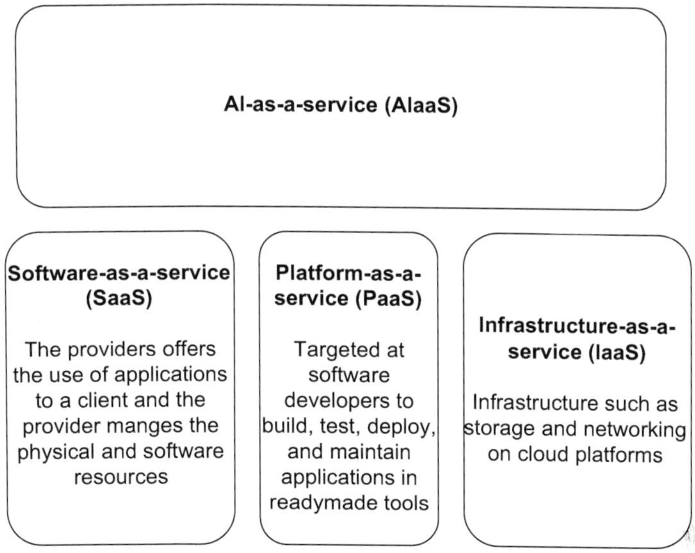

Figure 5.1 *Overview of AIaaS in relation to Software as a service, Platform as a service, and Infrastructure as a service*

in the cloud. It is possible to run and maintain applications on PaaS. Finally, IaaS provides virtualised computing resources, such as storage, network, and servers, on cloud services. AIaaS offers services across these different types of cloud services. AIaaS may, for instance, offer finished applications, such as SaaS, hardware solutions, IaaS, and development opportunities (PaaS).[12] The relationship between the different cloud service types is illustrated in Figure 5.1.

Different AIaaS vendors could either offer the technical cloud environment to process and develop the ML models or offer access to pre-trained models that can be used with the tenant's own data to fine-tune the pre-trained model to the tenant's data environment. Since the launch of generative pre-trained transformers in late 2022, the last alternative – access to pre-trained models that can be fine-tuned – is one of the most predominant types of AIaaS.[13]

12 Sebastian Lins et al. "Artificial intelligence as a service: Classification and research directions". In: *Business & Information Systems Engineering* 63 (2021), pp. 441–456. doi: https://doi.org/10.1007/s12599-021-00708-w.

13 Markets and Markets. *AI as a Service Market Global Forecast to 2028*. url: https://www.marketsandmarkets.com/Market-Reports/artificial-intelligence-ai-as-a-service-market-121842268.html. Last accessed: 01.08.2025. Medium.

One method often applied for such fine-tuning is Retrieval-Augmented Generation (RAG).[14] RAG is a method applied to fine-tune an LLM to the data applied in a specific domain. To illustrate the applicability of RAG, suppose that someone wants to develop a customer service chatbot for a tour operator. With an LLM, such as ChatGPT, the LLM could provide general answers to queries such as what to pack for the tour. However, the chatbot could not answer specific questions, such as how much the tour costs or when it starts. When using RAG, the chatbot would first generate a response based on the LLM, then test the response against domain knowledge outside of the training sources, for example, information scraped from the tour operators' website.[15] RAG does not require complete model retraining of the LLM; the RAG technology builds on query technology used in search engines to retrieve the information from the internal data, and then changes the output from the LLM.[16]

The market of AIaaS providers consists of both some of the world's largest technology companies and some smaller providers.[17] The largest providers include Microsoft Azure,[18] Amazon Web Services (AWS),[19] Google Cloud,[20]

Fine-tuning versus RAG in Generative AI Applications. url: https://harsha-srivatsa.medium.com/fine-tuning-versus-rag-in-generative-ai-applications-architecture-d54ca6d2acb8. Last accessed: 01.08.2025.

14 Patrick Lewis et al. *Retrieval-Augmented Generation for Knowledge-Intensive NLP Tasks*. 2021. arXiv: 2005.11401 [cs.CL]. url: https://arxiv.org/abs/2005.11401.

15 Ibid.

16 Ibid.

17 Markets and Markets. *AI as a Service Market Global Forecast to 2028*. url: https://www.marketsandmarkets.com/Market-Reports/artificial-intelligence-ai-as-a-service-market-121842268.html. Last accessed: 01.08.2025.

18 Microsoft. *Microsoft Azure*. url: https://azure.microsoft.com/. Last accessed: 01.08.2025.

19 Amazon Web Services. *Build and Scale the Next Wave of AI Innovation on AWS*. url: https://aws.amazon.com/ai/?nc2=h_ql_sol_use_ai. Last accessed: 01.08.2025.

20 Google. *AI and Machine Learning Products*. url: https://cloud.google.com/products/ai?hl=en. Last accessed: 01.08.2025.

OpenAI,[21] and IMB Watson.[22] Some of the smaller providers of AIaaS platforms include, for instance, Hugging Face,[23] DataRobot,[24] and BigML.[25]

Finished trained ML models offered through AIaaS are often accessed through an API.[26] The tenants of the AIaaS platform send an API request to the AIaaS platform together with the input data, the input data is computed in the AI model, and the output is returned to the application or system of the tenant through an API response. APIs are further elaborated in subsection 5.4.4 below. The overall flow of data from the AIaaS platform tenant to the platform traditionally follows these steps:

1. The input data is collected by the tenant from, e.g., sensors, usage data from third parties, data brokers, or similar.
2. The input data is transferred from the tenant to the AIaaS platform over a network through an API request.
3. The data is processed in the ML model at the AIaaS platform.
4. The output from the ML model is transmitted back to the tenant's system or application through an API response.[27]

The next section will address legal and compliance issues relating to AIaaS platforms, particularly those that arise when personal data is processed on AIaaS platforms. Data protection regulation, cybersecurity regulation, and requirements in the AI Act will be examined, starting with data protection regulation and requirements in the GDPR, especially relevant for AIaaS.

---

[21] OpenAI. *The Fastest and Most Powerful Platform for Building AI Products.* url: https://openai.com/api/. Last accessed: 01.08.2021.

[22] IBM. *IBM Watson.* url: https://www.ibm.com/watson. Last accessed: 01.08.2025.

[23] Hugging Face. *Hugging Face Enterprise.* url: https://huggingface.co/. Last accessed: 01.08.2025.

[24] DataRobot. *One Unified Platform for Generative and Predictive AI.* url: https://www.datarobot.com/. Last accessed: 01.08.2025.

[25] BigML. *Machine Learning Made Beautifully Simple for Everyone.* url: https://bigml.com/. Last accessed: 01.08.2025.

[26] Jennifer Cobbe and Jatinder Singh. "Artificial intelligence as a service: Legal responsibilities, liabilities, and policy challenges". In: *Computer Law & Security Review* 42 (2021), p. 105573. ISSN: 0267-3649. doi: https://doi.org/10.1016/j.clsr.2021.105573. url: https://www.sciencedirect.com/science/article/pii/S0267364921000467.

[27] Ibid.

5.3 AIaaS AND DATA PROTECTION REGULATION

5.3.1 Introduction

Section 5.3 will map out and analyse the requirements of the GDPR that are particularly relevant for the processing of personal data on AIaaS platforms.

Subsection 5.3.2 will analyse the legal basis for the reuse of personal data to develop ML models further on AIaaS platforms.

Subsection 5.3.3 focuses on the adjacent question of whether the tenant and the AIaaS platform provider assume joint controllership when personal data is used to develop the models on AIaaS platforms.

Several AIaaS platforms are established in countries outside the protected area under the GDPR – i.e., the countries in the European Economic Area (EEA). Section 5.3.4 will analyse requirements for third-country transfers under Chapter V of the GDPR, especially related to the definition of "transfer" in relation to the processing of personal data on AIaaS platforms.

Finally, subsection 5.3.5 summarises the overall findings related to data protection regulation and AIaaS and provides concluding remarks.

5.3.2 Reuse of Personal Data to Develop the Model: Legal Basis

When personal data is collected by the AIaaS tenant, sent to the AIaaS platform via an API request, and processed in the ML model on the platform to draw inferences, several AIaaS platforms use the personal data to further develop the models. The (personal) data applied in the model is applied to either continuously develop the model or develop the ML model to process data for other or new functionalities.

For instance, according to Section 3 of the Data Processing Addendum to the terms of service of Amazon Web Services (AWS), AWS uses customer data "to maintain or provide the Services".[28] In the terms of service of Microsoft Azure, Microsoft reserves the right to use data to keep "products up to date and performance, and enhancing user productivity, reliability, efficacy, quality, and security".[29]

---

[28] Amazon Web Services (AWS). *AWS Data Processing Addendum to the AWS Customer Agreement.* url: https://d1.awsstatic.com/legal/aws-dpa/aws-dpa.pdf. Last accessed: 26.08.2024.

[29] Microsoft. *Microsoft Products and Services Data Protection Addendum (DPA).* url: https://www.microsoft.com/licensing/docs/view/Microsoft-Products-and-Services-Data-Protection-Addendum-DPA?lang=1. Last accessed: 26.08.2024.

If, e.g., AWS or Azure intends to continuously train the ML models in the AIaaS platforms on personal data processed from the AIaaS platform tenants, this is possible in accordance with the terms of service and licensing agreements cited above. However, it is essential to analyse whether such product improvement – achieved by retraining the ML model and continuously improving the model by training it on the personal data from the tenants – would be regarded as a new purpose under the GDPR and whether such processing requires an additional legal basis.

The processing of personal data to improve products and services was one of the topics in the 2023 Meta Platforms Inc. judgement from the CJEU.[30] The following excerpts from paragraph (121) of the Meta Platform Inc. judgement are especially relevant:

> [A]s regards the "product improvement" objective, it cannot be ruled out from the outset that the controller's interest in improving the product or service with a view to making it more efficient and thus more attractive can constitute a legitimate interest capable of justifying the processing of personal data and that such processing may be necessary in order to pursue that interest.
>
> However, subject to final assessment by the referring court in that respect, it appears doubtful whether, as regards the data processing at issue in the main proceedings, the "product improvement" objective, given the scale of that processing and its significant impact on the user, as well as the fact that the user cannot reasonably expect those data to be processed by Meta Platforms Ireland, may override the interests and fundamental rights of such a user, particularly in the case where that user is a child.

The cited excerpt from the Meta Platform Inc. judgement presupposes that processing personal data for product improvement – such as retraining ML models on AIaaS platforms on personal data to develop the model – constitutes a new purpose distinct from the original processing purpose. When personal data is processed by the AIaaS platform tenant, it serves the tenant's interests. However, when personal data is utilised and processed to further develop and enhance the ML models on the platform, the primary purpose shifts to benefit the AIaaS platform provider. Although tenants would also benefit from continuous learning and improvement of the ML models, the primary interest in further processing for product improvement lies with the AIaaS platform provider. This distinction in whether the AIaaS tenant or the provider benefits from the processing underscores that product improvement and continuous training are new purposes that require a specific legal basis. Subsection 5.3.3

---

30 Judgement of the Court (Grand Chamber) in Case C-252/21 Meta Platforms Inc., Meta Platforms Ireland Ltd, Facebook Deutschland GmbH v. Budeskartellamt ECLI:EU:C:2023:537.

will examine the implications of processing personal data for AIaaS platforms in terms of joint controllership.

The legal analyses in subsection 3.2.7 in Chapter 3 are also relevant for the legal bases applied to process personal data for product improvement on AIaaS platforms. Consent, the performance of a contract, and legitimate interests can therefore – potentially – be applied to process data for such purposes, with Article 6 (1) (f) (legitimate interests) being the most relevant legal basis.

In its Meta Platforms Inc. judgement, the CJEU did not preclude the possibility for a controller's interest in improving the product to constitute a legitimate interest under Article 6 (1) (f) of the GDPR. However, the CJEU was doubtful whether the scale of processing of personal data and its significant impact on its users in Meta's applications made the legitimate interest in "product improvement" proportionate under Article 6 (1) (f). However, the specific proportionality assessment was an assessment deferred to the national court.

In order to contextualise the CJEU's assessment of "product improvement" as a legitimate interest under Article 6 (1) (f), it is relevant to understand how Meta Platforms processes personal data to improve its products. Neither the judgement from the CJEU, the application, nor the grounds in the request for a preliminary ruling to the CJEU provide detailed descriptions of Meta's personal data processing practices for product improvement. However, a decision from the Irish DPA – in which Meta Platforms were fined 210 million euros for violating the GDPR – characterises the product improvement purpose as "lacking clarity and concision". This vagueness renders it "difficult for the user to access meaningful information as to the processing operations".[31]

Hence, in order for personal data to be processed on AIaaS platforms to further develop the platform's ML models under Article 6 (1) (f) of the GDPR, the purpose and specific processing operations must be clearly communicated to the data subjects, and not just the AIaaS platform's tenants.

In conclusion, the reuse of personal data to continuously develop AI systems on AIaaS platforms primarily serves the interests of the AIaaS platform provider, although tenants may also benefit from product improvement. However, in order for such processing to be in line with the most relevant legal basis, Article 6 (1) (f) of the GDPR, the processing must be in line with the data subjects' reasonable expectations and be clearly communicated to the data subjects, not just the platform tenants. The processing must also be proportionate

31 Data Protection Commission. *Decision of the Data Protection Commission made pursuant to Section 113 of the Data Protection Act, 2018 and Articles 60 and 65 of the General Data Protection Regulation*. On page 72. url: https://www.dataprotection.ie/sites/default/files/uploads/2023-04/Meta%20FINAL%20DECISION%20%28ADOPTED%29%2031-12-22%20-%20IN-18-5-5%20%28Redacted%29.pdf. Last accessed: 01.08.2025.

under Article 6 (1) (f). Currently, the industry standard in terms of the AIaaS platform seems to obscure the processing of personal data to develop the platform's AI models through vague terms such as, e.g., "improving products and services".

5.3.3 Reuse of Personal Data to Develop the Model: Joint Controllership

The former subsection concluded that processing personal data to continuously develop and improve ML models on AIaaS platforms constitutes a distinct purpose from processing personal data to infer outputs from these ML models.

The focus of the current subsection will be on whether AIaaS platform providers may assume joint controllership or even sole controllership when processing personal data for the purpose of model improvement on AIaaS platform models.

Before analysing whether AIaaS platform providers and platform tenants could assume joint controllership when personal data is processed on these platforms to infer decisions and develop the models further, it is essential to define controllership and joint controllership under the GDPR.

A controller is defined in Article 4 (7) of the GDPR as "the natural or legal person, public authority, agency or other body which, alone or jointly with others, determines the purposes and means of the processing of personal data".

A processor is defined in Article 4 (8) of the GDPR as "a natural or legal person, public authority, agency or other body which processes personal data on behalf of the controller".

Controllers are the primary carriers of obligations of the GDPR and key actors in the operationalisation of the requirements of the regulation.[32] When allocating the role as controller, the predecessor of the EDPB, WP29,[33] the EDPB,[34] and the CJEU[35] have explicitly emphasised that the concept of con-

---

[32] Luca Tosoni and Lee A. Bygrave. "Article 4(7) Controller". In: *The EU General Data Protection Regulation (GDPR): A Commentary.* Ed. by Christopher Kuner, Lee A. Bygrave, and Christopher Docksey. Oxford: Oxford University Press, 2020, p. 146.

[33] Article 29 Working Party. *Opinion 01/2010 on the Concepts of "Controller" and "Processor" WP169, 16 February 2010.* On page 9.

[34] EDPB. *Guidelines 07/2020 on the Concepts of Controllers and Processor in the GDPR.* On page 10. url: https://www.edpb.europa.eu/system/files/2023-10/EDPB_guidelines_202007_controllerprocessor_final_en.pdf. Last accessed: 01.08.2025.

[35] Judgement of 13 May 2014 in Case C-131/12 Google Spain, ECLI:EU:C:2014:317, paragraph 68; Judgement of the Court (Grand Chamber)

troller shall be interpreted broadly with a basis on factual influence rather than formal analysis. Consequently, the designation of controllership in contractual arrangements or terms of service of AIaaS platforms is not a decisive factor. The decisive factor is whether an entity, in fact, determines the purpose and means of the processing.

To assume controllership under Article 4 (7), an entity must determine the purposes and means of processing personal data. The responsibilities of a controller require that the entity has the potential to assert influence over the processing, as indicated by the term "determines" in Article 4 (7) of the GDPR. In other words, the obligations as a controller presuppose that the entity can control the processing. In the context of an AIaaS platform, the "determine" criterion in Article 4 (7) can arise both from legal and factual influence over the processing.

The AIaaS platform provider could have control over the processing through legal provisions in the terms of service or through an obligation in law that prescribes some form of processing, such as collecting and further processing specific data for a particular reason. Additionally, with regard to factual influence, the AIaaS platform provider could exert decisive influence over the processing of personal data, in terms of both the technical measures used and the interest and the purpose of further processing.

For instance, if a controller (tenant) decides to make use of an AIaaS platform to process personal data for a specific purpose under a standard contract, where the AIaaS tenant has little to no influence over the standardised platform terms, and the personal data is solely used to infer the decision in the ML models on the platform, without further processing and strictly according to the tenant's instructions, the tenant would be considered the controller, and the platform provider the processor.

However, if the AIaaS provider processes the data further for its own purposes, such as model retraining, it could be argued that the platform provider also exerts influence over the processing, determines the purpose of the processing, and thus should be regarded as a controller for the processing related to the retraining.

The "purposes" relate to the objectives of the processing – the overarching goals, or the "why" – while the "means" relates to the technical and

of 5 June 2018 in case C-210/16 Unabhängiges Landeszentrum für Datenschutz Schleswig-Holstein v Wirtschaftsakademie Schleswig-Holstein GmbH ECLI:EU:C:2018:388; Judgement of the Court (Grand Chamber) of 29 July 2019 in case C-401/17 Fashion ID GmbH and Co. KG v Verbraucherzentrale NRW eV ECLI:EU:C:2019:629.

organisational measures of the processing, or the "how".[36] According to WP29, determining the purpose, the *why*, of the processing, is more decisive than the measures, the *how*, when allocating controllership status.[37] Certain aspects of the processing measures, such as minor technical means, may thus be delegated to a processor without the processor assuming controllership status.

Regarding potential joint controllership between the AIaaS platform provider and the platform tenant, the wording "alone or jointly with others" in Article 4 (7) of the GDPR is particularly relevant. According to the CJEU: "where several operators determine jointly the purposes and means of the processing of personal data, they participate in that processing as [joint] controllers".[38] Based on the guidance from WP29, the criteria for determining joint controllership are essentially equivalent to the criteria for determining sole controllership. However, the participation of the parties may take different forms and does not have to be equally shared.[39]

In the context of AIaaS platforms, the overall processing involves several stages, comprising the collection of the personal data by the tenant, the transmission of the data to the platform through an API request, the processing of the data in the model, and the retransmission of the model's output data to the tenant through an API response. Additionally, the AIaaS platform might process the data further, for instance, to develop the model or for other purposes. It is possible for the platform and the tenant to jointly or solely decide the purposes and means of the different stages. The tenant might be the controller of the overall processing, while the platform provider assumes controller status only for parts of the processing, the processing to develop the models. Therefore, the overall AIaaS processing chain might be divided into smaller processing operations, where the platform provider and the tenant are responsible for determining the purposes and means of each of the stages individually.

When deciding whether an entity would assume joint controllership, the requirements in Article 26 of the GDPR are relevant. According to the EDPB, the qualification of joint controllership will have main consequences related to

---

36 Luca Tosoni and Lee A. Bygrave. "Article 4(7) Controller". In: *The EU General Data Protection Regulation (GDPR): A Commentary.* Ed. by Christopher Kuner, Lee A. Bygrave, and Christopher Docksey. Oxford: Oxford University Press, 2020, p. 146.

37 Article 29 Working Party. *Opinion 01/2010 on the Concepts of "Controller" and "Processor" WP169, 16 February 2010.* On page 9.

38 Judgement of the Court (Grand Chamber) of 29 July 2019 in case C-401/17 Fashion ID GmbH and Co. KG v Verbraucherzentrale NRW eV ECLI:EU:C:2019:629.

39 Article 29 Working Party. *Opinion 01/2010 on the Concepts of "Controller" and "Processor" WP169, 16 February 2010.* On page 9.

the assignment of obligations to comply with data protection rules, in particular with respect to the rights of individuals.[40] When assessing joint controllership, the starting point is the same as controllership: Article 4 (7) of the GDPR. The assessment of joint controllership should mirror the assessment of normal "single" controllership status. The difference between a single controllership and a joint is that the determination of purposes and means of the processing of personal data is decided together by more than one party. Similar to assessing controllership, joint controllership has to be determined after a factual assessment, where terms in a contract or similar are assessed in relation to the actual processing of personal data.

With regard to the processing of personal data in AIaaS platforms, the starting criterion of joint controllership is fulfilled by default: there is more than one party in the processing chain, namely the AIaaS platform provider and the tenant. According to the EDPB, joint participation needs to include both the determination of purposes and the means. If each of these elements is determined by all the entities concerned, they should be considered joint controllers. In order for the AIaaS platform provider and the platform tenant to be regarded as joint controllers, the tenant and the provider need to determine both purposes and means.

To further shed light on the notion of joint controllership in Article 26 of the GDPR, it is necessary to analyse some of the case law from the CJEU regarding joint controllers. According to the CJEU in the Tietosuojavaltuutettu case,[41] both parties do not need to have access to the personal data processed to be joint controllers. In the context of the AIaaS platform, it would entail that even though the tenant does not have access to the processing for model improvement, the tenant could have the status of a joint controller.

Moreover, the CJEU held in the FashionID case[42] that an entity will be considered as a joint controller with the other(s) only with respect to those operations for which it determines, jointly with others, the means and the purposes

---

[40] EDPB. *Guidelines 07/2020 on the Concepts of Controllers and Processor in the GDPR*. On page 10. url: https://www.edpb.europa.eu/system/files/2023-10/EDPB_guidelines_202007_controllerprocessor_final_en.pdf. Last accessed: 01.08.2025.

[41] Judgement of the Court (Grand Chamber) of 10 July 2018 in Case C-25/17 Tietosuojavaltuutettu intervening parties: Jehovan todistajat — uskonnollinen yhdyskunta ECLI:EU:C:2018:551. [404]Judgement of the Court (Grand Chamber) of 29 July 2019 in case C-401/17 Fashion ID GmbH and Co. KG v Verbraucherzentrale NRW eV ECLI:EU:C:2019:629.

[42] Judgement of the Court (Grand Chamber) of 29 July 2019 in case C-401/17 Fashion ID GmbH and Co. KG v Verbraucherzentrale NRW eV ECLI:EU:C:2019:629.

of the same data processing, in particular in case of converging decisions. If one of these entities decides alone the purposes and means of operations that precede or are subsequent in the chain of processing, this entity must be considered the sole controller of this preceding or subsequent operation.

In relation to the processing of personal data in AIaaS platforms, it would entail that if the platform decides the purposes and means of the processing for model improvement alone, the platform provider would be regarded as the sole controller. However, if the purpose and means are decided together with the tenant in, e.g., the terms of service, both parties, dependent on the facts of the case, could be regarded as joint controllers.

Although formal aspects, such as whether the AIaaS platforms assume controllership or joint controllership in terms of service, are not decisive, such formal aspects might be a relevant starting point. As of September 2024, two of the largest AIaaS platforms – Microsoft Azure and Amazon Web Services – assume responsibility as processors and not controllers, according to their terms of service.[43] Microsoft assumes the controller status for some services, including incident response.[44] However, it is the factual situation and how the personal data is processed that is decisive for status as controller, and not contractual arrangements. It is therefore pertinent to analyse whether AIaaS platforms will assume controllership for the processing of personal data in such platforms based on a factual assessment of the processing of personal data in AIaaS platforms, in order to conclude on the controllership status.

The next paragraphs will illustrate how the different factual assessments related to personal data processing on AIaaS platforms might lead to different results regarding joint controllership. These factual assessments are illustrated in the flowchart in Figure 5.2, and how different facts lead to potentially different results is illustrated in Table 5.1.

The internal relationship between the joint controllers is regulated in Article 26 of the GDPR, where the duties of the controllers have to be shared between

---

[43] Microsoft. *Microsoft Products and Services Data Protection Addendum (DPA)*. url: https://www.microsoft.com/licensing/docs/view/Microsoft-Products-and-Services-Data-Protection-Addendum-DPA?lang=1. Last accessed: 26.08.2024. Amazon Web Services. *Build and Scale the Next Wave of AI Innovation on AWS*. url: https://aws.amazon.com/ai/?nc2=h_ql_sol_use_ai. Last accessed: 01.08.2025.

[44] Microsoft. *Microsoft Products and Services Data Protection Addendum (DPA)*. url: https://www.microsoft.com/licensing/docs/view/Microsoft-Products-and-Services-Data-Protection-Addendum-DPA?lang=1. Last accessed: 26.08.2024.

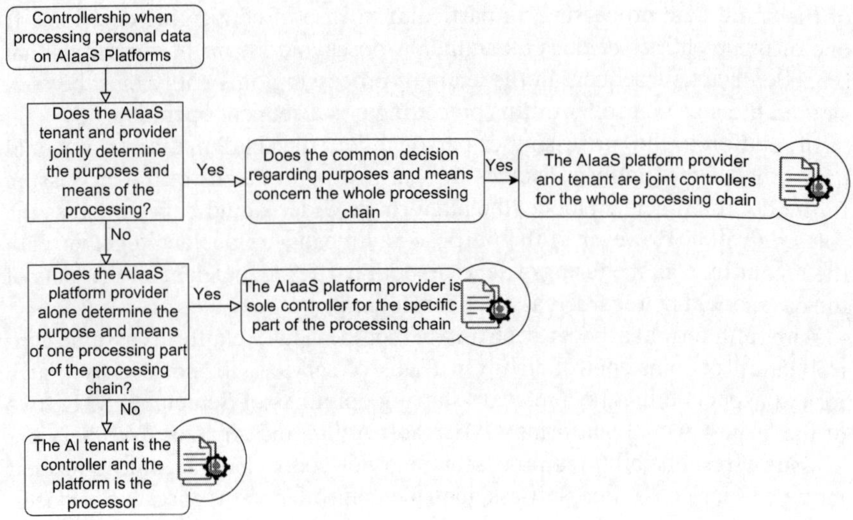

Figure 5.2 Flowchart of the controllership status on AIaaS platforms

Table 5.1 Table illustrating the different processor/controller relationships in AIaaS platform processing chains

Situation	Status of AIaaS platform provider	Status of AIaaS platform tenant
The tenant process personal data on the platform, the personal data is applied solely to draw inference	Processor	Controller
Personal data is processed on the platform, and both the provider and the tenant decide to process the data to develop the models further	Joint Controller	Joint Controller
Personal data is processed on the platform to draw inference and further processed by the provider to improve the models	Controller (for the processing for model improvement) and processor for the other processing	Controller

the parties in an arrangement. In the judgement in case C-683/21,[45] the CJEU held that the arrangement under Article 26 (1) should be viewed as a consequence of joint controllership and not a precondition for establishing joint controllership. The arrangement, or joint controllership agreement, has to be made available to the data subjects, according to Article 26 (2). Regardless of the arrangement or contract between the parties, the data subject might exercise their rights in respect of and against each controller, according to Article 26 (3) of the GDPR.

A specific issue regarding joint controllership is the situation where one of the parties of the joint controllership is from a European Economic Area (EEA) member state and the other party is established in a third country. Such a situation is very relevant in an AIaaS context where many of the largest providers are US companies.

In both the Wirtschaftsakademie[46] and Google Spain[47] cases, the CJEU established joint controllership with subsidiaries of Facebook and Google established in the EEA, Google Spain and Facebook Ireland. Joint controllership if a US AIaaS provider does not have an establishment in the EEA has not been adjudicated by the CJEU and is not expressly covered in the EDPB guidance.[48] The requirements for designating a lead supervisory authority (LSA) in Article 56 of the GDPR do not provide guidance on a matter of joint controllership between a controller in the EEA and a non-EEA controller either. Even if one party of a processing chain in the processing of personal data on an AIaaS platform does not have an establishment in the EU, Article 3 of the GDPR would entail that the non-EEA entity could enter the territorial scope of the GDPR and, thus, also assume joint controllership. The non-EEA entity would need to have processing activities related to the offering of goods and services to data subjects in the Union or the monitoring of data subjects' behaviour, according to Article 3 (2) (a) and (b) of the GDPR. If the processing does not relate to either of these two alternatives for the non-EEA entity, the situation

---

45 Judgement of the Court (Grand Chamber) of 5 December 2023 in case C-683/21 Nacionalinis visuomenės sveikatos centras prie Sveikatos apsaugos ministerijos v Valstybinė duomen apsaugos inspekcija ECLI:EU:C:2023:949.

46 Judgement of the Court (Grand Chamber) of 5 June 2018 in case C-210/16 Unabhängiges Landeszentrum für Datenschutz Schleswig-Holstein v Wirtschaftsakademie Schleswig-Holstein GmbH ECLI:EU:C:2018:388.

47 Judgement of 13 May 2014 in Case C-131/12 Google Spain, ECLI:EU:C:2014:317, paragraph 68.

48 EDPB. *Guidelines 07/2020 on the Concepts of Controllers and Processor in the GDPR*. On page 10. url: https://www.edpb.europa.eu/system/files/2023-10/EDPB_guidelines_202007_controllerprocessor_final_en.pdf. Last accessed: 01.08.2025.

would more likely constitute a transfer of personal data under Chapter V of the GDPR from the tenant to the provider than a joint controllership.

To conclude, the assessment of whether the AIaaS platform provider and platform tenant are sole controllers, joint controllers, or sole controllers for a part of the processing chain and joint controllers for the rest of the chain is an assessment dependent on the factual situation of the processing and not solely the terms of service of the platform. Relevant in this factual assessment is who decides the purposes and means of the processing and the interest each party has in the processing. As a general conclusion, when personal data is processed to further train the AI models on the platforms, the platform provider could assume sole or joint controllership status depending on the facts of the case.

5.3.4 Third-Country Transfers of Personal Data on AIaaS Platforms

5.3.4.1 Introduction

The overall purpose of the GDPR, as expressed in Article 1, is twofold: To promote the right to personal data protection and to promote the free movement of personal data internally in the EEA member states.[49]

In order to promote these two different objectives concurrently, a necessary consequence is that – as a general rule – personal data could be transferred and flow only to regions that have a similar protection of personal data as in the EEA. Thus, the GDPR has a general principle – with several exemptions – that prohibits the transfers of personal data outside the protected area in the EEA member states. Several of the largest AIaaS platform providers, such as AWS, Microsoft Azure, and Google Cloud, have server infrastructure in countries outside the EEA or are EEA subsidiaries of non-EEA companies.

The next subsections will address the rules relating to transfers of personal data outside the EEA in an AIaaS context.

First, the notion of "transfer" – a concept not defined in the GDPR – is analysed in an AIaaS platform setting in 5.3.4.2.

Then, relevant transfer mechanisms under the GDPR are analysed when transferring data outside the EEA to process the data in an AI model on an AIaaS platform in 5.3.4.3. In 5.3.4.3, some specific aspects of the European Data Protection Supervisor (EDPS) Microsoft 365 decision are also addressed.

In 5.3.4.4, technical aspects of transfers that could enhance the data protection of the transfer are addressed, and the implications of these technical aspects on the transfer rules are addressed.

---

[49] Subsection 5.3.4 is a rewritten version of Bjørn Aslak Juliussen et al. "The third country problem under the GDPR: Enhancing protection of data transfers with technology". In: *International Data Privacy Law* 13.3 [2023], pp. 225–243.

Lastly, 5.3.4.5 summarises the overall findings and provides concluding remarks.

5.3.4.2 The notion of transfers in an AIaaS context

The concept of "transfer" is not defined in either the Articles or the recitals of the GDPR, yet the regulation connects several legal requirements to the concept. The EDPB has, based on the Lindqvist judgement from the CJEU,[50] identified the following cumulative criteria in order for the processing of personal data to constitute a transfer:

1. A controller or processor is subject to the GDPR for the processing in question (the exporter).
2. The exporter discloses by transmission or otherwise makes personal data, subject to this processing, available to another controller, joint controller or processor which is importing the data (the importer).
3. The importer is located in a third country, i.e., a country outside the EU and the EEA, or is an international organisation, regardless of whether or not the importer is subject to the GDPR under Article 3.[51]

The previous subsections have established that when personal data is processed on an AIaaS platform, a commonly used processing chain is that the data is processed by the tenant, transmitted to the AIaaS platform in an API request, processed in the AI models on the platform, and then the output is retransmitted to the tenant through an API response. If the AIaaS tenant is located within the EU or an EEA member state and is subject to the GDPR, and the AIaaS platform is located outside the EEA, all three criteria above are fulfilled, and the data processing is, thus, subject to the rules for international transfers in Chapter V of the GDPR.

In order to shed some more light on the requirements for third-country transfers of personal data on AIaaS platforms, it is relevant to examine the terms of service of the largest AIaaS providers to determine whether the providers have server infrastructure in countries outside the EEA, thus potentially activating the transfer rules under Chapter V of the GDPR.

---

50 Judgement of the Court of 6 November 2003 in the case C-101/01 Bodil Lindqvist ECR 1-12971 ECLI:EU:C:2003:596.

51 EDPB. *Guidelines 05/2021 on the Interplay between the Application of Article 3 and the Provisions on International Transfers as per Chapter V of the GDPR*. url: https://edpb.europa.eu/system/files/2021-11/edpb_guidelinesinterplaychapterv_article3_adopted_en.pdf. Last accessed: 01.08.2025.

Table 5.2 indicates that, as of Q3 2024, some of the largest AIaaS platforms transfer data to third countries, according to publicly available information provided in the terms of service of the AIaaS platforms.

However, regarding Table 5.2, an important disclaimer must be made. The countries listed in the mid-section of the table are based on the countries the AIaaS providers have disclosed as possible receiving countries in their terms of service, data protection amendments, or similar. Transfers of personal data in AIaaS platforms are a highly complex and technical matter, and it is not certain that every type of processing will involve all the subprocessors in the various listed countries. However, the third countries listed are the countries and subprocessors that the AIaaS providers themselves have listed in their terms of service and must therefore be assessed as potential receiving third countries.

An AIaaS platform is – as indicated with all the different subprocessors and different countries in Table 5.2 – a complex and global ecosystem. However, before a controller under the scope of the GDPR could process personal data on such a platform, they would need to have a legal basis, and if the personal data processed is transferred to a third country, the controller would also need to have a valid transfer mechanism. As evident in Table 5.2, several of the largest commercial AIaaS platforms transfer personal data to third countries to provide AI services on the platforms. The risk of transferring personal data is very dependent on the receiving country and the facts of the case in question. The next paragraphs will thus address general aspects of all transfers, regardless of the receiving country.

A pertinent question before the different transfer mechanisms in the GDPR could be analysed in an AIaaS context is the situation where an AIaaS provider processes data in the protected area, but the AIaaS provider is a company established in a third country or a subsidiary of a third-country company. How does the GDPR, interpreted in line with Articles 7 and 8 of the Charter, relate to a situation where personal data is processed in the EEA but by an AIaaS provider established, or a subsidiary of, e.g., a US or Chinese company?

In the cloud and AIaaS platform service market, there is a development towards more data sovereignty. The overall concept in sovereign cloud models or sovereign AIaaS platforms is that the physical infrastructures necessitating third-country transfers, such as servers, are moved from third countries to the protected area in the EEA. In a sovereign AIaaS platform environment, personal data resides in the protected area under the GDPR, making the requirements for transfer to third countries excessive. Sovereign cloud models are therefore a technique applied to not transfer data out of the protected area.[52]

---

[52] Microsoft Corporation. *Microsoft Cloud for Sovereignty: The Most Flexible and Comprehensive Solution for Digital Sovereignty.* url: https://www.microsoft.com/en-us/industry/sovereignty/cloud. Last accessed: 26.08.2024.

Table 5.2 *Overview of international transfers on some of the largest AIaaS platforms*

AIaaS provider	Location	References
Microsoft Azure	• Most of Azures's AI services are storing the personal data at rest within the EU/EEA data boundary. The following services have a non-regional processing chain where data is stored in the EU, but where the processing chain includes other regions: Azure AI Bot Service; Azure AI Translator; Azure Open Datasets; Microsoft Copilot for Security; (and 60 other Azure AI services) • The following services are solely processed globally: Azure Bot Service; Azure Communication Service; Azure DevTest Labs; Azure Monitor; Azure Serial Console; Cloud Shell • The global processing chain includes these countries: South Africa; Israel; Qatar; The United Arab Emirates (UAE); Hong Kong; Singapore; Australia; China; India; Indonesia; Japan; South Korea; Malaysia; New Zealand; Saudi Arabia; Taiwan; USA; Mexico; Chile; Canada; Brazil.	[1–7]
IBM Watson	Australia Japan USA Canada Brazil	[8–15]
Google Cloud	USA Canada Chile India Singapore Indonesia Hong Kong Taiwan Japan Australia South Korea Israel Qatar Saudi Arabia South Africa	[16–17]

AIaaS provider	Location	References
AWS AI Services	USA Canada Brazil Bahrain UAE Israel South Africa Singapore Hong Kong China Japan South Korea Indonesia India Australia Argentina Colombia Kenya Oman Mexico Nigeria Panama The Philippines Taiwan Thailand Vietnam Peru	[18–20]
DataRobot	USA UAE Japan	[21–22]

AIaaS provider	Location	References
Oracle Cloud Infrastructure	India Mexico USA Candada Australia Phillippines Argentina Hong Kong China Ukraine Turkey Singapore Japan Malaysia UAE Brazil Costa Rica Colombia South Africa Egypt Israel Saudi Arabia New Zealand South Korea	[23–24]
OpenAI	USA	[25]

Notes: [1] Microsoft Azure. *Azure AI Bot Service*. url: https://azure.microsoft.com/en-us/products/ai-services/ai-bot-service/. Last accessed: 26.08.2024.
[2] Microsoft Azure. *Azure Geographies*. url: https://azure.microsoft.com/en-us/explore/global-infrastructure/geographies/#overview. Last accessed: 26.08.2024.
[3] Microsoft Azure. *Services That Will Temporarily Transfer a Subset of Customer Data or Pseudonymized Personal Data Out of the EU Data Boundary*. url: https://learn.microsoft.com/en-us/privacy/eudb/eu-data-boundary-temporary-partial-transfers#azure-services. Last accessed: 26.08.2024.
[4] Microsoft Azure. *Configuring Azure Non-regional Services for the EU Data Boundary*. url: https://learn.microsoft.com/en-us/privacy/eudb/eu-data-boundary-configure-azure-nonregional-services. Last accessed: 26.08.2024.
[5] Microsoft Azure. *Microsoft Azure Legal Information*. url: https://azure.microsoft.com/en-us/support/legal/. Last accessed: 26.08.2024.
[6] Microsoft Azure. *Privacy and Security Terms Microsoft Azure Core Services*. url: https://www.microsoft.com/licensing/terms/product/PrivacyandSecurityTerms/MCA. Last accessed: 26.08.2024.
[7] Microsoft Azure. *products Available by Region, Region: Non-regional*. url: https://azure.microsoft.com/en-us/explore/global-infrastructure/products-by-region/?products=all&regions=non-regional. Last accessed: 26.08.2024.
[8] IBM. *POV – Watson Privacy, Compliance, and Security*. url: https://www.ibm.com/watson/assets/duo/pdf/Watson-Privacy-and-Security-POV_final_062819_tps.pdf. Last accessed: 26.08.2024.

[9] IBM. *Keeping Your Data Secure and Compliant*. url: https://dataplatform.cloud.ibm.com/docs/content/wsj/getting-started/security.html?context=cpdaas&audience=wdp. Last accessed: 26.08.2024.
[10] IBM. *What Is the General Data Protection Regulation (GDPR)?* url: https://www.ibm.com/cloud/compliance/gdpr-eu. Last accessed: 26.08.2024.
[11] IBM. *Data Processing Addendum (DPA)*. url: https://www.ibm.com/support/customer/csol/terms/?id=Z126-7870&lc=en. Last accessed: 26.08.2024.
[12] IBM. *Transborder Data Processing and Country Required Terms*. url: https://www.ibm.com/support/customer/csol/terms/?id=Z126-8005&lc=en. Last accessed: 26.08.2024.
[13] IBM. *Service and infrastructure availability by location*. url: https://cloud.ibm.com/docs/overview?topic=overview-services_region. Last accessed: 26.08.2024.
[14] IBM. *Region and Data Center Locations for Resource Deployment*. url: https://cloud.ibm.com/docs/overview?topic=overview-locations. Last accessed: 26.08.2024.
[15] IBM. *IBM Cloud Catalog*. url: https://cloud.ibm.com/catalog?category=ai&search=watson#search_results. Last accessed: 26.08.2024.
[16] Google Cloud. *Google Cloud Platform Terms of Service*. url: https://cloud.google.com/terms. Last accessed: 26.08.2024.
[17] Google Cloud. *Products Available by Location*. url: https://cloud.google.com/about/locations/#multi-region. Last accessed: 26.08.2024.
[18] AWS. *AWS Data Processing Addendum*. url: https://d1.awsstatic.com/legal/aws-gdpr/AWS_GDPR_DPA.pdf. Last accessed: 26.08.2024.
[19] AWS. *Regions and Availability Zones*. url: https://aws.amazon.com/about-aws/global-infrastructure/regions_az/?p=ngi&loc=2. Last accessed: 26.08.2024.
[20] AWS. *AWS Infrastructure Entities*. url: https://aws.amazon.com/compliance/sub-processors/. Last accessed: 26.08.2024.
[21] Datarobot. *Subprocessors*. url: https://www.datarobot.com/privacy/subprocessors/. Last accessed: 26.08.2024.
[22] Datarobot. *DataRobot FAQ on International Transfer of Personal Data*. url: https://www.datarobot.com/wp-content/uploads/2022/03/FAQ-International-Transfer-of-Personal-Data-Post-Schrems-II.pdf. Last accessed: 26.08.2024.
[23] Oracle. *Data Flows and Oracle Services*. url: https://www.oracle.com/contracts/docs/corporate_privacy_shield_statement_071720.pdf?download=false. Last accessed: 26.08.2024.
[24] Oracle. *Oracle Affiliates*. url: https://www.oracle.com/corporate/oracle-affiliates/. Last accessed: 26.08.2024.
[25] OpenAI. *Production Best Practices*. url: https://platform.openai.com/docs/guides/production-best-practices/improving-latencies. Last accessed: 26.08.2024.

Several exporters of personal data are exploring sovereign cloud models with associated AIaaS platform services and functionalities. For instance, Microsoft announced the launch of Microsoft Cloud for Sovereignty in July 2022 and currently offers storage of data at rest in Microsoft Azure within the EU Data Boundary.[53] The sovereign cloud solution is offered to customers who

---

[53] Microsoft Azure. *Configuring Azure Non-regional Services for the EU Data Boundary*. url: https://learn.microsoft.com/en-us/privacy/eudb/eu-data-boundary-configure-azure-nonregional-services. Last accessed: 26.08.2024.

need to guarantee that personal data is processed only in a given region, for instance, in the protected area in the EEA. Other technology companies have announced similar products to mitigate the risk associated with the transfer of personal data to third countries.

The various sovereign cloud solutions incorporate different techniques to enforce personal data protection and confidentiality, including encryption and access controls. Nevertheless, the overall concept underlying such cloud infrastructures is to maintain the data within the jurisdictional boundaries of one specific geographical location. Consequently, the various sovereign cloud providers contend that they offer a solution where the transfer rules in Chapter V become inapplicable because the data is not transferred to a third country.

The following paragraphs will discuss a legal issue when a controller or processor established in the EEA makes use of a sovereign cloud solution, a sovereign AIaaS platform, or other AI services with sovereign functionality: how should a controller or processor in the protected area assess the situation where personal data is processed on a sovereign platform in the protected area and the cloud provider is registered in a third country or is an EU subsidiary of an enterprise registered in a third country?

To recapitulate, the GDPR does not define transfers out of the protected area. A common definition of such transfers is given in the EDPB guidelines.[54] In the situation where personal data is stored and processed in the protected area, but the AIaaS platform provider is an enterprise registered in a third country, the situation is not considered a transfer under the EDPB's guidelines.[55]

In the Council of Europe's Convention for the Protection of Individuals with regard to Automatic Processing of Personal Data (Convention 108+), Article 14, cross-border transfers to third countries are defined as a process where the data is transferred to a recipient that is subject to the jurisdiction of a state that is not a party to Convention 108+.[56] The definition of transfers in Convention 108+ is further elaborated in the Draft Explanatory Report to the Convention.[57]

---

54 EDPB. *Guidelines 05/2021 on the Interplay between the Application of Article 3 and the Provisions on International Transfers as per Chapter V of the GDPR*. url: https://edpb.europa.eu/system/files/2021-11/edpb_guidelinesinterplay chapterv_article3_adopted_en.pdf. Last accessed: 01.08.2025.

55 Ibid.

56 Council of Europe. *Convention for the Protection of Individuals with Regard to the Processing of Personal Data (Convention 108+) Article 14, 18.05.2018*. url: https://rm.coe.int/convention-108-convention-for-the-protection-of-individuals -with-regar/16808b36f1. Last accessed: 01.08.2025.

57 Council of Europe. *Draft Explanatory Report—Convention 108 Modernised*. url: https://rm.coe.int/convention-for-the-protection-of-individuals-with-regard-to -automatic-/16806b6ec2. Last accessed: 01.08.2025.

In the explanatory report, transborder data transfers are further explained as a process where "personal data are disclosed or made available to a recipient subject to the jurisdiction of another State or international organisation".[58] A transborder transfer under Convention 108+ would therefore also cover situations where personal data is made available to a jurisdiction of a non-party to the convention without the personal data being imported to the non-party state. This situation could occur when making personal data available on an AIaaS platform, even though the AIaaS platform server infrastructure is physically located in a state that is party to the Convention.[59]

Convention 108+ is an instrument of European data protection law as drafted and published by the Council of Europe (CoE) and is closely related to the right to data protection under Article 8 of the ECHR. Currently, as of Q3 2025, the Convention is not in force. Convention 108+ does, therefore, have relevance for the interpretation of the right to privacy and data protection in the Charter, according to the Charter Article 52 (3). Neither the GDPR nor the Convention has an explicit collision rule.[60] However, the GDPR does not define transfers. The definition is based on a recommendation from the EDPB[61] that is based on a judgement from the CJEU[62] under the predecessor of the GDPR.[63] The definition of transfers in Convention 108+ Article 14 could therefore represent a valid factor in the interpretation of the notion of "transfer" in EU data protection law.

---

58 Ibid.

59 Cécile de Terwangne. "Council of Europe Convention 108+: A modernised international treaty for the protection of personal data". In: *Computer Law & Security Review* 40 (2021), p. 105497. ISSN: 0267-3649. doi: https://doi.org/10.1016/j.clsr.2020.105497. url: https://www.sciencedirect.com/science/article/pii/S0267364920301023.

60 Jörg Ukrow. "Practitioner's corner – Data protection without frontiers? On the relationship between EU GDPR and amended CoE Convention 108". In: *European Data Protection Law Review* 4.2 (2018). doi: 10.21552/edpl/2018/2/14. url: https://doi.org/10.21552/edpl/2018/2/14.

61 EDPB. *Guidelines 05/2021 on the Interplay between the Application of Article 3 and the Provisions on International Transfers as per Chapter V of the GDPR*. url: https://edpb.europa.eu/system/files/2021-11/edpb_guidelinesinterplaychapterv_article3_adopted_en.pdf. Last accessed: 01.08.2025.

62 Judgement of the Court of 6 November 2003 in the case C-101/01 Bodil Lindqvist ECR 1-12971 ECLI:EU:C:2003:596.

63 Directive 95/46/EC of the European Parliament and of the Council of 24 October 1995 on the protection of individuals with regard to the processing of personal data and of the free movement of such data [1995] OJ L 281/31.

This preliminary conclusion must be somewhat elucidated. In Opinion of the Court 2/13, the CJEU concluded that the EU legal order constituted a distinct legal order and that the draft agreement regarding the EU accession to the ECHR was liable to affect the specific characteristics of EU law and its autonomy.[64] Consequently, the relationship between EU law and CoE law could be described as one marked by a certain tension. However, in May 2023, the CoE and the European Commission published a revised agreement on the EU accession to the ECHR.[65] The purpose of the revised agreement is to alleviate the concerns raised by the CJEU in Opinion 2/13 regarding the autonomy of EU law. This recent development would, most likely, facilitate the future accession of the EU to the ECHR, and therefore also underscores the relevance of Convention 108+ within the domain of EU data protection law.

Article 14 of Convention 108+ is an argument in favour of the entering into effect of the transfer rules in Chapter V of the GDPR when personal data is transferred to an AIaaS platform, within the EEA, but under the control of the authorities in a third country.

In a German judgement from the Administrative Court in Wiesbaden from December 2021, the Court interpreted a situation similar to when a sovereign cloud with AIaaS functionality is controlled by a third-country enterprise. The German Court concluded that even though the personal data never left the protected area under the GDPR, the situation could be defined as a transfer if the company processing the personal data is under the jurisdiction of a third country.[66] The German administrative court did not assess the EDPB transfer guidelines, and the opinion of the Court does, therefore, not represent a homogeneous European interpretation of the GDPR.

The question of whether processing personal data in the protected area by a processor under the jurisdiction of a third country could be regarded as a transfer is also the subject of a non-settled scholarly debate.[67]

---

64 Court of Justice of the European Union. *Opinion 2/13 of the Court ECLI:EU:C:2014:2454 (Full Court).* at paragraph 200. 2014.

65 Delegation of the European Union to the Council of Europe. *Major Progress on the Path to EU Accession to the ECHR: Negotiations Concluded at Technical Level in Strasbourg.* url: https://www.eeas.europa.eu/delegations/council-europe/major-progress-path-eu-accession-echr-negotiations-concluded-technical-level-strasbourg_en?s=51. Last accessed: 01.08.2025.

66 IAPP. *New EU Data Blockage as German Court Would Ban Many Cookie Management Providers.* url: https://iapp.org/news/a/new-eu-data-blockage-as-german-court-would-ban-many-cookie-management-providers/. Last accessed: 01.08.2025.

67 Laura Drechsler. "Defining personal data transfers for the context of the General Data Protection Regulation: A critical perspective on the Guidelines

The question was adjudged by the French Conseil d'État in March 2021. Unlike the German Administrative Court, the French Court concluded that a platform processing personal data where the processing took place in the protected area by a Dutch subsidiary of a US corporation did not constitute a transfer of personal data to a third country.[68] However, the Conseil d'État still assessed the risk of US authorities accessing personal data processed on the platform. The risk-based approach pursued by the Conseil d'État could mean that it is not that significant whether the situation is defined as a transfer to a third country or not, since the Court assessed the risks of US authorities getting access to the personal data even after concluding that the processing was not defined as a transfer.

In the situation where the data resides in a sovereign platform in the protected area, but the AIaaS platform is controlled by a third-country enterprise or a subsidiary of a third-country enterprise, several legal sources call for an assessment of the risks related to potential unauthorised access to the personal data on the platform by third-country authorities. In such a risk-based approach, relevant factors include the nature of the personal data, the purpose of the processing, and technical safeguards, for instance, encryption and logs on data access, according to Article 6 (4) (e), Article 24, and Article 32 (1) (a) of the GDPR.

To conclude on the legal status of sovereign AIaaS platforms in relation to transfers to third countries, a sovereign platform solution is a technical measure with the potential to render the processing outside of the scope of the transfer rules in Chapter V of the GDPR if the service provider is a company registered in the EEA. Both the legal status of the cloud in relation to the transfer rules and the risk of unauthorised access to personal data by authorities from third countries would depend on the nationality and jurisdiction of the AIaaS platform provider.

5/2021 of the European Data Protection Board". In: *Privacy in Germany* 10.1 (2022). On p. 24, pp. 24–29; Laura Drechsler and Irene Kamara. "Essential equivalence as a benchmark for international data transfers after Schrems II". In: *Research Handbook on EU Data Protection Law*. Cheltenham: Edward Elgar Publishing, 2022, pp. 314–352; Svetlana Yakovleva. *GDPR Transfer Rules vs Rules on Territorial Scope: A Critical Reflection on Recent EDPB Guidelines from Both EU and International Trade Law Perspectives*. url: https://europeanlawblog.eu/2021/12/09/gdpr-transfer-rules-vs-rules-on-territorial-scope-a-critical-reflection-on-recent-edpb-guidelines-from-both-eu-and-international-trade-law-perspectives/. Last accessed: 01.08.2025.

[68] Conseil d'État. *National Free Software and others CE N 444937*. url: https://www.conseil-etat.fr/content/download/157044/document/444937%20-%20CNLL%20et%20autres.pdf. Last accessed: 01.08.2025.

As an overall conclusion, the transfer concept is not defined in the GDPR; however, according to a guideline from the EDPB, a transfer presupposes an exporter in the EEA subject to the GDPR that discloses by transmission or otherwise makes personal data available to an importer established in a third country. A common structure of data processed in AIaaS is that the tenant transmits data to the platform through an API request, the data is processed in the models on the platform, and the output is retransmitted to the tenant through an API response. If the AIaaS platform provider is located in a third country, the GDPR Chapter V would be activated to process personal data on AIaaS platforms.

The subsection has also examined some of the largest AIaaS platform providers. According to publicly available terms of service, several of these providers have server infrastructure in third countries that, depending on the processing type, would be activated in the processing chain of the AIaaS service. The most common countries where personal data is processed are the United States, Canada, and Mexico; however, countries such as India, UAE, Australia, Japan, and Brazil follow as other common countries in the processing chain, according to the providers' data protection amendments.

The status of sovereign AIaaS platforms operated by third-country providers or subsidiaries of third-country providers in the protected area has also been analysed. According to a literal interpretation of the transfer concept from the EDPB, such processing would not be regarded as a transfer. However, several courts in the EU have called for an assessment of the risk associated with third-country authorities requesting data in such situations.

The next subsection will analyse relevant transfer mechanisms when personal data is transferred to third countries on the AIaaS platforms.

5.3.5 Relevant Transfer Mechanisms for AIaaS

5.3.5.1 Introduction

There are three main exemptions from the general prohibition of transferring personal data to third countries in the GDPR.[69]

1. The transfers may be based on an adequacy decision from the European Commission (EC) stating that the third country has an adequate level of personal data protection, according to Article 45.

---

[69] Subsection 5.3.5 is a rewritten version of Bjørn Aslak Juliussen et al. "The third country problem under the GDPR: Enhancing protection of data transfers with technology". In: *International Data Privacy Law* 13.3 (2023), pp. 225–243.

2. The transfer may be based on appropriate safeguards on a contractual level between the exporter and the importer, according to Article 46 of the GDPR. An example of a contractual safeguard is standard contractual clauses (SCCs), a standard contract adopted by the EC under Article 46 (2) (c). Another example is binding corporate rules for intra-corporation transfers that need to be assessed and pre-approved by either a national data protection authority or the Commission, under Article 46 (2) (b) and Article 47. SCCs are one of the most used transfer mechanisms, and SCCs will, thus, be focused on more in the following rather than approved binding corporate rules.
3. Lastly, the transfer might be based on derogations for specific situations under Article 49 for transfers on a case-by-case basis. According to recitals 111–112 of the GDPR, derogations may be employed exclusively as a transfer mechanism when the transfer of personal data is occasional and non-repetitive.

The CJEU held in paragraph 105 of the Schrems II case,[70] that the overall purpose and objective of the transfer mechanisms in Chapter V of the GDPR is to ensure that personal data protection in the receiving third country is essentially equivalent to the level of data protection in the protected area.

The transfer of personal data to third countries on a platform with several similarities to AIaaS platforms was the topic in the European Data Protection Supervisors (EDPS) investigation into the EU institutions' use of Microsoft 365.[71]

The investigation concerned the EU GDPR,[72] the regulation concerning data protection when personal data is processed in EU institutions, and not the GDPR. However, the transfer rules are similar under this regulation, and the investigation, therefore, also has relevance for the use of AIaaS providers under the GDPR.

---

[70] Judgement of the Court (Grand Chamber) 16 July 2020 in Case C-311/18 Data Protection Commissioner v Facebook Ireland Ltd, Maximillian Schrems ECLI:EU:C:2020:559.

[71] European Data Protection Supervisor. *EDPS Investigation into Use of Microsoft 365 by the European Commission (Case 2021-0518) Decision of 8 March 2024.* url: https://www.edps.europa.eu/system/files/2024-03/24-03-08-edps-investigation-ec-microsoft365_en.pdf. Last accessed: 01.08.2025.

[72] Regulation (EU) 2018/1725 of the European Parliament and of the Council of 23 October 2018 on the protection of natural persons with regard to the processing of personal data by the Union institutions, bodies, offices and agencies and on the free movement of such data, and repealing Regulation (EC) No 45/2001 and Decision No 1247/2002/EC [2018] OJ L 295/39.

In essence, the EDPS found that the European Commission had infringed the EU GDPR because it, on behalf of all the EU institutions' use of Microsoft 365, had not clearly provided to Microsoft what types of personal data could be transferred to which recipients in which third countries and for what purposes. Moreover, the Commission – according to the EDPS – had failed to provide appropriate safeguards ensuring that the transferred personal data enjoyed an essentially equivalent level of protection as in the EEA when transferred. This finding was supported by the fact that the EDPS had found that the Commission did not have a sufficient overview of the transfers in Microsoft 365 and thus could not decide whether additional safeguards were necessary.

In their investigation, the EDPS concluded that the most important starting point when assessing if a transfer of personal data to a third country is in compliance with the transfer rules is to have an overview and a clear understanding of what personal data are (or are proposed to be) transferred, to which recipients, to which destination, and for what purposes. This assessment should include an assessment of the risk of third countries' authorities remotely accessing personal data processed within the EEA. Such transfer mapping exercises must be conducted prior to personal data being transferred, in order to assess whether the transfer mechanism is compliant with the GDPR or whether additional safeguards need to be implemented to ensure compliance.

The EDPS also held that in cases where the receiving third country lacks an adequacy decision, the controller may transfer personal data only if appropriate safeguards are provided and on the condition that enforceable data subjects' rights and effective legal remedies are available. Moreover, the EDPS concluded that when the EU institutions relied on SCCs as a transfer mechanism, the exporter must assess and implement technical and organisational measures to ensure an essentially equivalent level of data protection in the country of destination as in the EEA, as identified in a transfer impact assessment.

Such a transfer impact assessment should include aspects of the legislation regarding secret surveillance in the receiving third country. According to the EDPS, with further reference to the EDPB, "problematic third country legislation" includes legal and regulatory requirements in the third country that impinge on the contractual safeguards in the SCC and legislation that does not respect the essence of fundamental rights and freedoms of the Charter or exceed what is necessary and proportionate.[73] In addition, practices that allow for a similar impact as the legislation should also be described in a transfer impact assessment. If problematic legislation and/or problematic practices

---

[73] European Data Protection Supervisor. *EDPS Investigation into Use of Microsoft 365 by the European Commission (Case 2021-0518) Decision of 8 March 2024.* url: https://www.edps.europa.eu/system/files/2024-03/24-03-08-edps-investigation-ec-microsoft365_en.pdf. Last accessed: 01.08.2025.

are identified in a transfer impact assessment, the exporter must implement supplementary measures of a technical or organisational character to ensure essentially equivalent protection. If such measures do not ensure essentially equivalent protection, the transfer cannot take place. The EDPS concluded that the EU institutions had not complied with the transfer rules when using Microsoft 365. The main reasons behind this conclusion were that third-country legislation and practices were not assessed and that additional measures and safeguards were to be implemented.[74]

The decision regarded Microsoft 365 and not specifically AIaaS. However, there are several aspects also relevant to AIaaS, and the underlying cloud infrastructure of Microsoft 365 is also applied in the AI services of Microsoft Azure. According to the documentation and terms of service referred to in Table 5.2, Microsoft has an EU storage guarantee where personal data in Microsoft Azure is guaranteed not to be transferred. However, as evident from the EDPS decision, certain Azure services require backup in other locations. One service that requires backups is Azure Active Directory, which is used for the management of user identities in Azure. On the basis of this finding, the EDPS found the Azure EU storage guarantee inefficient because its contractual basis allowed for exemptions.

Based on the fact that Azure Active Directory is also used in the AI services on Microsoft Azure, these findings are also relevant for AIaaS.

To summarise, the Microsoft 365 decision of the EDPS is referred to the general court and, therefore, is not final. However, the main conclusion from the decision is that the use of cloud-based services, such as AIaaS platforms, needs to be assessed in relation to whether the platform transfers personal data to third countries. If such transfers are identified, the legislation and practices in the third country need to be assessed, and if problematic legislation and or practices are identified, mitigating technical measures are required to be introduced in order to ensure essential equivalent protection of personal data.

5.3.5.2 Transfers of personal data, AIaaS, and adequacy decisions

Most of the largest AIaaS providers have transfers of personal data to the United States, according to the overview in Table 5.2. In July 2023, the European Commission adopted the adequacy decision on the adequate level of protection of personal data under the EU-US Data Privacy Framework.[75] According

---

74 Ibid.

75 European Commission. *Commission Implementing Decision of 10.7.2023 pursuant to Regulation (EU) 2016/679 of the European Parliament and of the Council on the adequate level of protection of personal data under the EU-US Data Privacy Framework C(2023) 4745 final.* url: https://commission.europa.eu/document/download/fa09cbad-dd7d-4684-ae60-be03fcb0fddf_en?filename

to recital 7 of the adequacy decision, the importer in the United States must be self-certified under the EU-US Data Privacy Framework in order for the transfer to be conducted in accordance with the adequacy decision. If the importer, i.e., the US AIaaS platform provider, is on the self-certified list,[76] the transfer might take place without any prior notification or procedure, according to recital 8 of the adequacy decision.

An adequacy decision is an *ex-ante* risk assessment of a specific third country where the Commission has assessed the adequacy of a specific third country's data protection based on the rule of law; respect for human rights; general and sectoral legislation; data protection rules, practices, case law, and commitments; and means of redress in the third country, according to the GDPR Article 45 (2) (a–c).

An adequacy decision does not require an identical level of personal data protection in the third country as in the protected area, as outlined in paragraph 73 in the Schrems I judgement.[77] The level of protection in the third country may differ from the protected area as long as the system as a whole, through the substance of privacy rights and their effective implementation, supervision, and enforcement, delivers an essentially equivalent level of data protection.

Although a transfer of personal data on an AIaaS platform to a self-certified importer in the United States can take place without any approval, it is important to keep in mind that the CJEU invalidated two different US adequacy decisions in 2015 and 2020.[78] The binding nature of an adequacy decision entails that it could be invalidated by the CJEU only and not by national supervisory authorities, according to Article 288 of the TFEU and the Schrems II judgement paragraph 188. The potential future inadequacy of the US importers would therefore require a judgement from the CJEU.

=Adequacy%20decision%20EU-US%20Data%20Privacy%20Framework_en.pdf. Last accessed: 01.08.2025.

76 US Department of Commerce. *Data Privacy Framework Program (DPF)*. url: https://www.dataprivacyframework.gov/list. Last accessed: 01.08.2025.

77 Judgement of the Court (Grand Chamber) of 6 October 2015 in case C-362/14 Maximillian Schrems v Data Protection Commissioner, joined party: Digital Rights Ireland Ltd ECLI:EU:C:2015:650.

78 Judgement of the Court (Grand Chamber) of 6 October 2015 in case C-362/14 Maximillian Schrems v Data Protection Commissioner, joined party: Digital Rights Ireland Ltd ECLI:EU:C:2015:650.; Judgement of the Court (Grand Chamber) 16 July 2020 in Case C-311/18 Data Protection Commissioner v Facebook Ireland Ltd, Maximillian Schrems ECLI:EU:C:2020:559.

As a result of the Schrems II judgement, the European Commission announced a new EU–US Privacy framework on 25 March 2022.[79] On 7 October 2022, US President Joe Biden issued an Executive Order with changes to US law regarding signal intelligence activities.[80] On 10 July 2023, the European Commission adopted the new adequacy decisions that entered into force the same day.[81]

EU law requires national laws that collect and retain personal data for national security purposes to be limited to what is strictly necessary.[82] In line with the consistent body of case law from the CJEU, with the exception of cases established under urgency, access to retained personal data must be subject to a prior review carried out by a court or independent body whose decision is designed to limit access to what is strictly necessary to the objective pursued.[83] According to the US Executive Order Section 2(ii)(A), bulk collection of personal data transferred to the United States could be authorised only when "it is determined to be necessary to engage in bulk collection in order to advance a validated intelligence priority". The Executive Order has a requirement of necessity rather than the requirement of strict necessity estab-

---

79 European Commission. *European Commission and the United States Joint Statement on Trans-Atlantic Data Privacy Framework 2022*. url: https://ec.europa.eu/commission/presscorner/detail/en/IP_22_2087. Last accessed: 01.08.2025.

80 The White House. *Executive Order on Enhancing Safeguards for United States Signals Intelligence Activities*. url: https://www.whitehouse.gov/briefing-room/presidential-actions/2022/10/07/executive-order-on-enhancing-safeguards-for-united-states-signals-intelligence-activities/. Last accessed: 01.08.2025.

81 European Commission. *Commission Implementing Decision of 10.7.2023 pursuant to Regulation (EU) 2016/679 of the European Parliament and of the Council on the adequate level of protection of personal data under the EU-US Data Privacy Framework C(2023) 4745 final*. url: https://commission.europa.eu/document/download/fa09cbad-dd7d-4684-ae60-be03fcb0fddf_en?filename=Adequacy%20decision%20EU-US%20Data%20Privacy%20Framework_en.pdf. Last accessed: 01.08.2025.

82 Joined Cases C-92/09 and C-93/09 Volker and Markus Schecke GbR, Hartmut Eifert v Land Hessen, joined party Bundesanstalt für Landwirtschaft und Ernährung ECLI:EU:C:2010:662 paragraph 47 and Amman v Switzerland app. no 27798/95 paragraph 30.

83 Joined Cases C-203/15 and C-698/15 Tele2 Sverige AB v Post- och telestyrelsen and others, Judgement of 21 December 2016 (Grand Chamber) (ECLI:EU:C:2016:970) para 115; Case C-2017/16 Ministerio Fiscal, Judgement of 2 October 2018 (Grand Chamber) (ECLI:EU:2018:788) para 52; Joined Cases C-511/18, C-512/18 and C-520/18 La Quadrature du Net and Others v Premier minister and Others, Judgement of 6 October 2020 (Grand Chamber) (ECLI:EU:C:2020:791) para 112.

lished by the consistent body of CJEU case law.[84] Another important aspect of the Executive Order is that it requires surveillance practices to be proportionate. The structured proportionality test conducted by the CJEU under EU law is, however, not part of the US constitutional doctrine.[85] A mere call for proportionality could therefore not amend disproportionate US surveillance practices. The EU–US Data Privacy Framework, therefore, has potential for future inadequate adequacy to be established by the CJEU.

The US adequacy decision only pre-approves transfers to organisations that are self-certified to the EU-US Data Privacy Framework and on a list from the US Department of Commerce. The following countries also have EC adequacy decisions as of August 2025, where the transfer could take place without self-certification:

- Andorra.
- Argentina.
- Canada (commercial organisations).
- Faroe Islands.
- Guernsey.
- Israel.
- Isle of Man.
- Japan.
- Jersey.
- New Zealand.
- South Korea.
- Switzerland.
- The United Kingdom (Under both the GDPR and the LED).[86]

The CJEU has, as of 2025, assessed adequacy decisions only regarding EU–US transfers.[87] Israel has an adequacy decision and similar surveillance

[84] Joined Cases C-92/09 and C-93/09 Volker and Markus Schecke GbR, Hartmut Eifert v Land Hessen, joined party Bundesanstalt für Landwirtschaft und Ernährung ECLI:EU:C:2010:662 paragraph 47 and Amman v Switzerland app. no 27798/95 paragraph 30.

[85] Vicki C Jackson. "Constitutional law in an age of proportionality". In: *Yale Law Journal* 124 (2014), p. 3094.

[86] European Commission. *Adequacy Decisions*. url: https://commission.europa.eu/law/law-topic/data-protection/international-dimension-data-protection/adequacy-decisions_en. Last accessed: 01.08.2025.

[87] Judgement of the Court (Grand Chamber) of 6 October 2015 in case C-362/14 Maximillian Schrems v Data Protection Commissioner, joined party: Digital Rights Ireland Ltd ECLI:EU:C:2015:650.; Judgement of the Court (Grand

practices to those of the USA.[88] After analysing surveillance laws and practices in Israeli law, Korff concludes that the Israeli privacy regulations do not provide "essentially equivalent" protection for EU data subjects.[89] A similar legal assessment has been made for the Adequacy Decision regarding Japan.[90] This legal assessment suggests that if these Adequacy Decisions are to be put under the scrutiny of the CJEU, there are indications that it might lead to invalidations.

The combination of a pragmatic Commission adopting adequacy decisions and the principle-based CJEU invalidating them in the two Schrems judgements indicates that there is a risk that the CJEU, in the future, will conclude that the EU–US transfer mechanism is regarded as inadequate. In case other adequacy decisions are put under the test in the CJEU, it is also an inherent risk that these decisions will experience a comparable result as in the Schrems judgements.

Such a resultant uncertainty necessitates the exploration of technical measures to secure the protection of personal data transferred to third countries on AIaaS platforms, even if such a transfer is based on an adequacy decision. Such technical measures are the focus of subsection 5.3.6 below.

5.3.5.3 Transfers of personal data, AIaaS, and standard contractual clauses

According to the overview in Table 5.2, several of the countries involved in the various AIaaS processing chains are countries without EC adequacy decisions, for instance, the UAE, Brazil, India, and Australia. If the processing of personal data on an AIaaS platform involves transfers of personal data from the EEA to one of these countries, the transfer has to be based on appropriate safeguards under Article 46 of the GDPR, such as standard contractual clauses (SCCs).

A decision adopted by the European Commission pursuant to Article 46 (2) (c) of the GDPR "standard data protection clauses" has a general character

---

Chamber) 16 July 2020 in Case C-311/18 Data Protection Commissioner v Facebook Ireland Ltd, Maximillian Schrems ECLI:EU:C:2020:559.

[88] BBC. *Pegasus Scandal: Are We All Becoming Unknowing Spies?* url: https://www.bbc.com/news/technology-57910355. Last accessed: 01.08.2025.

[89] Douwe Korff. *Opinion on the Future of Personal Data Transfers from the EU/EEA to Israel and the Occupied Territories.* url: https://www.ianbrown.tech/2022/02/23/israels-privacy-protection-act-amendments-and-eu-adequacy/. Last accessed: 01.08.2025.

[90] Ana Gascón Marcén. "The new personal data protection in Japan: Is it enough?" In: *Media Technologies for Work and Play in East Asia*. Bristol: University Press, 2021, pp. 101–120.

and does not refer to a specific third country, such as adequacy decisions. Prior to the Schrems II judgement,[91] exporters of personal data could, in essence, rely solely on the Standard Contractual Clauses adopted by the Commission prior to a third-country transfer. In the Schrems II judgement, the CJEU held that it is the exporters' responsibility not to export personal data to a country without essentially equivalent protection. The Schrems II judgement could be described as altering the nature of SCCs from being a guarantee that exporters could rely on to being a potential step to essentially equivalent personal data protection in the third country.[92]

Depending on the situation in the receiving third country, the exporter should assess the risk of the transfer not meeting the "essentially equivalent" requirement when SCCs are the chosen transfer mechanism. For instance, if an AIaaS platform tenant established in the EEA makes use of an AIaaS platform that transfers personal data to Brazil, India, or the UAE, the tenant must assess whether the receiving country has problematic legislation or practices that undermine the effectiveness of the SCCs. According to recital 19 of the SCC decision adopted by the Commission,[93] personal data must not be transferred if the laws and practices of the third country of destination prevent the data importer from complying with the clauses. When assessing the rules and practices of the receiving third country, the exporter should take into account the content, nature, and duration of the transfer, the type of recipient, the purpose of the processing, the laws and practices of the receiving country, and any relevant contractual, technical, or organisational measures applying to the transfer, according to recital 20 of the SCC decision. Such an assessment should be made in a Transfer Impact Assessment (TIA). If the transfer risks not meeting the essentially equivalent requirement, the exporters should introduce additional measures to safeguard the transfer.

The assessment of when the transfer, due to the implementation of additional measures, does provide "essentially equivalent" protection would vary based on the specifics of each transfer. The answer to whether personal data

---

[91] Judgement of the Court (Grand Chamber) 16 July 2020 in Case C-311/18 Data Protection Commissioner v Facebook Ireland Ltd, Maximillian Schrems ECLI:EU:C:2020:559.

[92] OneTrust DataGuidance. *International: Schrems II: What You Need to Know*. url: https://www.dataguidance.com/opinion/international-schrems-ii-what-you-need-know. Last accessed: 01.08.2025.

[93] European Commission. *Commission Implementing Decision (EU) 2021/914 of 4 June 2021 on standard contractual clauses for the transfer of personal data to third countries pursuant to Regulation (EU) 2016/679 of the European Parliament and of the Council OJ 2021 L 199/31*. url: https://eur-lex.europa.eu/eli/dec_impl/2021/914/oj. Last accessed: 01.08.2025.

protection is "essentially equivalent" would depend on the identified risk of data protection infringements in the third country due to the laws and practices, and whether the contractual, organisational, and technical measures would mitigate the identified risks. In case such additional measures do not make the situation in the receiving third country "essentially equivalent", the transfer cannot lawfully be made.[94] If the exporters transfer personal data to third countries where the third country's authorities could access the data in a manner not "essentially equivalent" to the GDPR, the exporters can risk fines of up to 20 million EUR or 4% of global annual turnover, under Article 83 (5) (c) of the GDPR.

When assessing the risk of a transfer on an AIaaS platform, relevant assessments would include the type of data transferred. The risk would, e.g., be lower if only diagnostic data that would need additional information to identify a data subject is transferred compared to if special categories of personal data of an individual are transferred to the AIaaS platform in plaintext.

In the next subsection, various technical measures are analysed to examine whether they could contribute to "essentially equivalent" protection in transfers of personal data based on SCCs to AIaaS platforms.

5.3.6 Technical Measures to Enhance Data Protection in AIaaS Transfers

5.3.6.1 Introduction

When the transfer of personal data on an AIaaS platform relies on SCCs as the transfer mechanism, the exporter is required to assess the legislation and practices in the third country and implement appropriate additional technical or organisational measures to ensure a level of data protection in the receiving third country that is essentially equivalent to that within the EEA.[95]

The EDPB has assessed possible additional measures in a Recommendation from 2020.[96] If there are identified problematic aspects in the third-country

---

94 Marcelo Corrales Compagnucci et al. "Supplementary measures and appropriate safeguards for international transfers of health data after Schrems II". In: *The Law and Ethics of Data Sharing in Health Sciences*. Ed. by Marcelo Corrales Compagnucci et al. Singapore: Springer Nature, 2024, pp. 151–172. isbn: 978-981-99-6540-3. doi: 10.1007/978-981-99-6540-3_9. url: https://doi.org/10.1007/978-981-99-6540-3_9.

95 Subsection 5.3.6 is a rewritten version of Bjørn Aslak Juliussen et al. "The third country problem under the GDPR: Enhancing protection of data transfers with technology". In: *International Data Privacy Law* 13.3 [2023], pp. 225–243.

96 EDPB. *Guidelines 05/2021 on the Interplay between the Application of Article 3 and the Provisions on International Transfers as per Chapter V of the*

legislation, organisational measures such as contractual terms between the exporter and importer cannot mitigate the problematic situation. The following paragraphs will address potential technical measures that might contribute to essentially equivalent protection when personal data is transferred based on SCCs.

AIaaS is offered through cloud infrastructure. The following example from the EDPB is especially relevant for AI services delivered on cloud platforms. For the following use case, the EDPB found no relevant technical measures that could mitigate a non-essential equivalent third country: "transfer to cloud service providers or other processors which require access to data in the clear".[97] For other transfers, the EDPB focused on encryption, pseudonymisation, and multi-party computation as potential technical measures that could mitigate a non-essentially equivalent third country. The next paragraphs will analyse various technical measures, especially relevant to AIaaS, and assess whether the technical measures could offer essentially equivalent data protection to the EEA.

An exporter of personal data relying on standard contractual clauses could be required, according to the SCC decision, to take both organisational and technical measures to ensure that a transfer to a third country is compliant with GDPR Chapter V interpreted in line with the Charter. In the following, these technical measures will be analysed: pseudonymisation, encryption, multi-party computation, differential privacy, and trusted execution environments.

5.3.6.2 Pseudonymisation as a technical safeguard in transfers to third countries

Pseudonymisation protects personal data by replacing the identifier between information in a dataset and a natural person, as defined in Article 4 (5) of the GDPR. Personal identifiers, for instance, a name, age, or an identification number, are replaced by a pseudonym, for instance, a random number or a hash, and the link between the identifier and the pseudonym is protected by keeping the additional information needed to identify the natural person separately and subject to technical and organisational safeguards.[98]

In relation to cross-border transfers to third countries on AIaaS platforms, the applicability of pseudonymisation could be illustrated with an example. Suppose that a patient in the EEA has a wearable sensor that monitors blood

---

GDPR. url: https://edpb.europa.eu/system/files/2021-11/edpb_guidelinesinterplay chapterv_article3_adopted_en.pdf. Last accessed: 01.08.2025.

[97] Ibid.

[98] European Agency for Cybersecurity (ENISA). *Deploying Pseudonymization Techniques*. url: https://www.enisa.europa.eu/publications/deploying-pseudonymisation-techniques. Last accessed: 01.08.2025.

pressure and heart rate. The wearable device sends data to be processed in an AI model on an AIaaS platform that has servers and a processing chain in a third country. The output from the analysis is retransmitted from the AIaaS platform to the patient's doctor. The doctor needs to link the results from the analysis with the identity of the patient. However, the identity of the patient is not necessary to perform the analysis of the patient's data on the AIaaS platform in the third country. Pseudonymisation could be applied to replace the name of the patient with a pseudonym, for instance, a number or a random hash. The number or hash is transmitted to the AIaaS platform together with the sensor data in API requests and responses. The computations of the sensor data in the AI model are performed and transmitted back to the protected area. The linking between the result of the analysis and the identity of the natural person behind the pseudonym is then performed in the protected area.

The example above illustrates that pseudonymisation could be applied to enhance the confidentiality of personal data and limit the identifiability of natural persons and thus contribute to the principle of data minimisation in third-country transfers on AIaaS platforms. To what extent could the pseudonymisation of natural persons' identifiers offer confidentiality protection? The level of confidentiality protection could also be illustrated with an example. Suppose that an AIaaS provider in the protected area stores the following data from its users: time-stamp with the users' time zone, IP address, type, and version of browser, set and preferences of natural languages in the browser settings, and the operating system of the user's computer. The IP address is pseudonymised and kept in a repository by the controller or processor.

Now, suppose that the controller and processor wish to compute something on the stored data on an AIaaS platform with servers in a third country. Is the pseudonymisation of the IP address sufficient to protect the data subject from re-identification attempts in a third country? The Panopticlick experiment has illustrated that although the IP address is pseudonymised, information on time-zone, language settings, type and version of the browser, and the operating system is sufficient to identify a browser and thus also a specific data subject.[99]

Unlike anonymisation, pseudonymisation is not a technique that enables the processing to fall outside the material scope of the GDPR. Personal data that has undergone pseudonymisation is still defined as personal data, and pseudonymisation is an example of an appropriate safeguard under Article 6 (4) (e), data protection by design and by default under Article 25, and as a security measure under Article 32 of the GDPR.

99 Electronic Frontier Foundation. *Cover Your Tracks*. url: https://coveryourtracks.eff.org/. Last accessed: 01.08.2025.

The recommendations on measures that supplement transfer tools to ensure compliance with the EU level of data protection protection from the EDPB[100] also regard pseudonymisation as an additional measure for essentially equivalent protection and not a measure that renders the processing on the importer's hand outside the scope of the GDPR. The EDPB concludes that pseudonymisation might represent a relevant additional measure for cross-border transfers to third countries. The conclusion from the EDPB is relevant for pseudonymisation techniques that fulfil the following requirements:

1. The personal data can no longer be attributed to a specific data subject or used to single out the data subject in a larger group.
2. The additional information necessary to identify the data subject is held exclusively by the exporter.
3. Disclosure or unauthorised use of the additional information is prevented by technical and organisational safeguards.
4. The exporter has thoroughly analysed the data in question and taken into account any information that the authorities in the recipient's third country may possess, and that the pseudonymised personal data cannot be attributed to an identified or identifiable natural person even if cross-referenced with such information.[101]

The recommendations from the EDPB call for the exporter to take into account "any information the authorities in the receiving third country may possess" when considering whether pseudonymisation is an efficient additional measure to secure personal data in a transfer to a third country.

The recommendations on pseudonymisation as an additional safeguard in transfer to third countries from the EDPB and the definition of pseudonymisation in Article 4 (5) of the GDPR are somewhat different. While the definition in Article 4 (5) of the GDPR presupposes that only information kept separately by the controller or processors should be assessed when evaluating whether natural persons are identifiable, Recommendation 01/2020 presupposes that the exporter of personal data should also assess the risk of indirect identification from information kept by third-country authorities.

---

100 EDPB. *Guidelines 05/2021 on the Interplay between the Application of Article 3 and the Provisions on International Transfers as per Chapter V of the GDPR*. url: https://edpb.europa.eu/system/files/2021-11/edpb_guidelinesinterplay chapterv_article3_adopted_en.pdf. Last accessed: 01.08.2025.

101 EDPB. *Guidelines 05/2021 on the Interplay between the Application of Article 3 and the Provisions on International Transfers as per Chapter V of the GDPR*. url: https://edpb.europa.eu/system/files/2021-11/edpb_guidelinesinterplay chapterv_article3_adopted_en.pdf. Last accessed: 01.08.2025.

To conclude on the legal status of pseudonymisation as a technical measure to safeguard transfers, the transfer of pseudonymised data may contribute to essentially equivalent protection, dependent on the specifics of the transfers, such as the sensitivity of the personal data and the laws and practices in the receiving third country. In such a situation, the analysis of laws and practices in the receiving third country is necessary. As an overall conclusion, pseudonymisation as a technical measure would contribute to securing the transfers of personal data to AIaaS providers with servers in third countries where the transfer is based on SCCs.

5.3.6.3 Encryption

An example of a technical safeguard described in the GDPR is encryption, mentioned in Articles 6 (4) (e) and 32 of the GDPR. Encryption can be applied to enforce the confidentiality of the personal data by making the data readable only to authorised principals.

Although encryption is widely adopted, there are certain assumptions that one needs to make when encrypting personal data. These assumptions impact the level of data protection, the level of data utility, and the level of additional measures necessary in order to reach "essentially equivalent" data protection if personal data are transferred outside the protected area on an AIaaS platform.

Symmetric encryption involves taking the information to be protected, termed as plaintext, and combining it with a secret value, referred to as the secret key, to produce an apparently random sequence of bits, known as the ciphertext. The ciphertext can be efficiently reversed to the original plaintext only by using the corresponding decryption process with the same secret key. Thus, only entities possessing the secret key can decrypt the ciphertext. As a result, encryption effectively conceals the information from anyone who does not possess the secret key.

Asymmetric encryption, also referred to as public-key encryption, uses pairs of related keys, a private key and a public key, to encrypt and decrypt information. In asymmetric encryption, anyone is able to encrypt data if they have access to the public key, but in order to decrypt the data, the receiver of the encrypted ciphertext would need a secret private key.[102] The keys for encryption and decryption are different but form a pair. Everyone can encrypt the data with a public key, but the data can be decrypted only with a secret key. A typical scenario involving asymmetric encryption would entail the following steps:

[102] Google Cloud. *Asymmetric Encryption.* url: https://cloud.google.com/kms/docs/asymmetric-encryption. Last accessed: 01.08.2025.

1. A sender obtains the public key, typically from a website.
2. The sender encrypts the message using the public key.
3. The public-key-encrypted ciphertext is sent to the receiver.
4. The recipient uses their secret key to decrypt the ciphertext and read the plaintext.

Generally, asymmetric encryption is computationally expensive and thus mostly possible on small plaintext sizes. Asymmetric encryption is frequently used for encryption keys.[103] One possibility for the use of asymmetric encryption on AIaaS platforms is to send the secret key used to symmetrically encrypt data in an asymmetrically encrypted manner. Hence, the encryption key used to symmetrically encrypt plaintext is available only to those with the secret key.

An ideal AIaaS platform would ensure both the highest level of confidentiality for tenants' personal data and the maximum utility for processing by AI models. Homomorphic encryption (HE) has been proposed as a mechanism to approximate this ideal. With HE, personal data may be encrypted using a secret key known only to the user, thereby ensuring confidentiality. Simultaneously, the AIaaS provider can perform specific computations on this encrypted data, preserving its utility. The fundamental attribute of HE is that conducting certain operations on homomorphically encrypted data and subsequently decrypting the result with the corresponding secret key will yield plaintext identical to the outcome of applying the same operations directly to the original data. Thus, with HE, users could encrypt their personal data, transmit the ciphertext to a third party such as an AIaaS provider, enable the provider to process the encrypted data using their AI models, receive the processed ciphertext, decrypt it, and access the plaintext equivalent to the computation's direct application to their original data.

However, HE is not without its drawbacks. There is a trade-off between the complexity of the computation that can be applied to the ciphertexts and the computational performance that can be achieved. The higher the complexity of the computation that one needs to apply to ciphertexts, the slower this computation becomes (compared to applying the same computation to plaintext), rendering HE impractical for general-purpose processing.[104] Although improving the performance of HE for a wider spectrum of computation is an active field

---

[103] Ibid.

[104] Furkan Turan, Sujoy Sinha Roy, and Ingrid Verbauwhede. "HEAWS: An accelerator for homomorphic encryption on the Amazon AWS FPGA". In: *IEEE Transactions on Computers* 69.8 (2020), pp. 1185–1196. doi: 10.1109/TC.2020.2988765.

of research,[105] an advanced type of processing, such as ML, is therefore, as of 2025, not applicable in commercial AIaaS platforms and conducted only in experimental solutions.[106]

Employing HE to enforce the data protection principles of confidentiality and purpose limitation in cross-border transfers to third countries could be a sensible proposal, as many other authors have already argued.[107] HE could be regarded as equivalent to original user-side encryption, with regard to protecting the confidentiality of personal data transferred to third countries.

5.3.6.4 Federated learning, multiparty computation, and differential privacy

Suppose that different institutions want to collaborate in the training of an AI model on an AIaaS platform, but without revealing their training data, which consists of personal data, to the other participants.

To address this limitation, federated learning has been introduced. In federated learning, participants collaborate by sharing the model and the partially trained model, without exchanging the training data itself. In this process, each participant receives a partially trained model from the previous participant, utilises their own training data to further refine the model, and subsequently passes the updated model to the next participant. This iterative procedure continues until the resultant trained model meets specific optimisation criteria.

---

[105] Vinod Vaikuntanathan. "Computing blindfolded: New developments in fully homomorphic encryption". In: *2011 IEEE 52nd Annual Symposium on Foundations of Computer Science*. 2011, pp. 5–16. doi: 10.1109/FOCS.2011.98.

[106] Xiaoqiang Sun et al. "Private machine learning classification based on fully homomorphic encryption". In: *IEEE Transactions on Emerging Topics in Computing* 8.2 (2018), pp. 352–364. doi: https://doi.org/10.1109/TETC.2018.2794611; Alexander Wood, Kayvan Najarian, and Delaram Kahrobaei. "Homomorphic encryption for machine learning in medicine and bioinformatics". In: *ACM Computing Surveys (CSUR)* 53.4 (2020), pp. 1–35. doi: https://doi.org/10.1145/3394658; Joon-Woo Lee et al. "Privacy-preserving machine learning with fully homomorphic encryption for deep neural network". In: *iEEE Access* 10 (2022), pp. 30039–30054. doi: https://doi.org/10.1109/ACCESS.2022.3159694.

[107] Luigi Sgaglione and Giovanni Mazzeo. "A GDPR-compliant approach to real-time processing of sensitive data". In: *Intelligent Interactive Multimedia Systems and Services*. Ed. by Giuseppe De Pietro et al. Cham: Springer International, 2019, pp. 43–52. isbn: 978-3-319-92231-7; Marcelo Corrales Compagnucci et al. "Homomorphic encryption: The 'holy grail' for Big Data analytics and legal compliance in the pharmaceutical and healthcare sector?" In: *European Pharmaceutical Law Review* 3.4 (2019). doi: 10.21552/eplr/2019/4/5. url: https://doi.org/10.21552/eplr/2019/4/5.

Employing federated learning offers high utility since the AI model is trained on the entire training data, even if this data is split among different participants.

In comparison to sending raw data to third parties, federated learning offers greater confidentiality protection. However, it has been established that the partially trained model, i.e., values of certain parameters of the model, might still reveal information about the training data.[108]

However, it is unclear whether the leaked information is sufficient to reconstruct personal data or identify a natural person. Nevertheless, one could conservatively conclude that in order to meet the "essentially equivalent" requirement, federated learning is not sufficient, depending on the transfer details and the receiving third country. Additional technical measures other than solely federated learning should be taken to protect personal data, especially if the training data is sensitive data, such as health data or other special categories of personal data under the GDPR Article 9 (1).

Increasing the confidentiality protection of federated learning can be achieved by slightly perturbing the partially trained model, i.e., the values of the parameters, so that information about the training data is not leaked from the model. Such a perturbation could be achieved through differential privacy.

The concept of differential privacy can be applied to any kind of data processing. A data processing method is considered differentially private if the outcome of this processing does not significantly depend on any single data entry. This means that removing an individual data entry should not significantly alter the processing result. Any data processing technique can achieve differential privacy by introducing a specific amount of noise to the final output.

Federating learning is a specific form of data processing, and researchers have developed differentially private federated learning (DPFL). In DPFL, the model is trained using differential privacy techniques. For instance, when a participant updates the model's parameters, a specified amount of noise is introduced to these values, ensuring that the resulting values do not overly depend on the individual training data items of that participant.[109]

The level of confidentiality protection provided by DPFL increases with the addition of more noise during the training process. At a certain threshold,

---

[108] David Enthoven and Zaid Al-Ars. "Fidel: Reconstructing private training samples from weight updates in federated learning". In: *2022 9th International Conference on Internet of Things: Systems, Management and Security (IOTSMS)*. New York: IEEE, 2022, pp. 1–8. doi: 10.1109/IOTSMS58070.2022.10062088.

[109] ICO. *Chapter 5: Privacy Enhancing Technologies (PETs)*. url: https://ico.org.uk/media/about-the-ico/consultations/4021464/chapter-5-anonymisation-pets.pdf. Last accessed: 26.08.2024.

personal data becomes irretrievable from the trained model. In this case, the exporter would comply with the "essentially equivalent" requirement and potentially also leave the scope of the GDPR. Under such conditions, the trained model could not be reversed back to an identifiable natural person and is therefore no longer defined as personal data under Article 4 (1) of the regulation interpreted in line with recital 26.

However, the addition of too much noise can affect the utility of the model. Excessive noise may degrade the model's accuracy to a point where it becomes ineffective when applied to unseen data.

Therefore, the challenge lies in determining the minimum amount of noise that must be added to a partially trained model to satisfy the "essentially equivalent" requirement when transferring data to a third country on AIaaS platforms.

Another confidentiality enforcement mechanism used in conjunction with federated learning is Secure Multi-Party Computation (MPC). MPC allows multiple parties, each holding separate datasets, to jointly compute a function over their combined data without explicitly sharing their individual datasets with one another. For instance, suppose that a conglomerate of different EU insurance providers wants to assess the risk of insurance fraud using an AI model on an AIaaS platform without revealing the data to the other participants or the platform. An MPC protocol can enable the participants to compute the risk of insurance fraud on the data without revealing to others or the AIaaS platform the data of each participant. However, MPC does not necessarily protect the privacy of the participant's data. This is because the very result of the function that an MPC protocol computes might reveal information about the personal data applied as input data. In the example above, by the end of the MPC protocol, every participant learns that at least one of the other participants has data that results in a high risk of insurance fraud, although they do not know which participant.

In the specific case of federated learning on AIaaS platforms, the participants can execute an MPC protocol to compute an aggregation function on their individual partially trained models. The result of the aggregation would be the final trained model. But similar to the example above, the final model might reveal information about individual partially trained models and, possibly, the corresponding training data sets.

Given that MPC alone does not guarantee the protection of private training data, it cannot, in itself, be used as a technical measure for satisfying the "essentially equivalent" requirement alone in cross-border transfers to third countries on the AIaaS platforms if the transfer is based on SCCs and problematic legislation or practices are identified.

5.3.6.5 Trusted Execution Environments

A Trusted Execution Environment (TEE) enables data to be processed while ensuring that unauthorised parties cannot access the data. Unlike homomorphic encryption, TEEs allow for practical applications of arbitrary computations on the data while maintaining its confidentiality.

In contrast to the previously discussed technical solutions, a TEE represents a hardware-based approach. An example of a TEE is Intel's Software Guard Extensions (SGX) processor. Within this framework, data is securely stored in an encrypted form within an isolated memory space known as an enclave. During computation, the processor accesses the data from the enclave, decrypts it, executes the necessary computations, and subsequently encrypts the results before storing them back in the enclave. Thus, no other processes on the same machine, including the operating system, can access the enclave's data without the appropriate secret key. Consequently, a TEE provides a high level of confidentiality protection and utility by enabling secure handling of arbitrary computations on sensitive data.

To determine whether the use of a TEE in a cross-border transfer to a third country on an AIaaS platform falls outside the scope of the transfer rules in Chapter V of the GDPR, it is essential to address two key issues. First, the deployment of a TEE necessitates confidence in the provider of that specific TEE. For instance, one must trust Intel to ensure that the SGX processor operates correctly and that the cryptographic keys are not susceptible to compromise or exposure to third-country authorities. The legal considerations regarding the TEE's status in this context are similar to those concerning sovereign AIaaS platforms and cloud services discussed above. Second, researchers have highlighted potential data leakages through timing side-channels when SGX is utilised.[110] If a TEE is certified and provided by a reliable entity within the protected area, and the timing side-channel leakages do not allow for the reconstruction of personal data, the use of a TEE could potentially render the data transfer outside the scope of Chapter V's transfer rules in the GDPR. At a minimum, it may fulfil the GDPR's requirement for "essentially equivalent" data protection.

AI services within TEEs on cloud platforms are an emerging research field. Google has, e.g., an active patent application for privacy-enhancing deep learning cloud services using TEEs.[111] If such a hardware-based solution were

---

[110] Johannes Götzfried et al. "Cache attacks on Intel SGX". In: EuroSec'17. Belgrade, Serbia: Association for Computing Machinery, 2017. isbn: 9781450349352. doi: 10.1145/3065913.3065915. url: https://doi.org/10.1145/3065913.3065915.

[111] Google Patents. *Privacy Enhancing Deep Learning Cloud Service Using a Trusted Execution Environment.* url: https://patents.google.com/patent/

offered in an AIaaS situation would make a cross-border transfer to a third country compliant with the transfer rules would depending on the situation in the receiving third country. This situation relies on the potentially identified problematic legislation or practices and the sensitivity of the personal data transferred. As a general conclusion, however, TEEs are a technical measure with potentially strong privacy guarantees since it is a hardware-based solution.

In conclusion, when considering the role of additional technical measures for third-country transfers on AIaaS platforms based on SCCs, it is essential to conduct a thorough assessment of the third country's legislation and practices. Such an assessment should particularly focus on secret surveillance measures and any legislation and practices that might infringe on the essence of the rights and freedoms of the Charter.

If such practices or legislation are identified, the exporter needs to implement additional measures to protect the transferred personal data. Generally, when problematic legislation or practices in the third country are identified, organisational measures are not suitable to mitigate the situation, and technical measures should be introduced. The subsections above have explored encryption and pseudonymisation, TEEs, federated learning, differential privacy, and multiparty computation as potential measures to enhance data protection in such contexts.

5.3.7 Summary of Relevant Data Protection Requirements in AIaaS

Subsection 5.3.6 examined data protection requirements when personal data is processed on AIaaS platforms. The most important findings are summarised as follows:

- Depending on the specific circumstances, processing of personal data to develop the AI models on an AIaaS platform is likely a distinct processing purpose that requires a specific legal basis.
- According to the terms of service of some of the largest AIaaS providers, these providers typically assume the responsibilities as processors under the GDPR. However, particularly in relation to the processing of personal data to further develop AI models, providers may assume the responsibility of a joint controller or even sole controller.
- AIaaS platforms process data on cloud platforms, often necessitating transfers of personal data to third countries. If the receiving third country does not have an adequacy decision, SCCs are the most relevant transfer

US11443182B2/en. Last accessed: 01.08.2025.

mechanism. If the exporter identified problematic legislation or practices in the third country relating to secret surveillance and or potential violations of the essence of the rights of the Charter, the exporter must introduce additional safeguards to ensure essentially equivalent protection.

5.4 AIaaS AND CYBERSECURITY REGULATION

5.4.1 Introduction

This subsection will analyse cybersecurity requirements within the EU acquis for AIaaS.

Subsections 5.4.2 and 5.4.3 will examine specific cybersecurity requirements relevant to AIaaS in the NIS 2 Directive and the CRA.

Subsection 5.4.4 will then shift the focus from compliance with cybersecurity regulations to exploring common attack vectors in APIs, a key component in AIaaS.

Finally, subsection 5.4.5 will summarise the overall findings related to cybersecurity regulation compliance for AIaaS platforms.

5.4.2 Requirements for Cloud Providers in the NIS 2 Directive

As discussed in the preceding subsections, AIaaS platforms rely on cloud infrastructure to deliver AI services to their tenants. Concerning the cybersecurity requirements in the NIS 2 Directive, the dependence on cloud infrastructure by the AIaaS platforms renders certain provisions of the Directive relevant for AIaaS providers.

Overall, the purpose of the NIS 2 Directive is to ensure a high common level of cybersecurity across the EU, according to Article 1 (1) of the NIS 2 Directive. To achieve this overall aim, the NIS 2 Directive requires that the EU member states adopt national cybersecurity strategies and designate a competent authority, implement cybersecurity risk-management measures and reporting obligations for specific types of entities, have rules on cybersecurity information sharing, and implement supervisory and enforcement obligations, according to Article 1 (2) (a–b) of the NIS 2 Directive.

The entities that are subject to the rules of the Directive are the entities referred to in Annexes I and II to the Directive and the entities under Directive (EU) 2022/2557 (the critical entities directive).[112] A critical entity under

[112] Directive (EU) 2022/2557 of the European Parliament and of the Council of 14 December 2022 on the resilience of critical entities and repealing Council Directive 2008/114/EC [2022] OJ L 333/164.

Directive 2022/2557 is an entity that has been identified by the member states as a public or private entity belonging to one of the categories of the annex to the critical entities directive, according to Article 2 (1). These categories are energy, transport, banking, financial market infrastructure, health, drinking water, wastewater, digital infrastructure, public administration, space, food production, processing, and distribution. Two of the subcategories under the category "digital infrastructure" are "providers of cloud computing services" and providers of data centre services. These categories are further defined in the NIS 2 Directive Article 6 (30 and 31) as follows:

> (30)
> "cloud computing service" means a digital service that enables on-demand administration and broad remote access to a scalable and elastic pool of shareable computing resources, including where such resources are distributed across several locations;
>
> (31)
> "data centre service" means a service "that encompasses structures, or groups of structures, dedicated to the centralised accommodation, interconnection and operation of IT and network equipment providing data storage, processing and transport services together with all the facilities and infrastructures for power distribution and environmental control".

A provider of AI services in cloud infrastructure, such as Microsoft Azure or AWS, would provide both "access to a scalable and elastic pool of shareable computing resources" and "processing and transport services", according to the NIS 2 Directive Article 6 (30) and (31). Thus, AIaaS services offered on a cloud computing network would be regarded as a critical entity under Directive 2022/2557 and, therefore, also come under the scope of the NIS 2 Directive, pursuant to Article 1 (2) (b) of the NIS 2 Directive.

Simultaneously, cloud computing service providers and data centre service providers are defined as sectors of high criticality under Annex 1, sector 8, points 4 and 5 of the NIS 2 Directive. Such providers activate the scope of the NIS 2 Directive both directly under the NIS 2 Directive and through the reference to Directive 2022/2557 in the NIS 2 Directive.

Entities must also exceed some thresholds for medium-sized enterprises and some other requirements for entering the scope of the NIS 2 Directive. For a flowchart illustrating the scope of the NIS 2 Directive, reference is made to Figure 5.3.

Once it has been established that cloud service providers and data centre service providers that are offering AIaaS on such platforms are under the scope of the NIS 2 Directive, what requirements are placed on such providers?

The NIS 2 Directive, in contrast to the CRA, which will be discussed in the next subsection, does not include many technical requirements for

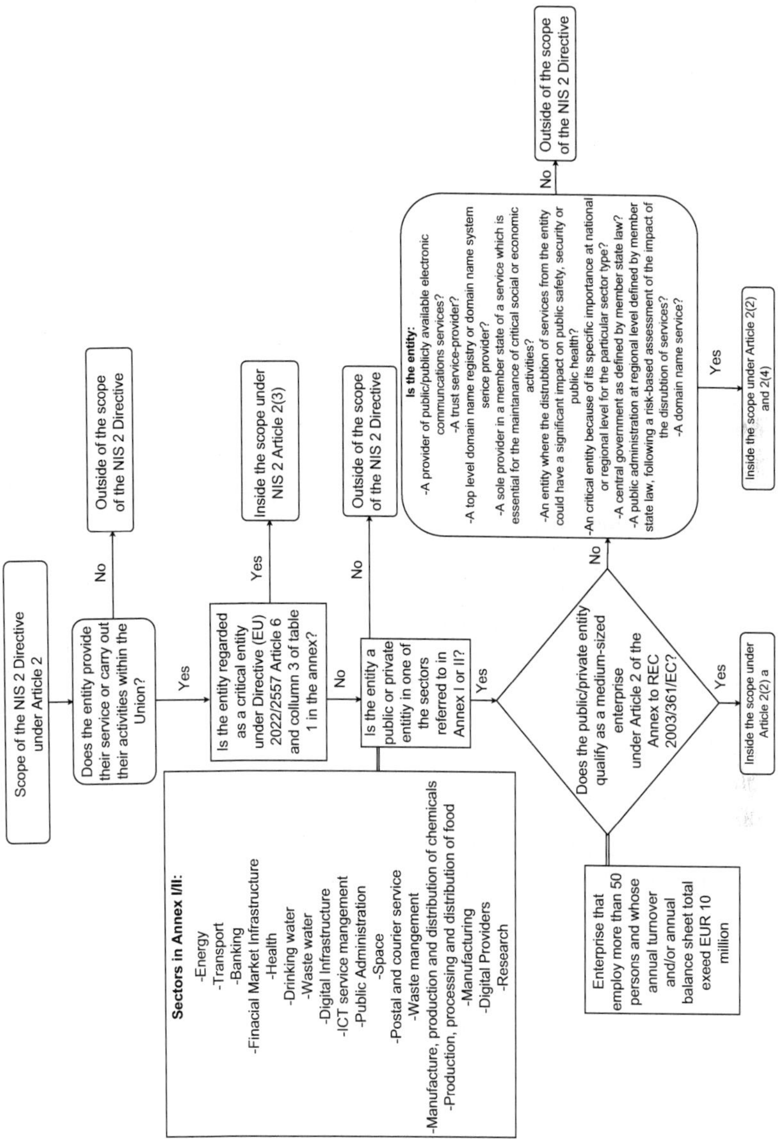

Figure 5.3 Flowchart of the scope of the NIS 2 Directive

critical sector entities or entities with high criticality. Instead, the focus of the Directive is to set out governance and management frameworks for cybersecurity. Some of the most crucial requirements of the NIS 2 Directive are placed in Chapter IV of the Directive.

According to Article 21, the entities under the scope of the Directive, e.g., AIaaS providers running on cloud infrastructure, are required to adopt appropriate and proportionate technical, operational, and organisational measures to manage cybersecurity risks. The aim of such measures is to manage the risk to the entities' operations and to prevent and minimise the impact of incidents on recipients of their services. Such risk management measures should have an all-hazard approach to protect the networks and information systems and their physical environments from incidents. According to Article 21 (2), such measures shall at least contain the following:

- Risk analysis and information security policies.
- Incident handling.
- Business continuity in the form of crisis handling and backup management.
- Security in network and information systems acquisition.
- Policies to assess the effectiveness of the cybersecurity measures.
- Cyber hygiene practices.
- Policies on cryptography and encryption.
- Human resource security.
- The use of multi-factor authentication.

Moreover, according to Chapter IV of the NIS 2 Directive, such risk management measures are the responsibility of the management bodies of the entities, according to Article 20 (1). The management bodies shall approve the cybersecurity measures, oversee their implementation, and can be held liable for infringement.

Entities under the scope of the NIS 2 Directive further have to notify cybersecurity incidents to computer security incident response teams (CSIRTs), under Article 22. The NIS 2 Directive further contains rules on cybersecurity certification schemes for certain products and the adoption of European and international standards, according to Articles 24 and 25.

Is a US provider of AIaaS on a cloud platform subject to the NIS 2 Directive? The jurisdiction and territoriality of the requirements in the Directive for cloud computing services are regulated in Article 26 (1) (b) of the Directive. Cloud service providers shall be considered to fall within the jurisdiction of member states where they have their main establishment. According to recital 114, the main establishment is where the entity exercises its activity through a stable arrangement. The legal form of the arrangement is not decisive. The physical presence of servers is not decisive either, according to recital 114.

The main establishment under the NIS 2 Directive shall be considered to be located in the member state where the decisions related to cybersecurity risk management are predominantly taken, typically where the central administration is located. If such a member state cannot be determined, the main establishment should be considered to be in the member state where the entity has the establishment with the highest number of employees in the Union. In cases where the services are carried out by a group of undertakings, the main establishment of the controlling undertaking should be considered to be the main establishment of the group of undertakings, according to Article 26 (2) and recital 114.

If a non-EU-established AIaaS service provider offers services within the Union without being established in a member state, it shall designate a representative in the Union, according to the NIS 2 Directive Article 26 (3).

In opposition to the GDPR and the AI Act, which place some of the responsibility on the entities making use of the products, as controllers under the GDPR and deployers under the AI Act, most of the responsibility of the NIS 2 Directive is placed on the entities providing the network and information systems. In order to have a common level of cybersecurity in the EU, it is necessary to place the responsibility of cybersecurity on those developing the products and offering the services. For AIaaS platforms to be as secure as possible, the NIS 2 Directive places requirements on the AIaaS provider through the requirements for cloud providers in the NIS 2 Directive.

To conclude, AIaaS providers must comply with the requirements in the NIS 2 Directive if such services are provided through a cloud-based infrastructure. The most relevant requirement in the NIS 2 Directive is to establish policies and risk management measures for cybersecurity incidents. If a non-EU AIaaS provider offers services within the Union, the provider must designate a representative if the provider does not have a main establishment in an EU country.

5.4.3 Requirements for Cloud Providers under the CRA

Does AIaaS provider enter the scope of the CRA and, if so, which requirements are placed on such providers under the Act?

The CRA lays down rules for products with digital elements to ensure their cybersecurity. A cloud service, such as AIaaS, is traditionally not regarded as a product but as a service offered to tenants.

However, the broad definition of both "products with digital elements" and remote data processing in the CRA also makes the act relevant for AIaaS. Products with digital elements are defined in Article 3 (1) as "a software or hardware product and its remote data processing solutions, including software or hardware components being placed on the market separately". "Remote data processing" is defined in Article 3 (2) as "data processing at a distance, the software for which is designed and developed by the manufacturer, or under the responsibility of the manufacturer, and the absence of which would prevent the product with digital elements from performing one of its functions".

AIaaS offered on a cloud solution would be regarded as remote data processing. However, according to Article 1 of the CRA, such AIaaS functionalities would be subject to the scope of the CRA only if they meet the definition of a product with digital elements. AI services enabled by the cloud will enter the scope of the CRA only if the AI services are necessary to ensure the functionality of a product with digital elements, according to recital 12 of the CRA.

To illustrate the applicability of the CRA on AIaaS, suppose that a provider of a smart home device is offering a new and improved system relying on an AI model offered through an AIaaS provider. This smart home system runs on an AI model offered through an AIaaS platform. The core new functionality of the system would not function without the AIaaS component. In such an instance, the smart home product is regarded as a product with digital elements, while the remote AI model offered on an AIaaS platform would be regarded as remote data processing under the scope of the CRA.

General AIaaS functionalities not necessary for the functionality of a product with digital elements would therefore enter the scope of the NIS 2 Directive, not the CRA, according to recital 12 of the CRA.

If a remote processing operation enters the scope of the CRA, the remote processing operation would be required to comply with the essential requirements set out in Annex I to the CRA. The overall purpose of these requirements is to ensure an appropriate level of cybersecurity based on the risk, according to Annex 1 (1). For an overview of some AI-specific attack types on deployed AI models and related mitigating measures, reference is made to subsection 4.3.2 in Chapter 4 of the book.

To conclude regarding the scope of the CRA for AIaaS providers, AIaaS functionality is under the scope of the CRA only if the AI services offered through a cloud interface are an integral part of a product with digital elements under the scope of the CRA, such as a smart home system or a baby monitor.

5.4.4 API Security in AIaaS

The previous subsections have identified that AIaaS providers might enter the scope of the NIS 2 Directive. According to the NIS 2 Directive, the providers shall assess the risk of cybersecurity incidents and introduce risk-mitigating measures. In Chapter 4, the focus was on AI-specific risks and risk-mitigating measures. The next subsections will address an AIaaS-specific risk and analyse corresponding risk-mitigating measures. AIaaS is characterised by communicating input and output through an Application Programming Interface (API), and the focus will be on the security of APIs in the following.

An API is a set of protocols designed to facilitate the communication and transfer of data between different software systems, applications, or AI models.[113] Given the widespread utilisation of APIs in AIaaS, the subsequent subsections will focus on how to embed data protection and cybersecurity compliance in APIs. However, before examining compliance with APIs, it is necessary to provide a high-level overview of how APIs function.

APIs are typically classified into three categories: private APIs, public APIs, and partner APIs.[114] In order to explain a private API, consider a large financial institution. The financial institution has many legacy systems, i.e., old and outdated software systems that fulfil their original purposes but do not allow for development and growth.[115] To circumvent the need for a complete software system overhaul while at the same time facilitating development, the financial institution might implement a private API to interconnect all the legacy systems within the organisation. As suggested by the name, private APIs are confined to data sharing within the organisation and are not accessible to third parties outside the organisation. Private APIs are instrumental in enhancing scalability, access, and modularity across software systems within an organisation.

Public APIs, on the other hand, provide public access to an organisation's data. For instance, a developer creating a home delivery application may want to access a governmental address database to ensure accurate delivery. This access – if granted – would likely be facilitated through a public API. Public APIs can, however, pose a security vulnerability since they can act as a backdoor to launch attacks against systems.

Lastly, partner APIs are custom-designed for data sharing between two or more collaborating parties. Unlike public APIs, partner APIs are not intended for public data access and thus incorporate specific authentication and access control measures to ensure that the data is shared exclusively with the intended parties.[116]

The primary objective of an API is to facilitate data sharing between disparate systems or applications. In the AIaaS field, APIs allow organisations to

113 Roy Thomas Fielding. *Architectural Styles and the Design of Network-Based Software Architectures*. Irvine: University of California, 2000.

114 Postman. *What Is an API?* url: https://www.postman.com/what-is-an-api/. Last accessed: 01.08.2025.

115 Santiago Comella-Dorda et al. "A survey of legacy system modernization approaches". In: *CMU/SEI* 18 (2000).

116 Postman. *What Is an API?* url: https://www.postman.com/what-is-an-api/. Last accessed: 01.08.2025.

access a trained AI model and include AI functionalities in their services. This is achieved through a cyclical process of requests and responses. When an end-user interacts with an application that utilises an API, the user first initiates a request for some data within the application. The request is then transmitted to the API, which retrieves the requested data from the other software system or AI model and returns it to the application.[117]

In essence, an API comprises three main components: an API client, an API server, and an API endpoint. The API client is tasked with compiling the data request from the application and transmitting it to the API server. Such a request may, e.g., be triggered by various user actions, such as clicking a button, entering a specific search term, or by sensory input.[118]

The API request is directed to the appropriate API endpoint within the API server. For example, in an AIaaS platform, the API server would be the AI model where the input data is processed.

API requests can take various forms and commonly include a method, for instance, that the API server should get, post, or delete the requested data. The API request may also specify the parameters of the requested data. It is common for the API request to include additional data, such as authentication credentials, to validate the request. Furthermore, the API request typically specifies the desired data format of the request.

The API server is responsible for authenticating the API request, retrieving and/or modifying the data from the API endpoint, and returning the requested data to the API client. The returned data typically includes the status of the request, indicating whether the request was successfully fulfilled or if the data was not found. The request may also include headers, such as instructions on how long the data can be stored in an internal cache. If the request is successful, the API response also includes the requested data and metadata. Several aspects can go wrong, and several issues can arise when data is shared across APIs. The next subsections will focus on how data protection and cybersecurity compliance can be embedded in APIs.[119]

In order to evaluate the potential for embedding compliance with data protection regulation and cybersecurity regulation within APIs, it is first essential to have a functional understanding of how the introduction of APIs could affect the overall security of a software system and the security of the processing of personal data, especially when data is processed in an AI model through the use of an API.

---

117 Neil Madden. *API Security in Action*. New York: Simon and Schuster, 2020, p. 32. isbn: 9781617296024.

118 Sascha Preibisch. *API Development*. Berkeley: Apress, 2018.

119 Postman. *What Is an API?* url: https://www.postman.com/what-is-an-api/. Last accessed: 01.08.2025.

The implementation of an API as part of a system potentially expands the attack vector, i.e., the means or manner by which an attacker can get access to a system or AI model. The expansion of the attack vector occurs because the API provides a potential additional entry point into the system. When an API is implemented, the boundary of the system shifts from a more secure internal boundary to API clients in external applications. Therefore, the introduction of APIs necessitates the incorporation of cybersecurity measures that protect the systems, the personal data processed, and the underlying AI model accessed through the API.

Hussain et. al. have outlined the most common cybersecurity attacks on a system via the API.[120] The most frequently employed attack vectors on an API are as follows:

- **API-Specific Distributed Denial of Service (DDoS) Attacks:** These attacks involve inundating specific parts of the API client with a significant amount of data, thereby overloading the API. If the API is integral to a critical part of the overall system, such as authentication or login solutions, the entire system could potentially become unavailable.
- **Buffer Overflow Attacks:** In these attacks, unexpected data types are uploaded in the API request, which can lead to the crashing of a specific part of the memory known as the buffer. The overflow of the buffer can lead to the possibility of entering malicious code into the API server and potentially the entire system.
- **SQL Injection Attacks:** These attacks manipulate the parameters of the API request to alter the data in the API server. This type of attack exploits vulnerabilities in the API server's query software to interfere with the operation of the API server in order to access data or potentially also personal data.
- **Script Insertion Attacks:** In these attacks, a malicious script is misinterpreted as content by the API client. The API thereby functions as a gateway to the system, where the script can cause harm.
- **Login Attacks:** These attacks involve testing the login credentials of the API against lists of breached login credentials or inputting random characters into the API until vulnerabilities are detected by an adversary.

Each of the examples of the different types of attacks against the API not only poses a threat to the API itself but also potentially to the overall system, the

[120] Fatima Hussain et al. "Enterprise API security and GDPR compliance: Design and implementation perspective". In: *IT Professional* 22.5 (2020), pp. 81–89. doi: 10.1109/MITP.2020.2973852.

personal data it processes, and the AI model. The attack types on AI models discussed in Chapter 4 are also relevant in this context. If an API-specific risk is identified in a risk assessment, risk-mitigating measures would be required to be implemented to lower the risk to an acceptable level.

Generally, both data protection by design measures under Article 25 of the GDPR and risk-mitigating measures in cybersecurity regulations, such as the CRA and the NIS 2 Directive, can be classified as either organisational or technical measures. In the context of API attacks, the mitigating measures embedded within the APIs tend to be of a more technical than organisational nature. The next paragraphs will address how the attacks on systems and AI models through the API – described in the list above – could be mitigated through technical data protection and security by design measures. Then, a table will present the mitigation technical "by design" measure that corresponds to the most typical attack vectors presented above.

Access control is a technical "by design" measure that could mitigate some of the vulnerabilities of attacks on an API. There are two main types of access controls typically applied in APIs: identity-based access control and capability-based access control.[121] The fundamental objective of both access control types is to ensure that only authorised users gain access to data or AI models through the API.

Identity-based access control operates by initially identifying the user attempting to access data through the API, subsequently granting the user access to the data they are authorised to receive. On the other hand, capability-based access control operates with a capability or a token that the user possesses, providing data access based on the information contained within the token. This token informs the API about the type of data the token bearer can access, without necessarily containing information about who the user is.

Such access control mechanisms could potentially prevent API-specific DDoS attacks and login attacks. In the case of DDoS attacks, access is denied to users attempting to overload the API with data. In the case of login attacks, the access control mechanism detects multiple access requests and denies access accordingly.

API Design Reviews are another measure that could potentially mitigate cybersecurity and data protection breaches in APIs.[122] Such a design review process bears resemblance to code reviews, i.e., a peer review process of the

[121] Neil Madden. *API Security in Action*. New York: Simon and Schuster, 2020, p. 32. isbn: 9781617296024.

[122] Fatima Hussain et al. "Enterprise API security and GDPR compliance: Design and implementation perspective". In: *IT Professional* 22.5 (2020), pp. 81–89. doi: 10.1109/MITP.2020.2973852.

code where the programming is scrutinised and potentially altered for clarity and quality.

An API design review is a procedure where the security, completeness, and quality of the API are evaluated prior to its integration into a larger system. The importance of API design and API reviews can be described with an example. A national coffee chain had implemented a mobile application enabling customers to order coffee and skip the queue. The coffee application utilised an API to transmit requests from the mobile applications to the Point of Sale (POS) system of the coffee shops. The API was equipped with state-of-the-art cybersecurity protocols.[123]

However, sometime post-implementation, the coffee shops observed a sudden surge in unclaimed coffee orders. After some inquiries, the coffee shop chain concluded that these unclaimed orders were sent to the API to elicit an API response in the form of an order confirmation. This confirmation included metadata and an order number, which contained information about the number of sales on that particular day. The API attacks in the form of unclaimed coffee orders were likely an advanced form of industry espionage perpetrated by a competitor to gain access to sales data.[124] This example illustrates the importance of reviewing the design of the API and the necessity for personnel other than the developers to review the design of the API. Such an API design review procedure could potentially ensure an evaluation of potential vulnerabilities and the implementation of appropriate mitigating measures.[125] Unlike the other mitigating measures elaborated above, API design reviews have a more organisational than technical character.

Authentication confidence levels represent a technical "by design" requirement implemented for embedded API security, with several similarities to access control. While access control is the process of auditing who gets access to an API, authentication is the process of verifying whether a user is the one they claim they are. It is the veracity of the credentials the user has that is authenticated, rather than the user themselves.

The primary objective behind authenticating a user's credentials in an API may be to prevent DDoS attacks by processing only authenticated requests in the API. Additionally, maintaining a record of users who have processed data in the API could be beneficial for accountability reasons. It may also be pertinent to authenticate both the user's identity and their pre-authorised actions in

---

123 Gerhard Giese. "Think like a hacker: Reducing cyber security risk by improving API design and protection". In: *Cyber Security: A Peer-Reviewed Journal* 4.1 (2020), pp. 48–57.

124 Ibid.

125 Ibid.

the API to uphold the confidentiality and integrity of the processed personal data.

Such a scheme – where the user is pre-authorised to perform certain actions through the API – is referred to as authentication confidence levels. This approach ensures that only users with the appropriate credentials and permissions can access and manipulate data, thereby enhancing the overall security of the system.[126]

Authorisation is another technical measure that is closely related to both access control and authentication. The distinction between authorisation and access control is primarily semantic, and access control and authorisation are sometimes used interchangeably. The main difference between access control and authentication lies in the fact that access control is sometimes used to refer to both authentication and authorisation processes. This implies that access control encompasses the verification of a user's identity (authentication) as well as the determination of a user's permissions (authorisation).[127]

Encryption is applied as a cybersecurity measure within APIs to protect the (personal) data against unauthorised access. Encryption can protect data both when the (personal) data is transmitted from the API to the client and when the data is at rest within the API server. Consequently, encryption plays a dual role in cybersecurity, shielding both the requests and the responses from the API as they traverse networks and preserving the integrity of data when stored in the API server. Such a dual functionality underscores the significance of encryption in securing the confidentiality and integrity of (personal) data in APIs.[128]

Input sanitation and input validation are two embedded cybersecurity measures in APIs that relate to the processing of input data, i.e., the request for data in the API client. These measures serve to either sanitise or validate the data prior to any further processing within the API or the AI model.[129]

The distinction between sanitising and validating input data lies in their respective functions. A validation check is a procedure that verifies whether the data contained in the request adheres to the policies and constraints specific to that particular API request. In the absence of input data validation in APIs, an adversary could potentially inject code directly into the API and execute the code in the database or elsewhere in the system.

---

126 Syafril Bandara et al. "Access control framework for API-enabled devices in smart buildings". In: *2016 22nd Asia-Pacific Conference on Communications (APCC)*. 2016, pp. 210–217. doi: 10.1109/APCC.2016.7581479.

127 Neil Madden. *API Security in Action*. New York: Simon and Schuster, 2020, p. 32. isbn: 9781617296024.

128 Ibid.

129 Postman. *What Is an API?* url: https://www.postman.com/what-is-an-api/. Last accessed: 01.08.2025.

Table 5.3 Summary of mitigating measures in API-specific attacks

-	DDoS	Buffer overflow	SQL injection	Script insertion	Login
Access Control	Yes	-	-	-	Yes
API Design Reviews	Yes	-	-	-	-
Authentication Confidence Levels	Yes	Yes	Yes	Yes	Yes
Authorization	-	Yes	Yes	Yes	-
Encryption	Yes	Yes	Yes	Yes	Yes
Input Sanitisation	Yes	-	Yes	Yes	-
Input Validation	-	-	Yes	Yes	-

API input sanitisation involves a two-step process. It first validates whether the data complies with the established policies and constraints and then removes any unsafe characters present in the API request.[130]

The technical measures that can function as "by design" requirements to mitigate cybersecurity attacks on APIs are summarised in Table 5.3.

To summarise, when a finished trained AI model is accessed through an API in AIaaS, it potentially offers an increased attack vector. This attack vector poses risks to the organisation's systems, the (personal) data it processes, and potentially also the AI model. In order to mitigate this risk, both Article 25 (1) and (2), and Article 32 of the GDPR and cybersecurity regulations such as the CRA mandate risk assessments and, if risks are identified, risk mitigating measures. Table 5.3 presents some of the most common attack vectors of APIs and related risk-mitigating measures. It is, however, important to interpret these API-specific vulnerabilities and mitigating measures in conjunction with the vulnerabilities for attacks on AI models elaborated in Chapter 4.

5.5 AIaaS AND REQUIREMENTS IN THE AI ACT

Overall, the AI Act has a system with providers and deployers of AI systems. Generally, an AIaaS platform tenant could assume the responsibilities of both provider and deployer.

If, for instance, a natural or legal person uses an AIaaS platform only to develop their own model on the basis of the infrastructure of the platform, they would, depending on the facts of the case, assume the responsibility as the

130 Neil Madden. *API Security in Action*. New York: Simon and Schuster, 2020, p. 32. isbn: 9781617296024.

provider. If the AI system is used for one of the high-risk purposes, the AIaaS platform tenant would also need to comply with the requirements for high-risk AI systems. If the tenant makes use of a finished developed AI model only on an AIaaS platform, the tenant would assume responsibility as a deployer of an AI system.

The definition of provider in Article 3 (3) of the AI Act includes entities that "put the AI system into service under its own name or trademark". Thus, an AIaaS platform provider could assume responsibility as a provider under the AI Act if it has developed an AI model on a platform, puts it into service, and is used in a high-risk application.

An AI model on an AIaaS platform might also be regarded as a general-purpose AI model or a general-purpose AI model with systemic risk.

The requirements for high-risk AI system providers, deployers, and general-purpose AI models have been the focus of Chapters 3 and 4 of the book and will not be recapitulated in the current chapter. Rather, the focus of the current chapter will be on some specific requirements for the AI value chain in the AI Act.

According to recital 9 to the AI Act, the Act places requirements on operators "involved in the AI value chain". In recital 83 to the Act, such operators are exemplified as "importers and distributors who may contribute to the development of AI systems". It is further highlighted in the same recital that the complexity of developing AI systems may lead to operators acting in more than one role at the same time. For instance, an AIaaS platform provider or tenant might fulfil the requirements for both the provider and the deployer of a high-risk AI system at the same time. In such a situation, recital 83 of the AI Act clarifies that the entity should fulfil cumulatively all relevant obligations associated with the roles they are assuming.

However, under certain specific situations, any distributor, importer, deployer, or other third party should be considered to be the provider of high-risk AI systems and assume all the relevant obligations for providers. According to Article 25 (1) of the AI Act, other entities than providers assume the responsibility as a provider if they put their name or trademark on a high-risk AI system already placed on the market or put into service or if they make a substantial modification to a high-risk AI system that has already been placed on the market or put into service in such a way that it remains a high-risk AI system. In such instances, the original provider shall no longer be regarded as a provider of that specific AI system, according to Article 25 (2).

The applicability of Article 25 of the AI Act on AIaaS platforms could be illustrated with some examples. In the examples below, it is assumed that the tenant has the role and the corresponding responsibilities as a deployer.

Suppose that an AIaaS platform tenant uses an existing high-risk AI system proposed for emotion recognition. Such a system is classified as high risk pursuant to Article 6 (2) and Annex III (1) (c). If the tenant makes use of this system and places it under its own name or trademark within the Union, regardless of whether the system makes use of an AI model on an AIaaS platform, the tenant would be regarded as a provider under Article 25 (1) (a).

Another example of an AIaaS platform tenant assuming responsibility as the provider under the AI Act is if the tenant makes a substantial modification to an already high-risk AI system placed on the market in such a manner that it remains a high-risk AI system. The term "substantial modification" is known from other examples of EU product safety regulation and is defined in the AI Act Article 3 (23) as:

> a change (...) which is not foreseen or planned in the initial conformity assessment carried out by the provider, and as a result of the compliance of the AI system with the requirements set out in Chapter II, Section 2 is affected or results in a modification to the intended purpose for which the AI system has been assessed.

If an AIaaS platform tenant makes such a substantial modification, e.g., if an AI model on an AIaaS platform is intended to detect people falling and the tenant develops the image recognition model to recognise natural persons' emotions, the tenant would assume responsibility as the provider, pursuant to the AI Act Article 25 (1) (b).

The last example is that an AIaaS platform tenant could assume the status of provider if the intended purpose of a non-high-risk AI system, including general-purpose AI models, is changed in such a way that the initial system becomes high risk. For instance, suppose that an AI model developed as a diagnostic tool for some sort of disease is applied for credit scoring, a high-risk purpose under Article 6 (2) and Annex III.

Article 25 of the AI Act does not concern AIaaS directly. However, the examples above have illustrated that the use of AIaaS could, in certain situations, change the roles under the AI Act if the tenant alters the models on the platform. Even though the AI Act has these specific requirements, it is fair to say that the overall system of the AI Act, with providers and deployers, would be challenged if AIaaS platforms become more widely adopted. The AI Act has some instruments for surveilling changes in commonly used AI models. For instance, the AI Board is tasked with issuing opinions on the trends in the evolving typology of AI value chains, in particular on the resulting implications of accountability, under Article 66 (e) (vi). Even though the AI Act has this requirement for monitoring changes in AI practices, AIaaS is a common business model not expressly addressed in the AI Act.

5.6 SUMMARY

Important findings of Chapter 5 are the following:

- First, with regard to data protection regulation, the sections above have established that the processing of personal data to develop models further could be regarded as a specific processing purpose that requires a legal basis and could also have consequences for the controllership status of the AIaaS platform provider. The data protection section also established that several AIaaS platforms have global processing chains that require cross-border transfers of personal data and compliance with the transfer rules in Chapter V of the GDPR.
- Second, the cybersecurity requirements section established that AIaaS platforms running on cloud infrastructure could enter the scope of the NIS 2 Directive. Moreover, if an AI model on an AIaaS platform forms a part of a product with digital elements, the model must comply with the CRA. AIaaS platforms function through transfers of data via cycles of API requests and responses. The cybersecurity requirements section addresses specific attack vectors for APIs and corresponding mitigating measures.
- The current chapter has analysed specific requirements where AIaaS tenants might assume responsibility as providers when developing and using AI systems offered through AIaaS platforms for high-risk purposes.
- In conclusion, the emerging use of AIaaS platforms could be described as challenging the different regulations that place responsibility on various actors. When drafting the GDPR, the NIS 2 Directive, and the AI Act, the legislators did not, most likely, take into account that AI models could be rented on platforms and thereby implemented in various systems and platforms. It is possible to address the responsibility of AIaaS providers through interpreting various requirements, e.g., controllership under the GDPR, broadly. However, the emerging use of AIaaS would most likely require reform of obligations placing liability on different static roles, such as controllers, processors, providers, and deployers, under the analysed legal frameworks.

6. Proportionality by design

6.1 INTRODUCTION

While the former chapters have focused on compliance in AI system development and during the use of AI systems at a micro level – specifically during model training, at the inference stage, and through the use of AIaaS – the current chapter aims to examine the "by design" approach from a broader macro perspective. This broader macro perspective will – to a larger extent than the previous chapters – include fundamental rights and the principle of proportionality.

The purpose of this chapter is to examine the relationship and interactions across the GDPR, the AI Act, and Articles 7 and 8 of the Charter when developing and using AI systems. This examination will be conducted through the lens of the principle of proportionality – specific subtests for lawfully interfering in non-absolute fundamental rights.[1] The framework established through such an analysis functions as a tool for understanding the interplay between the rule sets and provides a method for interpreting and analysing questions that arise under these regulatory frameworks, particularly those without clear-cut answers. Additionally, the established *proportionality by design* concept also functions as a basis for best practices for the development and deployment of AI systems that would entail interferences in fundamental rights.

The following sections introduce the concept of *proportionality by design* as an explanatory concept, focusing on its basis, function, and structure within the AI field:

---

[1] Aharon Barak. *Proportionality: Constitutional Rights and Their Limitations*. Cambridge, UK: Cambridge University Press, 2021; Jeremy McBride. "Proportionality and the European Convention on Human Rights". In: *The Principle of Proportionality in the Laws of Europe*. Ed. by Evelyn Ellis. Oxford: Hart Publishing, 1999, p. 23; Lorenzo Dalla Corte. "On proportionality in the data protection jurisprudence of the CJEU". In: *International Data Privacy Law* 12.4 (2022), pp. 259–275. doi: https://doi.org/10.1093/idpl/ipac014.

- Section 6.2 establishes the term *proportionality by design*, focusing on the essence and limitations of the term.
- In Section 6.3, the legal basis of the concept *proportionality by design* is presented.
- Section 6.4 discusses the advantages of *proportionality by design*, demonstrating that the term serves several functions: the concept acts as an interpretative tool, provides an explanatory taxonomy, and establishes a basis for best practices.
- Section 6.5 establishes the differences between material and procedural proportionality review.
- Building on section 6.5, section 6.6 analyses which types of proportionality review different AI systems entering the GDPR and the AI Act will, most likely, undergo.
- Section 6.7 summarises the overall findings of the chapter and concludes.

6.2 ESTABLISHING THE TERM "PROPORTIONALITY BY DESIGN"

While the term "compliance by design" in this book refers to how to comply with positive regulations while developing AI systems and using deployed AI models, the term "proportionality by design" has a wider function than merely guiding the compliance of AI system development and deployment. Proportionality by design focuses on the constitutional limits of AI system development and use established by interpreting the Charter of fundamental rights of the European Union and corresponding case law from the CJEU.

Suppose that the relationship between the means – the development or use of an AI system – and the ends – the overall intended purpose of the AI system or the inference made by the deployed AI model – is not assessed throughout the development and deployment phases. Under such circumstances, it becomes nearly impossible to determine whether the development or use of the AI system is violating pan-European constitutional norms under the Charter of Fundamental Rights. In the former chapters regarding compliance by design, the "by design" part has included various technical measures and alterations to the MLOps framework. The "design" part of the term "proportionality by design", however, refers to the inclusion of these different subtests – established in the next sections – throughout the development and deployment process of an AI system.

In order to define the term "proportionality by design", it is also necessary to describe the term in relation to the risk-based approach pursued in both the GDPR and the AI Act.

The GDPR pursues a risk-based approach – in which the controller processing personal data needs to assess the risks associated with the processing and introduce risk-mitigating measures, e.g., under Articles 24 and 32 of the GDPR.

The AI Act also pursues a risk-based approach where the overall regulation pursues a "clearly defined risk-based approach" where the rules are tailored to the type, content, and intensity of the risk that AI systems can generate, according to recital 26 of the AI Act.

A proportionality by design approach also functions as an explanatory model for a risk-based approach in secondary law, the GDPR and the AI Act. A risk-based approach – in essence – entails that controllers under the scope of the GDPR and providers and deployers under the scope of the AI Act shall assess the risks related to the processing of personal data or the overall risk to health, safety, and fundamental rights associated with the AI system. When the controller and provider assess such risks – especially the risks related to the rights in Article 8 of the Charter – it could be compared to assessing the interference with fundamental rights. The associated risk-mitigating measures could be compared to assessing whether the interference with the fundamental right is proportionate and thus lawful.

In Chapters 3, 4, and 5 of the book, cybersecurity regulation has been a focus in the compliance by design approach of AI system development and deployment. In the current chapter, cybersecurity regulations are not a core focus of the proportionality by design concept. The reason behind not including cybersecurity regulations in the concept is mainly due to the fundamental right basis of proportionality as a structure for lawfully interfering with fundamental rights. Cybersecurity regulations – such as the NIS 2 Directive and the CRA – also have a less individualistic focus where the risks the regulations attempt to mitigate are, first and foremost, societal risks and not risks of interference with individuals' rights. Although there are intersections between, e.g., the security of the processing of personal data and the proportionality of the interference, the cybersecurity regulations are left outside the scope of the current chapter, and the focus will be on the GDPR and the AI Act.

6.3 THE LEGAL BASIS FOR PROPORTIONALITY BY DESIGN

The focus of Chapter 3 of the book was on the fundamental rights structure, including the principle of proportionality, as a guideline for the processing of personal data during AI system development. The main essence of Chapter 3 was that throughout the development phase, the legality, legitimate aim, suitability, necessity, and proportionality *stricto sensu* need to be assessed for the interference – the processing of personal data – to be lawful. This assessment is necessary to determine whether the interference in the fundamental rights to privacy and data protection, which the development of the AI system entails, is proportionate and thus lawful.

The basis for proportionality as a guideline for the lawful processing of personal data during AI system development in Chapter 3 is case law from the CJEU interpreting the GDPR in light of Articles 7 and 8 in the Charter.[2] The rationale behind the relevance of proportionality when processing personal data for AI system development, is, therefore, that proportionality underpins the GDPR and that a compliance by design approach in breach of the Charter – an example of primary law with a *lex superior* nature in the EU – would be of little relevance.

The legal basis for this fundamental rights structure, in addition to the Charter, is Article 8 of the ECHR and national constitutions across European countries. Moreover, as evident from Chapter 3, the overarching structure of fundamental rights is reflected in both primary and secondary legislation, particularly the GDPR. The right to privacy and the right to data protection have both a negative and a positive obligation. Fundamental rights have traditionally covered protection from governmental interference. This is referred to as a states' negative obligation to protect fundamental rights, an obligation for states not to disproportionality interfere with the right under question.[3] The obligation under Article 51 (1) of the Charter to "observe the principles and promote the application thereof" could – in some instances – entail a positive obligation for the EU institutions and member states.[4] Article 51 could entail a positive obligation to promote the rights of the Charter when the EU institutions and member states are implementing EU law, because of the *lex superior*

---

[2] Joined Cases C-92/09 and C-93/09 Volker and Markus Schecke GbR, Hartmut Eifert v Land Hessen, joined party Bundesanstalt für Landwirtschaft und Ernährung ECLI:EU:C:2010:662 paragraph 47 and Amman v Switzerland app. no 27798/95 paragraph 30.; Judgement of 13 May 2014 in Case C-131/12 Google Spain, ECLI:EU:C:2014:317, paragraph 68; Judgement of the Court (Grand Chamber) in Case C-252/21 Meta Platforms Inc., Meta Platforms Ireland Ltd, Facebook Deutschland GmbH v Budeskartellamt ECLI:EU:C:2023:537.

[3] Malu Patricia Beijer. *The Limits of Fundamental Rights Protection by the EU: The Scope for the Development of Positive Obligations*. Cambridge, UK: Cambridge: Intersentia, 2017. isbn: 9781780684550.

[4] Mistale Taylor. "The EU's human rights obligations in relation to its data protection laws with extraterritorial effect". In: *International Data Privacy Law* 5.4 (Sept. 2015), pp. 246–256. ISSN: 2044-3994. doi: 10.1093/idpl/ipv023. eprint: https://academic.oup.com/idpl/article-pdf/5/4/246/9950994/ipv023.pdf. url: https://doi.org/10.1093/idpl/ipv023; Angela Ward. "Field of application". In: *The EU Charter of Fundamental Rights: A Commentary*. Bloomsbury Collections, 2014, p. 1416. doi: http://dx.doi.org/10.5040/9781849468350.ch-055.

nature of the Charter.[5] Moreover, according to the explanatory memorandum to the Charter, "the meaning and scope of the rights are determined not only by the text of those instruments but also by the case law of the European Court of Human Rights and by the Court of Justice of the European Union".[6] In a consistent body of case law from the CJEU, the requirements of the GDPR have been interpreted in light of the rights in the Charter establishing positive obligations under the Charter, for both member states and private sector controllers processing personal data.[7]

It is not just the GDPR and processing of personal data that need to be interpreted in light of the Charter, Articles 7 and 8, and where the purpose and aim of the regulation is to enhance fundamental rights of the Charter. The purpose and aim of the AI Act is – first and foremost – to improve the functioning of the internal market by laying down a uniform legal framework for the development and use of AI systems, according to recital 1 and Article 1 of the AI Act.

However, the purpose of the AI Act is also to ensure a high level of protection of health, safety, and fundamental rights enshrined in the Charter of Fundamental Rights of the European Union, according to recital 1 of the AI Act. Moreover, recital 2 of the AI Act requires the Act to be applied in accordance with the values of the Union enshrined in the Charter. Furthermore, according to recitals 5–6 of the AI Act, "AI may cause harm to public interest and fundamental rights" and it is therefore "vital for AI and its regulatory framework to be developed in accordance with Union values as enshrined in Article 2 of the Treaty of the European Union (TEU), the fundamental rights and freedoms enshrined in the Treaties and, pursuant to Article 6 TEU, the Charter".

---

[5] Mistale Taylor. "The EU's human rights obligations in relation to its data protection laws with extraterritorial effect". In: *International Data Privacy Law* 5.4 (Sept. 2015), pp. 246–256. ISSN: 2044-3994. doi: 10.1093/idpl/ipv023. eprint: https://academic.oup.com/idpl/article-pdf/5/4/246/9950994/ipv023.pdf. url: https://doi.org/10.1093/idpl/ipv023.

[6] Official Journal of the European Union. *Explanations Relating to the Charter of Fundamental Rights 2007/C 303/02*. url: https://eur-lex.europa.eu/legal-content/EN/TXT/PDF/?uri=CELEX:32007X1214(01). Last accessed: 01.08.2025.

[7] Joined Cases C-92/09 and C-93/09 Volker and Markus Schecke GbR, Hartmut Eifert v Land Hessen, joined party Bundesanstalt für Landwirtschaft und Ernährung ECLI:EU:C:2010:662 paragraph 47 and Amman v Switzerland app. no 27798/95 paragraph 30.; Judgement of 13 May 2014 in Case C-131/12 Google Spain, ECLI:EU:C:2014:317, paragraph 68; Judgement of the Court (Grand Chamber) in Case C-252/21 Meta Platforms Inc., Meta Platforms Ireland Ltd, Facebook Deutschland GmbH v Budeskartellamt ECLI:EU:C:2023:537.

According to the recitals of the AI Act, part of the purpose of the Regulation is to ensure fundamental rights protection during the development and use of AI systems. Moreover, the recitals to the AI Act establish that the material and procedural rules of the AI Act need to be interpreted and applied pursuant to the requirements in the Charter.

Article 52 (1) of the Charter contains the requirements for the scope and interpretation of the rights and principles in the Charter, including the requirements for interfering with Articles 7 and 8. According to the explanatory memorandum of the Charter, Article 52 of the Charter is based on well-established case law from the CJEU.[8] As stated in the explanatory memorandum to the Charter, with further references to the judgement in the case C-292/97, "restrictions may be imposed on the exercise of fundamental rights, in particular in the context of a common organisation of the market, provided that those restrictions in fact correspond to objectives of general interest pursued by the Community and do not constitute, with regard to the aim pursued, disproportionate and unreasonable interference undermining the very substance of those rights".[9] The principle of proportionality established through the case law of the CJEU, thus, constitutes the rational underpinning of the requirements for interfering with a fundamental right, under Article 52 of the Charter, according to the explanatory memorandum to the Charter and well-established case law from the CJEU.

Section 3.2 of Chapter 3 established the relevance of the principle of proportionality when processing personal data for AI system development. The subsections above further established that the purpose of the AI Act is partially to enhance fundamental right protection in AI system development and use, and that the requirements of the AI Act shall be interpreted in line with the obligations of the Charter. Hence, in order for an AI system under the scope of both the AI Act and the GDPR to lawfully interfere with Articles 7 and 8 of the Charter, the AI system needs to respect the principle of proportionality under Article 52 of the Charter. The principle of proportionality under the Charter includes the subtests of legitimate aim, suitability, necessity, and proportionality *stricto sensu* to assess whether the interference in a fundamental right is lawful.[10]

---

8 Official Journal of the European Union. *Explanations Relating to the Charter of Fundamental Rights 2007/C 303/02*. url: https://eur-lex.europa.eu/legal-content/EN/TXT/PDF/?uri=CELEX:32007X1214(01). Last accessed: 01.08.2025.

9 Judgement of the Court (Sixt Chamber) of 13 April 2000 in case C-292/97 Kjell Karlsson and Others, ECLI:EU:C:1999:24, paragraph 45.

10 Lorenzo Dalla Corte. "On proportionality in the data protection jurisprudence of the CJEU". In: *International Data Privacy Law* 12.4 (2022), pp. 259–275. doi: https://doi.org/10.1093/idpl/ipac014.

6.4 ADVANTAGES WITH THE TERM "PROPORTIONALITY BY DESIGN"

6.4.1 Compliance with Primary Law

All AI systems entering the scope of either the AI Act or the GDPR need to respect the fundamental rights of the Charter, according to Article 51 of the Charter. Due to the primary law nature of the Charter and the *lex superior* principle, secondary law in the EU acquis cannot provide more or less fundamental rights protection than primary law. Accordingly, the material and procedural requirements in the GDPR and the AI Act need to be interpreted in line with the fundamental rights structure of the Charter to represent lawful interferences in the fundamental rights of Articles 7 and 8 of the Charter.

Furthermore, it is evident from Chapters 3, 4, and 5 of the book that the requirements of both the GDPR and the AI Act are complex, detailed, and intertwined. The level of complexity in the two rule sets could potentially result in a negative consequence: the loss of oversight. The overall purpose of the GDPR, the AI Act, and the fundamental rights in Articles 7 and 8 of the Charter is that disproportionate AI systems should not be developed or deployed within the EU. When having a micro focus on the particular requirements of the AI Act and the GDPR, each and every one of the requirements in the rule sets could be fulfilled. However, the overall cumulative interference in Articles 7 and 8 of the Charter could result in disproportionate and thus unlawful AI systems. The proportionality by design approach, where the subtests legitimate aim, suitability, necessity, and proportionality *stricto sensu* are assessed throughout the development and deployment phase, could be a counterbalance and safeguard against such a narrow focus.

The purpose, or legitimate aim, of the AI system is crucial to guide the proportionality assessment of the interference. Suppose that the purpose and aim of the AI system is to protect national security and public safety against a current and imminent threat. In such an instance, the potential to interfere and the suitability, necessity, and proportionality *stricto sensu* would be assessed differently compared to if the purpose of the interference through the processing of the personal data in the AI system is to detect VAT fraud or to detect whether students in a public university has plagiarised their exams. The legitimate aim guides the assessment of proportionality. The necessity of the interference and the question of whether less intrusive means would fulfil the purposes are assessed in relation to the legitimate aim.[11] The suitability, often

[11] Mistale Taylor. "The EU's human rights obligations in relation to its data protection laws with extraterritorial effect". In: *International Data Privacy Law*

a factual assessment of whether the interference is appropriate, is also assessed against the legitimate aim. Finally, the proportionality *stricto sensu* assessment is a weighting exercise where the legitimate aim is weighed against the right that is interfered with.

There are examples of AI systems outside the scope of the GDPR and the AI Act which would hence also be outside the scope of the Charter, according to Article 51 of the Charter. Examples include AI systems for national security and military purposes, according to the AI Act Article 2 (3) and the GDPR recital 16. In such instances, the ECHR and the corresponding subtest of the fundamental rights structure would be applicable, and the proportionality by design approach would also be relevant in such circumstances.

The first advantage of the proportionality by design concept is thus to contribute to the concurrent compliance with primary and secondary law and to develop and deploy proportionate AI systems.

6.4.2 Proportionality by Design as an Explanatory Taxonomy

Another function of proportionality by design is as an explanatory model of the interrelations between secondary law – the GDPR and the AI Act – and the interrelations between primary law – the Charter – and secondary law – the GDPR and the AI Act.

Chapters 3, 4, and 5 of this book have illustrated that two primary purposes of both the GDPR and the AI Act are to contribute to the protection of the fundamental rights of Articles 7 and 8 of the Charter. Protection of the fundamental right to privacy and data protection is the core purpose of the GDPR, according to Article 1 of the GDPR. Moreover, according to subsection 3.3.3 in Chapter 3 of this book, privacy and data protection are one of the prominent purposes of the AI Act. Since the purpose of both these rule sets is, to some extent, overlapping, the proportionality by design framework could be a basis for structuring and understanding the connections across the GDPR and the AI Act in situations when both rule sets enter into effect.

This function of the proportionality by design concept is also relevant since the GDPR and the AI Act have several requirements that correspond to the fundamental rights structure of the Charter. As illustrated in Chapter 3, the GDPR is not a maze of bureaucratic and unstructured requirements. The GDPR is a collection of norms that contribute to two main purposes: The protection of personal data and the free flow of personal data in intra-EU transfers.

5.4 (Sept. 2015), pp. 246–256. ISSN: 2044-3994. doi: 10.1093/idpl/ipv023. eprint: https://academic.oup.com/idpl/article-pdf/5/4/246/9950994/ipv023.pdf. url: https://doi.org/10.1093/idpl/ipv023.

To illustrate the structuring function that the proportionality by design concept could have, the following examples from Chapters 3, 4, and 5 of the book are relevant.

Several of these examples illustrate the difference in the proportionality assessment when the interference is conducted by the state, the negative obligation, and by private parties, the positive obligation of protecting the fundamental rights in Articles 7 and 8 of the Charter. For instance, in 3.2.7.7, it was established that, according to Article 6 (1) (f) of the GDPR, public authorities cannot rely on Article 6 (1) (f) when processing personal data in the performance of their task. It is presupposed in the legal literature that Article 6 (1) (f) refers only to the interests of private sector controllers and that private bodies, vested in law with a task of public interest, also are precluded from relying on Article 6 (1) (f) as a legal basis.[12]

The rationale behind Article 6 (1) (f) is elaborated in recital 47 of the GDPR. According to recital 47, since it is the task of the legislator to provide by law the legal basis for public authorities, Article 6 (1) (f) should not apply to the processing by public authorities in the performance of their tasks. Article 6 (1) (f) as a legal basis contains a proportionality assessment of its own, where the legitimate aim, necessity, and proportionality *stricto sensu* have to be assessed and concluded for the processing to be lawful. In the context of public authorities, this proportionality assessment has to be assessed generally *ex-ante* in the legislative process and not by the authorities themselves on a per case basis, according to recital 47 of the GDPR.

The structure and content of the positive obligation under Article 6 (1) (f) of the GDPR were elaborated by the CJEU in the Meta Platforms Inc. judgement from 2023.[13] The judgement concerned several referred questions. The core topic of the judgement focused on the legal basis for personalised advertisement on Instagram and Facebook, a process involving the processing of personal data in AI models. In paragraph 108 of the judgement, the Court held that Article 6 (1) (f) requires that the legitimate interests pursued "cannot reasonably be achieved just as effectively by other means less restrictive of the fundamental rights and freedoms of the data subject, in particular, the rights to respect for private life and to the protection of personal data guaranteed by Articles 7 and 8 of the Charter". The CJEU further held, in the same

12 Waltraut Kotschy. "Article 6: Lawfulness of processing". In: *The EU General Data Protection Regulation (GDPR): A Commentary*. Ed. by Christopher Kuner, Lee A. Bygrave, and Christopher Docksey. Oxford: Oxford University Press, 2020.

13 Judgement of the Court (Grand Chamber) in Case C-252/21 Meta Platforms Inc., Meta Platforms Ireland Ltd, Facebook Deutschland GmbH v Budeskartellamt ECLI:EU:C:2023:537.

paragraph, that the necessity of the processing of personal data under Article 6 (1) (f) needs to be interpreted in conjunction with the data minimisation principle in Article 5 (1) (c). The requirement for necessity in Article 6 (1) (f) thus needs to be interpreted as whether less restrictive means of processing could achieve the processing purpose as effectively and in line with the data minimisation principle. The judgement illustrates that the necessity subtest under the principle of proportionality is relevant when assessing the proportionality of the interference under the GDPR, since the judgement calls for interpreting necessity in line with the data minimisation principle.

The CJEU also interpreted which interests can be regarded as "legitimate" under Article 6 (1) (f) in the Meta Platforms Inc. judgement. The CJEU concluded that direct marketing purposes, purposes related to network security, and product improvement could potentially constitute legitimate interests pursued by Meta. The Court further held, in paragraph 124 of the Meta Platforms Inc. judgement, that the objective of information sharing with law enforcement authorities cannot constitute a legitimate interest under Article 6 (1) (f) because the "objective is not capable, in principle, of constituting a legitimate interest pursued by the controller, within the meaning of point (f) of the first subparagraph of Article 6 (1) of the GDPR. A private operator such as Meta Platforms Ireland cannot rely on such a legitimate interest, which is unrelated to its economic and commercial activity. Conversely, that objective may justify processing by such an operator where it is objectively necessary for compliance with a legal obligation to which that operator is subject". The cited excerpt from the judgement is an example of the relevance of the structure with positive and negative obligations under the Charter. Law enforcement is a typically core member state competence, and information sharing with law enforcement authorities, thus, needs to be provided for by law and be based on a legal basis in Article 6 (1) (c) and not Article 6 (1) (f). The risk of interfering with the states' negative interference is higher when sharing personal data for law enforcement purposes. The proportionality, therefore, needs to be assessed by the legislator *ex-ante*, and not by controllers on a per case basis as it would be under Article 6 (1) (f).

Regarding the proportionality *stricto sensu* subtest under Article 6 (1) (f), the Court held that the balancing exercise between the fundamental rights of the Charter and the legitimate interests pursued with the processing depends on the specific circumstances of the particular case in the Meta Platforms Inc. judgement. In such a balancing exercise, it is, according to the wording of Article 6, necessary to pay special attention to the situation where the data subject is a child. Children merit specific protection because they may be less aware of the risks, consequences, and safeguards related to the processing of personal data. According to the CJEU, specific protection should apply to the processing of children's personal data for the purposes of marketing, creating personalised or user profiles, or offering services directed towards children. The Court also referenced recital 47 to the GDPR, where it is stated that the interests and fundamental rights of data subjects may, in particular, override the interests of the controller where personal data is processed in circumstances where data subjects do not reasonably expect such processing.

How do the identified requirements in the AI Act relate to the structuring function of the proportionality by design concept? First, the prohibitions under Article 5 of the AI Act – identified and analysed in Chapter 4 of the book – could be viewed as examples of the negative obligation under the rights of the Charter. Several of the prohibitions, e.g., real-time remote biometric identification systems for law enforcement purposes in publicly available spaces, emotion recognition systems in workplaces and education institutions, and systems based on untargeted scraping of facial images, are based on privacy and data protection concerns. Moreover, several of the prohibitions are also AI systems, mostly linked to traditional governmental purposes, e.g., law enforcement, public security, public benefits, and education. Based on the rationales behind several of the prohibitions under the AI Act Article 5 and that several of the prohibitions are closely linked to aims often pursued by the state, it is possible to frame these prohibitions under the negative obligation in the identified proportionality by design concept. The member states, thus, have an obligation not to breach the prohibitions under Article 5 of the AI Act and cannot derogate from the prohibitions.

Second, according to the AI Act Article 27 (1) and Annex III (5)(b) and (c), deployers that are governed by public law and private entities providing public services are required to conduct a fundamental rights impact assessment. The allocation of this requirement, especially on deployers governed by public law and private entities providing public services, exemplifies that the negative obligation is an obligation placed especially on the states and public authorities.

However, it is not solely deployers that are governed by public law who are required to conduct a fundamental rights impact assessment under the AI Act. Also, private entities providing public services, and deployers of high-risk AI systems intended to be used to assess the creditworthiness of natural persons or used for risk assessment and pricing of life and health insurance offered to natural persons, are required to conduct an assessment, according to the AI Act Article 27 (1) and Annex III (5) (b) and (c). The EU legislator has assessed that when private controllers process data to develop models to assess creditworthiness or for pricing of life and health insurance, the risk of interfering with the rights of the Charter – particularly the right to data protection in Article 8 – is substantial. Thus, the EU legislator has mandated that private deployers who make use of such AI systems need to assess and mitigate interference in fundamental rights. Article 27 (1) of the AI Act is also an example of the EU legislator expressing the positive obligation under the Charter through secondary law.

The difference between the member states' negative obligation to respect the Charter and the positive obligation to promote the application thereof is also evident in the pre-defined high-risk AI system areas in Annex III to the AI Act. Several of the areas, e.g., law enforcement, critical infrastructure, access to and enjoyment of public services and benefits, migration and border management, and administration of justice and democratic processes, are examples of core state competencies. Several of the listed high-risk areas in Annex III to the AI Act relate closely to AI systems that – provided they were deployed in the Union without any further process – would risk interfering with the member states' negative obligations under the Charter. Hence, the EU legislator has pre-listed certain purposes, where several have a close connection to core member states' functions, such as law enforcement and border control. The inclusion of such core member states functions as areas with high-risk AI systems, potentially reducing the risk of the member states violating their negative obligations under the Charter.

Another example of the structuring function of proportionality by design in the AI Act is that the provider needs to disclose the original purpose of the data processing when personal data is collected, as part of the data governance obligations for high-risk AI systems under Article 10 (2) (b) of the AI Act. Such disclosure may be the first necessary step for the data subject to invoke their rights under the GDPR. This requirement illustrates the interconnections between the GDPR, the AI Act, and the Charter.

Another illustration of proportionality by design expressed through the AI Act is the risk management measures for deployed high-risk AI systems, the post-market monitoring system, record-keeping, and serious incident reporting. These monitoring obligations should also – according to recital 93 of the AI Act – ensure that fundamental rights are protected when high-risk AI systems are developed and deployed. These obligations could, therefore, be viewed as the EU legislator fulfilling the positive obligation under the EU Charter through secondary legislation.

To summarise, the subsections above have established that the GDPR and the AI Act – two examples of secondary law that cover both private organisations and public authorities – have several requirements that are implemented to prevent the member states from breaching the negative obligations to "respect the rights" of the Charter. The subsections above have focused on requirements that have a close connection to the right to privacy and data protection because their rationale is related to these rights, and that are placed on public authorities.

In relation to the positive obligation under the Charter, both the AI Act and the GDPR have several relevant examples. The structure and function of the proportionality assessment under the positive obligation to ensure and fulfil the Charter is characterised by the interests of the private controller processing the personal data or the private provider developing the high-risk AI system being balanced against the fundamental right. The interest pursued by the controller needs to be related to the commercial and economic activity of the private organisation, be necessary, and proportionate, *stricto sensu*. The specificities of this assessment will vary from case to case, but the overall structure of the proportionality assessment will remain the same.

6.4.3 Proportionality by Design as a Basis for Best Practice

Proportionality by design is based on analysed case law that established the outer constitutional limits of the right to private life and the right to data protection in the EU acquis. These judgements are based upon interferences in these rights that have already taken place. When the proportionality is assessed before a potential interference (*ex-ante*) in a technology that is characterised by its autonomy and self-learning nature, it could be advisable not to test these constitutional limits, but to develop the technology with some distance from the pan-European constitutional boundaries. Therefore, proportionality by design also functions as a basis for best practices for AI development and use.

The proportionality by design concept could, therefore, also have an important function outside a purely legal dogmatics context. The concept could be applied as a basis for best practices for AI system development and deployment. The fundamental rights structure, including the assessment of legality and the principle of proportionality, could be characterised as the most important and internationally universal framework for assessing the lawfulness of interferences with fundamental rights.[14] AI systems that process personal data would represent an interference with the fundamental right to data protection. The proportionality by design concept, where the lawfulness of interferences is assessed through a structured and analytical approach, could, thus, also be applied in a more commercial and *lex ferenda* context.

The function of the proportionality by design concept is particularly relevant in an AI setting. The development and widespread deployment of AI systems have resulted in new legislation coming into effect in the EU in a relatively short timeframe, from being suggested in 2021 to being politically agreed in December 2023. However, both the self-learning nature and the rapid

---

[14] Aharon Barak. *Proportionality: Constitutional Rights and Their Limitations*. Cambridge, UK: Cambridge University Press, 2021; Jeremy McBride. "Proportionality and the European Convention on Human Rights". In: *The Principle of Proportionality in the Laws of Europe*. Ed. by Evelyn Ellis. Oxford: Hart Publishing, 1999, p. 23.

development of new technology would likely result in outdated legislation in a short amount of time. This phenomenon is known as the pacing problem, also referred to as the Collingridge dilemma.[15] The accelerating technological development would thus, most likely, necessitate new and updated regulations. However, new legislation takes a lot of effort, and trialogue negotiations in the EU are time-consuming. The proportionality by design concept and the fundamental rights basis of both data protection and AI regulation could function as an important mid-station during the waiting time for new legislation to be adopted or existing legislation to be revised in reopened trialogue negotiations.

6.5 MATERIAL VS PROCEDURAL PROPORTIONALITY

Section 6.5 will examine whether the constitutional review of AI systems that process personal data in the CJEU will take a material and substantive form or be conducted as a procedural review.

The previous sections of the current chapter have demonstrated that the principle of proportionality functions as an analytical instrument to manage and resolve conflicts between a public or private objective and a fundamental right, or a conflict between two or more rights. The application of the principle of proportionality by the CJEU and the constitutional review it entails can differ depending on several circumstances. For instance, the application varies depending on whether the interference has a basis in EU or national member state law, and the societal context in which the interference occurs.[16] The proportionality of the interference, i.e., the processing of personal data in an AI system, would therefore vary depending on whether the basis of the processing has a basis in EU law or in a national derogation from EU law and the societal context the processing of personal data in an AI system occurs.

The application of the principle of proportionality is likely to be applied differently depending on whether the interference relates to, e.g., public health, national security, or core commercial societal interests that involve both personal data protection and consumer protection. Legal scholars, through case law analysis, have suggested that the application of the principle of proportionality varies when the CJEU is assessing EU regulation (the horizontal application) compared to when the principle is applied to assess member

---

15 David Colingridge. *The Social Control of Technology*. New York: St Martins Press, 1982. isbn: 9780312731687.

16 Takis Tridimas. "Wreaking the wrongs: Balancing rights and the public interest the EU way". In: *Columbia Journal of European Law* 29 (2023), p. 185. url: https://cjel.law.columbia.edu/files/2023/04/10.-TRIDIMAS-PROOF.pdf.

state regulation (the vertical application), with the latter involving a stricter approach and a more rigorous constitutional review.[17]

Given the challenge of prognosticating whether future cases involving the processing of personal data in an AI system will be based on the GDPR, the AI Act, or member states' derogations, section 6.5 will not focus on the distinction between vertical and horizontal proportionality. Instead, the focus will be on the difference between material/substantial proportionality and procedural/process-oriented proportionality.

What is the difference between a material proportionality review and a procedural proportionality review? At its core, the distinction lies in the focus of the assessment. A material proportionality review evaluates the outcome of the interference with a fundamental right, examining the extent and impact of the interference through the subtests, legitimate aim, suitability, necessity, and proportionality *stricto sensu*. In contrast, a procedural proportionality review examines whether the legislator or the entity responsible for the interference has properly considered specific fundamental rights and adhered to relevant procedural steps. Often, these steps include ensuring that the legislator or the entity responsible for the interference itself has reviewed the proportionality before the interference.

The rationale behind a shift from a material to a procedural constitutional review in the CJEU is articulated by the president of the CJEU, Koen Lenaerts, who explains that this approach aims to "increase judicial scrutiny over the decision-making processes of the EU whilst preventing the Court from intruding into the realm of politics".[18]

A relevant question is whether procedural or material proportionality reviews are more prevalent in the CJEU cases involving Articles 7 and 8 of the Charter. Although the CJEU's President Lenaerts has expressed an overarching goal of adopting a more procedural proportionality review, case law concerning Articles 7 and 8 of the Charter reveals a trend not consistent with regard to a more procedural review. A consistent aspect in the case law from the CJEU is that a process-oriented proportionality review is typically applied in areas where the legislature has broad discretion, such as those involving political, economic, and social matters. However, when fundamental rights,

---

17 Tor-Inge Harbo. "The function of the proportionality principle in EU law". In: *European Law Journal* 16.2 (2010), pp. 158–185.

18 Koen Lenaerts. "The European Court of Justice and process-oriented review". In: *Yearbook of European Law* 31.1 (2012), pp. 3–16. doi: https://doi.org/10.1093/yel/yes009.

particularly the rights in Articles 7 and 8 of the Charter, are at stake, the CJEU tends to conduct a more substantive and material proportionality review.[19]

Regarding the distinction between material and procedural review, Dyzenhaus has observed that judges in several jurisdictions have "traditionally felt more comfortable reviewing decisions on procedural rather than on substantive grounds on the basis that procedural review does not interfere with the democratic mandate of the legislature both to make substantive decisions and to delegate authority to make such decisions to administrative officials".[20] However, when a case involves an interference with a fundamental right, as opposed to the democratic mandate of the legislature to make decisions and delegate authority to administrative officials, the situation differs. The EU Charter binds and applies to all EU institutions, including the CJEU, which means that the usual aversion and reluctance for concrete substantive review is, thus, not as pronounced in these contexts.

How does the existing landscape, where cases relating to the internal market have a more process-oriented review and fundamental rights receive a more substantial/material proportionality review, translate to cases under the scope of the GDPR and the AI Act?

As identified in the previous sections of this chapter and earlier chapters of the book, the AI Act serves multiple purposes, where it is intended both as a market instrument to ensure a single and unified European market for AI systems and as a mechanism to protect fundamental rights in the Charter. Therefore, it is plausible to contend that if the case in question is technical in nature and relates to the internal market for AI systems, the proportionality review will most likely have a process-oriented nature. Conversely, if the case relates to fundamental rights, the CJEU is likely to conduct a substantive and material proportionality review.

For instance, if the CJEU is referred a case of whether the harmonised or technical standards adopted under the AI Act are in breach of the AI Act because they, to some extent, place an extensive burden on providers or deployers of AI systems, the CJEU will, most likely, perform a process-oriented proportionality review. However, if the CJEU, for instance, is asked to interpret whether the wording under Article 5 (1) (a) of the AI Act "manipulative or deceptive techniques" includes a LLM trained on a potentially manipulative

---

19 Darren Harvey. "Towards process-oriented proportionality review in the European Union". In: *European Public Law* 23.1 (2017), pp. 93–121.

20 David Dyzenhaus. "Process and substance as aspects of the public law form". In: *The Cambridge Law Journal* 74.2 (2015), pp. 284–306.

Table 6.1 *Different cases under the GDPR and the AI Act and the corresponding proportionality review*

Case	Type of review
A core data protection case	Material/Substantial Proportionality Review
A case about technical/ market requirements in the AI Act	Procedural/Process-Oriented Review
A case about requirements in the AI Act reasoned in fundamental rights	Material/Substantial Proportionality Review

dataset, thus lacking a human intent to manipulate,[21] there are reasons to believe that the court would conduct a more substantive constitutional review.

If a case emanates from the GDPR or another data protection regulation, or if it involves the processing of personal data in some capacity, previous case law from the CJEU indicates that the case will be subjected to a substantive and material proportionality review.[22]

The different types of cases under the GDPR and the AI Act, along with the corresponding types of constitutional review, are summarised in Table 6.1.

To conclude, in cases where the legislature has broad discretion or when the issue concerns technical questions about the political, economic, or social integration of the EU member states, the CJEU has increasingly adopted a process-oriented or procedural proportionality test. In this test, the focus of

21 Micah Carroll et al. "Characterizing manipulation from AI systems". In: *Proceedings of the 3rd ACM Conference on Equity and Access in Algorithms, Mechanisms, and Optimization.* 2023, pp. 1–13. doi: https://doi.org/10.48550/arXiv.2303.09387.

22 Joined Cases C-92/09 and C-93/09 Volker and Markus Schecke GbR, Hartmut Eifert v Land Hessen, joined party Bundesanstalt für Landwirtschaft und Ernährung ECLI:EU:C:2010:662 paragraph 47 and Amman v Switzerland app. no 27798/95 paragraph 30.; Joined Cases C-203/15 and C-698/15 Tele2 Sverige AB v Post- och telestyrelsen and others, Judgement of 21 December 2016 (Grand Chamber) (ECLI:EU:C:2016:970) para 115; Case C-2017/16 Ministerio Fiscal, Judgement of 2 October 2018 (Grand Chamber) (ECLI:EU:2018:788) para 52; Joined Cases C-511/18, C-512/18 and C-520/18 La Quadrature du Net and Others v Premier minister and Others, Judgement of 6 October 2020 (Grand Chamber) (ECLI:EU:C:2020:791) para 112.; Judgement of the Court (Grand Chamber) of 6 October 2015 in case C-362/14 Maximillian Schrems v Data Protection Commissioner, joined party: Digital Rights Ireland Ltd ECLI:EU:C:2015:650; Judgement of the Court (Grand Chamber) 16 July 2020 in Case C-311/18 Data Protection Commissioner v Facebook Ireland Ltd, Maximillian Schrems ECLI:EU:C:2020:559.

the court is to review whether the proportionality has been assessed by the entity responsible for the interference. However, if a case concerns fundamental rights enshrined in the Charter, the traditional proportionality principle is applied, including the subtests of legitimate aim, suitability, and proportionality *stricto sensu* subtests.

For core data protection cases involving the GDPR or the rights in the Charter, the CJEU is likely to continue applying these traditional proportionality subtests. The AI Act, however, serves multiple purposes, one of which is the protection of fundamental rights. Therefore, if a case arises from a technical or internal market requirement in the AI Act, the CJEU will likely employ a process-oriented proportionality test. Conversely, if the case involves a requirement in the AI Act with a fundamental right protection rationale, the traditional proportionality test will likely be applied by the CJEU.

6.6 PROPORTIONALITY *EX-ANTE* AND *EX-POST*

To assess the proportionality of an interference in a fundamental right that has occurred and to prognosticate whether a future interference will be proportionate are two very different assessments. This difference is particularly relevant within the AI field, characterised by systems with a self-developing character. The next paragraphs will partially build on the former section regarding the two different types of proportionality review. Under both the GDPR and the AI Act, the controller and the provider are required to assess proportionality *ex-ante*. For instance, under the GDPR Article 35, the controller is obligated to conduct a Data Protection Impact Assessment (DPIA) when the processing, for instance, due to new technologies such as AI, is likely to result in a high risk to the rights and freedoms. When assessing whether the conditions under the legal basis in Article 6 (1) (f) are fulfilled, the controllers also need to conduct a proportionality assessment prior to the processing.

Under the AI Act, the providers are obligated to conduct fundamental rights impact assessments of certain high-risk AI systems under Article 27 and risk assessments under the risk management system in Article 9 of the AI Act.

The focus of this section is to analyse the difference in assessing the proportionality of interference in Articles 7 and 8 of the Charter prior to the interference (*ex-ante*), during the deployment of an AI system, and after the interference has taken place (*ex-post*). There are several differences in prognosticating a future interference in self-learning and developing technology, such as AI systems and reviewing an interference that has already taken place.

The legislative development, where assessments of, e.g., proportionality are assessed by different entities *ex-ante* instead of *ex-post*, is in line with principles for better regulation and better legislative techniques.[23] In recital 12 of the Interinstitutional agreement between the European Parliament, the Council of the European Union, and the Commission on Better Lawmaking,[24] it is highlighted that the principle of proportionality as well as fundamental rights should be "fully respected" in various impact assessments across Union legislation. The principle of proportionality is both a general principle of EU law and a principle for interfering with the Charter rights, according to the Charter Article 52. The emphasis on the relevance of the principle of proportionality in the interinstitutional agreement highlights that the principle of proportionality is not only relevant where direct interference with fundamental rights is identified, but also under impact assessments and *ex-ante* proportionality assessments when assessing potential future interference.

The factors that characterise the different risk assessments, impact assessments, and fundamental rights impact assessments across the GDPR and the AI Act, and how these assessments relate to the two types of constitutional review identified in the previous section, will be analysed in the following.

First, it is essential to analyse the various types of impact assessments under the GDPR. When assessing whether the requirements under the legal basis in Article 6 (1) (f) are fulfilled, the controller would need to prognosticate that the interest pursued by the future processing is legitimate, that the processing is suitable and strictly necessary for the(se) purpose(s), and that the right of the data subject does not override the legitimate aim pursued (proportionality *stricto sensu*). The assessment conducted by the controller prior to the processing and thus before the interference has the character of being a traditional material and substantive proportionality assessment, yet an assessment conducted *ex-ante*.

A DPIA, according to the GDPR Article 35, is a somewhat different proportionality assessment. Before digging deeper into the impact assessment, it is important to analyse which processing operations require a DPIA. According to the GDPR Article 35 (1), a DPIA is required "where a type of processing, in particular, using new technologies, and taking into account the nature, scope, context and purposes of the processing, is likely to result in a high risk to the rights and freedoms of natural persons". According to Article 35 (3), a DPIA shall specifically be required in the case of a systematic and extensive evaluation of personal aspects relating

23 Borja Sánchez Barroso. "Beyond the principle of proportionality: Controlling the restriction of rights under factual uncertainty". In: *Oslo Law Review* 2 (2023), pp. 74–91. doi: https://doi.org/10.18261/olr.9.2.1.

24 Interinstitutional agreement between the European Parliament, the Council of the European Union and the Commission on better lawmaking. Interinstitutional Agreement of 13 April 2016 [2016] OJ L 123/1.

to natural persons which are based on automated processing which decisions are based that produce legal effects or similarly affect the natural person, processing on a large scale of special categories of personal data, and a systematic monitoring of a publically accessible area on a large scale. Since new technologies are especially mentioned in Article 35 (1) and automated processing in Article 35 (3), DPIAs are particularly relevant for the processing of personal data in AI systems.

A DPIA shall, according to Article 35 (7), at least contain:

(a) a systematic description of the envisaged processing operations and the purposes of the processing, including, where applicable, the legitimate interest pursued by the controller;
(b) an assessment of the necessity and proportionality of the processing operations in relation to the purposes;
(c) an assessment of the risks to the rights and freedoms of data subjects referred to in Article 35 (1); and
(d) the measures envisaged to address the risks, including safeguards, security measures and mechanisms to ensure the protection of personal data and to demonstrate compliance with this Regulation, taking into account the rights and legitimate interests of data subjects and other persons concerned.

After examining the requirements for a DPIA, it becomes evident that the DPIA is intended to contribute to an acceptable risk of interfering with the right to personal data protection by identifying risks before the processing commences and implementing appropriate safeguards. Before the GDPR entered into force, the requirement to conduct a DPIA was viewed as having the potential to "act as an early warning system enabling all actors to systematically address potential deficiencies in a process (...) For controllers, it is an important instrument to demonstrate compliance with legal requirements and can build trust between controllers and its customers".[25] Based on the wording of Article 35 and the cited excerpt it is possible to contend that the obligation to conduct a DPIA is a type of proportionality assessment with both a material and a process-oriented character. The purpose is both to analyse the risk and introduce risk-mitigating measures in the form of safeguards (material

---

25 Felix Bieker et al. "A process for data protection impact assessment under the European General Data Protection Regulation". In: *Privacy Technologies and Policy*. Ed. by Stefan Schiffner et al. Cham: Springer International Publishing, 2016, pp. 21–37. isbn: 978-3-319-44760-5. doi: https://doi.org/10.1007/978-3-319-44760-5_2.

proportionality) and to demonstrate compliance for controllers (process-oriented proportionality).

However, after the GDPR entered into force in May 2018, it is possible to contend that Article 35 of the GDPR functions mostly as a process-oriented "tick-the-box" proportionality exercise to demonstrate paper compliance.[26] The *ex-ante* risk management tool in Article 35 of the GDPR, thus, has the potential to act both as a material and as a process-oriented proportionality assessment. Nevertheless, the process-oriented assessment, where the DPIA is applied mostly to demonstrate compliance, has become more prominent.

How do the different *ex-ante* risk management tools under the AI Act, risk management under Article 9 and fundamental rights impact assessment under Article 27 relate to the different proportionality assessments, material and procedural proportionality?

Under Article 9 (1) of the AI Act, a risk management system shall be established, implemented, documented, and maintained in relation to high-risk AI systems. AI risk management might be an integrated part of existing risk management procedures relating to relevant Union sectoral law, according to Article 9 (10). Under Article 9 (2) litra (a)–(d), such a system shall consist of a continuous iterative process running throughout the entire lifecycle of a high-risk AI system.

The purpose of the risk management system is to identify and analyse known and foreseeable risks and estimate and evaluate the risks that may emerge when a high-risk AI system is used. Moreover, the risk management system shall evaluate other possible risks based on the data gathered from the AI system and adopt suitable risk management measures.

According to Article 9 (2) (a) of the AI Act, the risks managed in the risk management system are risks to health and safety and risks of adverse interference with fundamental rights. The purpose of risk management of high-risk AI systems is to identify, estimate, and mitigate risks to health and safety and the risk of adverse impact on fundamental rights, according to Article 9 (1). An assessment of the risk of harm to health and safety and the risk of adverse impact on fundamental rights are two different assessments concerning the methodology typically applied. As argued by Beck: "How we assess the risk posed by the violation of freedom rights differs from our assessment

[26] Dara Hallinan and Nicholas Martin. "Fundamental rights, the normative keystone of DPIA". In: *European Data Protection Law Review* 6 (2020), p. 178. doi: https://doi.org/10.21552/edpl/2020/2/6; Niels van Dijk, Raphaël Gellert, and Kjetil Rommetveit. "A risk to a right? Beyond data protection risk assessments". In: *Computer Law & Security Review* 32.2 (2016), pp. 286–306. ISSN: 0267-3649. doi: https://doi.org/10.1016/j.clsr.2015.12.017. url: https://www.sciencedirect.com/science/article/pii/S026736491500182X.

of a perhaps health-related violation (...). Freedom dies without human beings being physically hurt".[27]

For instance, when assessing the risk to health and safety in a new AI system used for detecting gastrointestinal cancer through image recognition, a risk-based approach could be applied successfully. During such a risk assessment process, different risks associated with the AI system could first be identified. One potential identified risk in such a system is that a cancerous patient is left undiagnosed, a false negative outcome. After identifying the risk, the effect of the risk on affected persons and the likelihood of the materialisation could be assessed through different experiments and testing. In such an example, the risk of false negative outcomes could be quantified. The risk, i.e., the combination of the probability of an occurrence of harm and the severity of that harm, according to the definition in Article 3 (2) of the AI Act, could then be assessed and documented.

When assessing the risk of an AI system having an adverse impact on fundamental rights, an approach that enumerates and quantifies the risks has some constraints. For instance, when assessing whether an AI system adversely impacts the rights to privacy and data protection, it is possible to identify potential risks for adverse impacts. The difficult part is measuring the system's potential impact on fundamental rights, as well as balancing the legitimate aim of the system against the adverse effect on fundamental rights through a mere quantification.

Risk management under the AI Act is somewhat similar to DPIAs in data protection law. When conducting a DPIA, the controller needs to identify, assess, and mitigate risks in each processing operation. If the results of the risk assessment reveal that the risks cannot be effectively mitigated, the personal data cannot be processed. Similarly, when applying the principle of proportionality, the assessment is whether an interference with a fundamental right could be justified. This justification is dependent on the interference pursuing a legitimate aim, being suitable, necessary, and proportionate, *stricto sensu*. In 2007, de Sadeleer concluded that "the principle of proportionality is intertwined with risk management".[28]

Similar arguments can be made about the risk management system under Article 9 of the AI Act. If the identified risks cannot be eliminated or reduced, they should be mitigated and controlled to an acceptable level. Such

---

27 Ulrich Beck. "The digital freedom risk: Too fragile an acknowledgement". In: *22 Quaderns de la Mediterrània* (2015). On page 141, pp. 141–144.

28 Nicolas de Sedeleer. "The precautionary principle in European Community health and environment law: Sword or shield for the Nordic Countries?" In: *Implementing the Precautionary Principle: Approaches from the Nordic Countries, EU and USA*. London: Routledge, 2007, p, 37.

a risk-management system is consistent with the principle of proportionality under primary EU law. If an identified risk (or an identified interference in a fundamental right) pursues a legitimate aim, is necessary, and proportionate *stricto sensu*, it is justifiable.

The principle of proportionality could accordingly be viewed as intertwined with a risk management system under Article 9. However, it is possible to argue that due to the difference between adverse impact on fundamental rights and harm to health and safety, the two distinct sets of risks require somewhat different assessment methodologies, where the principle of proportionality is a prospective balancing assessment for the adverse effect an AI system could impose on fundamental rights.

If the risk management methodology under Article 9 of the AI Act is divided and applied as suggested above, the risk management system will function both as a material and as a process-oriented proportionality principle. It is material and substantive because, if the risks are identified and not possible to mitigate, the AI system cannot be deployed. The principle is, however, also process-oriented because the risk management system might be applied to demonstrate compliance with the AI Act.

Another example of an *ex-ante* assessment under the AI Act is Article 27, the fundamental rights impact assessment for high-risk AI systems. According to Article 27 (1) (a–f), the fundamental risk assessment shall consist of a description of the processes where the high-risk AI system will be used in line with its intended purpose, a description of the time period and frequency of the high-risk AI system, the categories of natural persons likely to be affected, the specific risks of harm likely to have an impact on these identified natural persons, a description of the implementation of human oversight measures, and measures to be taken in the case of the materialisation of those risks.

The purpose of the fundamental rights impact assessment is elaborated in recital 96 of the AI Act. According to the recital, the aim of the assessment is for the deployer to identify the specific risks to the rights of individuals or groups of individuals likely to be affected and identify measures to be taken in the case of materialisation of those risks. Moreover, "[t]he assessment should also include the identification of specific risks of harm likely to have an impact on the fundamental rights of those persons or groups. While performing this assessment, the deployer should take into account information relevant to a proper assessment of the impact, including but not limited to the information given by the provider of the high-risk AI system in the instructions for use. In light of the risks identified, deployers should determine measures to be taken in the case of a materialisation of those risks, including for example governance arrangements in that specific context of use, such as arrangements for human oversight according to the instructions of use or, complaint handling and redress procedures, as they could be instrumental in mitigating risks to fundamental rights in concrete use-cases".

As an assessment of the future risk to fundamental rights impact, the obligation in Article 27 of the AI Act could be described as a process-oriented assessment where the deployers should identify risk and plan risk mitigating measures in case the risk materialises. There is no trace of the obligation to conduct a fundamental rights impact assessment in Article 27 (1) of the AI Act to not deploy the AI system if the risk to natural persons is unacceptable. However, by analysing Article 27 (1) in light of not just the wording of the Article, but its purpose – to protect fundamental rights – it is possible to argue that if the identified risk is unacceptable, the AI system should not be deployed. Such a view could also be based on the fact that the requirements in the AI Act with a fundamental rights rationale also need to be interpreted in line with the rights of the Charter. Hence, the fundamental rights impact assessment requirement in Article 27 of the AI Act is a process-oriented proportionality assessment with material traces.

There are examples of *ex-ante* risk assessments of fundamental impact both in the GDPR (Article 6 (1) (f) and Article 35) and the AI Act (Article 9 and Article 27). Under the GDPR, the controllers must, under certain circumstances, assess the potential future impact of the rights of the data subject, for instance, when new technology such as AI systems is used. When assessing such impact, the subtests under the principle of proportionality might provide guidance. However, it is important to note that the requirement to conduct a DPIA is a substantial requirement, and not just a "tick-the-box" paper assessment.

Under the AI Act, *ex-ante* risk assessments of fundamental rights might occur both under Article 9 and in accordance with Article 27. Under the risk management system in Article 9, the previous paragraphs identified that assessing the risk to health and safety and fundamental rights are two very different assessments with regard to the assessment methodology applied. However, when assessing the fundamental rights impact, the principle of proportionality and its subtests are a relevant assessment tool. Under the fundamental rights impact assessment obligation in Article 27, the current section has concluded that the obligation has the character of being a process-oriented assessment with some material traces.

As a general conclusion, an *ex-ante* proportionality review would necessitate prognosticating a future interference in fundamental rights. When the interference is assessed before it has taken place in a self-learning, developing, and opaque technology, such as AI systems, the entity responsible for the interference would need to assess a future interference under factual uncertainty. The sections above have analysed several *ex-ante* risk management measures and impact assessments under the GDPR and the AI Act. These assessments mostly function as procedural assessments to document compliance with the rule sets. However, it is important to note that if the assessments result in an unacceptable interference, either because the subtests of the principle of proportionality are not fulfilled or because the factual uncertainty is too high, the impact assessments should result in the interference not taking place without safeguards, an example of *ex-ante* material proportionality review. Such an outcome, where the interference does not take place if the risk of disproportionate interferences is too high, has a basis in the purposes of the GDPR and the AI Act, interpreted in light of the Charter – to protect fundamental rights.

6.7 SUMMARY

The current chapter has addressed the following aspects and has identified the following findings:

- The chapter has established the term "proportionality by design" referring to an overall development method of AI systems processing personal data where the means – the development or use of an AI system – and the ends – the overall intended purpose of the AI system or the inference made by the deployed AI model – are assessed throughout the development and deployment phases. The term also functions in relation to the risk-based approach of the GDPR and the AI Act. When controllers and providers assess such risks – especially the risks related to the rights in Article 8 of the Charter – it could be compared to assessing the interference with fundamental rights. The associated risk-mitigating measures could be compared to assessing whether the interference with the fundamental right is proportionate.
- The basis for "proportionality by design" is case law from the CJEU that requires the GDPR to be interpreted in line with the rights of the Charter, and the partial purpose of the AI Act to develop AI systems in line with the fundamental rights of the Charter.
- "Proportionality by design" functions as an explanatory taxonomy, an interpretative tool, and as a basis for "best practice" of AI system development and use of deployed AI models.
- The model is divided into a negative obligation, when the AI system is developed or used by public authorities, and a positive obligation, when the AI system is developed or used by private organisations.
- Constitutional proportionality review is often assessed as either a material/substantial proportionality review, where the court assesses the interference and whether the subtests of legitimate aim, suitability, necessity, and proportionality *stricto sensu* are fulfilled, or a process-oriented/procedural proportionality review. The purpose of the process-oriented review is to

assess whether the proportionality has been assessed by the legislator or the entity responsible for the interference. In the AI field, the current chapter concluded that core data protection cases will, mostly likely, be subject to a material proportionality review, market requirements in the AI Act will be subjected to a procedural proportionality review, and requirements in the AI Act with a fundamental rights rationale will be scrutinised in the form of a material proportionality review.

7. Enforcement

7.1 INTRODUCTION

"Laws without enforcement are just good advice" is a well-known saying.[1]

The focus of the current chapter will be on the enforcement of the compliance by design concept and the proportionality by design approach identified in the book. More specifically, the chapter will examine how these two concepts could function as a basis for self-enforcement by controllers processing personal data and providers of AI systems. Additionally, the focus will be on how different supervisory authorities – under both the GDPR and the AI Act – could control and enforce the different proportionality assessments. Finally, the focus will be on future enforcement of cases entering the scope of both the GDPR and the AI Act in courts.

The current chapter is organised as follows. Section 7.2 focuses on enforcement authorities, more specifically, the current enforcement deficit of the GDPR and how the proportionality by design approach might potentially mitigate this deficit. Section 7.2 also analyses the enforcement authorities established under the AI Act. In section 7.3, emphasis is placed on future enforcement of the GDPR and the AI Act in courts. Section 7.4 focuses on how the identified proportionality by design concept from the previous chapter could function as an enforcement tool, for self-enforcing both the GDPR and the AI Act by enforcement authorities and by courts. Finally, section 7.5 provides a summary of the findings of the chapter.

1 Stephen Mulders. "Collective damages for GDPR breaches: A feasible solution for the GDPR enforcement deficit?" In: *European Data Protection Law Review* 8 (2022), p. 493.

7.2 ENFORCEMENT THROUGH ENFORCEMENT AUTHORITIES

7.2.1 The Enforcement Deficit

According to Article 8 (3) of the Charter, compliance with the rules of Article 8 and the right to data protection shall be subject to control by an independent authority. Such independent authorities are established under the GDPR Chapter VI. Chapter VI establishes the obligation for each member state to establish public authorities to be responsible for monitoring the application of the GDPR, to protect the fundamental rights and freedoms of natural persons in relation to processing, and to facilitate the free flow of personal data within the Union. In order to ensure these tasks, the supervisory authorities must act with complete independence, according to Article 52 of the GDPR.

After the GDPR entered into force in 2018, the supervisory authorities of the member states have had seven years of experience in enforcing the material and procedural requirements of the GDPR. The next subsections will address a tendency apparent in these seven years: the enforcement deficit.

The GDPR's enforcement deficit is a description of the gap between data protection in books and the actual compliance with data protection in action.[2] The reasons for this enforcement deficit are manifold. Lack of resources in national supervisory authorities, the cross-border nature of data protection cases, and the individual nature of data protection, where a case often requires initiative from individual data subjects, are some possible explanations. Supervisory authorities were also established under the previous Data Protection Directive.[3] Several have warned that the current enforcement deficit under the GDPR might lead to a risk of "a return to the business as usual scenario that we experienced under the 95/46 Directive when many companies

---

[2] Stephen Mulders. "Collective damages for GDPR breaches: A feasible solution for the GDPR enforcement deficit?" In: *European Data Protection Law Review* 8 (2022), p. 493; Orla Lynskey. "Regulating for the future: The law's enforcement deficit". In: *Studies: An Irish Quarterly Review* 112 (2023), pp. 15–72. doi: https://doi.org/10.1353/stu.2023.0007; Filippo Lancieri. "Narrowing data protection's enforcement gap". In: *Maine Law Review* 74 (2022), p. 15. url: https://digitalcommons.mainelaw.maine.edu/mlr/vol74/iss1/3?utm_source=digitalcommons.mainelaw.maine.edu%2Fmlr%2Fvol74%2Fiss1%2F3&utm_medium=PDF&utm_campaign=PDFCoverPages. Last accessed: 26.08.2024.

[3] Directive 95/46/EC of the European Parliament and of the Council of 24 October 1995 on the protection of individuals with regard to the processing of personal data and of the free movement of such data [1995] OJ L 281/31.

ignored the law because enforcement was slow or non-existent".[4] The next subsections will argue that "proportionality by design" could potentially mitigate some of the negative consequences of the GDPR enforcement deficit and potentially contribute to addressing systemic data protection structures, rather than small, trivial GDPR breaches. This analysis will be conducted after the enforcement mechanisms under the AI Act have been examined.

7.2.2 Enforcement of the AI Act

The enforcement of the AI Act consists of different layers and different authorities that have different responsibilities. At the Union level, the enforcement consists of an AI office, the European AI board, an advisory forum, a scientific panel of independent experts, and a pool of experts from each member state. In accordance with the AI Act Article 64, the European Commission shall develop Union expertise and capabilities by establishing an AI office. The AI office is tasked with supporting the governance bodies in each member state and enforcing the rules for general-purpose AI models. The AI office also has some tasks related to the development and support of regulatory sandboxes. The AI board, advisory forum, scientific panel, and pool of experts, according to Chapter VII of the AI Act, are mostly tasked with supporting, assisting, and contributing to the EU enforcement bodies and national member states' enforcement bodies, and they do not have any direct enforcement competencies.

At the national level in each member state, Article 70 (1) of the AI Act prescribes that every member state shall have as national competent authorities at least one notifying authority and at least one market surveillance authority for the purposes of the AI Act. These national competent authorities shall exercise their powers independently, impartially, and without bias so as to safeguard the objectivity of their activities and tasks.

The notifying authority is defined in Article 3 (19) of the AI Act as the "national authority responsible for setting up and carrying out the necessary procedures for the assessment, designation and notification of conformity assessment bodies and for their monitoring". Notification bodies bear resemblances to various accreditation bodies. Such bodies are responsible for receiving applications from conformity assessment bodies for notification, under Article 29 of the AI Act and approving applications from bodies that fulfil the requirements in Article 31 of the AI Act. Notified notification bodies have

---

4 Estelle Massé. "Two years under the EU GDPR: An implementation progress report". In: *Access Now Homepage* (2020). url: https://www.accessnow.org/wp-content/uploads/2020/05/Two-Years-Under-GDPR.pdf. Last accessed: 01.08.2025.

several operational requirements under the AI Act, the most important of which include verifying the conformity of high-risk AI systems under Article 34 (1) of the AI Act. The nature of the notifying authority, as part of the national member state layer of enforcement of the AI Act, could be described as a guarantee that the notifying bodies fulfil the requirements of the AI Act. Notifying authorities fulfils an enforcement function similar to data protection authorities accrediting certification bodies under Article 43 of the GDPR.

The market surveillance authority is the other enforcement body of the AI Act at the member state level. In Article 3 (26) of the AI Act, the market surveillance authority is defined as "the national authority carrying out the activities and taking measures pursuant to Regulation (EU) 2019/1020".[5] The purpose of Regulation 2019/1020 is to improve the functioning of the internal market by strengthening the market surveillance of products covered by Union harmonised legislation relating to products, according to Article 1 of Regulation (EU) 2019/1020. The reference to the market surveillance regulation in the definition of Article 3 (26) of the AI Act strengthens the view of AI systems being regarded as products in the AI Act. The tasks of the market surveillance authority are fragmented across the text of the AI Act; the main tasks are included in the list below:

1. Receive notifications from law enforcement authorities about real-time remote biometric identification systems in publicly available spaces for law enforcement purposes, according to Article 5 (4) of the AI Act.
2. Receive terminations of mandates from authorised representatives if the representative considers or has reasons to consider the provider to be acting contrary to the provider's obligations under the AI Act, according to Article 22 (4).
3. Receive notifications of high-risk AI systems representing a risk to the health, safety, or fundamental rights of persons from deployers and notifications of serious incidents, under Article 26 (5) of the AI Act.
4. Receive the results from fundamental rights impact assessments from deployers in accordance with Article 27 (3).
5. Act as a notifying body for conformity assessments related to high-risk AI systems intended to be put into service by law enforcement, immigration, or asylum authorities, or by Union institutions, bodies, offices, or agencies, according to Article 43 (1).

[5] Regulation (EU) 2019/1020 of the European Parliament and of the Council of 20 June 2019 on market surveillance and compliance of products and amending Directive 2004/42/EC and Regulations (EC) No 765/2008 and (EU) No 305/2011 [2019] OJ L 169/1.

6. Gives authorisation for derogations from the normal conformity assessments procedure for specific high-risk AI systems for a limited time period within territories of member states for exceptional reasons of public security or the protection of life and health of persons, environmental protection, or the protection of key industrial and infrastructural assets, according to Article 43 (1) of the AI Act.
7. Receive and approve real-world testing plans from providers or prospective providers of testing of high-risk AI systems in real-world conditions outside AI regulatory sandboxes, according to Article 60 of the AI Act.
8. Receive serious incident reports from providers immediately after the provider has established a causal link between the AI system and the serious incident, according to Article 73 (1).
9. Further inform national public authorities or bodies about the serious incident and take appropriate measures according to Regulation (EU) 2019/1020 Article 19 within seven days of a serious incident. Such appropriate measures include withdrawal, recall, or prohibition of the high-risk AI system producing the serious incident.
10. Carry out evaluations of AI systems where the market surveillance authority has sufficient reason to consider it presents a risk to health, safety, or fundamental rights, according to Article 79 (1) and (2) of the AI Act.
11. Carry out an evaluation of AI systems where there is sufficient reason to believe that the system presents a risk to health and safety and fundamental rights, according to Article 79 (1). Where risks to fundamental rights are identified, the market surveillance authority shall inform and cooperate with the public authority responsible for fundamental rights in each member state. If the market surveillance authority concludes that the AI system does not comply with the AI Act, it shall require the relevant operator to take all appropriate corrective actions.
12. Inform the Commission where non-compliance is not restricted to national territories, according to Article 79 (3).
13. Prohibit, recall, and restrict AI systems not complying with the requirements in the AI Act from the national market and inform the Commission, according to Article 79 (5).
14. Receive complaints from natural and legal persons regarding infringement of the AI Act, under Article 85 (1).

The powers of the market surveillance authority are not part of the AI Act, but Regulation (EU) 2019/1020 Article 14.[6] According to Article 14 (2), mar-

[6] Regulation (EU) 2019/1020 of the European Parliament and of the Council of 20 June 2019 on market surveillance and compliance of products and amending

ket surveillance authorities shall exercise their powers efficiently and effectively, in line with the principle of proportionality, and the nature and overall actual and potential harm resulting from the instances of non-compliance. Powers shall also be conducted in accordance with the Charter of fundamental rights and with the Union rules on data protection, according to Article 14 (1). According to Article 14 (4) of Regulation 2019/1020, the market surveillance authorities shall, at least, have the following powers:

- The power to require economic operators to provide relevant documents, technical specifications, data on compliance and technical aspects, and access to software.
- Power to require economic operators to provide relevant information about the supply chain.
- The power to conduct unannounced on-site inspections and physical checks of products.
- The power to enter premises.
- The power to start investigations on their own initiative.
- The power to require the operators to take appropriate action to end a state of non-compliance, withdraw, recall, and take corrective action against products.
- The power to impose penalties.
- The power to eliminate risks.
- The power to operate under a cover identity and acquire product samples.

In Regulation (EU) 2019/1020 Article 3 (19), "products presenting a risk is defined as products having the potential to affect health and safety of persons in general". In the AI Act, "fundamental rights" is added to the risk that the regulation aims to prevent, according to the AI Act recitals 1, 176, Articles 1, 4 (49), 3 (65), and 79 (1). Hence, a market surveillance authority under the AI Act is intended to enforce an area traditionally not covered by market surveillance authorities. According to Article 77 of the AI Act, in order to ensure proper enforcement of fundamental rights in the AI field, Article 77 of the AI Act contains specific enforcement powers of authorities protecting fundamental rights. National public authorities or bodies under national law which supervise or enforce the respect of obligations under Union law protecting fundamental rights, in relation to high-risk AI systems, shall have the power to request and access any document created and maintained under the AI Act in an accessible language format. When a document review is not sufficient

Directive 2004/42/EC and Regulations (EC) No 765/2008 and (EU) No 305/2011 [2019] OJ L 169/1.

to ascertain whether the infringement of a fundamental right has occurred, the national public authority responsible for fundamental rights might make a reasoned request for a technical test of the high-risk AI system to the market surveillance authority.

To recapitulate the enforcement measures under the AI Act, they consist of both an EU level, consisting of an AI office, and a national member state level, consisting of notifying authorities and market surveillance authorities. The market surveillance authorities shall perform market surveillance consistent with Regulation (EU) 2019/1020, where the risk of harm to fundamental rights is also one area the authority shall monitor.

The AI Act and the enforcement measures have not, as of July 2025, entered into effect, and the prioritisation of enforcement measures and market surveillance will need to develop through practice. However, several similar instruments to the AI Act have entered into force and might shed some light on the future enforcement of the AI Act.

In February 2024, the Digital Services Act (DSA)[7] entered into effect. The Regulation sets out harmonised rules for a safe, predictable, and trusted online environment that facilitates innovation and in which the fundamental rights of the Charter are effectively protected, according to Article 1 of the DSA. The DSA, thus, has a somewhat similar subject matter as the AI Act, which also attempts to achieve the balance between innovation and fundamental rights protection. The difference is that they cover different sectoral areas; the AI Act covers the AI field, and the DSA covers social media, information society services, and online platforms. Very Large Online Platforms (VLOPs) are subject to specific rules under the DSA, according to section 5 of the DSA. These are online platforms with more than 45 million average active monthly recipients in the Union and which are designated as a VLOP by the Commission. By a Commission Decision of 25 April 2024, TikTok Technology Ltd (TikTok) was designated as a VLOP.[8] In April 2024, the Commission launched an enforcement proceeding against TikTok regarding their service TikTok Lite in France and Spain. TikTok Lite is a reward program where users receive gift cards and monetary remuneration for doing "tasks" on TikTok, such as watching videos or liking content. The Commission concluded that TikTok Lite had the potential to be addictive and that it, therefore, required an *ex-ante* risk assessment

---

[7] Regulation (EU) 2022/2065 of the European Parliament and of the Council of 19 October 2022 on a Single Market For Digital Services and amending Directive 2000/31/EC (Digital Services Act) [2022] OJ L 2771/1.

[8] Commission Decision of 25.4.2023 designating TikTok as a very large online platform in accordance with Article 33(4) of Regulation (EU) 2022/2065 of the European Parliament and of the Council C(2023) 2720 final.

under the DSA to ensure fundamental rights compliance.[9] The development under the DSA supports the notions that *ex-ante* risk assessments and fundamental rights impact assessments are not just paper exercises but enforceable legal documents that can – and potentially will – be enforced by enforcement authorities. Similar developments could also be expected to take place under the enforcement of the AI Act in the future. However, the future effectiveness and impact of the enforcement of the AI Act will become apparent only over time.

7.3 ENFORCEMENT IN COURTS

Enforcement of regulations does not only take place within independent supervisory authorities. Also, courts will be relevant in the future enforcement of the GDPR, the AI Act, and the rights of the Charter. Since the entry into force of the GDPR in 2018, approximately 120 cases have been referred to preliminary rulings in the CJEU and adjudicated.[10] At the time of writing in July 2025, there are 46 pending GDPR cases in the CJEU.[11] Each of these cases gives guidance to interpretations of the Articles and underlying principles of the GDPR.

The AI Act, a detailed legislation in a rapidly changing area of society, will, most likely, also have several cases referred to the CJEU for preliminary rulings. This development, with a growing number of court cases and a corresponding growing complexity, makes data protection in AI systems an increasingly intricate area to work with. The next section will argue that the identified framework in the former chapter could potentially offer some guidance in this field.

The entry into force and application of the AI Act will have some specific consequences for the enforcement of the requirements in the Act. The AI Act was published in the *Official Journal of the European Union* on 12 July 2024 and entered into force on 1 August 2024, according to Article 113 of the AI Act. The AI Act applies with binding force from 2 August 2026. Chapters I and II apply from 2 February 2025, while the enforcement and governance

---

[9] European Commission. *Commission Opens Proceedings against TikTok under the DSA Regarding the Launch of TikTok Lite in France and Spain, and Communicates Its Intention to Suspend the Reward Programme in the EU.* url: https://ec.europa.eu/commission/presscorner/detail/en/ip_24_2227. Last accessed: 26.08.2024.

[10] GDPRHUB. *Category CJEU.* url: https://gdprhub.eu/index.php?title=Category:CJEU. Last accessed: 01.08.2025.

[11] Digibeetle. *Pending CJEU data protection cases.* url: https://app.digibeetle.eu/pending-cases/. Last accessed: 30.07.2025.

requirements apply from 2 August 2025, according to the AI Act Article 114 (b) and (c). The national enforcement authorities are therefore not operative when the prohibitions in Article 5 apply. The only manner to enforce the prohibitions in Article 5 in the time period from 2 February 2025 to 2 August 2025 (when the requirements for enforcement authorities enter into effect) is through private enforcement in courts. The enforcement of the prohibited AI systems is, therefore, dependent on private litigation from February to August 2025.

7.4 PROPORTIONALITY BY DESIGN AS AN ENFORCEMENT TOOL

In the growing number of examples of case law under the GDPR and the potential for a similar development under the AI Act, "proportionality by design" might potentially offer guidance for controllers under the GDPR, providers and deployers under the AI Act, enforcement authorities, and courts. This guidance, in essence, considers whether a new functionality or business model is not just in compliance with the requirements of the GDPR and the AI Act, but also if it is compliant with the GDPR and the AI Act interpreted in line with Articles 7 and 8 of the Charter and the principle of proportionality in Article 52. In this assessment, one criterion stands out as a core criterion: purpose limitation. The practicality of this test could be illustrated with some examples:

- In May 2024, Recall was launched as a feature in Microsoft Copilot +.[12] The function takes a screenshot of your computer every few seconds while in active use. The screenshots are archived and used to train generative AI features that allow for personalised searches and suggested content for each user. A searchable timeline is also made from the screenshots, with everything that is done on the Copilot + PC. The feature needs to be turned off to not take these snapshots. The recall feature will take screenshots of Zoom and Teams meetings, as well as all computer activity, without any notifications. The data is stored locally on every Copilot + PC.

  If this new feature is assessed, not just from a compliance by design perspective, but from a proportionality by design perspective, it is possible to contend that the feature is not proportionate. It is not purpose-oriented, and the data gathered does not have a specific pre-defined purpose, besides personalisation. The Recall feature is turned on by default and needs to be

---

12 Microsoft. *A new AI era begins*. url: https://www.microsoft.com/en-us/windows/copilot-plus-pcs?r=1#performance. Last accessed: 26.08.2024.

manually turned off. Moreover, it not only has a potential data protection aspect but also more generally privacy aspects because all computer activity is potentially used for future personalisation using generative AI. This perspective to assess the new feature could be applied by the developers, enforcement authorities, and courts, in case of future court cases concerning the functionality.

- On 13 May 2024, OpenAI launched GPT-4omni (GPT 4o), a new large language model that can compute across audio, video, and text in real time through a mobile app interface.[13] Under the video demonstration of GPT-4o, the presenter asked the model to recognise his emotions in real time.[14] Under the AI Act Article 5 (1) (f), such emotion recognition is prohibited in workplaces or educational institutions. When the AI Act enters into effect, OpenAI is required not to make such emotion recognition available to be use in workplaces or schools on the market. Non-compliance with the prohibition is punishable with 35 000 000 euros or 7% of total worldwide annual turnover, according to the AI Act Article 99 (3). In Chapter 6, it was argued that Articles in the AI Act with a fundamental rights rationale, such as Article 5 (1) (f) – according to recital 44 – would most likely be subject to a material proportionality review. Therefore, if the emotion recognition model launched by OpenAI is not just subject to review in line with compliance with the AI Act, but the AI Act interpreted in line with the Charter, providers and deployers could build in safeguards, for instance, so that it is possible to only infer your own emotions and not third parties or similar. Enforcement bodies and courts could also use the "proportionality by design" model, where the legitimate aim, suitability, necessity, and proportionality *stricto sensu* are applied to review the overall proportionality of the emotion recognition feature.
- The last example is about data scraping for training data acquisition. On 24 May 2024, the EDPB ChatGPT Taskforce launched its report.[15] The following excerpt is especially relevant:

> Regarding web scraping, OpenAI brought forward Article 6(1)(f) GDPR as a legal basis. It has to be recalled that the legal assessment of Article 6 (1) (f) GDPR should be based on the following criteria: i) existence of a legitimate interest, ii) necessity of processing, as the personal data should be adequate, relevant and limited to what is necessary in relation to the purposes for which they

---

[13] OpenAI. *Hello GPT-4o*. url: https://openai.com/index/hello-gpt-4o/. Last accessed: 26.08.2024.

[14] Ibid.

[15] EDPB. *Report of the Work Undertaken by the ChatGPT Taskforce*. url: https://www.edpb.europa.eu/system/files/2024-05/edpb_20240523_report_chatgpt_taskforce_en.pdf. Last accessed: 26.08.2024.

> are processed and iii) balancing of interests. Fundamental rights and freedoms of data subjects on the one hand and the controller's legitimate interests on the other hand have to be evaluated and balanced carefully. The reasonable expectations of data subjects should be taken into account in this assessment.

Even though the EDPB task force is merely writing out the subtests of Article 6 (1) (f) of the GDPR, the legal basis that OpenAI themselves have brought forward, several points could be read out of this, maybe self-evident, statement. First, the EDPB highlights the importance of proportionality when assessing the lawfulness of processing in AI systems and large language models. Second, the principle of proportionality, through a specific requirement in the GDPR, is applied by an enforcement body in their guidance, highlighting the importance of the principle also in an enforcement context. Lastly, the cited excerpt highlights that the EDPB interprets Article 6 (1) (f) in line with recital 47 and the reasonably expected interests of the data subjects. The view of the EDPB task force supports that proportionality, especially in web scraping, will be increasingly important in the times ahead.

7.5 SUMMARY

To conclude, the sections above have discussed the role of "proportionality by design" in enforcement, both in enforcement bodies and in courts. The chapter has analysed the existing enforcement landscape under the GDPR and the near future enforcement of the AI Act.

As a general conclusion, "proportionality by design" could be applied by controllers and providers for self-enforcement, by enforcement bodies to enforce Articles in the AI Act with a fundamental rights rationale, and by courts. Such proportionality enforcement development is already present under the GDPR in the EDPB, through the recent ChatGPT Taskforce report.

8. Overall conclusions, perspectives, and future research

8.1 OVERALL CONCLUSIONS

8.1.1 Conclusion on the Main Research Question

The primary research question (RQ) of this book was:

> How can data protection regulation, specific cybersecurity regulations, and requirements in the AI Act be implemented and complied with during the development and deployment of AI systems?

While individual sub-research questions have been addressed throughout the book, a comprehensive conclusion to the primary research question necessitates including some of the conclusions from the sub-research questions addressed throughout the book.

One of the most important findings of the book is the importance of distinguishing between the phases of AI systems when assessing regulatory compliance: the data collection and training phase, the inference phase, and a phase involving continuous training (AIaaS). Such a delineation is important as the legal basis of the GDPR, the risks under cybersecurity and AI regulations, and other legal requirements, such as the fundamental principles of processing under the GDPR, will vary substantially across these phases. It is therefore an important first step to separate the different phases of an AI system's development and deployment when assessing GDPR, cybersecurity regulation, and AI Act compliance.

Another finding of the book is that the different regulations assessed vary substantially regarding the complexity of implementing the requirements in the AI systems. Cybersecurity regulations, such as the CRA, generally present more binary and readily implementable requirements; for instance, when implementing mitigating measures against API-specific attacks related to a high-risk AI system.

In contrast, the GDPR is characterised by a greater reliance on legal assessments and procedures, rather than technical implementation. Some requirements in the GDPR, for instance, Article 25 "data protection by design and by default" require technical and organisational measures to be implemented in the processing solutions.

The AI Act presents a hybrid approach, combining both technically implementable requirements, e.g., various forms of Explainable AI (XAI) that could be applied to comply with the right to an explanation in Article 86 of the AI Act and process-oriented requirements that are less implementable to technical solutions. An example of the latter is process-related requirements such as various conformity assessments and risk management measures.

Another important compliance-related aspect the book has identified is the importance of continuous learning in AI systems, particularly through MLOps. This approach addresses the challenge of concept drift, where deployed AI models become misaligned with data distributions, potentially leading to inaccurate outputs. By continuously retraining the model in a deployed setting, the risk of concept drift and the corresponding risk of inaccurate model outputs could be lowered. However, such retraining for accuracy is a separate processing purpose that needs to have a valid legal basis in the GDPR and needs to be communicated to the data subjects.

To summarise, key steps towards comprehensive regulatory compliance with the GDPR, the AI Act, and relevant cybersecurity regulations in AI system development and deployment include:

- Differentiating between training, deployment, and continuous retraining phases when conducting compliance assessments.
- Addressing concept drifts and the misalignment between the data that the models are trained on and the live data used in a deployed setting.
- Conducting compliance assessments throughout the AI system's lifecycle.
- And, lastly, to employ multidisciplinary teams with shared understandings of concepts and terminology to address compliance issues.

8.1.2 The Importance of Proportionality

Another lesson learned through the analyses in the book is the importance of the principle of proportionality in "by design" approaches to regulatory compliance.

"By design" approaches are potentially highly effective solutions to achieve an end goal. Compliance with various laws and regulations, in essence, relies on the willingness of actors to comply with the laws. When such compliance is embedded in a technological solution, compliance with the laws and regulations becomes less dependent on such willingness. When a door is locked or a specific action within a system is impossible, compliance does not become a choice. However, this effectiveness is powerful and could potentially be misused for illicit purposes. Thus, compliance by design, within the EU acquis, must have a fundamental rights basis to ensure legitimacy.

When assessing the risk to rights, as several of the regulations analyses in the book call for, typical risk assessment methodologies are not especially suitable. In the current regulatory landscape, where different regulations overlap and have different main objectives, the principle of proportionality under the Charter marks itself as a cornerstone in assessing risk to rights, addressing overlap between different regulations, and when assessing specific issues that lack coherent interpretations.

Several of the regulations analysed in the book, for instance, the AI Act, have multiple end goals and multiple policy objectives. The AI Act intends to function as a product safety regulation that ensures a single EU market for AI systems, while at the same time ensuring fundamental rights. In relation to the fundamental rights purpose of the AI Act, the principle of proportionality and the proportionality by design concept elaborated in Chapter 6 of the book could contribute to ensuring legal consistency and achieving the fundamental rights purpose of the Act. The proportionality by design approach has the potential to be developed to also ensure the fundamental rights of other technology regulations that have multiple purposes and policy objectives.

8.2 PERSPECTIVES

The purpose of the current subsection is to critically examine and discuss some of the shortcomings of the findings of the book. Research, especially dogmatic and doctrinal research in an evolving field with regulations that have not entered into effect, should be scrutinised through a critical lens. The current section will address some of the evident pitfalls with the compliance by design approach and the proportionality by design concept, while also exploring the potential promises associated with these challenges.

One of the most apparent shortcomings of the compliance by design approach and the model identified in Chapter 6 is related to the discrepancy between law in books and law in action, particularly regarding the economic aspect of personal data processing and AI system development. For instance, NVIDIA, a leading producer of graphic processing units (GPUs) used in AI system development, was, as of February 2024, the third-largest company in the world measured in market capitalisation, with a net market value larger than the GDP of South Korea.[1] Additionally, personalisation of services through

1 MarketWatch. *Nvidia Is Now Worth More Than the GDP of Every Country Except These 11.* url: https://www.marketwatch.com/story/nvidia-is-now-worth-more-than-the-gdp-of-every-country-except-these-few-d58a3508. Last accessed: 26.08.2024.

the processing of personal data has emerged as one of the 21st century's most profitable business models. This can be further illustrated with an example.

In the early stages of Google's development in 2002, the search platform operated without ads. One morning, Google analysts observed a recurring pattern in the search queries. The previous night, a popular TV show aired across various US states, starting on the West Coast and then airing in different time zones towards the East Coast. The analysts noticed that the search patterns were specifically related to the broadcast schedule of the TV show.[2] Recognising that these patterns, when combined with other data, could be applied to predict search patterns and trends, these predictions could then be applied to create, in the words of Shoshana Zuboff, added value in the form of a behavioural surplus.[3] When Google started to commercialise this surplus to sell ads, their revenues increased by 3590%.[4]

In an economy where personalisation holds significant value and where ML models and AI systems further enhance this personalisation through the processing of personal data, it is conceivable that the economic operators might regard administrative fines as a budgetable business expense. However, there is an alternative perspective in which compliance with EU regulations and fundamental rights can be perceived as a competitive advantage and an economic asset. This potential asset of compliance, involving the development of proportionate solutions under the AI Act, the GDPR, and the fundamental rights of the Charter, is closely related to the allocation of liability under these regulations.

For instance, consider a small Norwegian municipality acquiring an AIaaS platform developed by a large multinational enterprise. Despite the municipality's lack of expertise and inability to tailor the solution, it holds the responsibility as the controller and would be subject to administrative fines in case of violations of the GDPR. Therefore, if the developer and provider of the AIaaS platform can demonstrate that their platform is developed in a manner compliant with relevant secondary regulations and fundamental rights, it becomes a selling point for the acquirer who assumes responsibility under the GDPR and the AI Act.

The economic perspective of the compliance by design approach and the "proportionality by design" model is, therefore, a two-sided coin that could be both a pitfall and a promise.

Scholars have argued that surveillance capitalism by private organisations challenges the governmental surveillance monopoly and should result in

---

2 Shoshana Zuboff. *The Age of Surveillance Capitalism: The Fight for a Human Future at the New Frontier of Power.* New York: PublicAffairs, 2011 p. 75.

3 Ibid.

4 Ibid.

privacy and data protection being considered as a collective value for national defence in addition to being an individual right.[5] The identified proportionality by design approach could be a preliminary step in this direction. The structure of the model with both negative and positive obligations could support the collective view of privacy and data protection while also serving as a tool to mitigate the risk of disproportionate governmental surveillance.

The enforcement chapter addressed several issues within data protection law, specifically the enforcement deficit and the growing corpus of case law from the CJEU regarding interpretations of the GDPR. Additionally, there are other issues and concerns with the GDPR. One of the most pertinent issues with the regulation is that the strict distinction between personal and non-personal data, due to more advanced technology, no longer matches reality. Another issue is the problem of consent, where several scholars have described consent fatigue from numerous cookie banners on websites.[6]

The compliance by design approach of the book is in no way a cure for all ills that fully resolves these issues. However, by shifting the focus from a mere tick-the-box GDPR compliance perspective to a fundamental rights perspective, it could be possible to provide, to some extent, a tool to address some of these concerns.

In a societal area characterised by disruption and "to move fast and break things",[7] it is important to preserve some lasting values. The book has argued that the GDPR and the AI Act interpreted in line with the fundamental rights of the Charter could contribute to such lasting values, which could guide the development and deployment of AI systems with the potential to violate fundamental rights.

8.3 FUTURE PERSPECTIVES

8.3.1 Need for More Sector Specificity

While this book has adopted a general perspective on compliance by design for AI systems, future research could benefit from developing sector-specific

---

[5] Vivi Ringnes Wilhelmsen. "Digital tracking – A matter of national security". In: *Internasjonal Politikk* 80.1 (2022). doi: https://doi.org/10.23865/intpol.v80.3096.

[6] Christine Utz et al. "(Un) informed consent: Studying GDPR consent notices in the field". In: *Proceedings of the 2019 ACM Sigsac Conference on Computer and Communications Security*. New York: Association for Computing Machinery, 2019, pp. 973–990. doi: https://doi.org/10.1145/3319535.3354212.

[7] Moshe Y Vardi. "Move fast and break things". *Communications of the ACM* 61.9 (2018), p. 7. 2018. doi: http://dx.doi.org/10.1145/3244026.

models. Different sectors, such as finance and health care, face distinct operational resilience and cybersecurity requirements compared to, for example, AI systems used in advertising. The general approach presented in this book provides a necessary foundation for such sector-specific approaches.

8.3.2 Legal Consistency in the EU Digital Market

The analyses in the book have identified that several of the regulations, e.g., the AI Act, have multiple policy objectives and purposes. Initially, it might seem like a difficult task to ensure innovation and fundamental rights protection concurrently, or accuracy and personal data minimisation at the same time. The approaches and suggestions of this book could be applied in future research on how to implement compliance in AI systems, specifically, and technology, generally, would affect the need for legal consistency and clarity in the law-making process and the resulting legal text.

8.3.3 Interdisciplinary Research

The book has identified a need for interdisciplinary research. When the codes of conduct and harmonised standards under the AI Act are published and enter into effect, there is a need to understand both the technical aspects of high-risk AI systems and the regulations. The legal aspects include the relationship, not particularly covered in the book, between codes of conduct, harmonised standards, regulations, case law, and primary law. This need for interdisciplinary collaboration covers both providers and deployers of high-risk AI systems, enforcement authorities, courts, and academia.

8.4 CLOSING REFLECTIONS

An overall common thread of the book has been the inconsistency between law in books (particularly the GDPR) and law in action (business models of large commercial entities not complying with the GDPR). Such business models have in some cases led to hundred million euro fines. However, in most cases, the EU technology landscape could be described as including disruptive players that move fast and break things and then pay an administrative fine ten years later.

Compliance by design, where positive regulations are implemented into the design of technology and in development methodologies such as MLOps, could be a first step in ensuring the rule of law and fundamental rights protection in this landscape. However, compliance by design is one of many different tools and not a panacea. Compliance by design needs to function side by side with traditional enforcement methods – private enforcement and public enforcement – to ensure compliance with positive regulations and fundamental rights protection. Historical evidence from the 1990s to the present time suggests that neither market self-regulation nor positive regulation alone is sufficient.

Compliance by design thus emerges as an important enabler of effective positive regulation in the technology sector.

References

CONVENTIONS

Convention for the Protection of Human Rights and Fundamental Freedoms (European Convention on Human Rights) (ECHR).

REGULATIONS AND DIRECTIVES

Directive 95/46/EC of the European Parliament and of the Council of 24 October 1995 on the protection of individuals with regard to the processing of personal data and of the free movement of such data [1995] OJ L 281/31.

Directive 2005/29/EC of the European Parliament and of the Council of 11 May 2005 concerning unfair business-to-consumer commercial practices in the internal market and amending Council Directive 84/450/EEC, Directives 97/7/EC, 98/27/EC and 2002/65/EC of the European Parliament and of the Council and Regulation (EC) No 2006/2004 of the European Parliament and of the Council ("Unfair Commercial Practices Directive") [2005] OJ L 149/22.

Directive 2006/24/EC of the European Parliament and of the Council of 15 March 2006 on the retention of data generated or processed in connection with the provision of publicly available electronic communications services or of public communications networks and amending Directive 2002/58/EC OJ L L 105/54.

Directive 2006/42/EC of the European Parliament and of the Council of 17 May 2006 on machinery, and amending Directive 95/16/EC [2006] OJ L 157/24 [as repealed by the Machinery Regulation].

Directive 2009/48/EC of the European Parliament and of the Council of 18 June 2009 on the safety of toys [2009] OJ L 170/1.

European Union, Charter of Fundamental Rights of the European Union, 26 October 2012, 2012/C 326/02.

Directive 2013/53/EU of the European Parliament and of the Council of 20 November 2013 on recreational craft and personal watercraft and repealing Directive 94/25/EC [2013] OJ L 354/90.

Interinstitutional agreement between the European Parliament, the Council of the European Union and the Commission on better lawmaking. Interinstitutional Agreement of 13 April 2016 [2016] OJ L 123/1.

Regulation (EU) 2016/679 of the European Parliament and of the Council of 27 April 2016 on the protection of natural persons with regard to the processing of personal data and on the free movement of such data, and repealing Directive 95/46/EC (General Data Protection Regulation) [2016] OJ L 199/1.

Directive (EU) 2016/680 of the European Parliament and of the Council of 27 April 2016 on the protection of natural persons with regard to the processing of personal data by competent authorities for the purposes of the prevention, investigation, detection or prosecution of criminal offences or the execution of criminal penalties, and on the free movement of such data, and repealing Council Framework Decision 2008/977/JHA [2016] OJ L 119/89.

Directive (EU) 2016/943 of the European Parliament and of the Council of 8 June 2016 on the protection of undisclosed know-how and business information (trade secrets) against their unlawful acquisition, use and disclosure [2016] OJ/L 157/1.

Regulation (EU) 2017/745 of the European Parliament and of the Council of 5 April 2017 on medical devices, amending Directive 2001/83/EC, Regulation (EC) No 178/2002 and Regulation (EC) No 1223/2009 and repealing Council Directives 90/385/EEC and 93/42/EEC [2017] OJ L 117/1.

Regulation (EU) 2017/746 of the European Parliament and of the Council of 5 April 2017 on in vitro diagnostic medical devices and repealing Directive 98/79/EC and Commission Decision 2010/227/EU [2017] OJ L 117/176.

Regulation (EU) 2018/1725 of the European Parliament and of the Council of 23 October 2018 on the protection of natural persons with regard to the processing of personal data by the Union institutions, bodies, offices and agencies and on the free movement of such data, and repealing Regulation (EC) No 45/2001 and Decision No 1247/2002/EC [2018] OJ L 295/39.

Regulation (EU) 2018/1807 of the European Parliament and of the Council of 14 November 2018 on a framework for the free flow of non-personal data in the European Union [2018] OJ L 303/59.

Regulation (EU) 2019/881 of the European Parliament and of the Council of 17 April 2019 on ENISA (the European Union Agency for Cybersecurity) and on information and communications technology cybersecurity certification and repealing Regulation (EU) No 526/2013 (Cybersecurity Act) [2016] OJ L 151/15 and Directive (EU) 2022/2555 of the European Parliament and of the Council of 14 December 2022 on measures for a high common level of cybersecurity across the Union, amending Regulation (EU) No 910/2014 and Directive (EU) 2018/1972, and repealing Directive (EU) 2016/1148 (NIS 2 Directive) [2022] OJ L 333/80.

Directive (EU) 2019/882 of the European Parliament and of the Council of 17 April 2019 on the accessibility requirements for products and services [2019] OJ L 151/70.

Regulation (EU) 2019/1020 of the European Parliament and of the Council of 20 June 2019 on market surveillance and compliance of products and amending Directive 2004/42/EC and Regulations (EC) No 765/2008 and (EU) No 305/2011 [2019] OJ L 169/1.

European Parliament resolution of 6 October 2021 on artificial intelligence and criminal law and its use by the police and judicial authorities in criminal matters [2021] OJ C 132.

Regulation (EU) 2022/2065 of the European Parliament and of the Council of 19 October 2022 on a single market for digital services and amending Directive 2000/31/EC (Digital Services Act) [2022] OJ L 2771/1.

Directive (EU) 2022/2555 of the European Parliament and of the Council of 14 December 2022 on measures for a high common level of cybersecurity across the Union, amending Regulation (EU) No 910/2014 and Directive (EU) 2018/1972, and repealing Directive (EU) 2016/1148 (NIS 2 Directive) [2022] OJ L 333/80.

Directive (EU) 2022/2557 of the European Parliament and of the Council of 14 December 2022 on the resilience of critical entities and repealing Council Directive 2008/114/EC [2022] OJ L 333/164.

Regulation (EU) 2024/1689 of the European Parliament and of the Council of 13 June 2024 laying down harmonised rules on artificial intelligence and amending Regulations (EC) No 300/2008, (EU) No 167/2013, (EU) No 168/2013, (EU) 2018/858, (EU) 2018/1139 and (EU) 2019/2144 and Directives 2014/90/EU, (EU) 2016/797 and (EU) 2020/1828 (Artificial Intelligence Act) [2024] OJ L 2024/1689.

Regulation (EU) 2024/2847 of the European Parliament and of the Council of 23 October 2024 on horizontal cybersecurity requirements for products with digital elements and amending Regulations (EU) No 168/2013 and (EU) 2019/1020 and Directive (EU) 2020/1828 (Cyber Resilience Act) OJ/L 2024/2847.

JUDGEMENTS AND DECISIONS

Handyside v the United Kingdom, 7 December 1976 Series A no 24.

Sporrong and Lönnroth v Sweden, 23 September 1982, Series A no. 52.

Amman v Switzerland app. no 27798/95

Y.G. v Russia, Judgement of 30 August 2022 Application No 8647/12.

Y.G. v Russia, Judgement of 30 August 2022 Application No 8647/12.

Glukhin v Russia, 4 July 2023 App No 11419/20 ECLI:CE:ECHR:2023:0704 JUD001151920.

Judgement of the Court (Sixth Chamber) of 13 April 2000 in case C-292/97 Kjell Karlsson and Others, ECLI:EU:C:1999:24.

Judgement of the Court 20 May 2003 in joined cases C-465/00, C-138/01 and C-139/01 Österreichischer Rundfunk and others ECLI:EU:C:2003:294.

Judgement of the Court of 6 November 2003 in the case C-101/01 Bodil Lindqvist ECR 1-12971 ECLI:EU:C:2003:596.

Joined Cases C-92/09 and C-93/09 Volker and Markus Schecke GbR, Hartmut Eifert v Land Hessen, joined party Bundesanstalt für Landwirtschaft und Ernährung ECLI:EU:C:2010:662.

Judgement of the Court 9 November 2010 joined Cases C-92/09 and C-93/09 Volker and Markus Schecke ECLI:EU:C:2010:662.

Judgement of the Court (Third Section) 14 February 2012 App No 7094/06 in the Case of Romet v The Netherlands.

Case C-2017/16 Ministerio Fiscal, Judgement of 2 October 2018 (Grand Chamber) (ECLI:EU:2018:788).

Joined Cases C-511/18, C-512/18 and C-520/18 La Quadrature du Net and Others v Premier minister and Others, Judgement of 6 October 2020 (Grand Chamber) (ECLI:EU:C:2020:791).

Judgement of the Court Fourth Chamber 17 October 2013, Schwarz, C-291/12, EU:C:2013:670.

Judgement of the Court (Grand Chamber) of 8 April 2014 in Joined Cases C-293/12 and C-594/12, Digital Rights Ireland Ltd (C-293/12) v Minister for Communications, Marine and Natural Resources, Minister for Justice, Equality and Law Reform, Commissioner of the Garda Síochána, Ireland, The Attorney General ECLI:EU:C:2014:238.

Judgement of 13 May 2014 in Case C-131/12 Google Spain, ECLI:EU:C:2014:317.

Judgement of the Court (Grand Chamber) of 6 October 2015 in case C-362/14 Maximillian Schrems v Data Protection Commissioner, joined party: Digital Rights Ireland Ltd ECLI:EU:C:2015:650.

Judgement of the Court (Grand Chamber) of 21 December 2016 in Joined Cases C-203/15 and C-698/15, Tele2 Sverige AB (C-203/15) v Post- och telestyrelsen, and Secretary of State for the Home Department (C-698/15) v Tom Watson, Peter Brice, Geoffrey Lewis, ECLI:EU:C:2016:970.

Judgement of the Court (Second Chamber) of 13 July 2017 In Case C-76/16 Ingsteel spol. s r. o., Metrostav a.s. v Úrad pre verejné obstarávanie, ECLI:EU:C:2017:549.

Judgement of the Court (Grand Chamber) of 5 June 2018 in case C-210/16 Unabhängiges Landeszentrum für Datenschutz Schleswig-Holstein v Wirtschaftsakademie Schleswig-Holstein GmbH ECLI:EU:C:2018:388.

Judgement of the Court (Grand Chamber) of 10 July 2018 in Case C-25/17 Tietosuojavaltuutettu intervening parties: Jehovan todistajat — uskonnollinen yhdyskunta ECLI:EU:C:2018:551.

Judgement of the Court (Grand Chamber) of 29 July 2019 in case C-401/17 Fashion ID GmbH and Co. KG v Verbraucherzentrale NRW eV ECLI:EU:C:2019:629.

Judgement of the Court (Grand Chamber) 16 July 2020 in Case C-311/18 Data Protection Commissioner v Facebook Ireland Ltd, Maximillian Schrems ECLI:EU:C:2020:559.

Judgement of the Court (Grand Chamber) of 6 October 2020 In Joined Cases C-511/18, C-512/18 and C-520/18, La Quadrature du Net (C-511/18 and C-512/18), French Data Network (C-511/18 and C-512/18), Fédération des fournisseurs d'accès à Internet associatifs (C-511/18 and C-512/18), Igwan.net (C-511/18) v Premier ministre (C-511/18 and C-512/18), Garde des Sceaux, ministre de la Justice (C-511/18 and C-512/18), Ministre de l'Intérieur (C-511/18), Ministre des Armées (C-511/18),ECL I:EU:C:2020:791.

Judgement of the Court (Grand Chamber) 21 June 2022 in the case C-817/19 Ligue des droits humains v Conseil des ministres ECLI:EU:C:2022:491.

Judgement of the Court (Grand Chamber) 1 August 2022 in case C-184/20 OT v Vyriausioji tarnybinės etikos komisija, third party: Fondas 'Nevyriausybinių organizacijų informacijos ir paramos centras ECLI:EU:C:2022:601.

Judgement of the Court (First Chamber) of 20 October 2022 in case C-77/21 Digi Távközlési és Szolgáltató Kft. v Nemzeti Adatvédelmi és Információszabadság Hatóság ECLI:EU:C:2022:805.

Judgement of the General Court (Eight Chamber, extended composition) of 26. April 2023 in Case T-557/20 Single Resolution Board (SRB) v European Data Protection Supervisor (EDPS).

Judgement of the Court (Grand Chamber) in case C-252/21 Meta Platforms Inc., Meta Platforms Ireland Ltd, Facebook Deutschland GmbH v Budeskartellamt ECLI:EU:C:2023:537.

Judgement of the Court (Third Chamber) of 9 November 2023 in case C-319/22 Gesamtverband Autoteile-Handel eV v Scania CV AB ECLI:EU:C:2023:837.

Judgement of the Court (Grand Chamber) of 5 December 2023 in case C-683/21 Nacionalinis visuomenės sveikatos centras prie Sveikatos apsaugos ministerijos v Valstybinė duomenų apsaugos inspekcija ECLI:EU:C:2023:949.

Judgement of the Court (First Chamber) in case C-634/21 OQ v Land Hessen and Schufa Holding AG ECLI:EU:C:2023:957.

Judgement of the Court (Fourth Chamber) 7 March 2024 in the Case C-604/22 IAB Europe v Gegevensbeschermingsautoriteit ECLI:EU:C:2024:214.

Judgement of the Court (Ninth Chamber) of 4 October 2024 in case C-621/22 Koninklijke Nederlandse Lawn Tennisbond v Autoriteit Persoonsgegevens, ECLI:EU:C:2024:858.

Judgement of the Court (First Chamber) of 27 February 2025 in case C-203/22 CK v Magistrat der Stadt Wien, other party: Dun and Bradstreet Austria GmbH ECLI:EU:C:2025:117.

Opinion of Advocate General Trstenjak on 8 September 2011 in Case C-282/10, ECLI: EU:C:2011:559 paragraphs 80–87, and Opinion of Advocate General Trstenjak delivered on 29 March 2007 in Case C-80/06 ECLI:EU:C:2007:200.

Opinion of Advocate General Villalón on 18 July 2013 in Case C-176/12 AMS or Association de Médiation Sociale ECLI:EU:C:2013:491.

Opinion of Advocate General Saugmandsgaard Øe in Case C-311/18.

Commission Decision of 25.4.2023 designating TikTok as a very large online platform in accordance with Article 33(4) of Regulation (EU) 2022/2065 of the European Parliament and of the Council C(2023) 2720 final.

LITERATURE AND OTHER SOURCES

(AWS), Amazon Web Services. *AWS Data Processing Addendum to the AWS Customer Agreement.* url: https://d1.awsstatic.com/legal/aws-dpa/aws-dpa.pdf. Last accessed: 26.08.2024.

Aguirre, Anthony et al. *AI Loyalty by Design: A Framework for Governance of AI.* Oxford Handbook on AI Governance (Oxford University Press), 2021. doi: https://doi.org/10.1093/oxfordhb/9780197579329.013.70.

AI, Clearview. *Privacy policy.* url: https://www.clearview.ai/privacy-policy. Last accessed: 26.08.2024.

Albahri, Ahmed Shihab et al. "A systematic review of trustworthy and explainable artificial intelligence in healthcare: Assessment of quality, bias risk, and data fusion". In: *Information Fusion* (2023). doi: https://doi.org/10.1016/j.inffus.2023.03.008.

Ali, Sajid et al. "Explainable artificial intelligence (XAI): What we know and what is left to attain trustworthy artificial intelligence". In: *Information Fusion* 99 (2023), p. 101805. doi: https://doi.org/10.1016/j.inffus.2023.101805.

Alla, Sridhar and Suman Kalyan Adari. "Beginning MLOps with MLFlow". In: *Begin. MLOps with MLFlow* (2021). doi: https://doi.org/10.1007/978-1-4842-6549-9.

Almada, Marco. "Human intervention in automated decision-making: Toward the construction of contestable systems". In: *Proceedings of the Seventeenth International Conference on Artificial Intelligence and Law.* 2019, pp. 2–11. doi: https://doi.org/10.1145/3322640.3326699.

— "Regulation by design and the governance of technological futures". In: *European Journal of Risk Regulation* (2023), pp. 1–13. doi: https://doi.org/10.1017/err.2023.37.

Almada, Marco and Nicolas Petit. "The EU AI Act: A medley of product safety and fundamental rights?" In: *Robert Schuman Centre for Advanced Studies Research Paper* 2023/59 (2023). doi: http://dx.doi.org/10.2139/ssrn.4308072.

Altobelli, Catherine et al. "To scrape or not to scrape? The lawfulness of social media crawling under the GDPR". In: *Deep Diving into Data Protection.* Ed. by J. Herveg. Namur: Larcier, 2021, p. 6. ISSN: 9782807926493.

Amazon Web Service. *Detecting Data Drift Using Amazon Sagemaker.* url: https://aws.amazon.com/blogs/architecture/detecting-data-drift-using-amazon-sagemaker/. Last accessed: 01.08.2025.

Amazon Web Services. *Build and Scale the Next Wave of AI Innovation on AWS.* url: https://aws.amazon.com/ai/?nc2=h_ql_sol_use_ai. Last accessed: 01.08.2025.

Antonopoulos, Nick and Lee Gillam. *Cloud Computing*. Vol. 51.7. Cham: Springer Nature, 2010. doi: https: //doi.org/10.1007/978-3-319-54645-2.

Apple Machine Learning Research. *Hey Siri: An On-Device DNN-Powered Voice Trigger for Apple's Personal Assistant*. url: https://machinelearning.apple.com/research/hey-siri. Last accessed: 01.08.2025

Article 29 Working Party. *Opinion 01/2010 on the Concepts of "Controller" and "Processor" WP169, 16 February 2010*. On p. 9

Aufschläger, Robert et al. "Anonymization procedures for tabular data: An explanatory technical and legal synthesis". In: *Information* 14.9 (2023), p. 487. doi: https://doi.org/10.3390/info14090487.

Ávila, Humberto. *Theory of Legal Principles*. Dordrecht: Springer, 2007, p. 114.

AWS. *AWS Data Processing Addendum*. url: https://d1.awsstatic.com/legal/aws-gdpr/AWS_GDPR_DPA.pdf. Last accessed: 26.08.2024.

— *AWS infrastructure Entities*. url: https://aws.amazon.com/compliance/sub-processors/. Last accessed: 26.08.2024.

— *Regions and Availability Zones*. url: https://aws.amazon.com/about-aws/global-infrastructure/regions_az/?p=ngi&loc=2. Last accessed: 26.08.2024.

Azure, Microsoft. *Azure AI Bot Service*. url: https://azure.microsoft.com/en-us/products/ai-services/ai-bot-service/. Last accessed: 26.08.2024.

— *Azure Geographies*. url: https://azure.microsoft.com/en-us/explore/global-infrastructure/geographies/#overview. Last accessed: 26.08.2024.

— *Configuring Azure Non-regional Services for the EU Data Boundary*. url: https://learn.microsoft.com/en-us/privacy/eudb/eu-data-boundary-configure-azure-nonregional-services. Last accessed: 26.08.2024.

— *Microsoft Azure Legal Information*. url: https://azure.microsoft.com/en-us/support/legal/. Last accessed: 26.08.2024.

— *Privacy and Security Terms Microsoft Azure Core Services*. url: https://www.microsoft.com/licensing/terms/product/PrivacyandSecurityTerms/MCA. Last accessed: 26.08.2024.

— *Products Available by Region: Non-regional*. url: https://azure.microsoft.com/en-us/explore/global-infrastructure/products-by-region/?products=all&regions=non-regional. Last accessed: 26.08.2024.

— *Services That Will Temporarily Transfer a Subset of Customer Data or Pseudonymized Personal Data Out of the EU Data Boundary*. url: https://learn.microsoft.com/en-us/privacy/eudb/eu-data-boundary-temporary-partial-transfers#azure-services. Last accessed: 26.08.2024.

Balboni, Paolo et al. "Designing connected and automated vehicles around legal and ethical concerns: Data protection as a corporate social responsibility". In: *SETN Workshops*. 2020, pp. 139–151. doi: https://doi.org/10.5281/zenodo.7291693.

Baltrušaitis, Tadas, Chaitanya Ahuja, and Louis-Philippe Morency. "Multimodal machine learning: A survey and taxonomy". In: *IEEE Transactions on Pattern Analysis and Machine Intelligence* 41.2 (2018), pp. 423–443. doi: https://doi.org/10.48550/arXiv.1705.09406.

Bandara, Syafril et al. "Access control framework for API-enabled devices in smart buildings". In: *2016 22nd Asia-Pacific Conference on Communications (APCC)*, 2016, pp. 210–217. doi: 10.1109/APCC.2016.7581479.

Baniecki, Hubert et al. "Dalex: Responsible machine learning with interactive explainability and fairness in python". In: *Journal of Machine Learning Research* 22.214 (2021), pp. 1–7. doi: https://doi.org/10.48550/arXiv.2012.14406.

Barak, Aharon. *Proportionality: Constitutional Rights and Their Limitations*. Cambridge, UK: Cambridge University Press, 2012, p. 342.

— *Proportionality: Constitutional Rights and Their Limitations*. Cambridge, UK: Cambridge University Press, 2021, p. 341.

— *Proportionality: Constitutional Rights and Their Limitations*. Cambridge, UK: Cambridge University Press, 2021, p. 340.

— *Proportionality: Constitutional Rights and Their Limitations*. Cambridge, UK: Cambridge University Press, 2021, p. 482.

Bareis, Jascha. *BigTech's Efforts to Derail the AI Act*. url: https://verfassungsblog.de/bigtechs-efforts-to-derail-the-ai-act/. Last accessed: 26.08.2024.

Barroso, Borja Sánchez. "Beyond the principle of proportionality: Controlling the restriction of rights under factual uncertainty". In: *Oslo Law Review* 2 (2023), pp. 74–91. doi: https://doi.org/10.18261/olr.9.2.1.

BBC. *Pegasus Scandal: Are We All Becoming Unknowing Spies?* url: https://www.bbc.com/news/technology-57910355. Last accessed: 01.08.2025.

Beck, Ulrich. "The digital freedom risk: Too fragile an acknowledgement". In: *22 Quaderns de la Mediterrània* (2015), p. 141, pp. 141–144.

Beijer, Malu Patricia. *The Limits of Fndamental Rights Protection by the EU: The Scope for the Development of Positive Obligations*. Cambridge, UK: Intersentia, 2017. isbn: 9781780684550.

Biasin, Elisabetta. "Why accuracy needs further exploration in data protection". In: *CAIP 2021: Proceedings of the 1st International Conference on AI for People: Towards Sustainable AI, CAIP 2021, 20–24 November 2021, Bologna, Italy*. Ghent: European Alliance for Innovation, 2021, p. 96. doi: http://dx.doi.org/10.4108/eai.20-11-2021.2314205.

Bieker, Felix et al. "A process for data protection impact assessment under the European General Data Protection Regulation". In: *Privacy Technologies and Policy*. Ed. by Stefan Schiffner et al. Cham: Springer International Publishing, 2016, pp. 21–37. isbn: 978-3-319-44760-5. doi: https://doi.org/10.1007/978-3-319-44760-5_2.

Biggio, Battista and Fabio Roli. "Wild patterns: Ten years after the rise of adversarial machine learning". In: *Proceedings of the 2018 ACM SIGSAC Conference on Computer and Communications Security*. New York: Association for Computing Machinery, 2018, pp. 2154–2156. doi: https://doi.org/10.48550/arXiv. 1712.03141.

BigML. *Machine Learning Made Beautifully Simple for Everyone*. url: https://bigml.com/. Last accessed: 01.08.2025.

Billeter, Yann et al. "MLOps as an enabler of trustworthy AI". In: *11th IEEE Swiss Conference on Data Science (SDS), Zurich, Switzerland, 30–31 May 2024*. ZHAW Zürcher Hochschule für Angewandte Wissenschaften, 2024. doi: https://doi.org/10.21256/zhaw-30443.

Bloomberglaw. *OpenAI's Legal Woes Driven by Unclear Mesh of Web-Scraping Laws*. url: https://news.bloomberglaw.com/ip-law/openais-legal-woes-driven-by-unclear-mesh-of-web-scraping-laws. Last accessed: 01.08.2025.

Bogdandy, Armin von. "Founding principles of EU law: A theoretical and doctrinal sketch". In: *European Law Journal* 16.2 (2010), pp. 95–111. doi: https://doi.org/10.1111/j.1468- 0386.2009.00500.x.

Bradford, Anu. "The Brussels Effect". In: *Northwestern University Law Review* 107 (2012), p. 1. url: https://ssrn.com/abstract=2770634.

Brems, Eva and Laurens Lavrysen. "'Don't use a sledgehammer to crack a nut': Less restrictive means in the case law of the European Court of Human Rights". In:

Human Rights Law Review 15.1 (2015), pp. 139–168. doi: https://doi.org/10.1093/hrlr/ngu040.

Bygrave, Lee A. "Core principles of data privacy law". In: *Data Privacy Law: An International Perspective.* Oxford: Oxford University Press, 2014, pp. 145–168. doi: https://doi.org/10.1093/acprof:oso/9780199675555.003.0005.

— "Machine learning, cognitive sovereignty and data protection rights with respect to automated decisions". In: *The Cambridge Handbook of Information Technology, Life Sciences and Human Rights.* Ed. by Marcello Ienca et al. Cambridge, UK: Cambridge University Press, 2022, pp. 166–188. doi: https://doi.org/10.1017/9781108775038.016.

— "Minding the machine v2. 0: The EU general data protection regulation and automated decision making". In: *Algorithmic Regulation.* Oxford:Oxford University Press 2019, Forthcoming, University of Oslo Faculty of Law Research Paper No. 2019-01 (2019). doi: https://doi.org/ 10.1093/oso/9780198838494.003.0011.

— "Security by design: Aspirations and realities in a regulatory context". In: *Oslo Law Review* 8 (3 2021), pp. 126–177. doi: https://doi.org/10.18261/olr.8.3.2.

Carroll, Micah et al. "Characterizing manipulation from AI systems". In: *Proceedings of the 3rd ACM Conference on Equity and Access in Algorithms, Mechanisms, and Optimization.* New York: Association for Computing Machinery, 2023, pp. 1–13. doi: https://doi.org/10.48550/arXiv.2303.09387.

Casaletto, James et al. "Federated analysis for privacy-preserving data sharing: A technical and legal primer". In: *Annual Review of Genomics and Human Genetics* 24 (2023), pp. 347–368. doi: https://doi.org/10.1146/annurev-genom-110122-084756.

Cavukian, Ann. *Privacy by Design: The 7 Foundational Principles.* Tech. rep. Information and privacy commissioner of Ontario, Canada, 2009.

Celeste, Edoardo. "Digital constitutionalism: A new systematic theorisation". In: *International Review of Law, Computers & Technology* 33.1 (2019), pp. 76–99. doi: 10.1080/13600869.2019.1562604.

Chami, Ines et al. "Machine learning on graphs: A model and comprehensive taxonomy". In: *Journal of Machine Learning Research* 23.1 (2022), pp. 3840–3903. doi: https://doi.org/10.48550/arXiv.2005.03675.

Chang, Yupeng et al. "A survey on evaluation of large language models". In: *ACM Transactions on Intelligent Systems and Technology* 15.3 (2023), pp. 1–45. doi: https://doi.org/10.48550/arXiv.2307. 03109.

Chiara, Pier Giorgio. "Towards a right to cybersecurity in EU law? The challenges ahead". In: *Computer Law & Security Review* 53 (2024), p. 105961. ISSN: 0267-3649. doi: https://doi.org/10.1016/j.clsr.2024.105961. url: https://www.sciencedirect.com/science/article/pii/S0267364924000281.

Cloud, Google. *Asymmetric Encryption.* url: https://cloud.google.com/kms/docs/asymmetric-encryption. Last accessed: 01.08.2025.

— *Cloud Billing Overview.* url: https://cloud.google.com/billing/docs/concepts. Last accessed: 26.08.2024.

— *Google Cloud Platform Terms of Service.* url: https://cloud.google.com/terms. Last accessed: 26.08.2024.

— *Products Available by Location.* url: https://cloud.google.com/about/locations/#multi-region. Last accessed: 26.08.2024.

CNIL. *Defining a Purpose.* url: https://www.cnil.fr/en/defining-purpose. Last accessed: 01.08.2025.

Cobbe, Jennifer and Jatinder Singh. "Artificial intelligence as a service: Legal responsibilities, liabilities, and policy challenges". In: *Computer Law &*

Security Review 42 (2021), p. 105573. ISSN: 0267-3649. doi: https://doi.org/10.1016/j.clsr.2021.105573. url: https://www.sciencedirect.com/science/article/pii/S0267364921000467.

Colaner, Nathan. "Is explainable artificial intelligence intrinsically valuable?" In: *AI & Society* (2022), pp. 1–8. doi: https://doi.org/10.1007/s00146-021-01184-2.

Colburn, Timothy. "Methodology of computer science". In: *The Blackwell Guide to the Philosophy of Computing and Information*. Ed. by Luciano Floridi. Hoboken: Blackwell Publishing, 2003, pp. 318–326. doi: https://doi.org/10.1002/9780470757017.ch24.

Colingridge, David. *The Social Control of Technology*. New York: St Martin's Press, 1982. isbn: 9780312731687.

Comella-Dorda, Santiago et al. "A survey of legacy system modernization approaches". In: *CMU/SEI* 18 (2000), pp. 1–21.

Compagnucci, Marcelo Corrales et al. "Homomorphic encryption: The 'holy grail' for Big Data analytics and legal compliance in the pharmaceutical and healthcare sector?" In: *European Pharmaceutical Law Review* 3.4 (2019), pp. 144–155. doi: 10.21552/eplr/2019/4/5. url: https://doi.org/10.21552/eplr/2019/4/5.

Conseil d' État d'. *National Free Software and others CE N 444937*. url: https://www.conseil-etat.fr/content/download/157044/document/444937%20-%20CNLL%20et%20autres.pdf. Last accessed: 01.08.2025.

Corrales Compagnucci, Marcelo et al. "Supplementary measures and appropriate safeguards for international transfers of health data after Schrems II". In: *The Law and Ethics of Data Sharing in Health Sciences*. Ed. by Marcelo Corrales Compagnucci et al. Singapore: Springer Nature, 2024, pp. 151–172. isbn: 978-981-99-6540-3. doi: 10.1007/978-981-99- 6540-3_9. url: https://doi.org/10.1007/978-981-99-6540-3_9.

Council of Europe, Committee of Ministers of the Council of Europe. *Recommendation Concerning the Protection of Personal Data Collected and Processed for Statistical Purposes (Rec(1997)18, 30 September 1997)*. url: https://rm.coe.int/cmrec-97-18-concerning-the-protection-of-personal-data-collected-and-p/1680a43b63. Last accessed: 01.08.202.

Council of Europe. *Convention for the Protection of Individuals with Regard to the Automatic Processing of Individual Data, 28 January 1981, ETS 108*.

Court of Justice of the European Union. *Opinion 2/13 of the Court ECLI:EU:C:2014:2454 (Full Court)*. at paragraph 200. 2014.

Crawford, Stuart L. "Extensions to the CART algorithm". In: *International Journal of Man-Machine Studies* 31.2 (1989), pp. 197–217. ISSN: 0020-7373. doi: https://doi.org/10.1016/0020-7373(89)90027-8. url: https://www.sciencedirect.com/science/article/pii/0020737389900278.

Custers, Bart and Anne-Sophie Heijne. "The right of access in automated decision-making: The scope of article 15(1)(h) GDPR in theory and practice". In: *Computer Law & Security Review* 46 (2022), p. 105727. ISSN: 0267-3649. doi: https://doi.org/10.1016/j.clsr.2022.105727. url: https://www.sciencedirect.com/science/article/pii/S026736492200070X.

Dalla Corte, Lorenzo. "On proportionality in the data protection jurisprudence of the CJEU". In: *International Data Privacy Law* 12.4 (July 2022), pp. 259–275. ISSN: 2044-3994. doi: 10.1093/idpl/ipac014. eprint: https://academic.oup.com/idpl/article-pdf/12/4/259/47703258/ipac014.pdf. url: https://doi.org/10.1093/idpl/ipac014.

— "On proportionality in the data protection jurisprudence of the CJEU". In: *International Data Privacy Law* 12.4 (2022), pp. 259–275. doi: https://doi.org/10.1093/idpl/ipac014.

Danish Data Protection Authority. *ISO/IEC 27001.* url: https://www.datatilsynet.dk/hvad-siger-reglerne/vejledning/sikkerhed/katalog-over-foranstaltninger. Last accessed: 01.08.2025.

Das, Sibanjan Debeeprasad and Pradip Kumar Bala. "What drives MLOps adoption? An analysis using the TOE framework". In: *Journal of Decision Systems* 33.3 (2024), pp. 376–412. doi: https://doi.org/10.1080/12460125.2023.2214306.

Data Protection Commission. *Data Protection Commission launches inquiry into Google AI model.* url: https://www.dataprotection.ie/en/news-media/press-releases/data-protection-commission-launches-inquiry-google-ai-model. Last accessed: 01.08.2025.

— *Decision of the Data Protection Commission made pursuant to Section 113 of the Data Protection Act, 2018 and Articles 60 and 65 of the General Data Protection Regulation.* On page 72. url: https://www.dataprotection.ie/sites/default/files/uploads/2023-04/Meta%20FINAL%20DECISION%20%28ADOPTED%29%2031-12-22%20-%20IN-18-5-5%20%28Redacted%29.pdf. Last accessed: 01.08.2025.

DataGuidance, OneTrust. *International: Schrems II: What you need to know.* url: https://www.dataguidance.com/opinion/international-schrems-ii-what-you-need-know. Last accessed: 01.08.2025.

DataRobot. *One Unified Platform for Generative and Predictive AI.* url: https://www.datarobot.com/. Last accessed: 01.08.2025.

DataRobot. *DataRobot FAQ on International Transfer of Personal Data.* url: https://www.datarobot.com/wp-content/uploads/2022/03/FAQ-International-Transfer-of-Personal-Data-Post-Schrems-II.pdf. Last accessed: 26.08.2024.

— *Subprocessors.* url: https://www.datarobot.com/privacy/subprocessors/. Last accessed: 26.08.2024.

Datatilsynet. *Etablering og dealing av datasæt.* url: https://www.datatilsynet.dk/afgoerelser/afgoerelser/2024/jan/etablering-og-deling-af-datasaet#_ftn1. Last accessed: 01.08.2025.

— *NAV – sluttrapport.* url: https://www.datatilsynet.no/regelverk-og-verktoy/sandkasse-for-kunstig-intelligens/ferdige-prosjekter-og-rapporter/nav-sluttrapport/rettslig-grunnlag/. Last accessed: 01.08.2025.

— *Uttalelse om behandlingsgrunnlag til utvikling av AI løsning.* url: https://www.datatilsynet.dk/afgoerelser/afgoerelser/2023/nov/udtalelse-om-behandlingsgrundlag-til-udvikling-og-drift-af-ai-loesning-inden-for-sundheds-og-omsorgsomraadet. Last accessed: 01.08.2025.

Datatrade. *Explore AI ML Training Datasets and Providers.* url: https://datarade.ai/data-categories/ai-ml-training-data. Last accessed: 01.08.2025.

De Gregorio, Giovanni. "The rise of digital constitutionalism in the European Union". In: *International Journal of Constitutional Law* 19.1 (Apr. 2021), pp. 41–70. ISSN: 1474-2640. doi: 10.1093/icon/moab001. eprint: https://academic.oup.com/icon/article-pdf/19/1/41/38501964/moab001.pdf. url: https://doi.org/10.1093/icon/moab001.

de Terwangne, Cécile. "Council of Europe convention 108+: A modernised international treaty for the protection of personal data". In: *Computer Law & Security Review* 40 (2021), p. 105497. ISSN: 0267-3649. doi: https://doi.org/10.1016/j.clsr.2020.105497. url: https://www.sciencedirect.com/science/article/pii/S0267364920301023.

Denning, Peter J et al. "Computing as a discipline". In: *Communications of the ACM* 32.1 (1989), pp. 9–23.
Dietterich, Tom. "Overfitting and undercomputing in machine learning". In: *ACM Computing Surveys (CSUR)* 27.3 (1995), pp. 326–327.
Digibeetle. *Pending CJEU data protection cases.* url: https://app.digibeetle.eu/pending-cases/. Last accessed: 30.07.2025.
Dimitrova, Diana. "The rise of the personal data quality principle: Is it legal and does it have an impact on the right to rectification?" In: *EJLT European Journal of Law and Technology* 12.3 (2021). doi: http://dx.doi.org/10.2139/ssrn.3790602.
Ditzler, Gregory et al. "Learning in nonstationary environments: A survey". In: *IEEE Transactions on Knowledge and Data Engineering* (2015), pp. 2346–2363. doi: https://doi. org/10.1109/MCI.2015.2471196.
Diver, Laurence. *Digisprudence: Code as Law Rebooted.* Edinburgh: Edinburgh University Press, 2022, p. 26. isbn: 9781474485340. doi: doi:10.1515/9781474485340.
Drechsler, Laura. "Defining Personal Data Transfers for the Context of the General Data Protection Regulation: A Critical Perspective on the Guidelines 5/2021 of the European Data Protection Board". In: *Privacy in Germany* 10.1 (2022). On page 24., pp. 24–29.
Drechsler, Laura and Irene Kamara. "Essential equivalence as a benchmark for international data transfers after Schrems II". In: *Research Handbook on EU Data Protection Law.* Cheltenham: Edward Elgar Publishing, 2022, pp. 314–352.
Dwivedi, Rudresh et al. "Explainable AI (XAI): Core ideas, techniques, and solutions". In: *ACM Computing Surveys* 55.9 (2023), pp. 1–33. doi: https://doi.org/10.1145/3561048.
Dyzenhaus, David. "Process and substance as aspects of the public law form". In: *The Cambridge Law Journal* 74.2 (2015), pp. 284–306.
Ebert, Christof et al. "DevOps". In: *IEEE Software* 33.3 (2016), pp. 94–100. doi: 10.1109/MS. 2016.68.
EDPB. *European Data Protection Board, Guidelines 3/2019 on Processing of Personal Data through Video Devices v2.0, (EDPB Guidelines, 2020).* Page 68. url: https://edpb.europa.eu/our-work-tools/our-documents/guidelines/guidelines-32019-processing-personal-data-through-video_en. Last accessed: 01.08.2025.
— *Guidelines 05/2020 on Consent under Regulation 2016/679.* url: https://edpb.europa.eu/sites/default/files/files/file1/edpb_guidelines_202005_consent_en.pdf. Last accessed: 01.08.2025.
— *Guidelines 05/2021 on the Interplay between the Application of Article 3 and the Provisions on International Transfers as per Chapter V of the GDPR.* url: https://edpb.europa.eu/system/files/2021-11/edpb_guidelinesinterplaychapterv_article3_adopted_en.pdf. Last accessed: 01.08.2025.
— *Guidelines 07/2020 on the Concepts of Controllers and Processor in the GDPR.* On page 10. url: https://www.edpb.europa.eu/system/files/2023-10/EDPB_guidelines_202007_controllerprocessor_final_en.pdf. Last accessed: 01.08.2025.
— *Guidelines 4/2019 on Article 25 Data Protection by Design and by Default Version 2.0 Adopted on 20 October 2020.* url: https://edpb.europa.eu/sites/default/files/files/file1/edpb_guidelines_201904_dataprotection_by_design_and_by_default_v2.0_en.pdf. Last accessed: 01.08.2025.
— *Guidelines on Automated Individual Decision-Making and Profiling for the Purposes of Regulation 2016/679 (wp251rev.01).* url: https://ec.europa.eu/newsroom/article29/items/612053. Last accessed: 01.08.2025.

— *Report of the Work Undertaken by the ChatGPT Taskforce.* url: https://www.edpb.europa.eu/system/files/2024-05/edpb_20240523_report_chatgpt_taskforce_en.pdf. Last accessed: 26.08.2024.

Electronic Frontier Foundation. *Cover your tracks.* url: https://coveryourtracks.eff.org/. Last accessed: 01.08.2025.

Emmert-Streib, Frank and Matthias Dehmer. "Taxonomy of machine learning paradigms: A data-centric perspective". In: *Wiley Interdisciplinary Reviews: Data Mining and Knowledge Discovery* 12.5 (2022), e1470. doi: https://doi.org/10.1002/widm.1470.

ENISA. *Privacy Enhancing Technologies.* 2022. url: https://www.enisa.europa.eu/news/enisa-news/promoting-data-protection-by-design-exploring-techniques. Last accessed: 01.08.2025.

Enqvist, Lena. "'Human oversight' in the EU artificial intelligence act: What, when and by whom?" In: *Law, Innovation and Technology* 15.2 (2023), pp. 508–535. doi: 10.1080/17579961. 2023.2245683.

Enthoven, David and Zaid Al-Ars. "Fidel: Reconstructing private training samples from weight updates in federated learning". In: *2022 9th International Conference on Internet of Things: Systems, Management and Security (IOTSMS).* New York: IEEE, 2022, pp. 1–8. doi: 10.1109/IOTSMS58070. 2022.10062088.

— "Fidel: Reconstructing private training samples from weight updates in federated learning". In: *2022 9th International Conference on Internet of Things: Systems, Management and Security (IOTSMS).* New York: IEEE, 2022, pp. 1–8. doi: https://doi.org/10.1109/IOTSMS58070.2022.10062088.

— *Convention for the Protection of Individuals with Regard to the Processing of Personal Data (Convention 108+) Article 14, 18.05.2018.* url: https://rm.coe.int/convention-108-convention-for-the-protection-of-individuals-with-regar/16808b36f1. Last accessed: 01.08.2025.

— *Draft Explanatory Report—Convention 108 Modernised.* url: https://rm.coe.int/convention-for-the-protection-of-individuals-with-regard-to-automatic-/16806b6ec2. Last accessed: 01.08.2025.

— *EU Accession to the ECHR ("46+1" Group).* url: https://www.coe.int/en/web/human-rights-intergovernmental-cooperation/accession-of-the-european-union-to-the-european-convention-on-human-rights. Last accessed: 01.08.2025.

Europe Treaty Series – No. 225, Council of. *Council of Europe Framework Convention on Artificial Intelligence and Human Rights, Democracy and the Rule of Law.* url: https://rm.coe.int/1680afae3c. Last accessed: 01.08.2025.

European Agency for Cybersecurity (ENISA), European Agency for. *Deploying Pseudonymization Techniques.* url: https://www.enisa.europa.eu/publications/deploying-pseudonymisation-techniques. Last accessed: 01.08.2025.

European Commission. *Adequacy Decisions.* url: https://commission.europa.eu/law/law-topic/data-protection/international-dimension-data-protection/adequacy-decisions_en. Last accessed: 01.08.2025.

— *Assessment List for Trustworthy Artificial Intelligence (ALTAI) for Self-Assessment.* url: https://digital-strategy.ec.europa.eu/en/library/assessment-list-trustworthy-artificial-intelligence-altai-self-assessment. Last accessed: 26.08.2024.

— *Commission Implementing Decision (EU) 2021/914 of 4 June 2021 on standard contractual clauses for the transfer of personal data to third countries pursuant to Regulation (EU) 2016/679 of the European Parliament and of the Council OJ 2021 L 199/31.* url: https://eur-lex.europa.eu/eli/dec_impl/2021/914/oj. Last accessed: 01.08.2025.

— *Commission Implementing Decision of 10.7.2023 pursuant to Regulation (EU) 2016/679 of the European Parliament and of the Council on the adequate level of protection of personal data under the EU-US Data Privacy Framework C(2023) 4745 final*. url: https://commission.europa.eu/document/download/fa09cbad-dd7d-4684-ae60-be03fcb0fddf_en?filename=Adequacy%20decision%20EU-US%20Data%20Privacy%20Framework_en.pdf. Last accessed: 01.08.2025.

— *Commission opens proceedings against TikTok under the DSA regarding the launch of TikTok Lite in France and Spain, and communicates its intention to suspend the reward programme in the EU*. url: https://ec.europa.eu/commission/presscorner/detail/en/ip_24_2227. Last accessed: 26.08.2024.

— *Commission signed the Council of Europe Framework Convention on Artificial Intelligence and human rights, democracy and the rule of law*. url: https://digital-strategy.ec.europa.eu/en/news/commission-signed-council-europe-framework-convention-artificial-intelligence-and-human-rights. Last accessed 16.09.2024.

— *Commission welcomes political agreement on Cyber Resilience Act*. url: https://ec.europa.eu/commission/presscorner/detail/en/ip_23_6168. Last accessed: 26.08.2024.

— *European Commission and the United States Joint Statement on Trans-Atlantic Data Privacy Framework 2022*. url: https://ec.europa.eu/commission/presscorner/detail/en/IP_22_2087. Last accessed: 01.08.2025.

— *High-Level Expert Group on Artificial Intelligence*. url: https://digital-strategy.ec.europa.eu/en/policies/expert-group-ai. Last accessed: 26.08.2024.

European Data Protection Supervisor. *EDPS Investigation into use of Microsoft 365 by the European Commission (Case 2021-0518) Decision of 8 March 2024*. url: https://www.edps.europa.eu/system/files/2024-03/24-03-08-edps-investigation-ec-microsoft365_en.pdf. Last accessed: 01.08.2025.

European Union, Official Journal of the. *Explanations Relating to the Charter of Fundamental Rights 2007/C 303/02*. url: https://eur-lex.europa.eu/legal-content/EN/TXT/PDF/?uri=CELEX:32007X1214(01). Last accessed: 01.08.2025.

European Union to the Council of Europe, Delegation of the. *Major Progress on the Path to EU Accession to the ECHR: Negotiations Concluded at Technical Level in Strasbourg*. url: https://www.eeas.europa.eu/delegations/council-europe/major-progress-path-eu-accession-echr-negotiations-concluded-technical-level-strasbourg_en?s=51. Last accessed: 01.08.2025.

Fielding, Roy Thomas. *Architectural Styles and the Design of Network-Based Software Architectures*. Irvine: University of California Press, 2000.

Finck, Michèle and Asia Biega. "Reviving purpose limitation and data minimisation in data-driven systems technology and regulation," in: *Techreg* (2021). doi: https://doi.org/ 10.26116/techreg.2021.004.

Finck, Michèle and Frank Pallas. "They who must not be identified—distinguishing personal from non-personal data under the GDPR". In: *International Data Privacy Law* 10.1 (Mar. 2020), pp. 11–36. ISSN: 2044-3994. doi: 10 . 1093 / idpl / ipz026. eprint: https://academic.oup.com/idpl/article-pdf/10/1/11/33151834/ipz026.pdf. url: https://doi.org/10.1093/idpl/ipz026.

Fredrikson, Matthew et al. "Privacy in pharmacogenetics: An end-to-end case study of personalized warfarin dosing". In: *23rd USENIX Security Symposium (USENIX Security 14)*. 2014, pp. 17–32. url: https://www.usenix.org/system/files/conference/usenixsecurity14/sec14-paper-fredrikson-privacy.pdf.

Fuster, Gloria Gonzáles. *Study on the Essence of the Fundamental Right to Privacy and to Protection of Personal Data*. Tech. rep. Vrije Universiteit Brussel (VUB) and EDPS, 2022. url: https://www.edps.europa.eu/system/files/2023-11/edps-vub-study_on_the_essence_of_fundamental_rights_to_privacy_and_to_protection_of_personal_data_en.pdf. Last accessed: 26.08.2024.

Fuster, Gloria González. "Inaccuracy as a privacy-enhancing tool". In: *Ethics and Information Technology* 12 (2010), pp. 87–95. doi: https://doi.org/10.1007/s10676-009-9212-z.

Garcia, Katherine R et al. "Drivers' understanding of artificial intelligence in automated driving systems: A study of a malicious stop sign". In: *Journal of Cognitive Engineering and Decision Making* 16.4 (2022), pp. 237–251. doi: https://doi.org/10.1177/15553434221117001.

Garg, Satvik et al. "On continuous integration/continuous delivery for automated deployment of machine learning models using MLOps". In: *2021 IEEE Fourth International Conference on Artificial Intelligence and Knowledge Engineering (AIKE).* New York: IEEE, 2021, pp. 25–28. doi: https: //doi.org/10.1109/AIKE52691.2021.00010.

GDPRHUB. *Category CJEU.* url: https://gdprhub.eu/index.php?title=Category:CJEU. Last accessed: 01.08.2025.

Gelder, Pieter van et al. "Safe-by-design in engineering: An overview and comparative analysis of engineering disciplines". In: *International Journal of Environmental Research and Public Health* 18.12 (2021), p. 6329. doi: 10.3390/ijerph18126329.

Georgieva, Ludmila and Christopher Kuner. "Article 9: Processing of special categories of personal data". In: *The EU General Data Protection Regulation (GDPR): A Commentary.* Ed. by Christopher Kuner et al. Oxford: Oxford University Press, Feb. 2020. isbn: 9780198826491. doi: 10.1093/oso/9780198826491.003.0038. eprint: https://academic.oup.com/book/0/chapter/352296960/chapter-pdf/52771138/isbn-9780198826491-book-part-38.pdf. url: https://doi.org/10.1093/oso/9780198826491.003.0038.

Giese, Gerhard. "Think like a hacker: Reducing cyber security risk by improving API design and protection". In: *Cyber Security: A Peer-Reviewed Journal* 4.1 (2020), pp. 48–57.

Goldsteen, Abigail et al. "Data minimization for GDPR compliance in machine learning models". In: *AI and Ethics* 2.3 (2022), pp. 477–491. doi: https://doi.org/10.48550/arXiv.2008.04113.

Goodman, Bryce and Seth Flaxman. "EU regulations on algorithmic decision-making and a 'right to explanation.'" In: *ICML Workshop on Human Interpretability in Machine Learning (WHI 2016),* New York. *http://arxiv. org/abs/1606.08813 v1.* 2016. doi: https://doi.org/10. 1609/aimag.v38i3.2741.

Google. *AI and Machine Learning Products.* url: https://cloud.google.com/products/ai?hl=en. Last accessed: 01.08.2025.

Google Patents. *Privacy Enhancing Deep Learning Cloud Service Using a Trusted Execution Environment.* url: https://patents.google.com/patent/US11443182B2/en. Last accessed: 01.08.2025.

Götzfried, Johannes et al. "Cache attacks on Intel SGX". In: *EuroSec'17.* Belgrade, Serbia: Association for Computing Machinery, 2017. isbn: 9781450349352. doi: 10.1145/3065913. 3065915. url: https://doi.org/10.1145/3065913.3065915.

Graver, Hans Petter. "Vanlig juridisk metode? Om rettsdogmatikken som juridisk sjanger". In: *Tidsskrift for Rettsvitenskap* 2 (2008). doi: https://doi.org/10.18261/ISSN1504-3096-2008-02-01.

Gunning, David et al. "XAI—Explainable artificial intelligence". In: *Science Robotics* 4.37 (2019), eaay7120. doi: https://doi.org/10.1126/scirobotics.aay7120.

Habermas, Jürgen. *Between Facts and Norms: Contributions to a Discourse Theory of Law and Democracy*. Cambridge, MA: MIT Press, 1998.

Hallinan, Dara and Nicholas Martin. "Fundamental rights, the normative keystone of DPIA". In: *European Data Protection Law Review* 6.2 (2020), pp. 178–193. doi: https://doi.org/10.21552/edpl/2020/2/6.

Hallinan, Dara and Frederik Zuiderveen Borgesius. "Opinions can be incorrect (in our opinion)! On data protection law's accuracy principle". In: *International Data Privacy Law* 10.1 (Jan. 2020), pp. 1–10. ISSN: 2044-3994. doi: 10 . 1093 / idpl / ipz025. eprint: https://academic.oup.com/idpl/article-pdf/10/1/1/33151826/ipz025 .pdf. url: https://doi.org/10.1093/idpl/ipz025.

Han, Meng et al. "A survey of active and passive concept drift handling methods". In: *Computational Intelligence* 38.4 (2022), pp. 1492–1535. doi: https://doi.org/10.1111 /coin.12520.

Harbo, Tor-Inge. "PA: Between rationality and reasonableness". In: *The Function of Proportionality Analysis in European Law*. Leiden: Brill Nijhoff, 2015, pp. 201–214.

— "The function of proportionality analysis in European law". In: *The Function of Proportionality Analysis in European Law*. Leiden: Brill Nijhoff, 2015, p. 72.

— "The function of the proportionality principle in EU law". In: *European Law Journal* 16 (2 2010), pp. 158–185.

Harvey, Darren. "Towards process-oriented proportionality review in the European Union". In: *European Public Law* 23.1 (2017), pp. 93–121.

Hausken, Kjell. "The Shapley value of coalitions to other coalitions". In: *Humanities and Social Sciences Communications* 7.1 (2020), pp. 1–10. doi: https://doi.org/10 .1057/s41599-020- 00586-9.

Helbing, Dirk et al. "Ethics of smart cities: Towards value-sensitive design and co-evolving city life". In: *Sustainability* 13.20 (2021), p. 11162. doi: 10.3390/ su132011162.

Hermsen, Felix and Avikarsha Mandal. "Privacy and utility evaluation of synthetic tabular data for machine learning". In: *Privacy and Identity Management: Sharing in a Digital World*. Ed. by Felix Bieker et al. Cham: Springer Nature, 2024, pp. 265–281. isbn: 978-3-031-57978-3.

Heuvel, Willem-Jan van den and Damian A. Tamburri. "Model-driven ML-Ops for intelligent enterprise applications: Vision, approaches and challenges". In: *Business Modeling and Software Design*. Ed. by Boris Shishkov. Cham: Springer International Publishing, 2020, pp. 169–181. doi: https://doi.org/10.1007/978-3-030 -52306-0_11.

Hildebrandt, Mireille. "Legal protection by design: Objections and refutations". In: *Legisprudence* 5.2 (2011), pp. 223–248. doi: https://doi.org/10.5235 /175214611797885693.

— "The public(s) on life: A call for legal protection by design". In: *The Onlife Manifesto: Being Human in a Hyperconnected Era*. Cham: Springer International, 2015, pp. 181–193. doi: https://doi.org/10.1007/ 978-3-319-04093-6_19.

Hjelkrem, Lars Ole and Petter Eilif de Lange. "Explaining deep learning models for credit scoring with SHAP: A case study using open banking data". In: *Journal of Risk and Financial Management* 16.4 (2023), p. 221. doi: https://doi.org/10.3390/ jrfm16040221.

Hoepman, Japp-Henk. "Privacy design strategies". In: *ICT Systems Security and Privacy Protection. SEC 2014. IFIP Advances in Information and Communication Technology*. Ed. by Nora Cuppens-Boulahia et al. Cham: Springer Nature, 2014. doi: https://doi.org/10.1007/978-3-642-55415-5_38.

Householder, Allen D et al. *The Cert Guide to Coordinated Vulnerability Disclosure.* 2017. url: https://insights.sei.cmu.edu/documents/1945/2017_003_001_503340.pdf.

Huang, Jianglin, Yan-Fu Li, and Min Xie. "An empirical analysis of data preprocessing for machine learning-based software cost estimation". In: *Information and Software Technology* 67 (2015), pp. 108–127. doi: https://doi.org/10.1016/j.infsof.2015.07.004.

Huang, Tao and Shuyuan Zheng. "Using differential privacy to define personal, anonymous and pseudonymous data". In: *IEEE Access* 11(2023), pp. 109226–109236. doi: https://doi.org/10.1109/ACCESS.2023.3321578.

Huang, Xuanxiang and Joao Marques-Silva. "On the failings of Shapley values for explainability". In: *International Journal of Approximate Reasoning* 171 (2024), p. 109112. ISSN: 0888-613X. doi: https://doi.org/10.1016/j.ijar.2023.109112. url: https://www.sciencedirect.com/science/article/pii/S0888613X23002438.

Hugging Face. *Hugging Face Enterprise.* url: https://huggingface.co/. Last accessed: 01.08.2025.

Hungarian National Authority for and Freedom of Information and Data Protection. *Case No NAIH-85 – 3/2022 Budapest Bank.* url: https://naih.hu//hatarozatok-vegzesek?download=517:mesterseges-intelligencia-alkalmazasanak-adatvedelmi-kerdesei?. Last accessed: 01.08.2025.

Hussain, Fatima et al. "Enterprise API security and GDPR compliance: Design and implementation perspective". In: *IT Professional* 22.5 (2020), pp. 81–89. doi: 10.1109/MITP. 2020.2973852.

IAPP. *New EU Data Blockage as German Court Would Ban Many Cookie Management Providers.* url: https://iapp.org/news/a/new-eu-data-blockage-as-german-court-would-ban-many-cookie-management-providers/. Last accessed: 01.08.2025.

IBM. *Data Processing Addendum (DPA).* url: https://www.ibm.com/support/customer/csol/terms/?id=Z126-7870&lc=en. Last accessed: 26.08.2024.

— *IBM Cloud Catalog.* url: https://cloud.ibm.com/catalog?category=ai&search=watson#search_results. Last accessed: 26.08.2024.

— *IBM Watson.* url: https://www.ibm.com/watson. Last accessed: 01.08.2025.

— *Keeping Your Data Secure and Compliant.* url: https://dataplatform.cloud.ibm.com/docs/content/wsj/getting-started/security.html?context=cpdaas&audience=wdp. Last accessed: 26.08.2024.

— *POV – Watson Privacy, Compliance, and Security.* url: https://www.ibm.com/watson/assets/duo/pdf/Watson-Privacy-and-Security-POV_final_062819_tps.pdf. Last accessed: 26.08.2024.

— *Region and Data Center Locations for Resource Deployment.* url: https://cloud.ibm.com/docs/overview?topic=overview-locations. Last accessed: 26.08.2024.

— *Service and Infrastructure Availability by Location.* url: https://cloud.ibm.com/docs/overview?topic=overview-services_region. Last accessed: 26.08.2024.

— *Transborder Data Processing and Country Required Terms.* url: https://www.ibm.com/support/customer/csol/terms/?id=Z126-8005&lc=en. Last accessed: 26.08.2024.

— *What Is the General Data Protection Regulation (GDPR)?* url: https://www.ibm.com/cloud/compliance/gdpr-eu. Last accessed: 26.08.2024.

ICO. Chapter 5: *Privacy Enhancing Technologies (PETs).* url: https://ico.org.uk/media/about-the-ico/consultations/4021464/chapter-5-anonymisation-pets.pdf. Last accessed: 26.08.2024.

— *Generative AI Second Call for Evidence: Purpose Limitation in the Generative AI Lifecycle.* url: https://ico.org.uk/about-the-ico/what-we-do/our-work-on-artificial-intelligence/generative-ai-second-call-for-evidence/. Last accessed: 01.08.2025.

— *ISO/IEC 27001*. url: https://ico.org.uk/for-organisations/the-guide-to-nis/security-requirements/. Last accessed: 01.08.2025.

Information Commisioner's Office. *How Should We Assess Security and Data Minimisation in AI?* url: https://ico.org.uk/for-organisations/uk-gdpr-guidance-and-resources/artificial-intelligence/guidance-on-ai-and-data-protection/how-should-we-assess-security-and-data-minimisation-in-ai/. Last accessed: 01.08.2025.

Islam, Mir Riyanul et al. "A systematic review of explainable artificial intelligence in terms of different application domains and tasks". In: *Applied Sciences* 12.3 (2022), p. 1353. doi: https://doi.org/10.3390/app12031353.

ISO. *ISO/IEC 27001 and Related Standards*. url: https://www.iso.org/isoiec-27001-information-security.html. Last accessed 01.08.2025.

Italian Data Protection Authority. *Garante per la protezione dei dati personali (Italy) – 9685994*. url: https://gdprhub.eu/index.php?title=Garante_per_la_protezione_dei_dati_personali_(Italy)_-_9685994. Last accessed: 01.08.2025.

Jackson, Vicki C. "Constitutional law in an age of proportionality". In: *The Yale Law Journal* 124.8 (2015), pp. 3094–3196.

Jain, Prince. "Interaction between software engineering and artificial intelligence – A review". In: *International Journal on Computer Science and Engineering* 3.12 (2011), pp. 3774–3779.

Johansen, Stian Øby et al. "The revised draft agreement on the accession of the EU to the ECHR: Third time's a charm?" In: *European Papers: A Journal on Law and Integration* 9.2 (2024), pp. 641–646. doi: https://doi.org/10.15166/2499-8249/774.

Johnson, Jeff. "Rethinking floating point for deep learning". In: *arXiv preprint arXiv:1811.01721* (2018). doi: https://doi.org/10.48550/arXiv.1811.01721.

Jordan, Michael I and Tom M Mitchell. "Machine learning: Trends, perspectives, and prospects". In: *Science* 349.6245 (2015), pp. 255–260. doi: https://doi.org/10.1126/science.aaa8415.

Juliussen, Bjørn Aslak, Jon Petter Rui, and Dag Johansen. "Algorithms that forget: Machine unlearning and the right to erasure". In: *Computer Law & Security Review* 51 (2023), p. 105885. doi: https://doi.org/10.1016/j.clsr.2023.105885.

Juliussen, Bjørn Aslak et al. "The third country problem under the GDPR: Enhancing protection of data transfers with technology". In: *International Data Privacy Law* 13.3 (2023), pp. 225–243.

Karkliniewska, Iwona. "Building transparency and robustness of AI/ADM management in public sector". In: *AIxPA@ AI* IA*. 2022, pp. 1–7.

Kera, Denisa Reshef. "Experimental algorithmic citizenship in the sandboxes: An alternative to ethical frameworks and governance-by-design interventions". In: *Proceedings of the III Ibero-American Conference on Smart Cities (ICSC-2020)* (2020).

Khder, Moaiad Ahmad. "Web scraping or web crawling: State of art, techniques, approaches and application". In: *International Journal of Advances in Soft Computing & Its Applications* 13.3 (2021), pp. 145–168.

Kilkenny, Monique F and Kerin M Robinson. "Data quality: 'Garbage in–garbage out.'" In: *Health Information Management Journal* 47.3 (2018), pp. 103–105. doi: https://doi.org/10.1177/1833358318774357.

Klatt, Matthias and Moritz Meister. *The Constitutional Structure of Proportionality*. Oxford: Oxford University Press, 2012.

Knott, Brian et al. "Crypten: Secure multi-party computation meets machine learning". In: *Advances in Neural Information Processing Systems* 34 (2021), pp. 4961–4973. doi: https://doi.org/10.48550/arXiv.2109.00984.

Knowledge Base. *Understand Measures of Supercomputer Performance and Storage System Capacity.* url: https://kb.iu.edu/d/apeq. Last accessed: 01.08.2025.

Kokott, Juliane and Christoph Sobotta. "The distinction between privacy and data protection in the jurisprudence of the CJEU and the ECtHR". In: *International Data Privacy Law* 3.4 (Sept. 2013), pp. 222–228. ISSN: 2044-3994. doi: 10 . 1093 / idpl / ipt017. eprint: https://academic.oup.com/idpl/article-pdf/3/4/222/2160080/ipt017.pdf. url: https://doi.org/10.1093/idpl/ipt017.

Korff, Douwe. *Opinion on the Future of Personal Data Transfers from the EU/EEA to Israel and the Occupied Territories.* url: https://www.ianbrown.tech/2022/02/23/israels-privacy-protection-act-amendments-and-eu-adequacy/. Last accessed: 01.08.2025.

Kotschy, Waltraut. "Article 6. Lawfulness of processing". In: *The EU General Data Protection Regulation (GDPR): A Commentary.* Ed. by Christopher Kuner, Lee A. Bygrave, and Christopher Docksey. Oxford: Oxford University Press, 2020, pp. 321–344.

— "Article 6: Lawfulness of processing". In: *The EU General Data Protection Regulation (GDPR): A commentary.* Ed. by Christopher Kuner, Lee A Bygrave, and Christopher Docksey. Oxford: Oxford University Press, 2020, p. 333.

Kotsiantis, Sotiris B, Dimitris Kanellopoulos, and Panagiotis E Pintelas. "Data preprocessing for supervised learning". In: *International journal of computer science* 1.2 (2006), pp. 111–117.

Kramcsák, Pablo Trigo. "Can legitimate interest be an appropriate lawful basis for processing artificial intelligence training datasets?" In: *Computer Law & Security Review* 48 (2023), p. 105765. ISSN: 0267-3649. doi: https://doi.org/10.1016/j.clsr.2022.105765. url: https://www.sciencedirect.com/science/article/pii/S026736492200108X.

Kranenborg, Herke. "Protection of personal data". In: *The EU Charter of Fundamental Rights: A Commentary.* Ed. by Steve Peers et al. Oxford: Hart Publishing, 2014, pp. 223–266 on p. 230. doi: http://dx.doi.org/10.5040/9781849468350.ch-009.

Kremnitzer, Mordechai, Talya Steiner, and Andrej Lang. *Proportionality in Action: Comparative and Empirical Perspectives on the Judicial Practice.* Vol. 22. Cambridge, UK: Cambridge University Press, 2020, p. 1.

Krishnamoorthy, CS and S Rajeev. *Artificial Intelligence and Expert Systems for Engineers.* Boca Raton: CRC Press, 2018, p. 18.

Kroll, Joshua A. "The fallacy of inscrutability". In: *Philosophical Transactions of the Royal Society A: Mathematical, Physical and Engineering Sciences* 376.2133 (2018), p. 20180084. doi: https://doi.org/10.1098/rsta.2018.0084.

Kumar, Ram Shankar Siva et al. "Failure modes in machine learning systems". In: *arXiv preprint arXiv:1911.11034* (2019). doi: https://doi.org/10.48550/arXiv.1911.11034.

Kuru, Taner. "Lawfulness of the mass processing of publicly accessible online data to train large language models". In: *International Data Privacy Law* 14.4 (2024), pp. 326–351. doi: https://doi.org/10.1093/idpl/ipae013.

Lancieri, Filippo. "Narrowing data protection's enforcement gap". In: *Maine Law Review* 74.1 (2022), pp. 15–74. url: https://digitalcommons.mainelaw.maine.edu/mlr/vol74/iss1/3?utm_source=digitalcommons.mainelaw.maine.edu%2Fmlr%2Fvol74%2Fiss1%2F3&utm_medium=PDF&utm_campaign=PDFCoverPages. Last accessed: 26.08.2024.

Lawson, Anton E. "Hypothetico-deductive method". In: *Encyclopedia of Science Education*. Ed. by R Gunston. Dordrecht: Springer, 2015. doi: https://doi.org/10.1007/978-94-007-2150- 0_260.

LeCun, Yann, Yoshua Bengio, and Geoffrey Hinton. "Deep learning". In: *Nature* 521.7553 (2015), pp. 436–444. doi: https://doi.org/10.1038/nature14539.

Lee, Joon-Woo et al. "Privacy-preserving machine learning with fully homomorphic encryption for deep neural network". In: *iEEE Access* 10 (2022), pp. 30039–30054. doi: https://doi.org/ 10.1109/ACCESS.2022.3159694.

Lenaerts, Koen. "The European Court of Justice and process-oriented review". In: *Yearbook of European Law* 31.1 (2012), pp. 3–16. doi: https://doi.org/10.1093/yel/yes009.

Lewis, Patrick et al. *Retrieval-Augmented Generation for Knowledge-Intensive NLP Tasks*. 2021. arXiv: 2005.11401 [cs.CL]. url: https://arxiv.org/abs/2005.11401.

Li, Li et al. "A review of applications in federated learning". In: *Computers & Industrial Engineering* 149 (2020), p. 106854. doi: https://doi.org/10.1016/j.cie.2020.106854.

Linardatos, Pantelis, Vasilis Papastefanopoulos, and Sotiris Kotsiantis. "Explainable AI: A review of machine learning interpretability methods". In: *Entropy* 23.1 (2020), p. 18. doi: https://doi.org/10.3390/e23010018.

Lins, Sebastian et al. "Artificial intelligence as a service: Classification and research directions". In: *Business & Information Systems Engineering* 63 (2021), pp. 441–456. doi: https://doi.org/10.1007/s12599-021-00708-w.

Luqman, Alka, Riya Mahesh, and Anupam Chattopadhyay. "Privacy and security implications of cloud-based AI services: A survey". In: *arXiv preprint arXiv:2402.00896* (2024). doi: https://doi.org/10.48550/arXiv.2402.00896.

Lynskey, Orla. "Deconstructing data protection: The 'added-value'of a right to data protection in the EU legal order". In: *International & Comparative Law Quarterly* 63.3 (2014), pp. 569–597. doi: https://doi.org/10.1017/S0020589314000244.

— "Regulating for the future: The law's enforcement deficit". In: *Studies: An Irish Quarterly Review* 112.445 (2023), pp. 104–119. doi: https://doi.org/10.1353/stu.2023.0007.

Madden, Neil. *API Security in Action*. New York: Simon and Schuster, 2020, p. 32. isbn: 9781617296024.

Marcano, Néstor J Hernández et al. "On fully homomorphic encryption for privacy-preserving deep learning". In: *2019 IEEE Globecom Workshops (GC Wkshps)*. New York: IEEE, 2019, pp. 1–6. doi: https://doi.org/10.1109/GCWkshps45667.2019.9024625.

Marcelo, Marcelo Marinho, John Noll Ita Richardson, and Sarah Beecham. "Plan-driven approaches are alive and kicking in agile global software development". In: *2019 ACM/IEEE International Symposium on Empirical Software Engineering and Measurement (ESEM)*. New York: IEEE, 2019, pp. 1–11. doi: https://doi.org/10.48550/arXiv.1906.08895.

Marcén, Ana Gascón. "The new personal data protection in Japan: Is it enough?" In: *Media Technologies for Work and Play in East Asia*. Bristol: Bristol University Press, 2021, pp. 101–120.

Markets and Markets. *AI as a Service Market Global Forecast to 2028*. url: https://www.marketsandmarkets.com/Market-Reports/artificial-intelligence-ai-as-a-service-market-121842268.html. Last accessed: 01.08.2025.

MarketWatch. *Nvidia is now worth more than the GDP of every country except these 11*. url: https://www.marketwatch.com/story/nvidia-is-now-worth-more-than-the-gdp-of-every-country-except-these-few-d58a3508. Last accessed: 26.08.2024.

Massé, Estelle. "Two years under the EU GDPR: An implementation progress report". In: *Access Now Homepage* (2020). url: https://www.accessnow.org/wp-content/uploads/2020/05/Two-Years-Under-GDPR.pdf. Last accessed: 01.08.2025.

Mast, Tobias and Christian Ollig. "The lazy legislature: Incorporating and horizontalising the Charter of Fundamental Rights through secondary union law". In: *European Constitutional Law Review* 19.3 (2023), pp. 462–486. doi: 10.1017/S1574019623000238.

McBride, Jeremy. "Proportionality and the European Convention on Human Rights". In: *The Principle of Proportionality in the Laws of Europe*. Ed. by Evelyn Ellis. Oxford: Hart Publishing, 1999, p. 23.

McCarthy, John et al. "A proposal for the Dartmouth summer research project on artificial intelligence, August 31, 1955". In: *AI Magazine* 27.4 (2006), p. 12.

Medium. *Fine-Tuning versus RAG in Generative AI Applications*. url: https://harsha-srivatsa.medium.com/fine-tuning-versus-rag-in-generative-ai-applications-architecture-d54ca6d2acb8. Last accessed: 01.08.2025.

— *Fraud Detection via LLM*. url: https://medium.com/@aevalone/fraud-detection-via-llm-9c88a6a9f0dc. Last accessed: 01.08.2025.

Mehta, Sanket Vaibhav et al. "An empirical investigation of the role of pre-training in lifelong learning". In: *Journal of Machine Learning Research* 24.214 (2023), pp. 1–50. url: http://jmlr.org/papers/v24/22-0496.html.

Mell, Peter and Tim Grance. *The NIST Definition of Cloud Computing*. Washington, DC: National Institute of Standards and Technology, 2011.

Microsoft. *A New AI Era Begins*. url: https://www.microsoft.com/en-us/windows/copilot-plus-pcs?r=1#performance. Last accessed: 26.08.2024.

— *Microsoft Azure*. url: https://azure.microsoft.com/. Last accessed: 01.08.2025.

— *Microsoft Products and Services Data Protection Addendum (DPA)*. url: https://www.microsoft.com/licensing/docs/view/Microsoft-Products-and-Services-Data-Protection-Addendum-DPA?lang=1. Last accessed: 26.08.2024.

Microsoft Corporation. *Microsoft Cloud for Sovereignty: The Most Flexible and Comprehensive Solution for Digital Sovereignty*. url: https://www.microsoft.com/en-us/industry/sovereignty/cloud. Last accessed: 26.08.2024.

Microsoft Learn. *Security Engineering Threat Modeling Aim*. url: https://learn.microsoft.com/en-us/security/engineering/threat-modeling-aiml. Last accessed: 26.08.2024.

Miller, Tim. "Explanation in artificial intelligence: Insights from the social sciences". In: *Artificial Intelligence* 267 (2018), pp. 1–38. doi: https://doi.org/10.48550/arXiv.1706.07269. arXiv: 1706.07269 [cs.AI].

Mitchell, Eric et al. "Detectgpt: Zero-shot machine-generated text detection using probability curvature". In: *International Conference on Machine Learning*. PMLR. 2023, pp. 24950–24962.

Mitchell, Tom M. *Machine Learning*. New York: McGraw-Hill, 1997, p. 2.

Mitsilegas, Valsamis and Emmanouil Billis. "Article 49 – Principles of legality and proportionality of criminal offences and penalties". In: *The EU Charter of Fundamental Rights: A Commentary*. Ed. by Steve Peers et al. London: Bloomsbury Publishing, 2021, pp. 1473–1508.

Molnar, Christoph. *Interpretable Machine Learning*. Lulu.com, 2020.

Mosier, Kathleen L and Linda J Skitka. "Automation use and automation bias". In: *Proceedings of the Human Factors and Ergonomics Society Annual Meeting*. Vol. 43. 3. Los Angeles: SAGE Publications, 1999, pp. 344–348. doi: https://doi.org/10.1177/154193129904300346.

Mühlhoff, Rainer and Hannah Ruschemeier. "Updating purpose limitation for AI: A normative approach from law and philosophy". In: *Available at SSRN 4711621* (2024).
Mulders, Stephen. "Collective damages for GDPR breaches: A feasible solution for the GDPR enforcement deficit?" In: *European Data Protection Law Review* 8.4 (2022), pp. 493–500.
Mulligan, Deirdre K and Kenneth A Bamberger. "Saving governance-by-design". In: *California Law Review* 106.3 (2018), pp. 697–784. doi: https://doi.org/10.15779/Z38QN5ZB5H.
Murray, Andrew and Colin Scott. "Controlling the new media: Hybrid responses to new forms of power". In: *The Modern Law Review* 65.4 (2002), pp. 491–516.
Nadeem, Farrukh. "Evaluating and ranking cloud IaaS, PaaS and SaaS models based on functional and non-functional key performance indicators". In: *IEEE Access* 10 (2022), pp. 63245–63257. doi: https://doi.org/10.1109/ACCESS.2022.3182688.
Nasr, Milad et al. "Scalable extraction of training data from (production) language models". In: *arXiv preprint arXiv:2311.17035* (2023). doi: https://doi.org/10.48550/arXiv.2311.17035.
Nemitz, Paul. "Constitutional democracy and technology in the age of artificial intelligence". In: *Philosophical Transactions of the Royal Society A: Mathematical, Physical and Engineering Sciences* 376.2133 (2018), p. 20180089. doi: https://doi.org/10.1098/rsta.2018.0089.
Neutatz, Felix et al. "From cleaning before ML to cleaning for ML". In: *IEEE Data Engineering Bulletin* 44.1 (2021), pp. 24–41.
Norwegian Data Protection Authority. *ISO/IEC 27001*. url: https://www.datatilsynet.no/rettigheter-og-plikter/virksomhetenes-plikter/informasjonssikkerhet-internkontroll/etablere-internkontroll/iverksette-styringssystem-for-informasjonssikkerhet/. Last accessed: 01.08.2025.
Nouwens, Midas et al. "Dark patterns after the GDPR: Scraping consent pop-ups and demonstrating their influence". In: *Proceedings of the 2020 CHI Conference on Human Factors in Computing Systems*. New York: Association for Computing Machinery, 2020, pp. 1–13. doi: https://doi.org/10.1145/3313831.3376321.
OpenAI. *ChatGPT*. url: https://chat.openai.com/. Last accessed: 01.08.2025.
— *Hello GPT-4o*. url: https://openai.com/index/hello-gpt-4o/. Last accessed: 26.08.2024.
— *Production Best Practices*. url: https://platform.openai.com/docs/guides/production-best-practices/improving-latencies. Last accessed: 26.08.2024.
— *The Fastest and Most Powerful Platform for Building AI Products*. url: https://openai.com/api/. Last accessed: 01.08.2021.
OpenAI OpCO, LLC. *Privacy Policy*. url: https://openai.com/policies/privacy-policy. Last accessed: 26.08.2024.
Oracle. *Data Flows and Oracle Services*. url: https://www.oracle.com/contracts/docs/corporate_privacy_shield_statement_071720.pdf?download=false. Last accessed: 26.08.2024.
— *Oracle Affiliates*. url: https://www.oracle.com/corporate/oracle-affiliates/. Last accessed: 26.08.2024.
Organisation for Economic Co-operation and Development (OECD). *AI Principles Overview*. Paris: OECD. url: https://oecd.ai/en/ai-principles. Last accessed: 01.08.2025.

Pagallo, Ugo. "Cracking down on autonomy: Three challenges to design in IT law". In: *Ethics and Information Technology* 14 (2012), pp. 319–328. doi: https://doi.org/10.1007/s10676- 012-9295-9.

— "On the principle of privacy by design and its limits: Technology, ethics and the rule of law". In: *European Data Protection: In Good Health?* Ed. by Serge Gutwirth et al. Dordrecht: Springer, 2012, pp. 331–346. isbn: 978-94-007-2903-2. doi: 10.1007/978-94-007- 2903-2_16. url: https://doi.org/10.1007/978-94-007-2903-2_16.

Palladino, Nicola. "The role of the epistemic communities in the 'constitutionalization' of Internet governance: The example of the European Commission High-Level Expert Group on Artificial Intelligence". In: *Telecommunications Policy* 45.6 (2021), p. 102149. ISSN: 0308-5961. doi: https://doi.org/10.1016/j.telpol.2021. 102149. url: https://www.sciencedirect.com/science/article/pii/S0308596121000537.

Panigutti, Cecilia et al. "The role of explainable AI in the context of the AI Act". In: *Proceedings of the 2023 ACM Conference on Fairness, Cccountability, and Transparency*. New York: Association for Computing Machinery, 2023, pp. 1139–1150. doi: https://doi.org/10.1145/3593013.3594069.

Papernot, Nicolas et al. "Sok: Security and privacy in machine learning". In: *2018 IEEE European Symposium on Security and Privacy (EuroS&P)*. New York: IEEE, 2018, pp. 399–414. doi: 10.1109/ EuroSP.2018.00035.

Parliament, European. *Artificial Intelligence Act: MEPs Adopt Landmark Law*. url: https://www.europarl.europa.eu/news/en/press-room/20240308IPR19015/artificial-intelligence-act-meps-adopt-landmark-law. Last accessed: 26.08.2024.

— *Legal Aspects of EU Multilingualism*. url: https://www.europarl.europa.eu/RegData/etudes/BRIE/2017/595914/EPRS_BRI%282017%29595914_EN.pdf. Last accessed: 01.08.2025.

Parola, Alberto et al. "Voice patterns in schizophrenia: A systematic review and Bayesian meta-analysis". In: *Schizophrenia Research* 216 (2020), pp. 24–40. doi: https://doi.org/10.1016/j.schres.2019.11.031.

Patterson, Dan. *Introduction to Artificial Intelligence and Expert Systems*. Englewood Cliffs: Prentice Hall, 1990, p. 10.

Pena, Jose Manuel et al. "Dimensionality reduction in unsupervised learning of conditional Gaussian networks". In: *IEEE Transactions on Pattern Analysis and Machine Intelligence* 23.6 (2001), pp. 590–603.

personale, Garante per la protezione dei data. *ChatGPT: Italian DPA notifies breaches of privacy law to OpenAI*. url: https://gpdp.it/home/docweb/-/docweb-display/docweb/9978020#english. Last accessed: 01.08.2025.

Peters, Anne. "Proportionality as a global constitutional principle". In: *Handbook on Global Constitutionalism*. Cheltenham: Edward Elgar Publishing, 2023, pp. 346–362. doi: https://doi.org/10.4337/9781783477357.00028.

Phi, Michael. *Illustrated Guide to Transformers: Step by Step Explanation*. url: https://towardsdatascience.com/illustrated-guide-to-transformers-step-by-step-explanation-f74876522bc0. Last accessed: 01.08.2025.

Postman. *What Is an API?* url: https://www.postman.com/what-is-an-api/. Last accessed: 01.08.2025.

Pra, Marco Del. *Large Language Models*. url: https://medium.com/@marcodelpra/large-language-models-1a6eec644b30. Last accessed: 01.08.2025.

Preibisch, Sascha. *API Development*. Springer, 2018.

Prifti, Kostina et al. “Regulation by design: Features, practices, limitations, and governance implications”. In: *Minds and Machines* 34.2 (2024), p. 13. doi: https:// doi.org/10.1007/ s11023-024-09675-z.

Purtova, Nadezhda. “The law of everything: Broad concept of personal data and future of EU data protection law”. In: *Law, Innovation and Technology* 10.1 (2010), pp. 40–81. doi: 10.1080/17579961.2018.1452176.

Ramberg, Christina. *Erfarenheter som kan vara til nytta för doktorandar i juridik.* Stockholm: Jure Forlag, 2003.

Rani, Pooja et al. “Taxonomy of machine learning algorithms and its applications”. In: *Journal of Computational and Theoretical Nanoscience* 17.6 (2020), pp. 2508–2513. doi: https://doi. org/10.1166/jctn.2020.8922.

Registratiekamer, Information and Privacy Commissioner Ontario. *Privacy-Enhancing Technologies: The Path to Anonymity.* Tech. rep. Achtergrondstudies en Verkenningen 5B, vols. I and II, Rijswijk, 1995.

Renggli, Cedric et al. “A data quality-driven view of MLOps”. In: *arXiv preprint arXiv:2102.07750* (2021). doi: https://doi.org/10.48550/arXiv.2102.07750.

Ribeiro, Mauro, Katarina Grolinger, and Miriam AM Capretz. “Mlaas: Machine learning as a service”. In: *2015 IEEE 14th International Conference on Machine Learning and Applications (ICMLA).* New York: IEEE. 2015, pp. 896–902. doi: https://doi.org/10.1109/ICMLA.2015.152.

Rising, Lind and Norman S. Janoff. “The Scrum software development process for small teams”. In: *IEEE Software* 17.4 (2000), pp. 26–32. doi: https://doi.org/10.1109 /52.854065.

Rokach, Lior and Oded Maimom. *Data Mining with Decision Trees: Theory and Applications.* Singapore: World Scientific, 2014. doi: https://doi.org/10.1142/9097.

Sandhu, Aqilah. *Grundrechtsunitarisierung durch Sekundärrecht: Zur Reichweite des mitgliedstaatlichen Grundrechtsschutzes im Anwendungsbereich von Öffnungsklauseln am Beispiel des europäischen Datenschutzsekundärrechts.* Tübingen: Mohr Siebeck, 2021, p. 188. doi: https: //doi.org/10.1628/978-3-16-16 0897-1.

Sangwan, Raghvinder S, Youakim Badr, and Satish M. Srinivasan. “Cybersecurity for AI systems: A survey”. In: *Journal of Cybersecurity and Privacy* 3.2 (2023), pp. 166–190. ISSN: 2624-800X. doi: 10.3390/jcp3020010. url: https://www.mdpi .com/2624-800X/3/2/10.

Sarker, Iqbal H. “Machine learning: Algorithms, real-world applications and research directions”. In: *SN Computer Science* 2.3 (2021), p. 160. doi: https://doi.org/10.1007 /s42979-021- 00592-x.

Sarker, Iqbal H, Md Hasan Furhad, and Raza Nowrozy. “AI-driven cybersecurity: An overview, security intelligence modeling and research directions”. In: *SN Computer Science* 2.3 (2021), p. 173. doi: 10.1007/s42979-021-00557-0.

Sedeleer, Nicolas de. “The precautionary principle in European Community health and environment law: Sword or shield for the Nordic countries?” In: *Implementing the Precautionary Principle: Approaches from the Nordic Countries, EU and USA.* London: Routledge, 2007, pp. 37–85.

Selbst, Andrew D and Julia Powles. “Meaningful information and the right to explanation”. In: *International Data Privacy Law* 7.4 (Dec. 2017), pp. 233–242. ISSN: 2044-3994. doi: 10.1093/idpl/ipx022. eprint: https://academic.oup.com/idpl/ article-pdf/7/4/233/22923065/ipx022.pdf. url: https://doi.org/10.1093/idpl/ipx022.

Senapathi, Mali, Jim Buchan, and Hady Osman. “DevOps capabilities, practices, and challenges: Insights from a case study”. In: *Proceedings of the 22nd International*

Conference on Evaluation and Assessment in Software Engineering 2018. New York: Association for Computing Machinery, 2018, pp. 57–67. doi: https://doi.org/10. 48550/arXiv.1907.10201.

Sgaglione, Luigi and Giovanni Mazzeo. "A GDPR-compliant approach to real-time processing of sensitive data". In: *Intelligent Interactive Multimedia Systems and Services*. Ed. by Giuseppe De Pietro et al. Cham: Springer International Publishing, 2019, pp. 43–52. isbn: 978-3-319-92231-7.

Shapley, Lloyd S. *A Value for N-Person Game*. Santa Monica: RAND, 1952. url: https://www.rand.org/pubs/papers/P295.html. Last accessed: 01.08.2025.

Smits, Jan M. "What is legal doctrine? On the aims and methods of legal-dogmatic research". In: *Rethinking Legal Scholarship: A Transatlantic Dialogue*. Ed. by Rob van Gestel, Hans-W Micklitz, and Edward L Rubin. Cambridge, UK: Cambridge University Press, 2017, pp. 207–228.

Spano, Robert. "Foreword". In: *Proportionality in Crime Control and Criminal Justice*. Ed. by Emmanouil Billis, Nandor Knust, and Jon Petter Rui. Oxford: Bloomsbury Publishing, 2021. url: https://papers.ssrn.com/sol3/papers.cfm?abstract_id=3979696.

Speith, Timo. "A review of taxonomies of explainable artificial intelligence (XAI) methods". In: *Proceedings of the 2022 ACM Conference on Fairness, Accountability, and Transparency*. New York: Association for Computing Machinery, 2022, pp. 2239–2250. doi: https://doi.org/10.1145/3531146.3534639.

Spring, Jonathan M et al. "On managing vulnerabilities in AI/ML systems". In: *Proceedings of the New Security Paradigms Workshop 2020*. 2020, pp. 111–126. doi: https://doi.org/10. 1145/3442167.3442177.

Staab, Robin et al. "From principle to practice: Vertical data minimization for machine learning". In: *arXiv preprint arXiv:2311.10500* (2023). doi: https://doi.org/10.48550/arXiv.2311.10500.

Ståhl, Niclas et al. "Evaluation of uncertainty quantification in deep learning". In: *International Conference on Information Processing and Management of Uncertainty in Knowledge-Based Systems*. Cham: Springer Nature, 2020, pp. 556–568. doi: https://doi.org/10.1007/978-3-030-50146- 4_41.

Stewart, Matthew. *The Actual Difference between Statistics and Machine Learning*. url: https://towardsdatascience.com/the-actual-difference-between-statistics-and-machine-learning-64b49f07ea3. Last accessed: 26.08.2024.

Stöffelbauer, Andreas. *How Large Language Models Work: From Zero to ChatGPT*. url: https://medium.com/data-science-at-microsoft/how-large-language-models-work-91c362f5b78f. Last accessed: 01.08.2025.

Sun, Xiaoqiang et al. "Private machine learning classification based on fully homomorphic encryption". In: *IEEE Transactions on Emerging Topics in Computing* 8.2 (2018), pp. 352–364. doi: https://doi.org/10.1109/TETC.2018.2794611.

Tamburri, Damian A. "Sustainable MLOPs: Trends and challenges". In: *2020 22nd International Symposium on Symbolic and Numeric Algorithms for Scientific Computing (SYNASC)*. 2020, pp. 17–23. doi: 10.1109/SYNASC51798.2020.00015.

Taylor, Mistale. "The EU's human rights obligations in relation to its data protection laws with extraterritorial effect". In: *International Data Privacy Law* 5.4 (Sept. 2015), pp. 246–256. ISSN: 2044-3994. doi: 10.1093/idpl/ipv023. eprint: https://academic.oup.com/idpl/article-pdf/5/4/246/9950994/ipv023.pdf. url: https://doi.org/10.1093/idpl/ipv023.

Terwagne, Cécile de. "Article 5. Principles Relating to processing of personal data". In: *The EU General Data Protection (GDPR): A Commentary*. Ed. by Christopher Kuner et al. Oxford: Oxford University Press, 2020, p. 317.

Testi, Matteo et al. "MLOps: A taxonomy and a methodology". In: *IEEE Access* 10 (2022), pp. 63606–63618. doi: 10.1109/ACCESS.2022.3181730.

Thirlway, Hugh. "Reflections on *lex ferenda*". In: *Netherlands Yearbook of International Law* 32 (2001), pp. 3–26. doi: 10.1017/S0167676800001148.

TOGAF Standard, Version 9.2. 22 Architecture patterns. https://pubs.opengroup.org/architecture/togaf9-doc/arch/chap22.html. Last accessed: 26.08.2024.

Tom, Edith, Aybüke Aurum, and Richard Vidgen. "An exploration of technical debt". In: *Journal of Systems and Software* 86.6 (2013), pp. 1498–1516. doi: https://doi.org/10.1016/j.jss.2012.12.052.

Torpmann-Hagen, Birk et al. "Segmentation consistency training: Out-of-distribution generalization for medical image segmentation". In: *2022 IEEE International Symposium on Multimedia (ISM)*. 2022, pp. 42–49.

Tosoni, Luca. *The Fundamental Right to Cybersecurity*. University of Oslo, 2023. url: http://urn.nb.no/URN:NBN:no-nb_digibok_2023033148096.

Tosoni, Luca and Lee A. Bygrave. "Article 4(7) Controller". In: *The EU General Data Protection Regulation (GDPR): A Commentary*. Ed. by Christopher Kuner, Lee A. Bygrave, and Christopher Docksey. Oxford: Oxford University Press, 2020, p. 146.

Towards Data Science. *Categorical Variables for Machine Learning Algorithms*. url: https://towardsdatascience.com/categorical-variables-for-machine-learning-algorithms-d2768d587ab6. Last accessed: 01.08.2025.

Tridimas, Takis. "Proportionality in European Community law: Searching for the appropriate standard of scrutiny". In: *The Principle of Proportionality in the Laws of Europe*. Ed. by Evelyn Ellis. Oxford: Hart Publishing, 1999, pp. 65–84.

— "The general principles of EU law and the Europeanisation of national laws". In: *Review of European Administrative Law* 13.2 (2020), pp. 5–31. doi: 10.7590/187479820X15930701852193.

— "Wreaking the wrongs: Balancing rights and the public interest the EU way". In: *Columbia Journal of European Law* 29.2 (2023), pp. 185–212. url: https://cjel.law.columbia.edu/files/2023/04/10.-TRIDIMAS-PROOF.pdf.

Troncoso Reigada, Antonio. "The principle of proportionality and the fundamental right to personal data protection: The biometric data processing". In: *Lex Electronica* 17 (2012), p. 1. url: https://www.lex-electronica.org/en/s/159.

Truyens, Maarten and Patrick Van Eecke. "Legal aspects of text mining". In: *Computer Law & Security Review* 30.2 (2014), pp. 153–170. ISSN: 0267-3649. doi: https://doi.org/10.1016/j.clsr.2014.01.009. url: https://www.sciencedirect.com/science/article/pii/S0267364914000260.

Turan, Furkan, Sujoy Sinha Roy, and Ingrid Verbauwhede. "HEAWS: An Accelerator for Homomorphic Encryption on the Amazon AWS FPGA". In: *IEEE Transactions on Computers* 69.8 (2020), pp. 1185–1196. doi: 10.1109/TC.2020.2988765.

Ugartemendia, Juan Ignacio. "The horizontal effect of the EU Charter of Fundamental Rights in the case law of the Court of Justice". In: *Fundamental Rights Challenges: Horizontal Effectiveness, Rule of Law and Margin of National Appreciation*. Ed. by Cristina Izquierdo-Sans, Carmen Martínez-Capdevila, and Magdalena Nogueira-Guastavino. Cham: Springer International Publishing, 2021, pp. 11–21. isbn: 978-3-030-72798-7. doi: 10.1007/978- 3-030-72798-7_2. url: https://doi.org/10.1007/978-3-030-72798-7_2.

Ukrow, Jörg. "Practitioner's corner – Data protection without frontiers? On the relationship between EU GDPR and amended CoE Convention 108". In: *European Data Protection Law Review* 4.2 (2018). doi: 10 . 21552 / edpl / 2018 / 2 / 14. url: https://doi.org/10.21552/edpl/2018/2/14.

Urquhart, Lachlan and Tom Rodden. "A legal turn in human computer interaction? Towards 'regulation by design' for the Internet of Things". In: *Towards "Regulation by Design" for the Internet of Things (March 11, 2016)* (2016). doi: https://dx.doi.org/10.2139/ssrn.2746467.

Usama, Muhammad et al. "Unsupervised machine learning for networking: Techniques, applications and research challenges". In: *IEEE Access* 7 (2019), pp. 65579–65615. doi: 10.1109/ACCESS.2019.2916648.

US Department of Commerce. *Data Privacy Framework Program (DPF)*. url: https://www.dataprivacyframework.gov/list. Last accessed: 01.08.2025

Utz, Christine et al. "(Un) informed consent: Studying GDPR consent notices in the field". In: *Proceedings of the 2019 ACM Sigsac Conference on Computer and Communications Security*. New York: Association for Computing Machinery, 2019, pp. 973–990. doi: https://doi.org/10.1145/3319535.3354212.

Vaikuntanathan, Vinod. "Computing blindfolded: New developments in fully homomorphic encryption". In: *2011 IEEE 52nd Annual Symposium on Foundations of Computer Science*. New York: IEEE, 2011, pp. 5–16. doi: 10.1109/FOCS.2011.98.

Vale, Daniel, Ali El-Sharif, and Muhammed Ali. "Explainable artificial intelligence (XAI) post-hoc explainability methods: Risks and limitations in non-discrimination law". In: *AI and Ethics* 2.4 (2022), pp. 815–826. doi: https://doi.org/10.1007/s43681-022-00142-y.

van Bekkum, Marvin. "Using sensitive data to de-bias AI systems: Article 10 (5) of the EU AI act". In: *Computer Law & Security Review* 56 (2025), p. 106115. doi: https://doi.org/10.1016/j.clsr.2025.106115.

van Bekkum, Marvin and Frederik Zuiderveen Borgesius. "Using sensitive data to prevent discrimination by artificial intelligence: Does the GDPR need a new exception?" In: *Computer Law & Security Review* 48 (2023), p. 105770. ISSN: 0267-3649. doi: https://doi.org/10.1016/j.clsr.2022.105770. url: https://www.sciencedirect.com/science/article/pii/S0267364922001133.

van Cleynenbreugel, Pieter. "By-design regulation in the algorithmic society: Promising way forward or (EU) constitutional nightmare in-the-making?" In: *Inaugural Conference of the IACL Research Group on Algorithmic State Market & Society–Constitutional Dimensions*. 2019. doi: https://doi.org/10.1017/9781108914857.011.

van Dijk, Niels, Raphaël Gellert, and Kjetil Rommetveit. "A risk to a right? Beyond data protection risk assessments". In: *Computer Law & Security Review* 32.2 (2016), pp. 286–306. ISSN: 0267-3649. doi: https://doi.org/10.1016/j.clsr.2015.12.017. url: https://www.sciencedirect.com/science/article/pii/S026736491500182X.

Vardi, Moshe Y. "Move fast and break things". In: *Communications of the ACM* 61.9 (2018), p. 7. doi: http://dx.doi.org/10.1145/3244026.

Vaswani, Ashish et al. *Attention Is All You Need*. 2023. arXiv: 1706.03762.

Wachter, Sandra, Brent Mittelstadt, and Luciano Floridi. "Why a right to explanation of automated decision-making does not exist in the General Data Protection Regulation". In: *International Data Privacy Law* 7.2 (June 2017), pp. 76–99. ISSN: 2044-3994. doi: 10.1093/idpl/ipx005. eprint: https://academic.oup.com/idpl/article-pdf/7/2/76/17932196/ipx005.pdf. url: https://doi.org/10.1093/idpl/ipx005.

— "Why a right to explanation of automated decision-making does not exist in the General Data Protection Regulation". In: *International Data Privacy Law* 7.2

(June 2017), pp. 76–99. ISSN: 2044-3994. doi: 10.1093/idpl/ipx005. eprint: https://academic.oup.com/idpl/article-pdf/7/2/76/17932196/ipx005.pdf. url: https://doi.org/10.1093/idpl/ipx005.

Wachter, Sandra, Brent Mittelstadt, and Chris Russell. "Why fairness cannot be automated: Bridging the gap between EU non-discrimination law and AI". In: *Computer Law & Security Review* 41 (2021), p. 105567. ISSN: 0267-3649. doi: https://doi.org/10.1016/j.clsr.2021.105567. url: https://www.sciencedirect.com/science/article/pii/S0267364921000406.

Wang, Haiying and Huiru Zheng. "Positive predictive value". In: *Encyclopedia of Systems Biology*. Ed. by Werner Dubitzky et al. New York: Springer, 2013, pp. 1723–1724. isbn: 978-1-4419-9863-7. doi: 10.1007/978-1-4419-9863-7_256. url: https://doi.org/10.1007/978-1-4419-9863-7_256.

Wang, Qi et al. "A comprehensive survey of loss functions in machine learning". In: *Annals of Data Science* 9 (2022), pp. 187–212. doi: https://doi.org/10.1007/s40745-020-00253-5.

Ward, Angela. "Article 51: Field of application". In: *The EU Charter of Fundamental Rights: A Commentary*. Ed. by Steve Peers et al. London: Bloomsbury Publishing, 2014, pp. 1553–1610. doi: http://dx.doi.org/10.5040/9781849468350.ch-055.

Weitzenboeck, Emily M et al. "The GDPR and unstructured data: Is anonymization possible?" In: *International Data Privacy Law* 12.3 (Mar. 2022), pp. 184–206. ISSN: 2044-3994. doi: 10.1093/idpl/ipac008. eprint: https://academic.oup.com/idpl/article-pdf/12/3/184/45690911/ipac008.pdf. url: https://doi.org/10.1093/idpl/ipac008.

The White House. *Executive Order on Enhancing Safeguards for United States Signals Intelligence Activities*. url: https://www.whitehouse.gov/briefing-room/presidential-actions/2022/10/07/executive-order-on-enhancing-safeguards-for-united-states-signals-intelligence-activities/. Last accessed: 01.08.2025.

Wilhelmsen, Vivi Ringnes. "Digital tracking – A matter of national security". In: *Internasjonal Politikk* 80.1 (2022). doi: https://doi.org/10.23865/intpol.v80.3096.

Wood, Alexander, Kayvan Najarian, and Delaram Kahrobaei. "Homomorphic encryption for machine learning in medicine and bioinformatics". In: *ACM Computing Surveys (CSUR)* 53.4 (2020), pp. 1–35. doi: https://doi.org/10.1145/3394658.

Yakovleva, Svetlana. *GDPR Transfer Rules vs Rules on Territorial Scope: A Critical Reflection on Recent EDPB Guidelines from Both EU and International Trade Law Perspectives*. url: https://europeanlawblog.eu/2021/12/09/gdpr-transfer-rules-vs-rules-on-territorial-scope-a-critical-reflection-on-recent-edpb-guidelines-from-both-eu-and-international-trade-law-perspectives/. Last accessed: 01.08.2025.

Yeung, Karen. "Hypernudge: Big Data as a mode of regulation by design". In: *The Social Power of Algorithms*. New York: Routledge, 2019, pp. 118–136. doi: https://doi.org/10.1080/1369118X.2016.1186713.

Yeung, Karen, Andrew Howes, and Ganna Pogrebna. "AI governance by human rights–centered design, deliberation, and oversight: An end to ethics washing". In: *The Oxford Handbook of Ethics of AI*. Ed. by Markus D Dubber, Frank Pasquale, and Sunit Das. Oxford: Oxford University Press, 2020, pp. 77–106.

Yin, Ming, Jennifer Wortman Vaughan, and Hanna Wallach. "Understanding the effect of accuracy on trust in machine learning models". In: *Proceedings of the 2019 Chi Conference on Human Factors in Computing Systems*. 2019, pp. 1–12. doi: https://doi.org/10.1145/3290605.3300509.

Zafar, Muhammad Rehman and Naimul Khan. "Deterministic local interpretable model-agnostic explanations for stable explainability". In: *Machine Learning and Knowledge Extraction* 3.3 (2021), pp. 525–541. doi: https://doi.org/10.3390/make3030027.

Zalnieriute, Monika, Lyria Bennett Moses, and George Williams. "Rule of law by design?" In: *Tulane Law Review* 95.5 (2021), pp. 1063–1101.

Zemčík, Tomáš. "Failure of chatbot Tay was evil, ugliness and uselessness in its nature or do we judge it through cognitive shortcuts and biases?" In: *AI & Society* 36 (2021), pp. 361–367. doi: https://doi.org/10.1007/s00146-020-01053-4.

Zenisek, Jan, Florian Holzinger, and Michael Affenzeller. "Machine learning-based concept drift detection for predictive maintenance". In: *Computers & Industrial Engineering* 137 (2019), p. 106031. doi: https://doi.org/10.1016/j.cie.2019.106031.

Zhang, Kai and Minxia Luo. "Outlier-robust extreme learning machine for regression problems". In: *Neurocomputing* 151 (2015), pp. 1519–1527. doi: https://doi.org/10.1016/j.neucom.2014.09.022.

Zhang, Xinrui and Jason Jaskolka. "Conceptualizing the Secure Machine Learning Operations (SecMLOps) paradigm". In: *2022 IEEE 22nd International Conference on Software Quality, Reliability and Security (QRS)*. New York: IEEE, 2022, pp. 127–138. doi: 10.1109/QRS57517.2022.00023.

— "Security patterns for machine learning: The data-oriented stages". In: *Proceedings of the 27th European Conference on Pattern Languages of Programs*. New York: Association for Computing Machinery, 2022, pp. 1–12. doi: https://doi.org/10.1145/3551902.3565070.

Zhang, Yuheng et al. "The secret revealer: Generative model-inversion attacks against deep neural networks". In: *Proceedings of the IEEE/CVF Conference on Computer Vision and Pattern Recognition*. 2020, pp. 253–261. doi: 10.1109/CVPR42600.2020.00033.

Zuboff, Shoshana. *The Age of Surveillance Capitalism: The Fight for a Human Future at the New Frontier of Power*. New York: PublicAffairs, 2011.

Zuiderveen Borgesius, Frederik J. "Singling out people without knowing their names – Behavioural targeting, pseudonymous data, and the new Data Protection Regulation". In: *Computer Law & Security Review* 32.2 (2016), pp. 256–271. ISSN: 0267-3649. doi: https://doi.org/10.1016/j.clsr.2015.12.013. url: https://www.sciencedirect.com/science/article/pii/S0267364915001788.

Index